SHOW ME HOW

TO **ILLUSTRATE**

EVANGELISTIC

SERMONS

Other Books by R. Larry Moyer

21 Things God Never Said
31 Days to Contagious Living
31 Days to Living as a New Believer
31 Days to Walking with God in the Workplace
31 Days with the Master Fisherman
Free and Clear
Growing in the Family
Show Me How to Answer Tough Questions
Show Me How to Preach Evangelistic Sermons
Show Me How to Share the Gospel
Show Me How to Share the Gospel in the Workplace (forthcoming)
Welcome to the Family

R. Larry Moyer is the founder and CEO of EvanTell, Inc., an evangelistic training ministry in Dallas Texas. EvanTell empowers ministry organizations and churches to train and equip their members and staff to share the gospel in the context and cultures they serve. For more information go to www.evantell.org.

R. Larry Moyer

SHOW
ME
HOW
S·E·R·I·E·S

SHOW ME HOW
TO **ILLUSTRATE**
EVANGELISTIC
SERMONS

Kregel
Academic & Professional

Show Me How to Illustrate Evangelistic Sermons

© 2012 by R. Larry Moyer

Published by Kregel Publications, a division of Kregel, Inc., P.O. Box 2607, Grand Rapids, MI 49501.

The author wishes to express thanks and appreciation to Radio Bible Class for use of selected material—taken from *Our Daily Bread*, copyright by RBC Ministries, Grand Rapids, Michigan. Reprinted by permission. All rights reserved.

All Scripture quotations are from The New King James Version. © 1979, 1980, 1982, Thomas Nelson, Inc. Used by permission. All rights reserved.

Scripture quotations marked ASV are from the American Standard Version.

Scripture quotations marked NASB are from the NEW AMERICAN STANDARD BIBLE, updated edition. Copyright © 1960, 1962, 1963, 1968, 1971, 1972, 1973, 1975, 1977, 1995 by The Lockman Foundation. Used by permission. (www.Lockman.org)

Library of Congress Cataloging-in-Publication Data

Moyer, R. Larry (Richard Larry), 1947-
    Show me how to illustrate evangelistic sermons / R. Larry Moyer.
        p. cm.
    Includes bibliographical references (p. 36) and index.
    1. Homiletical illustrations. 2. Evangelistic work. 3. Preaching. I. Title.
    BV4226.M69 2009
    251'.08—dc22

                                                                    2009035649

ISBN 978–0–8254–3356–6

Printed in the United States of America
12 13 14 15 16 / 5 4 3 2 1

Dedicated to
Dr. John W. Reed

*You consistently encouraged me
to take what I learned and share it
with those who want their audience
to both hear and "see" truth.*

Contents

Acknowledgments / 9

Introduction / 11

1. Why Illustrate? / 13

2. Why Humor? / 17

3. How Do Illustrations Help Communicate? / 21

4. Where Do You Find Illustrations? / 27

5. What Topics Do You Illustrate? / 33

6. Let's Talk About Illustrating Sin / 37
   Illustrations About Sin / 39

7. Let's Talk About Illustrating Substitution / 167
   Illustrations About Substitution / 171

8. Let's Talk About Illustrating Saving Faith / 261
   Illustrations About Saving Faith / 263

9. Your Illustration Check List / 357

Index of Illustration Topics / 359

Notes / 363

Acknowledgments

TO THE MANY VOLUNTEERS, typists, researchers, and assistants who over a course of ten years played a part in making this book a reality. Special acknowledgment must go to Jonathan Graham, whose vision for the project, tireless effort, and attention to detail brought this book to fruition.

Introduction

IT STARTED AS A THOUGHT but became a hunger. It became crystallized through what I most love.

I'm an evangelist. From the day I met Christ, a passion to evangelize consumed me. To tell non-Christians how to get to heaven is the most exciting thing on earth. Like strawberry shaved ice on a hot summer day, it's refreshing, stimulating, reviving.

One day I got an idea. It crossed my mind the more I spoke. Even as I jogged before breakfast or drove to an appointment, I couldn't get it off my mind. The idea consumed me. I wanted to write a book on illustrations—but a very different book.

As I considered that thought, one thing weighed heavily on me. Illustrations help non-Christians of the twenty-first century relate to the gospel message. Yet I want to provide more than just thought-provoking stories. Illustrations alone don't excite me. I want to do for you, the reader, what I wish someone would have done for me years ago—explain how to use them. The effectiveness of an illustration depends on the way you walk into it or out of it. Walking in without direction is like shooting an arrow into the air. The purpose is unclear. Walking out clumsily is like shooting an arrow with no tip. The penetration is blunted. My goal is to give you a book that will enhance your ability to communicate with non-Christians. It is designed to guide you in how to effectively use *any* illustration in your message, not just the ones in this book.

Notice I keep emphasizing non-Christians. Again, I'm an evangelist. *My* burden is to explain how to use illustrations effectively before a non-Christian audience. I hope this will serve you in your outreach opportunities.

God wants non-Christians not just to hear—He wants them to understand. As the Holy Spirit works through an effectively used illustration, unbelievers will say, "I understand what God is saying to me." When your Savior becomes their Savior by truth, illuminated through a well-used illustration, that is something of eternal value.

Chapter 1

Why Illustrate?

GOD IS A PROMISE KEEPER, not a promise breaker. What does God promise to use to bring people to Christ? The Word of God. Romans 10:17 says, "So then faith comes by hearing, and hearing by the word of God."

That's why it's important not to speak around the Word. No, we must speak the Word. Paul's exhortation to Timothy was unmistakable: "Preach the Word" (2 Tim. 4:2). We, as evangelists, need to be expositors. We should convey the truth in such a way that non-Christians know we are repeating what God has already said. Once we've read the text, we ought to jump into it, not leap from it. We are explaining God's Word, not ours. His Word is relevant, authoritative, and penetrating. When unbelievers struggle with what they hear, they need to know their struggle is with Him, not us. He authored the text. We're just explaining it.

So Why Do We Need Illustrations?

Illustrations help both in the explanation of the text and in understanding it. Jesus Christ was the number one communicator of all time. Count the number of times He told a story or, as the Bible calls it, a parable. In the Gospel of Matthew, Jesus gave sixteen parables. Dwight Pentecost said, "The story parable was the figure Christ used most commonly to teach truth to His hearers."[1] Approximately one-third of Christ's teaching was through parables. Jesus knew that stories communicate. Truth from the mouth of the speaker becomes understanding in the mind of the listener. The Master Communicator knew the importance of illustrations.

A careful student of Scripture might ask, "What was the purpose of the parables?" Matthew 13:10–13 reveals that with greater revelation comes greater responsibility. The more one understands and rejects, the more severely will one be judged. Through parables, Christ revealed truth to believers to help them spiritually. He hid it from unbelievers to protect them from more severe judgment. Parables in the New Testament, then, were often designed more for Christians than non-Christians. Through parables Jesus revealed truth about the kingdom of heaven to His disciples.

What Purpose Do Illustrations Serve for Non-Christians?

The point is, as a communicator, Christ used stories. Even when we use stories to illustrate truth, we don't use them the way Christ used divinely inspired parables—to teach truth to believers and hide it from unbelievers. Our stories are not divinely inspired. Only the Word has such claim. We are simply following a principle that Christ demonstrated: a story drives home truth. Haddon Robinson notes, "Ordinary people responded to Jesus' parables with such interest that they walked miles to be in His audience. Stories are inductive; they resemble stealth bombers slipping in under people's defenses to deliver their load."[2]

Christ wasn't the first to use illustrations. The Old Testament is full of them. When the prophet Nathan confronted David about his sin with Bathsheba, he told the story of a rich man who took a little lamb from a poor man to feed a traveler (2 Sam. 12:1–15). That story convicted David of his sin with Bathsheba.

Why Are Illustrations Effective?

Illustrations use something people do understand to explain what they don't understand. Non-Christians understand newspapers, magazines, bumper stickers, and billboards. They see these daily. Illustrations from such sources help drive home the truth from God's Word. Charles Spurgeon viewed the sermon as the house, and the illustrations as the windows that let in the light. Listeners hear the truth you proclaim; through an illustration they see it. So when you use an illustration, you turn an ear into an eye. Seeing a sermon is always better than just hearing one.

Keep in mind, though, that understanding happens only through the power of the Holy Spirit. First Corinthians 2:14 reminds us, "But the natural man does not receive the things of the Spirit of God, for they are foolishness to him; nor can he know them, because they are spiritually discerned." But illustrations are what the Holy Spirit often uses to cause people to understand truth, not just hear it.

Another reason illustrations are effective is they add interest. What happens when you hear a speaker make one of the following comments?

- You won't believe what happened to me just two days ago.
- Did you see the article in the newspaper this morning?
- A friend e-mailed this story to me.
- The evening news last night reported an interesting event.

14

- You're going to laugh when I tell you what happened to a good friend last week.

Instantly, you look up. If you're starting to doze, you wake up. Your eyes are focused, you listen more keenly, your attention is captured. Which messages cause you to glance at your watch the most—the ones with illustrations or the ones without? Illustrations enliven a message and keep your attention. If told well, a three-minute story seems more like thirty seconds. When listening to speakers who illustrate well, you're surprised when they're finished instead of wishing they were. Illustrations, then, make a message interesting. Ralph Waldo Emerson summarized it well: "I cannot hear a sermon without being struck by the fact that amid drowsy series of sentences, what a sensation a historical fact, a biographical name, a sharply objective illustration makes."[3] Spurgeon captured the thought in seven words: "Illustrations make a sermon pleasurable and interesting."[4]

When a speaker doesn't use illustrations, the message comes across as academic, not quite connected with life. Beyond that, the speaker cannot hold the attention of an audience as well. Spurgeon told his students, "A house must not have thick walls without openings, neither must a discourse be all made up of solid slabs of doctrine without a window of comparison or a lattice of poetry; if so, our hearers will gradually forsake us, and prefer to stay at home and read their favorite authors whose lively tropes and vivid images afford more pleasure to their minds."[5]

USA Today once carried a special article titled, "When giving speech, tell a good story." It featured thoughts from Mark Wiskup, a professional communicator coach. The article read, "At different points in your speech, insert stories so that you can 'paint the picture with words.' Well crafted and well delivered stories build connections, make people comfortable, and make cold figures and seemingly distant concepts reassuring. 'Audiences want to follow and learn from speakers who are inspiring and who make actual messages come alive,' [Wiskup] says."[6]

If listeners understand Scripture more easily and you can hold their attention, God has used illustrations to bring them one step closer to the kingdom.

Chapter 2

Why Humor?

NEVER BEEN THERE. SO when I received an invitation to Delhi, India, for an evangelistic outreach I was excited. Preaching the gospel in a country steeped in Hinduism thrills any evangelist. I began my homework, asking questions about the audience. Sensing my desire to be effective, the host pastor said, "There are two things you need to communicate in India. Stories and humor."

When I was in Russia, I prepared to speak at a city-wide outreach. As I talked through my messages with my interpreter, I shared a humorous story I planned to use. He said, "Don't use that. Russians don't identify with humor." I removed all humor from my messages. Then I got to know the people of Russia. They *loved* humor. The pastors just weren't using any. I wondered, "Is that why many churches in Russia have no young people in them? What image are they presenting of God? Aren't Christians, of all people, the ones who should laugh and enjoy life?" So I convinced my interpreter that if I used humor the people would respond. Attendance climbed each night. Thoughts about God, life, and laughter changed. As the week concluded, pastors asked, "Will you teach us how to use humor when we speak?"

What Makes Humor Effective?

Humor is universal. Everyone appreciates it and loves to laugh. Humor also communicates. It conveys a message. When people are laughing, they are listening, and you can tell them anything you want to tell them. In fact, telling your audience something through humor makes the truth more digestible. Talk to a man about his conceit, and he might become defensive. A humorous illustration makes him laugh and say, "You're right. That sounds a lot like me." Talk to a woman about her dishonesty and she may attempt to deny it. Use an illustration that contains humor, she might respond, "Okay, I *have* done wrong."

Humor relaxes the audience—an audience that is often on edge. The listeners are apprehensive about how long the program will last, what the participants will be like, how dull the speaker might be. Humor will make them glad they came.

Another advantage of using humor is what it says about the speaker. Humor tells the audience that the speaker is an engaging person. People are drawn to speakers with a good sense of humor. We enjoy speakers who can laugh, particularly at themselves.

Perhaps the most important advantage of humor is that it gives non-Christians, who often have a negative view of God, a positive view of His people and eventually of Him. I love the story told by Chuck Swindoll in *Living on the Ragged Edge*. He writes:

> When I was growing up, my family lived next door to a family that had many of the world's goods we didn't have, but they didn't have the joy Christ can bring—which we had in abundance. I remember one Christmas when we were singing together as a family. My dad was playing his harmonica; my brother was playing the piano; and my sister, mother, brother, and I were singing some of the old carols and some of the folk songs of the Christmas season. We were laughing like crazy, singing to the top of our voices.

Suddenly, my mom said, "We're making so much noise, we better close the windows or we'll disturb all the neighbors." So we closed the windows.

Within moments our phone rang. It was a girl who lived next door. She asked, "Why did you close your windows?" "Well, we didn't want to disturb you," was mom's answer. The girl blurted out, "Disturb us? That's the most laughter we've had the entire Christmas season! Please open your windows. That's beautiful music!"[1]

Are There Subjects to Avoid Joking About?

Humor must enhance your message, not *be* your message. So I'm not suggesting you tell jokes for twenty-five minutes and then say, "Come to Christ." God desires that we be communicators, not stand-up comics.

Humor should never be used for humor's sake. It should be used for communication's sake. Make a point and use humor to communicate that idea. Avoid humor that doesn't fit. Humor might make us laugh for five seconds, but it should make us think for ten minutes.

Some subjects, though, are inappropriate for humor. A. W. Tozer once said, "Your sense of humor doesn't have to dry up and die [because you're a Christian]. There's plenty to laugh at in the world—just be sure you don't laugh at that which God takes seriously."[8] Some topics should never be laughed at, such as the holiness of God or the substitutionary death of His Son. Use proper boundaries.

Avoid humor that would offend lost people. Never tell ethnic jokes or jokes about particular people. If you tell a joke on a political figure that you don't respect, people in your audience might be offended if they see that person as a hero.

Use caution with jokes on occupations. Should you tell an "attorney" joke there could be an attorney in the audience. That's why in using occupation-related humor, you might consider using your own occupation first.

Did Christ Use Humor?

I believe He did—and I have two reasons. First, consider who He was—the perfect Son of God, totally balanced in all areas, committed to grace, and a person who lived life to the fullest and wanted that for others. John 1:14 says of Christ, He "was full of grace and truth." Graceful living allows us to enjoy life and humor. In John 10:10 Jesus declared, "The thief does not come except to steal, and to kill, and to destroy. I have come that they may have life, and that they may have it more abundantly." *Abundance* speaks of the quality of life Jesus wants for us. Not only does He desire that we live forever, but also He wants us to experience life to the fullest. A life of that nature gives reason to smile and even enjoy humor.

Second, consider His mind as evidenced by the way He spoke and the words He used. Look at Matthew 23:24. Christ characterizes the Pharisees' behavior by saying, "Blind guides, who strain out a gnat and swallow a camel!" That statement is hyperbole, or exaggeration, which is often used to point out the irony in a situation. In this case, the basis is the Old Testament. Leviticus 11:41–43 prohibited eating any insect that swarmed, crawled on its belly, walked on all fours, or had many feet. The Pharisees were meticulous with that regulation. They would strain out the smallest insect—the gnat—with a cloth filter before drinking liquids, especially wine. Christ stated they would, however, easily swallow such a large unclean animal as a camel. No one can swallow a camel, but His exaggeration was for the purpose of exposing their hypocrisy.

Someone who would use "swallow a camel" to convey hypocrisy *probably* said things that struck one as being humorous. While the Pharisees may or may not have smiled at such an analogy, some of the people listening in might have. I think that Christ, who was such an effective communicator, said things that caused people to smile. While smiling, they were also convicted by the truth behind whatever humor He used.

Since we weren't present when His messages were spoken, it's difficult to pick up on that humor. Additionally, we don't have every word He uttered. Whether or not He used humor doesn't change anything. If He did, we're following His pattern. If He didn't, that doesn't negate the fact that God can use humor to speak to lost people.

Chapter 3

How Do Illustrations Help Communicate?

ILLUSTRATIONS ARE LIKE LOCOMOTIVES. They only help if they're on a track and move the passenger (in this case, the listener) to a particular destination the speaker has in mind. What does that track look like? As stories and humor are used of the Holy Spirit, what makes them move listeners?

Illustrations Must Be Relevant

Stories have to interest non-Christians, not just you. They need to be relevant. A book like this could contain an entire chapter on the need to spend time with non-Christians. Otherwise, you forget what interests them. Stories and humor used in evangelistic speaking are often different from ones used with believers. They are prepared for unbelievers and given to unbelievers. The illustration is relevant to where they are *now*, not where they will be *after* they come to Christ.

Suppose you choose a story about a mission trip to Africa. The fact that it was a mission trip doesn't need to be mentioned. Use aspects of the story relevant to non-Christians. You may, for example, relate the confusion experienced in determining how to get from one city to another when the people around you give conflicting directions. Then you use that frustrating experience to illustrate the confusion your listeners experience in knowing how to get to heaven when people give conflicting messages. Use the part relevant to non-Christians, not the part that isn't. Non-Christians can't identify with the "mission" part of the trip. They can, however, identify with the confusion about conflicting directions.

If you're using an illustration about prayer, use aspects of prayer that interests non-Christians. Where and how often your church meets for prayer is immaterial. Telling about encouraging answers received to prayer might be helpful to your listeners. Though it may be difficult, step outside your circle of believers and think non-Christian.

Illustrations Must Address a Particular Point

The most effective illustrations are not like a shotgun shell full of pellets that scatter. They're like a rifle shell with a single tip, or in this case, a point that penetrates. There must be a single truth the illustration drives home. Never use an illustration unless you have a purpose for using it. We use illustrations, after all, to communicate.

Purpose, then, is the critical area. An illustration you have chosen to address the need for honesty may actually address the benefits of honesty. An illustration selected for the deceitfulness of sin might actually address the consequences of sin. If you have any questions, ask a trusted friend for feedback. Encourage your friend to tell you what you need to hear, not what you want to hear.

Illustrations Should Have the Proper Amount of Detail

Details also make illustrations effective. Whey you say "office building on a busy street," that doesn't catch my attention. Neither does it help me envision the building. When you tell me, though, it was a dark granite, five-story office building, at a crowded intersection in downtown Philadelphia, I see it. Was the woman blonde or gray? Did she amble or jog? Was the man a businessman or a plumber? Was the vehicle a VW or an SUV? Did the man jump out of bed, or did he stumble his way into the kitchen? Was the cake chocolate with icing dripping down the sides or was it a bland sponge cake? Did the accident occur as the sun was coming up or going down? Such details help your listeners visualize those people, places, buildings, circumstances, and events. Details make the stories come alive.

Suppose you don't know the details. To make up the details can destroy the integrity of the illustration. If, though, you can reasonably determine as much as possible about the circumstances, the more you can share, the better. If you don't know the details, the illustration (if it's a good one) can and should be used. But any available details are helpful.

Yet balance is critical. It's possible to share so many details one loses the main point of the story. Here's a helpful question to ask when considering how many details to use: "Will these details help the illustration without overwhelming the listener?" If so, use them. If not, leave them out. Again, the key word is *balance*. It's possible not to have enough details but it's also possible to have too many. Also, as you'll see when we examine illustrations that use quotations, the person who made the quote sometimes matters. Other times it doesn't. The year of the occurrence may be important. Other times it isn't.

Illustrations Must Be Believable

An illustration that lacks believability hinders communication. It might fascinate the listener but distract from the truth. We don't want our listeners to doubt the accuracy of the story. That doubt can lead to a lack of trust in what we're saying. The listener might wonder, if we're not truthful with the illustration, are we truthful in other areas?

What about an illustration that sounds unbelievable but is true? If you can convince the audience it is real, use it. If nothing you say would convince the audience of the illustration's integrity, it has to be laid aside. Illustrations that don't sound truthful—even if they are—will hurt more than help.

Be careful how you use illustrations from your own life. Personal illustrations have the advantage of being fresh. They've never been heard. But every illustration shouldn't be about you. Warren Wiersbe and David Wiersbe in *The Elements of Preaching* state, "Some preachers talk about themselves so much, you could reconstruct their lives from their sermons. Others are so private that their personal experiences are told as anonymous anecdotes. Both extremes should be avoided."[9]

Also, with non-Christians, personal illustrations should deal with where you have failed, not where you have succeeded. Most people can handle you being transparent about your failures. When you share that you received two speeding tickets within two weeks, they can relate. C. S. Lewis speaks to this issue when he says, "I cannot offer you a water-tight technique for awakening the sense of sin. I can only say that, in my experience, if one begins from the sin that has been one's own chief problem during the last weeks, one is very often surprised at the way this shaft goes home."[10] Listeners cannot handle your bragging about your accomplishments. You may have trained hard to win a triathlon, but someone else needs to mention it, not you.

Illustrations Must Grab Attention

An illustration that is true, has a point, and is believable still won't do any good if it doesn't grab and hold the listener's attention. That's why the newer the illustration, the better. It's important to consistently add to your collection of illustrations.

Some illustrations, however, are applicable even if they happened twenty years ago because the event could happen today. A story about someone who rushes into the path of an approaching car to save a child is relevant because that act could just as easily occur today. A quote about death made forty years ago may be just as applicable today. For many illustrations, the date doesn't matter. The content makes it timeless. Also, it's sometimes difficult to find a current illustration on a specific topic.

One suggestion in using a familiar illustration is to tell it in a way the audience may not have heard it or add a detail often overlooked. That makes even a familiar illustration interesting.

Are historical illustrations out? No. They deal with what has happened, not what might happen. They are about fact, not fiction. Also, many people love history. And sometimes the best illustration is one that happened thirty years ago, not last week. *What* happened matters. *When* it happened isn't always important.

Illustrations Must Be Understandable

If the story is difficult to explain, it's difficult to comprehend. Some stories and humor are hard to grasp. Those stories may not be worth your time and effort.

Illustrations Must Be in the Right Amount

It's possible to use too many illustrations. The greater danger, however, is using too few, not too many. In *Illustrating the Sermon*, Michael Hostetler makes the point, "Very few sermons are over-illustrated; multitudes are under-illustrated."[11] We are speaking to a generation of people who watch. They don't read. Illustrations help them watch. They see truth, not merely hear it. Think of illustrations consisting of quotes, stories, statistics, analogies, and so forth. As a general rule, you need ten to fifteen per message. This, of course, depends on time, the message, and your audience. You need fewer illustrations for a fifteen-minute evangelization message than for one that takes thirty minutes. Certain messages, such as unfolding a biblical drama, may require fewer illustrations than a message from the book of Proverbs. A message to young people may require more illustrations than one to middle-aged parents.

Be sure to use a wide variety of illustrations in each message. Every quote should not be from a sports figure. Two "lost at sea" illustrations are too many. The illustrations should cover a spectrum of circumstances.

Illustrations Must Be a Good Mix of Humor and Serious

Humor is enhanced when it's properly mixed with serious illustrations. Serious illustrations are enhanced when they are properly mixed with humor. At times humorous illustrations are placed back-to-back after consecutive points in a message. If, for example, you deal with four ways we try to relieve guilt, two of those ways might lend themselves to humorous illustrations. The more you can spice the message throughout with humor the better.

Humor is more appropriate in the beginning and middle of the message than at the closing. As you approach your conclusion, you're going to call upon your listeners to make a serious decision about their eternal destiny. Humor no longer fits at that point. It would distract from the seriousness of the moment.

Using effective illustrations makes you a communicator, not just a speaker. The proper use of stories and humor keep your message from becoming an abandoned train. Illustrations can instead help your message be a power-driven locomotive. The train is on a track toward its destination. Illustrations help the message arrive there.

Chapter 4

Where Do You Find Illustrations?

HOW DO YOU FIND a wedding ring on a 30,000-acre ranch? That was my dilemma.

My wife and I love the outdoors. While enjoying an outing on a large ranch in Texas, we had covered a considerable amount of acreage. Returning to our SUV, I suddenly realized my wedding ring was gone. Sure, it could be replaced, but *that one* represented more than thirty years of the greatest love I've ever felt toward and from anyone.

I knew it was gone. "Wait a minute," I thought. "Maybe not." I remembered clearing some brush from a spot so we could sit and relax for a moment. Perhaps the perspiration had caused the ring to slide off my hand. Still, even if we searched that location, how would we find it? One wrong step could press the ring into the dusty Texas soil.

Then an idea hit me. Gold sparkles in the dark when exposed to light. After dark we could take our brightest lantern and cover the same ground. That night, with light and eyes focused downward and prayers directed upward, we began the search. Close to the spot where we'd cleared the brush, something gleamed in the darkness. To our amazement, it was the ring. It was level with the ground, but the top edge of it had caught the light. Picking it up, I returned it to the only place it was helpful to me—the ring finger of my left hand.

Illustrations are like my ring buried in the soil. They're of no use unless you find them. You can't use an illustration you haven't heard, can't remember, or haven't read. Let's look at how you find and store illustrations.

How Do You Find Them?

Before you think sources, think principles. Two principles are more important than anything else I could suggest.

Principle 1: Never Be Without a Way to Record

I carry 3 x 5 cards everywhere I go. I've used them for years and found that this works best for me. They fit easily into my pocket, and I keep a large supply. If you do what is taught in this chapter, you'll need more than one. While waiting for appointments in reception areas, I often find good illustrations by reading magazines, but I occasionally run out of cards. The office usually has some, and the receptionist will let me have one or two. Whether using 3 x 5 cards, electronic devices, or a small notepad, find something that is convenient and that you'll use consistently. You need to record illustrations when you find them, not later. You won't remember them later. How many times have you said, "What was that story someone told me?"

If you do remember the story, you may forget the details. As noted earlier, details make the illustration engaging. Was it a sports arena or a high-rise apartment complex? Was the person a teenager or an elderly man? Was the couple enjoying a rib-eye steak or a value meal at McDonald's? What color was her hair? Without details, an illustration loses its warmth and some of its communicative ability. Recording those details in whatever fashion you choose saves them and enables you to recall the details when your mind can't. An old Chinese proverb states, "The faintest ink has a better memory than the sharpest brain."

Principle 2: Set a Goal

"Aim at nothing, hit nothing" is true in many areas, including illustrations. If you don't start collecting illustrations this week, you may never start. You'll put it off until another time, and that "another time" may never arrive.

My goal is ten a week. I always go over that amount, though, not under it. For some goals in my life I'll say, "Well, I tried—just didn't make it." This is *not* one of them. It's because I know it is a reachable goal. Also, it's imperative to how I earn my living—communicating truth.

If you follow these two principles you'll begin looking for illustrations wherever you turn. As Jay Adams says in *Pulpit Speech*, "One way to begin to 'see' illustrations of truth wherever you turn is to discipline yourself to do so."[12] Illustrations are everywhere. You'll find them on the side of a bus or back bumpers of cars, the front page of a newspaper or the back side of a community bulletin. A news commentator will quote a sports figure, or a special-feature TV program will quote a historian. A coworker will share a humorous story, or a neighbor will share a thought-provoking paragraph from a best seller.

Without something to record illustrations when you find them and without a goal, they will remain hidden in the soil. The eye will not be developed to see them, and an instrument will not be handy to retain them.

Now Think Sources

Reading is the biggest source of illustrations. Television programs supply illustrations, as do conversations, but nothing surpasses reading. The more you read, the more quickly your illustration file grows.

Newspapers and weekly magazines top the list. They are frequent and current. Choose those that view life from a broad perspective. *USA Today*, for example, features sections on current news, sports, money, and life. *Time* magazine often presents things the way non-Christians view them.

Don't stop with the weekly publications. *Reader's Digest* is published once a month but is filled with human life adventures and humor. The point is, read as much as possible. Consume books. I read at least two a month. Rarely do I read a book without finding one and often dozens of illustrations. Keep a 3 x 5 card as a bookmark in anything you read. Then it's handy to write down the illustration and the page number of each illustration in that book. Devotions like *Our Daily Bread* published by Radio Bible Class offer many. Other sources include the Internet and newsletters.

Speakers who use illustrations in their messages also use them when they write. So read what those speakers have authored. I've been privileged to sit under the ministry of Dr. Chuck Swindoll on numerous occasions. He averages twelve illustrations per message. When he writes he also uses illustrations. When I read his books, I receive the blessing of his ministry as well as obtain illustrations.

Your mate can be a big help in finding illustrations. Returning from an engagement, I'll often find on my desk an illustration my wife found. And remember, you're looking for illustrations for all people, not just for non-Christians. Your messages to believers need supporting material, too. Everyone loves stories. So another source for illustrations is the people to whom you minister. Become known as a person who uses illustrations frequently, and when your people read statistics, quotations, and stories, they often think of you. They may forward an e-mail to you or mail an article with an illustration. You can discern later which illustrations are suitable for a non-Christian audience.

And don't feel like you're taking some illicit shortcut by using someone else's illustrations. Very few speakers use original illustrations, and they are borrowed from other sources without apology. Having collected over 20,000 illustrations over more than thirty years, I seldom hear one I haven't already heard. Even those featured in *Reader's Digest* are frequently from other sources. When I file them, I always record my source so I know where I found them, but I'm aware that often that source was not the original one.

For accountability purposes, it's best to locate the original source whenever possible.

Pray! God is more concerned about communication of truth than you are. The God who supplies food and finances to meet physical needs will supply illustrations that meet spiritual needs. I regularly come to the Lord as I prepare a message and ask, "Give me the supporting material to drive this truth home." He directs me to some I already have and helps me obtain what I don't have.

How Do You File Them?

"It will take me a while to find that," a church leader once remarked. "My filing system is deplorable." If that's true of your illustration file, it will be of little use. Time is critical in message preparation. You have only so many hours set aside to put a message together. You don't have an entire evening to find one illustration.

Start your filing system by giving each illustration a main heading—one word that captures the illustration. Try this: for each illustration, ask two questions:

1. What is it talking about?
2. What is it saying about what it is talking about?

How does the illustration strike *you*? I might read the illustration and humility pops to my mind. When you read it you think of brokenness. You need to file it under brokenness.

Next, using one to five words, put your illustrations under subheadings. Is it telling about "brokenness—cause of" or "brokenness—example of" or perhaps "brokenness—means to"? If your message needs an "example of" brokenness, you don't need to spend time looking at all the illustrations that speak to the "means of" brokenness.

Understand that when you first read an illustration, you could probably think of five different headings to file it under. Choose the one that you're most comfortable with, and don't spend an inordinate amount of time deciding upon the heading. The idea is that you'll eventually have plenty of illustrations, and this frustration with filing will cease to be a problem.

Keep in mind, too, that humorous illustrations need to be spread throughout the file. You don't need a separate section called humor. You want applicable humorous illustrations under every heading and subheading, be it lying, temptation, excuses, honesty, pride, or anything else. Should you need an illustration on how we try to hide our sin instead of confess it, you want to have under your "sin—hiding it" subheading both varieties—humorous and serious.

What started out as my file box has now been converted to a computerized system. This has greatly aided me when searching for specific illustrations. I use Microsoft Access, a software program that allows me to create a database of my illustrations. By entering key words into the software's search field, I can now search by topic and subtopic, and a multitude of other search options. If, for instance, I remember a quote from a current or previous president, even though I can't recall what heading I gave it, I can enter the president's name. I can also type in a partial phrase of the quote in the search field and the software can locate it within seconds.

If you use an illustration, designate in your file system how you used it. Which message, what occasion, or what radio program? You may think you'll remember the ones you've used, but you won't. I give each of my messages a number, then I record the message number on the "used" line of my Access program. The number reminds me of the message that I've used this illustration in.

Ready, Set, Collect!

Available illustrations don't build up your illustration file. Collecting them does. But the time to start is today. Go back to the two most important principles: (1) never be without a way to record; (2) set a goal. If you act on these two principles, one month from now you'll be a measurable distance from where you started. A good habit will have been formed—one that sets you apart from many speakers. Most importantly, when your audience leaves, they know how truth written two thousand years ago fits life today.

Chapter 5

What Topics Do You Illustrate?

IT WAS ONLY A DREAM but it seemed so real. I stood on the edge of the pit called hell. What lay before me was dark and bottomless—the worst sight I'd ever seen. The Savior was there. His eyes reflected love, yet sorrow. It was clear that He had not rejected me. I had rejected Him.

I awoke in a sweat. Why didn't He ask what church I belonged to? Hadn't He observed my good life and community service? Wouldn't those have made a difference? I knew it was only a dream, but it still bothered me.

I kept studying the Bible—the wrong way. I placed it on its binder, let it fall open, and pointed to a verse. Some verses confused me. Others helped me. Through the ministry of the Holy Spirit, I started to understand. God saw me as a sinner, not as a church-going son of an honest dairy farmer. I was a sinner whose sin had to be punished by death. My good living would not pay for my sins. Jesus Christ already died in my place. He died, though, not to show me how to live—loving others. Neither did He die to show me how to die—without complaining. He died for more than that. He died as my substitute. They nailed Him to the cross when they should have nailed me.

When I fully understood that, Easter became more meaningful. He arose the third day, proving He is the One He claimed to be. To get to heaven, I had to accept what God accepted. I had to trust in Christ alone as the only way. One night, with the bedroom door closed, knees on the floor, hands cupped on my bed, I told God I was trusting His Son to save me.

No two conversions are exactly alike. In one sense, however, mine *was* like everyone's. Before I could be saved I had to understand three things.

I had to know I was a sinner. I had to know I had a substitute. I had to believe.

Whenever you present the gospel to a lost person, whether one on one or through public speaking, you must stress those three things. Your listeners must know they are sinners. Otherwise, they will never see their need. Christ plainly said, "For the Son of Man has come to seek and to save that which was lost" (Luke 19:10). Unless we see ourselves as God sees us—lost people—we will never come to Christ. Spurgeon was noted for his comment, "Before you can get a person saved, you have to get him lost." His point was biblical. Unless we see ourselves as sinners, we see no need for a Savior.

Your listeners must also know they have a substitute. If one person takes another person's punishment, the guilty can go free. In our lost condition, the payment is death and eternal separation from God. God declared, "The wages of sin is death" (Rom. 6:23). Whoever took our punishment, though, had to be a perfect person. One murderer cannot pay for another murderer's crime. One thief cannot pay for another thief's wrong. That's because neither is innocent and both deserve punishment. Second Corinthians 5:21 says about Christ, "For He made Him who knew no sin to be sin for us." Rising three days later, Christ could proclaim to the world, "I have conquered sin and death." Sin can now be pardoned instead of punished.

That pardon, though, has to be received. Scripture says the same thing to a lost person again and again. Believe! Jesus said, "Most assuredly, I say to you, he who believes in Me has everlasting life" (John 6:47). As a sinner deserving of hell, I must recognize that Jesus Christ has already taken my punishment and rose again. I must trust in Christ alone to save me. I can't depend on my good living, church attendance, baptism, or taking of the sacraments to get me to heaven. When it comes to my salvation, I can't depend on Christ *plus* anything that I have done. Instead, I must trust in Christ alone as my only way to heaven.

With that understood, we now have the three broad areas where illustrations are needed in evangelistic speaking—sin, substitution, and faith. Those three areas, properly illustrated, help lost people understand their condition, God's remedy, and the only thing God asks them to do in order to be saved.

You need many illustrations, though, for each subject. When you go to your illustration file, you want to have many to choose from and not be restricted to one or two. Two illustrations, for example, might illustrate the same thing. But because of the circumstances of the people in the illustration and those of your audience, one might be better than another. Also, one message may call for a serious illustration while another may need a humorous one.

We're about to look in detail at the "how to" of using particular illustrations. For one thing, you must enter and exit each illustration properly. In some of the illustrations I've given ideas to stir your thinking for both. With some illustrations, notice the wording, *"Possible Entrance"* and *"Possible Exit."* Remember, you can alter the effectiveness of an illustration by the way you walk into or out of it. Sometimes an illustration has to be adjusted through paraphrase, deletion of words, or removal of details. Different speakers also have their own styles and will use the same illustration differently. So I can give only a *Possible Entrance* and *Exit,* and depending on the message, the actual entrance and exit will vary. If I gave every *Possible Entrance* and *Exit* for every illustration, you'd have volumes to read. In each major topic, however, I've tried to give you enough to help you capture the idea of how to walk in and out of illustrations.

I've attempted to give the source of each one. Sometimes the source is unknown, so please be patient—and, if necessary, forgiving. I've been collecting illustrations every week for more than forty years, and I may have erred unintentionally with the source. Also, I often see the same illustration in more than one source. Stories get around!

Use these illustrations but aggressively add to them. Remember, I'm more interested in teaching you the "how" of illustrating than giving you illustrations. Let these excite you into finding other illustrations. Not only will you then have an abundance of illustrations on sin, substitution, and faith but also you'll know how to use them.

Chapter 6

Let's Talk About Illustrating Sin

NO ONE LIKES BAD news. We all prefer good news.

A squeak developed in one of the front wheels of our Chevy Tahoe. When my wife took it to our mechanic, we feared the worst. New brakes. Axle problem. Large bill. We were relieved when he told us that a piece of dirt on the brake lining was the only problem and the bill was twenty-five dollars. Good news.

The pain in my lower back hurt more each time I ran. It was irritating. Annoying. I was afraid the doctor might tell me to stop running or that I had a disc problem. I was relieved when he said the tiny calcium deposit would break up and disappear and that I should keep running. One week later, it was gone. Good news.

It was a thrilling time overseas, training nationals to reach their own people. But I was ready to come home to my family and the people at the office. The return flight was canceled. The news wasn't good. The next flight wasn't until the following morning. I remembered the key word in overseas travel—flexibility. Then the airline agent had more news. A seat had just opened up on the flight leaving in five minutes. If I hurried I could make it. I did. Good news.

Everyone would rather hear good news instead of bad. But in evangelism, if your listeners don't understand the bad news, they won't appreciate the good news. That's why each person must face his or her sinful and lost condition. We must see ourselves as God sees us. It's painful for us to recognize that we are sinners, but through that pain we see our need of a Savior.

What is involved in talking to people about sin? First, it depends on the text used before a lost audience. As an expositor, you may be speaking on John 3, the account of Christ's conversation with Nicodemus. At the appropriate time of the message, you might need to explain that our religious upbringing could keep us from seeing our need of Christ. Pharisees didn't always see themselves as sinners. If you are speaking on Luke 19, Christ's conversation with Zacchaeus, you have to explain that unless we see ourselves as Zacchaeus did—a person who has done wrong—we will never see our need of a Savior.

The second thing involved in talking about sin is the audience. When I first spoke in Russia, I discovered I didn't have to convince the people that they needed to be saved. Instead, I had to convince them that they *could* be saved. After seventy years of atheistic Communist rule, many believed they were destined to hell. People said, "It's too late. I can no longer be saved." In America, it's the opposite. I don't have to convince people they can be saved. I have to convince them they *need* to be saved. Our prideful society pats itself on the back and thinks, "I'm not half as bad as a lot of people I know."

The text and the audience make a difference in the illustrations needed. That's why an illustration file needs to include the different aspects of telling people, "You are a sinner."

Sometimes we need to explain people are sinners regardless of whether they think they are. Our sinful condition is based on fact, not feelings. Other times we need to alert them to the dangers of making excuses for sin. God desires confession, not excuses. The severity of sin must be understood. The punishment for sin is physical and spiritual. It is eternal death. Life does not stop at the grave. For an unbeliever, it continues in an eternal hell.

Some must recognize their own pride. Conceit blinds us to our sinfulness and depravity. Others have to recognize that their sin is against God, not just man. Still others have to understand what keeps them from thinking about the hereafter. The "somethings" of life and its materialism obscures their need of Someone. While focusing on what they do have, they miss out on Who they don't have.

Here, more than any other topic of evangelistic speaking, is where humor can help. Pride, stubbornness, and materialistic attitudes are hard to admit. But while laughing, we listen. By laughing at someone else's stubbornness, we see our own. Such humor tears down defenses, causes listeners to lower their guards, and opens their eyes for self-examination.

On the following pages are some helpful illustrations to use when talking about sin. (An index of illustration topics can be found at the end of this book.) Note that humorous illustrations are marked with a ☺. Whether humorous or not, each illustration can help when explaining to a lost person, "You are a sinner."

Illustrations
About Sin

ACCEPTANCE/REJECTION

❖ **POSSIBLE ENTRANCE:** *We sometimes feel like we're worthless, worthless to others and worthless to God. We may even feel that others see us as trash.*

In *Lincoln's Daughters of Mercy*, Marjorie Greenbie tells about Mother Bickerdyke, who worked with General Sherman during the Civil War. She brought relief to thousands of wounded and dying Union soldiers.

Once, when Mother Bickerdyke was giving special attention to a man considered worthless by his comrades, she was asked, "Why do you waste your time on trash like that?" "Because," she replied, "when there's any creature around here so miserable that there's nobody to care for him, he still has two friends in this army. One is God, and the other is me."

—Our Daily Bread, 1994

POSSIBLE EXIT: *With God, the issue is not how you feel about yourself or how others feel about you, but how He feels about you.*

❖ **POSSIBLE ENTRANCE:** *Before God can do anything, we must see ourselves as God sees us—sinners who cannot save themselves.*

The reason why many are still troubled, still seeking, still making little forward progress is because they have not yet come to the end of themselves.

—A. W. Tozer, sermon "Dark, Dark Night of the Soul"

POSSIBLE EXIT: *How about you? Have you come to the end of yourself?*

❖ When you say a situation or a person is hopeless, you are slamming the door in the face of God.

—Charles L. Allen, God's Psychiatry

ACHIEVEMENTS

❖ **POSSIBLE ENTRANCE:** *One way God draws us to Himself is to show us all the things in life that can't satisfy us.*

Duane Thomas, star running back for the Dallas Cowboys in the 1970s, had it right. He kept hearing writers refer to the Super Bowl as the ultimate game, so he asked the obvious question: "If this is the ultimate game, why do they play it again next year?" That's the way things are in the world. You climb to the top of the heap only to discover that next year you've got to start all over again. Nothing in this life satisfies forever.

—Ray Pritchard, *He's God and We're Not*

POSSIBLE EXIT: *How many things have you looked at as the ultimate, only to discover how quickly those things pass?*

Note: Here the name and position is more important than the year. Also remember to adapt the illustration to your message. Instead of using the first two lines as they appear here, simply say, "Duane Thomas, who years ago was the star running back for the Dallas Cowboys, made an interesting observation. After hearing the Super Bowl referred to as the ultimate game, he asked . . ."

❖ The sensitive person who lives only for earthly things cannot truly feel good about himself or face the end of life with contentment. In 1966, about a year before he died, the brilliant physicist Robert Oppenheimer said, "I am a complete failure!" This man had been the director of the Los Alamos Project, a research team that produced the atomic bomb, and he had served as the head of the Institute for Advanced Study at Princeton. Yet, in looking back, he saw his achievements as meaningless. When asked about them, he replied, "They leave on the tongue only the taste of ashes."

—*Our Daily Bread*, 1984

❖ I began wrestling in the seventh grade, having set as my goal the state championship. My junior high and high school wrestling career had its ups and downs, but finally my sophomore year in junior college I won the state championship. I had attained my goal, but to my surprise, it wasn't satisfying. I began to feel that there must be something more to life than just achievements.

After trusting Christ I said, "With Christ in control of my life, I find I'm not as likely to be offended by what others think about me, and when I came up against tough competition on the mat or a bad call by the referee I can trust Christ with that situation and know He will use it to strengthen me, rather than my losing my temper or giving in to frustration."

—Sam Hieronymous, *Athletes in Action*, January 1972

Note: With this illustration, all the listener needs to know is that the comment came from a person who played on his university wrestling team or competed in collegiate sports.

❖   The following came from a UPI news release: "Isaac Singer, 77, who won the Nobel prize for literature at 73, said he was surprised and happy after his 1978 Nobel selection, but twenty minutes later was the same man 'with the same worries and troubles.'"

The failure of human achievements to bring lasting satisfaction was expressed well by Mr. Singer. Less than half an hour after being so highly acclaimed, he realized that he was burdened with the same cares as before.

—*Our Daily Bread*, 1983

ATHEISTS

❖   Today, it seems to me, there is no good reason for an intelligent person to embrace the illusion of atheism or agnosticism, to make the same intellectual mistakes I made. I wish—how often do we say this in life?—I had known then what I know now.

—Patrick Glynn, *God The Evidence*

❖   **POSSIBLE ENTRANCE:** *We have a struggle. We are not convinced God exists. But if there is a God, we are afraid of what He might do to us if we admitted those feelings to Him.*

A young boy wrote a letter he wished to send God. It read,

Dear Mr. God,

How do you feel about people who don't believe in you? Somebody else wants to know.

A friend,
Neil

Stephen Fortosis, *A Treasury of Prayers*, Kregel, 2001

POSSIBLE EXIT: *Go ahead—tell God your feelings. You will discover something exciting. Your feelings about Him don't change His feelings about you.*

☺   Son to atheistic Dad: Does God know we are atheists?
Dad: Yes, He does.

—Ramesh Richard

BLAME

☺ At times every leader feels like Lucy when she was leaning against a fence with Charlie Brown. "I would like to change the world," she said. Charlie Brown asked, "Where would you start?" She replied, "I would start with you!"

—John C. Maxwell, *Developing the Leader Within You*

☺ Boss to employee: "We've decided, Sherman, to give you more responsibility. From now on, you'll be responsible for everything that goes wrong."

—http://nithya.tripod.com/offi0007.htm

☺ **POSSIBLE ENTRANCE:** *We are so accustomed to blaming others for our problems.*

A woman angrily jumped out of her car after a collision with another car. "Why don't people ever watch where they're driving?" she shouted wildly. "You're the fourth car I've hit today!"

—Source unknown

POSSIBLE EXIT: *Everything you do is not someone else's fault. Some of it is your fault.*

☺ Teacher: "Yes, Johnny, what is it?"
Johnny: "I don't want to scare you, but Dad said if I didn't get better grades someone is going to get punished."

—Source unknown

❖ **POSSIBLE ENTRANCE:** *We often try to blame our sin on someone else. Some are not willing to take the blame for everything wrong they've done because they already feel they take the blame for everything.*

One evening my sister was sleeping in her bedroom upstairs while her eight-year-old son, Jason, was in his room on the first floor. Suddenly she was awakened by a loud crash. A van had run off the road, smacked into the side of the house, and come to a stop in the living room. Her first thought was of her son.

"Jason!" she yelled out.

From downstairs her son yelled back, "I didn't do it, Ma!"

—Submitted by Tammy Bonneau. Reprinted with permission from the July 1989 *Reader's Digest*. Copyright ©1989 by The Reader's Digest Assn., Inc.

POSSIBLE EXIT: *We can't keep blaming others. Sometimes we have to blame ourselves.*

CONFUSION
❖ Speaking of the current culture, the late Leonard Bernstein observed, "Half of the people are drowned . . . and the other half are swimming in the wrong direction."

—*Bibliotheca Sacra*, January–March 2000

☺ As I was driving to a speaking engagement, a car passed me with a bumper sticker that said: "I don't know if I am coming or going. Stay back in case I find out."

—R. Larry Moyer

Note: Here is an example of how in everything you do, illustrations come across your path. You simply have to be observant, set a goal of finding a certain number, and write them down.

☺ Some people are confused and feel as beaten down as a sparrow who flies into the middle of a badminton game.

—Source unknown

CONSCIENCE
❖ J. W. Mawson once had a long talk with a man of considerable intellectual powers, during which he pressed the claims of Christ upon him. Mawson said, "Several times in the course of our conversation he said, 'I'll never believe in hell.'" Mawson's answer was, "I am not asking you to believe in hell. What I want is that you should know the once crucified, but now risen and glorified Savior as our Lord." His final words were, "I'll never believe in hell."

That night he found it hard to sleep as his conscience and his mind were in conflict, and he argued with himself until, very weary, he dozed off to sleep early in the morning. It was the month of December. He awoke suddenly to see his bedroom in flames with fire and his first thought was, "I'm in hell."

It was a great factory on the opposite side of the road that was ablaze, flames leaping from the windows. His relief was beyond words, but he began to ask himself, "If there is no hell, why should I have thought that I was there on seeing the fire?" He realized that his conscience had spoken before he had had time to marshal his arguments. A thoroughly sobered man, he came to listen to the gospel and fled for refuge to the one and only Savior, Jesus Christ the Lord.

—S. Lewis Johnson

❖ The definition of conscience is "that still, small voice that warns us someone is watching."

—Source unknown

❖ Without God there is no absolute right and wrong that imposes itself on our conscience. But we know deep down that objective moral values do exist—some actions like rape and child torture, for example, are universal moral abominations—and, therefore, this means God exists.

—Lee Strobel, *The Case for Faith*

❖ There is no pillow so soft as a clear conscience.

— *Pulpit Helps*, July 1992

❖ A good conscience is a continual Christmas.

—Benjamin Franklin

☺ A mother was helping her son with his spelling assignment and came to the words "conscious" and "conscience." When she asked him if he knew the difference between the two, he responded, "Sure, Mom, conscious is when you are aware of something, and conscience is when you wish you weren't."

—Source unknown

❖ **POSSIBLE ENTRANCE:** *Even though we try to deny when we do wrong, we know it's wrong. Our conscience tells us so.*

Members of the housing authority board in Evansville, Indiana, thought they had come up with a good fundraising idea. They observed that many residents were living together without being married. Assuming that some would marry if they could afford a wedding, the board organized a raffle and offered as the winning prize an all-expense-paid wedding. Applications were distributed, but not one was returned.

45

Apparently the raffle wasn't such a good idea. The reason may have been that some couples would be embarrassed if it became known that they were living together.

Daily Bread, 1991

POSSIBLE EXIT: *Why be embarrassed by what you've done when God offers forgiveness for all our sins?*

❖ A bad conscience has a good memory.

—*Our Daily Bread*, 1982

❖ A conscience is what hurts when everything else feels good.

—Source unknown

CONSEQUENCES OF SIN

❖ Our For What It's Worth Department knows there's a roadside sign on I-95 as you approach DeLand, Florida. The yellow diamond-shaped sign warns travelers, *Narcotics Inspection Ahead*. There is no inspection. But the drivers who see the sign panic and make an immediate illegal U-turn. They are stopped and searched. The American Civil Liberties Union is objecting.

—Paul Harvey's *For What It's Worth*, May 1989

Note: Whether right or wrong, this tactic does not have to disqualify its use as an illustration. Instead you can say, "Regardless of how we feel about such a practice, there is one inspection we can't escape—the day when we have to answer to God for all the wrongs we have done." The weight of this illustration is that it puts an inspection we can negotiate up against an inspection we can't negotiate.

☺ **POSSIBLE ENTRANCE:** *Sometimes our sins come back to haunt us in ways we never anticipated.*

When Harry was a young boy in Louisiana, he was always getting into trouble. One morning while waiting for the school bus, he pushed the out-house into the bayou and went off for school as if nothing had happened. When he returned, his father was waiting for him. He said, "Son, did you push the outhouse into the bayou?" "Yes, Father," said Harry, "like George Washington, I cannot tell a lie." Harry's father took off his belt and said, "All right, son, bend over. I'm going to have to whip you." Harry tried to explain that Mr. Washington didn't spank George when he admitted chopping down the cherry tree. "Yes, son," said Harry's father, "but George's father wasn't in the tree."

—Source unknown

POSSIBLE EXIT: *Just because you can't foresee the consequences of your sin does not mean you won't experience them.*

❖ If you step on a rusty nail and don't do something about it, it will poison your system and eventually cause death.

It is the same with your sin. If you don't do something about it, it will poison your spiritual health and eventually cause eternal death.

—R. Larry Moyer

❖ **POSSIBLE ENTRANCE:** *Sin never pays. Sometimes the consequences are greater than we ever imagined.*

One Halloween, two boys who lived close to my hometown in Pennsylvania threw a log across the road. They thought it would be fun to watch surprised drivers when they came to the log and had to get out of their car to remove it. They watched and waited in the bushes. What they didn't anticipate was that with the sun beginning to fade, drivers might not see the dark log on the black road. A car came, and the driver, not seeing the log, crashed into it. The jolt killed both occupants—the parents of the two boys.

—R. Larry Moyer

POSSIBLE EXIT: *Do you know what the greatest consequence was? The damage could not be undone. Sin's consequences are sometimes like that.*

❖ A boy went to a lady's house to sell some berries he had picked. "Yes, I'll buy some," said the lady as she took the pail and went inside. Without concern for the berries, the boy stayed at the door, whistling to some birds perched in a cage. "Don't you want to come in and see that I don't take more than I should? How do you know I won't cheat you?" she asked. The boy responded from the porch, "I'm not worried. Besides, you'd get the worst of it." "Get the worst of it," said the lady. "What do you mean by that?" "Oh, I would only lose a few berries, but you would make yourself a thief."

—*Our Daily Bread*, 1982

☺ Two men tried to pull the front off a cash machine by running a chain from the machine to the bumper of their pickup truck. Instead of pulling the front panel off the machine, though, the machine pulled the bumper off their truck. Scared, they left the scene and drove home with the chain still attached to the machine. With their bumper still attached to the chain. With their vehicle's license plate still attached to the bumper.

—Internet humor

☺ Our For What It's Worth Department wonders if you heard about the customer who presented a credit card at David Burr, a clothing store in Irving, Texas.

The cashier asked, "What is your name?"
Customer said, "Diane Klos.
Cashier asked, "And what is your address?"
Customer gave her address. It was the address on the credit card.
But the cashier announced, "You came to the wrong place. I am Diane
    Klos; that is my address and that is *my* credit card."
And *then* she summoned police.

—Paul Harvey's *For What It's Worth*, February 1998

DEATH

❖ **POSSIBLE ENTRANCE:** *Death is a subject we'd rather not talk about but we can't escape. We never know when it is going to strike or what the circumstances will be.*

In Thomas Lynch's popular book *The Undertaking: Life Studies from the Dismal Trade* he reflects on his work as a funeral director in a small Michigan town. In twenty-five years, he has overseen some five thousand burials. How has it shaped his thinking?

"It tends to make me want to resolve conflicts a little quicker," Mr. Lynch says, "because I've seen people go off to work who don't come home."

—*Our Daily Bread*, 1999

POSSIBLE EXIT: *When you know Christ, you know where you're going whenever death strikes. You can live as a person prepared to die, then die as a person prepared to live.*

❖ Every person will either die a hopeless death or a deathless hope.

—Rich McCarrell

❖ When death knocks, it's come as you are!

—Marquee Motivators

❖ **POSSIBLE ENTRANCE:** *When we know Christ, we no longer need to fear death. He has gone ahead of us and come out on the other side victorious. Max Lucado, in Six Hours One Friday, tells the story of a missionary in Brazil who discovered a tribe of Indians in a remote part of the jungle.*

They lived near a large river. The tribe was in need of medical attention. A contagious disease was ravaging the population. People were dying daily.

A hospital was not too terribly far away—across the river, but the Indians would not cross it because they believed the river was inhabited by evil spirits. And to enter its water would mean certain death.

The missionary explained how he had crossed the river and was unharmed. But they were not impressed. He then took them to the bank and placed his hand in the water. They still wouldn't go in. He walked into the water up to his waist and splashed water on his face. It didn't matter. They were still afraid to enter the river.

Finally, he dove into the river, swam beneath the surface until he emerged on the other side. He raised a triumphant fist into the air. He had entered the water and escaped. It was then that the Indians broke into a cheer and followed him across.

Isn't that what Jesus did? He entered the river of death and came out on the other side so that we might no longer fear death, but find eternal life in Him.

—Reprinted by permission. *Six Hours One Friday*, Max Lucado, 2009,
Thomas Nelson Inc., Nashville, Tennessee. All rights reserved.

POSSIBLE EXIT: *Since Jesus Christ conquered death, when we have placed our trust in Him, we experience His same victory.*

❖ We need to own our own needs, to express our own feelings, to put our hope and trust in God, who will see us through. Perhaps the most crucial war in our nation's history was not the Revolutionary War but the Civil War. It was during one of those heated times of conflict that our president, Abraham Lincoln, was touring some of the battlefield hospitals. There he came upon a young man who would not live very long. The young man was in such a state that he did not recognize who Lincoln was.

The president said, "Son, is there anything I can do for you?" He said, "Yes, sir, if you would, please. I cannot write, I can barely see. If you would just please write a letter to my mother." The president sat down beside the bed and wrote the letter for the young man as he dictated it. The young man said, "Would you please sign it? I cannot do that." The young man then recognized the President of the United States.

He said, "Oh, I'm sorry, Mr. President, I did not know I was hindering or bothering you." He replied, "It's no bother, my son. Is there anything else I can do for you?" He said, "Yes, sir, since you are here, would you just wait a moment and see me through. It won't be long now."

Eleven o'clock, twelve o'clock, one o'clock, three o'clock, five o'clock. The President of the United States stayed by the bedside of that dying young man, and as the sun began to rise, the young man went on to claim his reward. The president closed the young man's sightless eyes and placed his hands across his breast with the satisfaction that he had kept his word—he had stayed, he had seen him through.

And that, beloved, is God's promise to you. When everything seems so out of control, Jesus who gave Himself for you and loved you will keep His word. He will stay with you, and He will see you through.

—Gary L. Carver, pastor, First Baptist Church, Chattanooga, Tennessee, cited in Michael Duduit, ed., *Great Preaching*

❖ In 1981, when President Ronald Reagan was nearly assassinated, his pastor from California came to see him in the hospital in Washington, D.C. Pastor Don Moomaw took the president's hand and asked him, "How is it with you and the Lord?"

"Everything is fine with me and the Lord," replied Mr. Reagan.

"How do you know?"

The answer was simple and profound: "I have a Savior."

—Ray Pritchard, *Beyond All You Could Ask or Think*

❖ At death we cross from one territory to another, but we'll have no trouble with visas. Our representative is already there, preparing for our arrival. As citizens of heaven, our entrance is incontestable.

—Erwin W. Lutzer quoted by George Sweeting in *Who Said That?*

❖ When a Christian dies, he has just begun to live.

—*Our Daily Bread*, 1990

❖ A person who knew the Lord stated how excited he was as he looked forward to death. He saw America as a death-denying, death-hating culture in contrast to what Scripture says is something believers can look forward to.

He is right. For the believer, death is the most exciting adventure of life. One doesn't go from life to death, but from life to life.

—R. Larry Moyer

❖ Death is not outside the boundaries of His love but inside the design of His glory.

—Pastor Jim Rose

❖ When a friend of ours, who was a believer, was in the hospital dying of cancer and they were discussing her coming through or not coming through, she said, "Either way, I'm a winner."

—R. Larry Moyer

❖ On Friday, December 22, 1899, D. L. Moody awoke to his last winter dawn. Having grown increasingly weak during the night, he began speaking in slow measured words: "Earth recedes, heaven opens before me!" Son Will, who was nearby, hurried across the room to his father's side.

"Father, you are dreaming," he said.

"No. This is no dream, Will," said the elder Moody. "It is beautiful. It is like a trance. If this is death, it is sweet. God is calling me and I must go. Don't call me back."

—*Moody Monthly*, July–August 1989

Note: In identifying D. L. Moody to a non-Christian audience, all one needs to say is, "a prominent preacher of the past."

❖ A man dying with cancer said to me, "The life of faith is a series of adventures. I am about to experience the last and best of them as I take my journey home."

—*Our Daily Bread, Special Edition*

❖ **POSSIBLE ENTRANCE:** *We sometimes use the expression, "The best is yet to come." For Christians, that is the absolute truth.*

A bright young girl of fifteen was suddenly cast upon a bed of suffering, completely paralyzed on one side and nearly blind. She heard the family doctor say to her parents as they stood by the bedside, "She has seen her best days, poor child."

"No, doctor," she exclaimed, "my best days are yet to come, when I shall see the King in His beauty."

—D. L. Moody

POSSIBLE EXIT: *If you trust Christ, you can have good days on earth, but the best is yet to come.*

❖ Now she is dead—as if everything she endured weren't enough to earn her a long life. On the other hand, maybe it means she gets to heaven, where she belongs, that much sooner.

—Referring to Jackie Kennedy, *Town and Country*

❖ **POSSIBLE ENTRANCE:** *When two people know Christ and one dies, they don't say "good-bye," they only say "so long." It will only be "so long" before they see each other again.*

Pastor Maynard Belt told of an elderly Christian couple who, after more than fifty years of marriage, were parted when the husband finally succumbed to a fatal disease. When their pastor went to call on the bereaved wife he found her sorrowing, yet triumphant. "I'm pleased to see you doing so well," he commented. "But I'm sure you miss your husband." "Oh yes," she replied. "I miss him more than I could ever say. But I think of it this way: For years and years I would wait all day for Bill to come home from his job. I'd work busily around the house, and I'd look forward eagerly to the time he'd come through the door. I'd have his dinner ready and we would enjoy being together. All these years I waited for him to come home, and now he's waiting for me to come home!"

—*Our Daily Bread*, 1983

POSSIBLE EXIT: *If you have not trusted Christ, Christ is waiting for you to come to Him. If you come to Christ, your loved ones who have died will be eagerly waiting for you to come home!*

❖ In the *Choice Gleanings* calendar, Alex Ross tells of an elderly Christian lady who lay dying. Her beloved husband sat by her bedside, tenderly holding her hand. They both knew that the end was near and that they soon would be parted. As their eyes met, a tear flowed down the old woman's wrinkled cheek. Gently, her husband wiped it away. Then, with a quaver in his voice, he said, "Thank God, Mary, that's the last!"

—*Our Daily Bread*, 1986

❖   A little girl looked up toward the beautiful sky one day and said, "Man, if it's that beautiful on this side, what is the other side going to be like?"

—Source unknown

❖   Separation is the law of earth. Reunion is the law of heaven.

—*Our Daily Bread*, 1983

❖   When the people in Colorado Springs, Colorado, learned that Jed Jackson, a popular local TV sportscaster, was losing his battle with cancer, they sent thousands of e-mails, letters, and cards to him. In response to the outpouring of encouragement, Jed wrote an article that was printed on the front page of the newspaper the day after his death. In it he said, "It has been my sincere privilege to serve this wonderful community, which has given me so much in return. The Lord has blessed my life in every possible way. He has given me my wife of nineteen years, my three splendid children, and more friends than a man should be allowed to have. I am overwhelmed by the kind regards so many of you have sent. Truly, my cup runneth over. Never forget that, with Jesus, the best is yet to come."

—*Our Daily Bread*, 2001

❖   No matter what is happening in your life, know that God is waiting for you with open arms.

—*Pulpit Helps*, Bulletin Inserts, November 2001

❖   Someone asked a Scotsman, "Are you on the way to heaven?" He replied, "Why man, I live there."
    What he meant was he was only a pilgrim here. Heaven was his home.

—Source unknown

❖   Over the door of a printer's shop, which is on the ground floor, are the words written, "Residence above: Here we have no continuing city, but we seek one to come (Hebrews 13:14). Our citizenship is in heaven; from where also we look for the Savior, the Lord Jesus Christ" (Philippians 3:20).

—Source unknown

❖ Going to heaven is not so much going to a place as it is going to a Person.

—Ray Pritchard, *Beyond All You Could Ask or Think*

❖ **POSSIBLE ENTRANCE:** *Christ changes not only your perspective on life, but also on death. Instead of being something you dread, it can be a moment you live for.*

Corporal, as an old slave was called, believed with an unalterable firmness in the truths brought to him.

Finally, the time came for Corporal to leave this world. The doctor said to him, "Corporal, it is only right to tell you that you must die."

"Bless you, doctor; don't let that bother you; that's what I've been living for," said Corporal with a smile.

—*The Earnest Worker*

POSSIBLE EXIT: *Can you look forward to death with anticipation? If not, the time to do something about that is not tomorrow. Tomorrow may never come. Do something about it today!*

Note: This can be greatly condensed and enhanced by saying. "Years ago a man was told by his doctor, 'It's only fair to tell you that you are dying.' The man said, 'Great, that's what I've been living for.'"

❖ Dr. G. Campbell Morgan tells of an incident that took place while he was a pastor in London. A young girl from his church lay dying. She had given birth to a child, and it appeared that it would cost her life. Dr. Morgan went to visit the girl and stood back in the shadow of her room while the doctor did his best to take care of her. She was delirious and kept saying, "Doctor, I don't want to go on alone. Doctor, please, I want to take my baby with me."

The doctor tried to say something that would help her. "My dear, your baby will have loving care. You need not be afraid. You can't take the baby with you. The gate through which you must go is only wide enough for one." Campbell Morgan stepped forward and touched the physician's shoulder and said, "Doctor, don't tell her that. Tell her that the gate through which she is about to pass is wide enough for two—for herself and her Shepherd. He who has brought her to this place will not desert her now, but He'll see her safely home to the other side."

—Haddon Robinson, *The Good Shepherd*

❖ Recently a weathered woodsman from the North Country told me how he had become a Christian only six months earlier. He said when he was young, in his twenties, he had seen his mother die—full of faith, with peace and confidence that God would receive her into heaven. He had never forgotten the witness of her life and realized that her whole life, full of hardships, had been lived in fellowship with God. Now, many years later, his father had died—bitter, full of fear, and without hope and without God. He was overwhelmed with the contrast and said, "I got myself over to the preacher's house to say I wanted to believe what mother believed because it was good for living and good for dying."

—Gladys M. Hung, "Don't Be Afraid to Die"

❖ When Corrie ten Boom was a girl, her first realization of death came after a visit to the home of a neighbor who had died. It impressed her that someday her parents would die. Corrie's father comforted her. "Corrie, when you and I go to Amsterdam—when do I give you your ticket?" Corrie answered, "Why, just before we get on the train." "Exactly," responded her father, "and our wise Father in heaven knows when we're going to need things too. Don't run out ahead of Him, Corrie. When the time comes that some of us will have to die, you will look into your heart and find the strength you need—just in time."

—Corrie ten Boom, *The Hiding Place*

❖ As a great Baptist missionary, Adoniram Judson, lay sick and about to die, he said, "I am not tired of my work, neither am I tired of the world; yet when Christ calls me home, I shall go with the gladness of a boy bounding away from his school. Perhaps I feel something like the young bride when she contemplates resigning the pleasant associations of her childhood for a yet dearer home—though only a little like her, for there is no doubt resting on my future."

—Edward Judson, *The Life of Adoniram Judson*

Note: There is no one in your audience who cannot identify with the statement, "I shall go with the gladness of a boy bounding away from his school." This statement is all you need. I have found it helpful to change the word "away" to "home." And as a speaker you may take this liberty as long as you don't change the meaning.

❖ When Augustine's mother lay dying, she whispered, "Bury my body wherever you wish. Nowhere is far from God."

—*Bible Expositor and Illuminator*, March–May, 1973

Note: The audience may not know who Augustine is, so you will want to refer to him as an early church father and/or the author of *The City of God* and *Confessions*.

❖ Voltaire said, "I hate life, and yet I hate to die."
Paul said, "For me to live is Christ, to die is gain."
—*Pulpit Helps*, August 2004

❖ When you are born again you never die; you just ascend.
—R. Larry Moyer

❖ Dr. Peter Conally, who has gone on to be with the Lord now, was a great preacher from Ireland. He was living when the *Titanic* sank. He told the story about an old preacher who was on board the ship and was thrown out into the cold waters of the Atlantic. (Remember, those waters were freezing, mushy ice.) When the old preacher realized that he couldn't save his own life, he literally swam from lifeboat to lifeboat, raft to raft, piece of debris to piece of debris, piece of ship to piece of ship crying out to the people, "Trust Christ. Take Him as Savior."

Finally, when the old preacher could stand it no longer, he started to sink. When he started to sink he cried out, "I'm going down!" Then all of the sudden, with a last great effort, he said, "No! No! I'm going up!" With that, he breathed his last.
—Greg Dixon, "The Sinking of the *Titanic*"

❖ **POSSIBLE ENTRANCE:** *When you have trusted Christ, death is not the end; it's only the beginning.*

A girl was greatly loved her brother, who was killed in World War II. One night she dreamed that she found her brother standing with a group of soldiers. She exclaimed, "I thought you were dead!"

"Dead? No! I'm not dead," he said. "I am only waiting for my new uniform. I am going to parade before the King!"
—Source unknown

POSSIBLE EXIT: *When you trust in Christ, knowing you will be in His presence is not a dream—it's a certainty!*

☺ Isaac Asimov tells the story of a rough ocean crossing during which a Mr. Jones, a believer, became terribly seasick. At an especially rough time, a kind steward patted Jones on the shoulder and said, "I know, sir, that it seems awful. But remember, no one ever died of seasickness." Mr. Jones lifted his green countenance to the steward's concerned face and replied, "Oh, don't say that! It's only the wonderful hope of dying that keeps me alive."

—Our Daily Bread, 2001

❖ Death for the Christian is a door, not a wall!

—Source unknown

❖ In the early days of her illness, Mom said to me, "Christine, I've taught you how to live. Now I'm going to teach you how to die."

—Christine Wyrtzen

Note: Many on the East Coast knew Mr. and Mrs. Jack Wyrtzen, Christine's in-laws. Jack was one of the cofounders of Word of Life International. The quote is pertinent and can be effective for an evangelistic message on Mother's Day. You can enhance the illustration by adding, "In the early days of an illness that eventually took her life, Mrs. Jack Wyrtzen, whose husband cofounded Word of Life International, said to her daughter-in-law, 'Christine . . .'"

❖ For the Christian, death is not gloom but glory!

—Our Daily Bread, 1976

❖ **POSSIBLE ENTRANCE:** *In many ways Jesus Christ renamed death. Instead of being "point of defeat" it's the "point of victory."*

The cape at the extreme southern point of Africa used to be called "Cape of Storms." It was a dangerous place, where many vessels were lost. The time came, however, when the voyage was successfully made and the name of the cape was changed to "Cape of Good Hope." Adventurers and sailors found that, once they had rounded the cape, they came into a quieter and more peaceful sea.

—Hugh T. Kerr

POSSIBLE EXIT: *This is similar to what happened to death. Because Christ arose, instead of being a place of dread, death is the entrance into eternal life. It's not a point of defeat; it's a point of victory.*

❖ The chariot has come, and I am ready to step in.
—Jordan Antie quoted by John Lawrence in *The Death of Death*

❖ Before his decapitation in the Tower of London, Sir Walter Raleigh said, "If the heart be right, it matters not which way the head lies."
—Source unknown

❖ Four minutes is all the warning we are likely to get for an all-out nuclear attack, according to the experts. . . . A national newspaper asked its readers to say how they would spend the last four minutes on earth. . . . A lady in Bristol said that she would read the 23rd Psalm, while someone in Kent declared that they would pray as they had never prayed before. From Washington came the searching comment, "Four minutes is quite a long time if you're prepared."
—Victory Tracts, "Four Minutes Warning," London

Note: Instead of using those locations, you could use the quote without them or interview a few local people to get their responses.

❖ A pious Scotch minister, being asked by a friend during his last illness whether he thought himself dying, answered, "Really, I care not whether I am or not; for, if I die, I shall be with God; if I live, He will be with me."
—Arvine quoted by C. H. Spurgeon in *Spurgeon's Sermon Notes*

❖ The finest epitaph for a Christian's tombstone are the words "Asleep in Jesus."
—J. Vernon McGee, *The Empty Tomb*

❖ When King Saul made his ignominious suicidal exit from life, he said, "I have played the fool" (1 Sam. 26:21). When Paul departed to be forever with the Lord, he said, "I have kept the faith" (2 Tim. 4:7).
—Source unknown

Note: Non-Christians do not know who King Saul and Paul were. If you use this, give a brief synopsis of each one that a non-Christian could identify with. Also, as you find illustrations, make sure the facts are correct. In 2 Samuel 26:21, King Saul is not making his "exit from life." It would be more accurate to say, "When King Saul came toward the end of his life . . ."

❖ **POSSIBLE ENTRANCE:** *When you know Christ, you don't have to worry about how death comes—you are prepared.*

Three Doolittle flyers were shot down over Japan during World War II. They were captured and sentenced to death. Before his death, one of them wrote a letter to his loved ones. It said in part, "Don't let this get you down. Just remember, God will make everything right. I'll see you all again in the hereafter. My faith in God is complete. I am unafraid!"

—Walter B. Knight

POSSIBLE EXIT: *Think of those you know who have trusted Christ. Would you be able to say to them, "I'll see you again in the hereafter. I am not afraid"?*

Note: The Doolittle flyers were named after James Doolittle, who led a force of U.S. planes in a bombing attack upon Tokyo in 1942, the first U.S. air raid upon Japan.

❖ Augustus Toplady, the author of "Rock of Ages," was jubilant and triumphant as he lay dying at the age of thirty-eight. "I enjoy heaven already in my soul," he declared, "My prayers are all converted into praises."

When Joseph Everett was dying he said, "Glory! Glory! Glory!" and he continued exclaiming glory for over twenty-five minutes.

In my own life I have been privileged to know what some of the dying saints said before they went to heaven. My grandmother sat up in her bed, smiled, and said, "I see Jesus, and He has His hand outstretched to me. And there is Ben, and he has both of his eyes and both of his legs." (Ben, my grandfather, had lost a leg and an eye at Gettysburg.)

There was an old Welsh grocer who lived near us, and my father was at his side when he was dying. He said, "Frank, can you hear that music! I've never heard such music in all my life—the orchestras, the choirs, angels singing"—and then he was gone.

—Billy Graham, *Unto the Hills*

❖ A Moslem said, "What did you do to our daughter?" The Moslem woman's child had died at sixteen years of age. "We did nothing," answered the missionary. "Oh yes, you did," protested the mother. "She died smiling. Our people do not die like that." The girl had found Christ and believed on Him a few months before.

—John Lawrence, *The Death of Death*

❖ The best of all is, God is with us.

—John Wesley, on his deathbed

☺ A boy named Mike, who was very fond of his pastor, was saddened to hear that his beloved minister had died and gone to heaven. That night Mike added a postscript to his prayer: "Dear, God, our pastor is on his way up. Please be good to him when he gets there."

—Dick Van Dyke

❖ I have pain—but I have peace, I have peace.

—Richard Baxter's last words

❖ Many years ago, the ship known as the *Empress of Ireland* went down with 130 Salvation Army officers on board, along with many other passengers. Only 21 of those Christian workers' lives were spared—an unusually small number. Of the 109 who drowned, not one body had on a life preserver! Many of the survivors told how those brave people, seeing that there were not enough life belts, took off their own and strapped them onto others, saying, "I know Jesus, so I can die better than you can." Their supreme sacrifice and faithful words set a beautiful example that for many years inspired the Salvation Army to carry on courageously for God. Millions came to recognize that born-again individuals can face death fearlessly.

—*Our Daily Bread*, 1980

> Note: An illustration like this is particularly beneficial over the holidays when people are accustomed to seeing Salvation Army workers.

❖ **POSSIBLE ENTRANCE:** *You may know and have everything there is in life, but all of that is immaterial if you haven't prepared for death.*

Once a boy was rowing an old-timer across a wide river. The old-timer picked a floating leaf from the water, studied it for a moment, and then asked the boy if he knew anything about biology. "No, I don't," the boy replied. The old timer said, "Son, you have missed twenty-five percent of your life."

As they rowed on, the old timer took a rock from the bottom of the boat. He turned it in his hand, studying its coloration, and asked the boy, "Son, do you know anything about geology?" The boy sheepishly replied, "No, I don't, sir." The old-timer said, "Son, you have missed fifty percent of your life."

Twilight was approaching and the old-timer gazed raptly at the North Star that had begun to twinkle. After a while he asked the boy, "Son, do you know anything about astronomy?" The boy admitted, "No I don't, sir." The old-timer nodded, "Son, you have missed seventy-five percent of your life."

Just then the boy noticed the huge dam upstream beginning to crumble and torrents of water pouring through the break. Quickly, he turned to the old-timer and shouted, "Sir, do you know how to swim?" The old-timer replied, "No," to which the boy shouted back, "You just lost your life."

—Charlie "Tremendous" Jones, *Life Is Tremendous*

POSSIBLE EXIT: *If you have prepared for everything but death, you haven't prepared for the one thing that really matters.*

❖   No man is truly ready to live until he is fully prepared to die!

—*Our Daily Bread*, 1974

❖   **POSSIBLE ENTRANCE:** *Death is something at times we can't prevent. All we can do is prepare for it.*

A woman who watched her son-in-law die wrote a poem:

I watched you suffer. I watched you die.
But all I could do was just stand by.

—*Winnipeg Free Press*, February 16, 1985

POSSIBLE EXIT: *No one else can prepare you for your death. You have to prepare for your own.*

❖   Heaven is a nice place to go, but nobody is in a rush to get there.

—Diane P., age 10

Note: Don't *assume* people understand your point. This would be helped if it were introduced by a statement such as, "We want to go to heaven, but we wish we didn't have to go through the channel of death."

❖   One person said, "If death is merely a period at the end of something, there's no problem. But it's more. There's another life."

—Source unknown

❖   The fear of death and torment is the fear that justice will be done.
—*Esquire*, March 1970

❖   On a talk show, a popular actress spoke of death as the end of the road where all you did was lie in the ground. She also referred to that as happiness. I wondered if that was her actual belief or if she was denying her own fears.
—R. Larry Moyer

❖   As I walked out of the chapel after a memorial service for a Christian friend, the funeral home director remarked, "You know, there's a big difference between the funerals of those who are Christians and those who are unsaved."
—*Our Daily Bread*, 1995

❖   Dr. Frances Schaeffer once said that when he wanted to keep up on the events of the day, he read the newspaper. But when he wanted a perspective on life and death, he read the Bible.
—Donald Campbell

> Note: Some may not know who Dr. Frances Schaeffer was, particularly unbelievers. Here all one needs to say is, "A person once observed . . ." This then becomes a thought-provoking statement.

❖   A celebrity once described death as an escape. Unfortunately, for the non-Christian, death is a bigger tragedy than life without God; it is eternity separated from God.
—R. Larry Moyer

❖   I have talked to doctors and nurses who have held the hands of dying people, and they say that there is as much difference between the death of a Christian and a non-Christian as there is between heaven and hell.
—Editor Cort R. Flint, *Billy Graham Speaks!*

❖   **POSSIBLE ENTRANCE:** *The irony of life is that regardless of our great plans, we never know when they will be interrupted by our sudden death.*

"A Loss in the Family"—Harold Washington (1922–1987)

When the near religious fervor of black voters combined with enough support from white "lakefront liberals" to propel him to a second term last spring, Harold Washington predicted that he would serve twenty years as Chicago's first black mayor. But his bid to establish a political dynasty that would rival Richard J. Daley's legendary machine came to a sudden end last week. Seated at the desk in his city hall office, the portly sixty-five-year-old Washington collapsed from a massive coronary while going over the day's appointments. Despite the speedy intervention of bodyguards and para-medics, the mayor suffered irreversible brain damage and was pronounced dead at Northwestern Memorial Hospital two and a half hours later.

—*Time*, December 7, 1987

POSSIBLE EXIT: *That is why the time to prepare for death is not tomorrow but today.*

Note: This illustration is effective because many people know of Richard J. Daley's dynasty, even though they may not know of Harold Washington.

❖   John Lennon's widow, Yoko Ono, said they always taught their son he could do anything he wanted to. Several months after John Lennon died, his boy said to his mom, "There's one thing you cannot do." She said, "What's that?" He said, "You can't bring Daddy back."

—Radio announcer at the time of Lennon's death, Source unknown

❖   Until this moment I thought there was neither a God nor a hell. Now I know and feel that there are both, and I am doomed to perdition by the just judgment of the Almighty.

—Sir Thomas Scott quoted by John Lawrence in *The Death of Death*

❖   George Whitefield, the famous Methodist preacher, noted in his journal on a voyage to Georgia that the ship's cook had a bad drinking problem. When reproved for that and other sins, the cook boasted that he would be wretched until the last two years of his life, and then reform. But within six hours the cook had died of an illness related to his drinking.

—Roy B. Zuck, ed., *Devotions for Kindred Spirits*

☺   **POSSIBLE ENTRANCE:** *We often joke about death. Some time ago, I read the actual reason for demise given on seven death certificates. Although not meant to be so, they were quite humorous.*

Actual reasons for demise listed on seven real death certificates:

1. "Went to bed feeling well. Woke up dead."
2. "Don't know: Never fatally ill before."
3. "Don't know. Died with aid of doctor."
4. "Nothing seriously wrong."
5. "Blow to head with an axe."
6. "Contributory cause was another man's wife."

—St. Louis Genealogical Society, *Dallas Times Herald*, March 16, 1991

POSSIBLE EXIT: *But we all know that when death strikes, it is no laughing matter. It's very serious.*

❖ The fear of death keeps us from living, not from dying.
—Paul C. Roud, *Making Miracles*

❖ Thomas Paine wrote "Age of Reason," declaring that enlightened man should cast aside their superstitious belief in God. Through his writings, he destroyed the faith of many. But as he viewed the dark gate of death, he sobbed, "Oh, Lord, help me. Oh, Christ help me! Stay with me! It is hell to be left alone."
—Neil William Rodenberg, *How to Explain Your Faith* (unpublished document)

❖ All of us need to make specific plans for our departure from this life. If we don't, we can be left in a predicament similar to that of a young man who became stranded in an Alaskan wilderness. His adventure began in the spring of 1981 when he was flown into the desolate north country to photograph the natural beauty and mysteries of the tundra. He had photo equipment, 500 rolls of film, several firearms, and 1400 pounds of provisions. As the months passed, the entries in his diary, which at first detailed his wonder and fascination with the wildlife around him, turned into a pathetic record of a nightmare. In August he wrote, "I think I should have used more foresight about arranging my departure. I'll soon find out." He waited and waited, but no one came to his rescue. In November, he died in a nameless valley, by a nameless lake, 225 miles northeast of Fairbanks. An investigation revealed that he had carefully mapped out his venture but had made no provision to be flown out of the area.
—*Our Daily Bread*, 1983

Note: Here, the year should be excluded because of other helpful details, which are more important. An illustration like this becomes more meaningful if introduced with the thought, "We make great preparation for coming into this life." Then explain what parents go through in preparing for a baby—crib to clothing. Then continue, "We even enjoy the beauty and resorts offered us during our lives on earth and prepare for everything. Often, however, we make no preparations for how we are going to leave this life."

❖ Henry Goodear, a merchant living in London, was very much inclined to scoff at the Bible and its teaching. One day his niece persuaded him to go to church "just to please her." Greatly to her grief the lesson was from the fifth chapter of Genesis. As the verses were read she could only shrink back in her place. Why had God permitted such an uninteresting list to be read that day?

Mr. Goodear made no comment as they walked home. The only difference was that he was a little quieter and more thoughtful. And yet with every passing footstep, every tread of his own feet, every throb of his heart, came the refrain, "And he died."

Up in his room that night, Mr. Goodear seemed to hear the clock strike the words, "And he died."

The next morning, busy at his ledger as usual, his pen seemed to trace the words, "And he died." Finally he could stand it no longer, and he reached for his half-forgotten family Bible, and read the words from the Bible lesson again: "All the days that Adam lived were nine hundred and twelve years: and he died." "All the days of Seth were nine hundred and thirty years: and he died." "All the days of Enos were nine hundred and five years: and he died." Right to the end of the chapter he read. Wicked or good, the same simple story was told of each. "He lived . . . and he died."

The Spirit of God can use the most unlikely of instruments. By this uninteresting list of facts, Mr. Goodear's life was entirely changed. He was living—but he would have to die, and what then?

That very night Mr. Goodear decided to give his life to the Lord, who has said, "Whosoever believeth in me shall never die" [see John 11:26].

—Valley Station Church of Christ
Web site, http://vscoc.org/Bulletinfdr/And_he_died.htm

Note: Since the merchant is not known to the audience, his name is unnecessary. Also when we discuss "Illustrating Faith" we will explain that the terminology to use in explaining salvation and inviting people to Christ is "trust Christ." For the sake of clarity, when illustrating, *do not use the terminology as stated in this illustration.* It's best to use the appropriate wording. So here, one would say, "That very night, that merchant decided to trust Christ . . ." instead of "That very night, Mr. Goodear decided to give his life to the Lord . . ."

❖   An acquaintance of mine was dying of terminal cancer. Like Job's comforters, some Christians told him that he must have some secret sin. . . . I will never forget the words that came from this friend's lips after a series of bombarding, accusing questions. He answered his accusers with great confidence: "God has been very good to me. I know I will be leaving this life soon. I know my date. My house is in order, I am ready to meet Jesus Christ face to face. Maybe you should pray for yourselves. You forget that you are terminal also. You just don't know your date."

—Harold L. Bussell, *Unholy Devotion: Why Cults Lure Christians*

❖   POSSIBLE ENTRANCE: *We are tempted to think we have all the time in the world to think about our eternal destiny. The graveyard proves us wrong.*

Once long ago, a prince asked that his tutor prepare him for the life beyond. "There is plenty of time for that when you are old," the tutor replied.

"No!" exclaimed the prince, "I have been to the cemetery and measured the graves and there are many shorter than I am."

—George Sweeting, *Tomorrow May Be Too Late*

POSSIBLE EXIT: *How many people can you think of right now who met what many would call a premature death?*

☺   God doesn't tell you when you're going to die because He wants it to be a big surprise.

—Alan K., age 7, quoted by Michael J. Imperiale in sermon
"In Life and in Death: We Belong to God," February 5, 2006

☺   When you die, God takes care of you like your mother did when you were alive—only God doesn't yell at you all the time.

—Steve K., age 8

❖   A man who worked in a funeral home and had an angina attack said, as he was facing death, "I've seen hundreds of people come in here to claim bodies, but all of a sudden it's frightening to think that someone will soon be coming in here to claim mine."

—Man in Bristol, PA

☺   I drink a lot on the plane. Who knows? This could be my last chance.
—Man on flight to Amsterdam, March 1990

Note: It's easy to dismiss a comment like this and consider it useless due to a man's obvious drinking problem. But when speaking to non-Christians this illustration can be very effective. Introduce it by saying, "We focus on what we'd like to enjoy before we die instead of focusing on where we will be the moment death strikes." Always bear in mind you are speaking to non-Christians. What a Christian cannot identify with, a non-Christian might.

❖   A man whose mother died confessed how hard it was to see his mom lying in a casket and described his futile attempts to block that image from his mind. The casket kept him from thinking of the happy moments from the past.

When the deceased knew the Lord, it's a lot different. We can look at a casket with a smile on our face because we know that the one we are looking at is smiling in the presence of Christ.
—R. Larry Moyer

☺   Dear Pastor, I hope to go to heaven someday, but later than sooner.
—Ellen, age 9

❖   **POSSIBLE ENTRANCE:** *We think of a sudden death as something that happens to others. One person came to Christ because a friend reminded him that the "other person" could be himself.*

One day a fellow member of the Guardian Angels got Jerry's attention in a dramatic way. He walked up to him, pointed his finger at him as if it were a gun, and said, "You're good at kung fu. Bang!" Jerry immediately got the point. His skill at self-defense was no match for a loaded gun. Then the other Angel asked, "Where will you spend eternity if you're blown away on patrol?" Jerry admitted he had never thought about that. When Jerry mentioned the incident to his brother, they both realized their need for God in their lives. Today, Jeff and Jerry are Christians, and they now use their kung fu demonstrations to tell others about the ultimate defense, the one King David celebrated in the 59th Psalm.
—*Our Daily Bread*, 1986

POSSIBLE EXIT: *Let me be your friend. What if today were your last? Do you know where you'd spend eternity?*

Note: Since non-Christians don't know Psalm 59, you could rephrase the end of this by saying "the one King David spoke about in the Bible."

❖ **POSSIBLE ENTRANCE:** *Perhaps, the greatest favor we could do for ourselves is to put some type of a reminder before us that we are not promised another day.*

When Daniel Boone died they didn't have to hunt to find a coffin for him. He had one already. He had acquired it long before. It was made of cherry wood, and for years he'd kept it under his bed. Most of us would not like to have that daily reminder of the certainty of death, but on occasion we do need to be reminded that "it is appointed unto man once to die, but after this the judgment" [Heb 9:27].

—*Preaching Today*, May–June 1996

POSSIBLE EXIT: *Putting before us a reminder that we have no guarantee of tomorrow is not a morbid way to live. It is a realistic way to approach life.*

❖ Dying is one of the few events in life certain to occur—and yet one we are not likely to plan for. We will spend more time getting ready for two weeks away from work than we will for our last two weeks on earth. Consequently, says Frank Ostaceski, who runs a San Francisco home for the dying, "We have more preparation on how to operate our VCRs than we do for how to die."

—*Time*, September 18, 2000

Note: Consistently keep in mind that illustrations, even if dated, should spark ideas of our own. The first two lines of this illustration make an impact. We could use this to make our own observation. "We know better how to operate our DVD players, or mp3 players than we know how to die."

☺ When you die, you don't have to do homework in heaven unless your teacher is there too.

—Marsha W., age 9

❖ On the back of a truck transporting caskets, "Please drive safely. Yours might be on this load."

—Source unknown

Note: A speaker must identify with his audience. If you have seen a sign like this, make it a testimonial by saying, "I was reminded of my own mortality when I saw a sign the other day on the back of a truck transporting caskets. It read . . ."

❖ **POSSIBLE ENTRANCE:** *When you see a hearse, a funeral procession, or any other reminder of death, what is your first thought?*

A short time before his own death, a soldier wrote about how sad it was to watch soldiers being sent back to America in caskets covered with American flags. Then he said, "I can't help but think what might happen if it had been me in one of those caskets."

—Adapted from *Time*, October 18, 1993

POSSIBLE EXIT: *The most helpful question any of us can ask ourselves when we see a casket is, "What if it were me?"*

Note: Whenever you read anything, ask yourself, "How can I use this one day in speaking?" Then write it down. Otherwise you won't remember it.

❖ What would you do if you knew you had only one day left to live? That's what Gunther Klempnauer recently asked 625 young German students in twelve vocational schools. As I read about his project, I was interested in the varied responses he received. For instance, his book reveals that 20 percent of the young men questioned would spend their last day on earth drinking, taking drugs, and pursuing the opposite sex. A different response came from an eighteen-year-old girl who wrote, "I would like to spend my last evening in church (to be alone with God) to thank Him for a full and happy life."

—*Our Daily Bread*, 1980

Note: Because of the source, this survey must have been done before 1980. Because similar responses could be expected today, it can still be used. You can also use the Internet to locate more recent surveys. Also, it is the quote of the eighteen-year-old that you want to emphasize. Then ask, "Are you as excited about meeting God as she was?"

❖ **POSSIBLE ENTRANCE:** *Think about it. Many who die every day intended to live at least one day longer. Some intended to live for many years.*

Magazine publisher J. I. Rodale, a zealous advocate of health foods, claimed at the age of seventy-two that he would live to be a hundred. The same week that his prediction appeared in the *New York Times*, he was being interviewed for a television program, again claiming that his bones were as strong as ever. Moments after making his boast, he died of a heart attack.

Dr. Stuart Berger, a nutritionist, claimed that he had the formula for living past the century mark. Although he had supposedly found the secret of youthfulness and had convinced many to follow his advice, he died in his sleep at the age of forty, grossly overweight.

Then there was author Jim Fixx, who advocated running to prevent coronary trouble. Yet at the age of fifty-two he died of a heart attack—yes, ironically, while running.

—*Our Daily Bread*, 1995

POSSIBLE EXIT: *None of us know how long we have. Today and even this hour is the time to think about your eternal destiny. Tomorrow and even one hour from now might be too late.*

❖ I always say that death can be one of the greatest experiences ever. If you have lived each day of your life right, then you have nothing to fear.

—*USA Today*, "Living Fully," August 11, 1997

> Note: An illustration like this can be used two ways. One would be to point out the wrong thinking of many that all we have to do is "live right" and we'll be prepared to meet the Lord. The other way is to say, "That person was right—all you have to do is live right and you're prepared to see the Lord." But don't forget, with God, "living right" means "being right"—being rightly related to God through faith in Christ. It is not what you've done that will get you to heaven but who you know. Since you are speaking to non-Christians, be careful of wording that would allow them to think they can work their way into heaven.

❖ John Wayne, at age seventy-one, sometimes had difficult moments watching his old movies. "It's kind of irritating to see I was a good looking forty-year-old and suddenly I can look over and see this seventy-one-year-old . . . I'm not squawking . . . I just want to be around for a long time."

—Interview with Barbara Walters in January 1979

> Note: What adds to the impact of this quote is that the interview took place just a few months before he died.

❖ Overconfidence, coupled with negligence, can lead to sad consequences. This is the case when a person is so sure of himself that he becomes careless about little things that may pose a threat. I'm thinking, for example, of a stuntman named Bobby Leach. In July 1911, he went over Niagara Falls in a specially designed steel drum and lived to tell about it. Although he suffered minor injuries, he survived because he recognized the tremendous dangers involved in the feat, and because he had done everything he could to protect himself from harm.

Several years after that incident, while skipping down a street in New Zealand, Bobby Leach slipped on an orange peeling, fell, and badly fractured his leg. He was taken to a hospital, where he later died of complications from that fall. He received a greater injury walking down the street than he sustained in going over Niagara Falls. He was not prepared for danger in what he assumed to be a safe situation.

—*Our Daily Bread*, 1987

> Note: The illustration becomes effective because of people's familiarity with Niagara Falls. Be certain to capitalize on the thought that he prepared for what he knew could cause death but overlooked other possible causes of death. Then give pertinent examples of what your audience does. Example: We prepare for a cross-country flight two weeks from now, aware this could be the next plane to crash. But we overlook that we could more likely be killed in an accident at those busy intersections two miles from our houses.

❖ **POSSIBLE ENTRANCE:** *Some people are so afraid to die, they try to plan everything.*

A terminally ill man who admitted that he was afraid of death tried to arrange the details of his own death to avoid suffering. The country where he lived permitted euthanasia, so he was able to have his doctor assist in his demise. In contrast, a friend of mine said to me, "I get excited thinking about death. I don't know when or where it will come, but I know where I'll be." What's the different between these two responses to death? A person named Jesus Christ.

—R. Larry Moyer

POSSIBLE EXIT: *With Christ, you don't have to be afraid to die. And because He is there whatever the circumstances, you don't have to be afraid to live.*

❖ Tony Reno, a software engineer, is only thirty-three, but he's taking no chances.
"I love life," says Mr. Reno, of Pepperell, Massachusetts. "I love the way technology is going, and I want to see how it all ends up."

So, as if it were the most natural thing in the world, Mr. Reno has signed up to be frozen upon his death for as long as it takes scientists to figure out how to thaw people and bring them back to the future.

—*Dallas Morning News*, April 11, 1993

Note: Let an illustration cause you to think of the *most* effective way to use it. This illustrates the fear of death. It can also be used to say, "What is exciting about knowing Christ is that you have no interest in being frozen. Because when life stops here it starts there—you are already in His presence forever." In this way you've used the illustration to reinforce a positive truth.

❖ I heard of a popular senator who was swept out of office after only one term. His defeat came as a complete surprise to opponents and supporters alike. In his concession speech, the losing candidate wryly commented that recent events reminded him of an epitaph he once saw on an old tombstone. It said, "I expected this—but not so soon."

—*Our Daily Bread*, 1995

Note: This illustration proves the need to read a variety of sources. The biggest portion of this illustration is of little help. One is not likely to speak to politicians who lose elections, although that was the subject of this article. But the epitaph or the tombstone is very relevant when addressing the suddenness of death.

❖ **POSSIBLE ENTRANCE:** *Even famous athletes question the importance and brevity of life.*

Legendary basketball player Michael Jordan was dynamically and dramatically affected by the sudden death of his father. After his father died, Jordan reportedly said that his father's death caused him to realize how valuable life is and how quickly it can be taken away.

—Adapted from Richard Stengel, "I'll Fly Away," *Time*, October 18, 1993

POSSIBLE EXIT: *Jordan is right. Life is valuable, and the thing that adds to its value is realizing how quickly it can end.*

❖ **POSSIBLE ENTRANCE:** *There are many ways we are unlike others. But there is at least one way we are like everyone we meet. We will all die.*

In May 1981, writer William Saroyan lay dying of cancer. Picking up the phone next to his hospital bed, he dialed the Associated Press and said to the reporter who answered, "Everyone has to die, but I always thought an exception would be made in my case. Now what?"

—Roy B. Zuck

POSSIBLE EXIT: *There are no exceptions when it comes to death. Never has been and never will be.*

❖ John Connally was in the motorcade with President John F. Kennedy on November 22, 1963, the day Kennedy was assassinated. In his memoir, Connally wrote about the impact Kennedy's death had on him: "In the weeks after the assassination, the weeks spent in Parkland Hospital, my temperament changed. John Kennedy's death gave me a different perspective on life, its frailties and its meaning. It made me impatient with trivia and egos and self-aggrandizement."

—Adapted from *In History's Shadow,* John Connally

> Note: An illustration like this is timeless because of the Kennedy assassination. Be careful not to overwhelm the audience with the details about John Connally or they'll lose the main point. The fact that he was a three-term Texas governor and Democrat turned Republican is not important. What is important is that he was in the car on the infamous afternoon of November 22, 1963.

❖ A woman began attending meetings of a Cryonics group after learning that they were exploring the possibility that people who died of an incurable disease could be frozen until a cure was discovered. Her reason for attending? The fear of death.

—Adapted from *Dallas Times Herald,* May 24, 1981

❖ **POSSIBLE ENTRANCE:** *Whenever you attend a funeral, you do it with the keen awareness that yours may be next. Something very unusual was mentioned in a Dallas, Texas, newspaper. It illustrates the suddenness of death.*

The preacher had just told mourners at a country cemetery, "We never know who is going next," when a bolt of lightning killed the grandson of the woman he had buried, witnesses say.

Services for ninety-one-year-old Liza Poteet of Alpharetta had just been concluded when the lightning hit like "a ball of fire out of the sky," the Rev. Ray Hewett said.

"It was like—bang! It happened like that. I never witnessed nothing like that in my thirty years of preaching."

The lightning bolt Sunday afternoon killed Donald Metcalf, twenty-seven. His wife, Martha Metcalf, twenty-four, was knocked unconscious and was in fair and stable condition in Union County Hospital.

—*Dallas Times Herald*, July 13, 1982

POSSIBLE EXIT: *Regardless of how death may occur—if it were today, do you know where you'd end up?*

Note: With an illustration like this, you must prepare your audience with the strangeness of this happening. Admitting the strangeness prepares your audience. The fact that it was reported in the newspaper gives it credibility.

❖ "On his tombstone were two dates over which he had no control."—Man remarking on the death of Joe Louis, heavyweight boxing champion

—*Elkhart Truth*, April 22, 1981

❖ President McKinley was assassinated in Buffalo. At his deathbed his wife pleaded, "I want to go too, I want to go too." He replied, "We are all going."

—Patrick M. Morley, *Man in the Mirror*

❖ A man on the way to the electric chair refused to let his attorney try to get the Supreme Court to postpone his execution. His reason was, "We're all going to die anyway. Let's get it over with."

—Source unknown

❖ One person once defined death as "an inevitable nuisance that hopefully comes during sleep."

—Elisabeth Kubler-Ross, *On Death and Dying*

❖ Acceptance of death takes many forms. Some grant a grudging acceptance, such as W. C. Fields, who had these words chiseled on his tombstone: "I'd rather be in Philadelphia." He was saying, in essence, that he looked at death, didn't like it, and would rather ignore it; but he would have to accept it.

—Jim Conway, *Men in Midlife Crisis*

❖ A man who was suffering from poor health decided to move to a warmer climate. Wanting to make sure he would choose the area best suited to his needs, he visited several locations. While in Arizona, he asked those who lived there, "What's the average temperature?" "What about the humidity?" "How many days of sunshine are there?" When he asked, "What's the death rate?" he received this answer: "Same as where you come from, friend—one death for every birth!"

—*Our Daily Bread*, 1991

❖   The man is a fool who does not put death on his schedule every day.

—C. H. Spurgeon

❖   **POSSIBLE ENTRANCE:** *A sixteen-year-old wrote a newspaper columnist and expressed what we all feel.*

Dear Ann Landers:
I hope you won't think this letter is too dumb to print. It took a lot of nerve for me to write it. I'm sixteen, a girl, and for the last six months I've been terribly afraid that I will get sick and die.
There is no real reason for this. I'm in good health. In fact, I've always been healthy, but I keep thinking I'll catch a terrible disease, something incurable, and die young. How can I get these hideous thoughts out of my head?
Signed, Creepy Louise

—Ann Landers

POSSIBLE EXIT: *With Christ, you no longer have to fear death. It doesn't have to be a hideous thought in your head. Instead you can look forward to it.*

Note: Since you're not quoting the newspaper columnist's reply, her name is immaterial. It's the teenager's comment and question that matters.

❖   It's not the fact that you can't think it over, but that it might all be over before you have time to think.

—R. Larry Moyer

❖   **POSSIBLE ENTRANCE:** *It doesn't matter how many achievements we have made. Those achievements won't change the fact that we still have an appointment with death and death may strike sooner than we think.*

Died. Jim ("Catfish") Hunter, 53, Hall of Fame pitcher; of Lou Gehrig's disease; in Hertford, N.C. During his fifteen-year career with the Oakland

A's and the New York Yankees, Hunter won five World Series, pitched a perfect game, won a Cy Young Award and became the first multimillion-dollar player when he declared free agency in 1974. "He taught us how to win," said his onetime boss George Steinbrenner.

—*Time*, September 20, 1999

POSSIBLE EXIT: *When death strikes, the issue is not what you've done. The issue is Who you know.*

❖ I hate life, but I'm afraid to die.

—Voltaire

❖ A very good friend of mine was killed in a one-car accident last Friday night. They buried him Monday. Even though I saw him lying in the coffin, I can't really believe he is dead. I keep thinking I'll see him tomorrow or the next day, talk to him, hear him laugh, and find it all a dream. He was twenty-four, married but separated the last two years. He had a very rotten childhood, a marriage wrecked by a jealous wife, and now death.

—Letter to R. Larry Moyer, January 1972

Note: These illustrations are timeless. These words could have been written yesterday.

❖ Died. Andy Hug, 35, world champion Swiss kick boxer, karate expert, and aspiring film actor, of acute leukemia, in Tokyo. Growing up an orphan in Switzerland and teased by schoolmates, Hug was inspired by the *Rocky* movies and trained relentlessly in martial arts from age twelve. Considered the Michael Jordan of his sport, he was mobbed in Europe and Japan. Last week, after enduring nausea and nosebleeds, Hug was admitted to a Tokyo hospital with a high fever and was found to have leukemia. He was put on chemotherapy but suffered immediate organ failure and brain damage.

—*Time*, September 4, 2000

❖ Live every day like it's your last, 'cause one day you're gonna be right.

—Ray Charles quoted in *Esquire*, August 2003

Note: Comments like this could be considered humorous or serious. It all depends on how you say it.

❖ **POSSIBLE ENTRANCE:** *Time* *magazine featured an article dealing with a horrible situation relating to many deaths. The last line of the article is particularly interesting.*

"Most people don't want to deal with death until it happens, and not even then."

—*Time*, "Dead and Forsaken," March 4, 2002

POSSIBLE EXIT: *What about you? Are you waiting until it is too late to deal with death or are you dealing with it now?*

Note: In collecting illustrations, it's best to keep more facts than you need even if you don't use all of them. That way you know the circumstances. Here it's the last line that matters. One can say, "*Time* magazine featured an article that dealt with a horrible situated related to many deaths. The last line of that article was particularly interesting. The writer said, '. . .'"

❖ We free ourselves from the womb, but there is no knife sharp enough to cut the umbilical cord that binds us to our grave.

—Paul Eldridge

❖ Ancient merchants often wrote the words *memento mori*—"think of death"—in large letters on the first page of their accounting books. Philip of Macedon, father of Alexander the Great, commissioned a servant to stand in his presence each day and say, "Philip, you will die." In contrast, France's Louis XIV decreed that the word "death" not be uttered in his presence. Most of us are more like Louis than Philip, denying death and avoiding the thought of it except when it's forced upon us. We live under the fear of death.

—Randy Alcorn, *Heaven*

❖ Ted Turner referred to death as the greatest fear of all. He wanted to overcome the fear so that he would have freedom to go forward in life (*Time*, January 6, 1992). Turner is right about this: Our attitude about death affects our attitude about life.

—R. Larry Moyer

❖ It's not the pace of life that concerns me, it's the sudden stop at the end.

—Source unknown

❖   A college girl was fatally injured in a car accident. Her last words to her mother were these: "Mother, you taught me everything I needed to know to get by in college—how to light my cigarette, how to hold my cocktail glass, and how to have intercourse safely. But, Mother, you never taught me how to die. You'd better teach me quickly! Mother, I'm dying."

—Billy Graham quoted in *Christianity Today*

❖   Died. Salvador Sanchez, 23, World Boxing Council featherweight champion and one of the sport's best fighters, of injuries after his Porsche 928 collided with two trucks just north of Queretaro, Mexico. A school dropout at 16, Sanchez once explained, "I found out that I liked hitting people, and I didn't like school, so I started boxing." A peppery tactician, he wore opponents down for late round knockouts. "I'd like to step down undefeated," he said last month. "I'm only twenty-three and I have all the time in the world."

—*Time*, August 23, 1982

☺   **POSSIBLE ENTRANCE:** *Death can be such a depressing subject, we try to relieve our sadness by laughing.*

Phoning a patient, a doctor says, "I have some bad news and some worse news. Here is the bad news. You have only twenty-four hours left to live."
"That is bad news," the patient replies. "What could be worse?"
The doctor replied, "I should have told you yesterday."

—Internet humor

POSSIBLE EXIT: *But we all know death is not a laughing matter.*

☺   It's not that I'm afraid to die. I just don't want to be there when it happens.

—Woody Allen

❖   After retiring, Hall of Fame basketball great Pete Maravich (aka Pistol Pete) became a health enthusiast and, reportedly, became a Christian. Just before his death at age 40, he remarked about how good he felt.

—Adapted from *Time*, January 18, 1988

❖   As human beings, we have a terminal disease called mortality. The current death rate is 100 percent.

—Randy Alcorn, *Heaven*

DENIAL

❖ **POSSIBLE ENTRANCE:** *As those who have sinned before God, we often fail to realize the seriousness of our situation.*

For twenty-one years, I was part of a group that conducted drive-in gospel services. I recall that at one of these outdoor meetings a Christian physician gave a message on the subject, "The People Jesus Won't Save!" He used this illustration: "While I was in residence at the Mayo Clinic, a lady who had suffered for many years came for an examination. We found that she could be helped through surgery and proper medication. Before leaving the clinic she suggested that her husband have a checkup, although he appeared to be in good physical condition. At first he refused, saying, 'I'm not sick; I'm perfectly healthy. I don't need a doctor.' But at his wife's insistence, he finally yielded and received the tragic news that he had a cancerous tumor in his chest that would soon end his life! Since it had not affected any nerves, he experienced no pain. Yet he was a dying man."

—*Our Daily Bread*, 1975

POSSIBLE EXIT: *We may not feel that bad about our spiritual condition, but feelings are not the issue. The fact is, we are facing eternal separation from God in what the Bible calls hell.*

☺ Patient: "This hospital is terrible. They treat me like I'm a dog."
Orderly: "Mr. Jones, that is just not true. Now, roll over."

—Internet joke

☺ A certain man used to come home dead drunk each night. He was always so inebriated that he would fall into bed fully clothed, pass out, and then snore loudly all night long. His wife was losing so much sleep because of his snoring that she went to a doctor and said, "Doctor, I can't stand it any longer. If you'll tell me how to keep him from snoring, I'll pay you anything!" The doctor told her that there was no problem and that he would not even charge her. He told her that whenever her husband passed out and started snoring, she was to take a ribbon and tie it around his nose and his snoring would stop. That night, her husband came in as usual, fell across the bed fully dressed, passed out, and started snoring. The wife got up, pulled a blue ribbon from her dresser, and tied it around his nose. Sure enough, the snoring stopped. The next morning, the wife, fully refreshed, was preparing breakfast and asked the husband as he was awakening, "Honey, where were you last night?" The husband, still fully clothed, looked in the mirror and seeing the blue ribbon around his nose, replied, "I don't know, but wherever I was, I won first prize!"

—Adapted from www.sermoncentral.com

☺ My wife claims I'm a baseball fanatic. She says all I ever read about, and talk about, and think about is baseball. I told her she's way off base.

—Internet humor

DEPRAVITY

❖ Show me a worm that fully comprehends a man and I'll show you a man that can comprehend God.

—from *Encyclopedia of 7700 Illustrations* by Paul L. Tan

❖ No clever arrangement of bad eggs will make a good omelet.

—C. S. Lewis

❖ There is a saying, "If you drop a lot of wine into sewage, all you have is sewage." But if you drop just a little bit of sewage into a whole lot of wine, you still have sewage. So whether we see ourselves as the sewage into which a lot of wine is added (an evil person with a few good qualities), or if we see ourselves as a lot of wine with just a little sewage added (a good person with a few problems), we are all the same from God's perspective—corrupt.

—"Schopenhauer's Law of Entropy," Arthur Schopenhauer, German philosopher

> Note: Let an illustration like this provoke your thinking. For example, purified water and a clump of dirt would be a good analogy as well.

❖ Suppose we pour a measure of salt into a container of water. The salt affects every drop of the water to the extent that all the pure water becomes salty. From that time on, every bit of water drawn from that container is salty, and no pure water can be drawn. This is similar to the condition of man. The first sin was an act; one act brought sin into the race. Since that one act the very bloodstream of the human race has been polluted.

—John L. Miles, *Perfectionism*, unpublished master's thesis

❖ **POSSIBLE ENTRANCE:** *Most of us find it hard to look into our own hearts and depravity. If we did, we wouldn't like what we saw.*

Jonathan Edwards, eighteenth-century Puritan leader, wrote, "When I look into my heart and take a view of my wickedness, it looks like an abyss infinitely deeper than hell."

—Alexander Hill, *Just Business*

POSSIBLE EXIT: *The problem is God doesn't like what He sees in us either. But although He abhors our sin, and our depravity is repulsive to Him, He loves us still.*

❖ Surely what a man does when he is taken off his guard is the best evidence of what sort of man he is. If there are rats in a cellar, you are most likely to see them if you go in suddenly. But the suddenness does not create the rats: it only prevents them from hiding. In the same way the suddenness of the provocation does not make me ill-tempered; it only shows me what an ill-tempered man I am.

—C. S. Lewis, *Mere Christianity*

❖ By nature I was too blind to know Him, too proud to trust Him, too obstinate to serve Him, too base-minded to love Him.

—John Newton, *Cardiphonia, or, The Utterance of the Heart*

❖ Man was created a little lower than the angels, and he has been getting a little lower ever since.

—Josh Billings in *Mark Twain's Library of Humor*

❖ A Jewish man stepped in and watched a part of Eichmann's trial and burst into tears.
Someone next to him said, "Your anger must be unbearable."
He said, "No, it isn't anger. The longer I sit here, the more I realize I have a heart like his."

—Charles Colson, "The Enduring Revolution," 1993 Templeton Address

Note: Don't assume your audience knows who Eichmann was. It better to be certain they do so you don't lose the effectiveness of the illustration. Explain that Adolf Eichmann was responsible for the murder of millions of Jews in the death camps in Europe during World War II.

❖ The root of the problem is the moral disease of the human heart, leading either to pride and assumed superiority or to fear because of imaginary or real competition.

—Richard Wolff, *Riots in the Streets*

❖ According to Jay Adams, the state of California made a study of two hundred plus criminals over a twelve-year period. The study "never found a criminal who believed he was evil. Each criminal thought of himself as a basically good person."

—Jay Edward Adams, *Biblical View of Self-esteem, Self-love, and Self-image*

❖ **POSSIBLE ENTRANCE:** *It doesn't matter how much we try to clean up ourselves on the outside, we are the same on the inside.*

Years ago the children of a family vacationing on the Gulf Coast in Texas came across a soaked and scraggly little dog. They wanted to keep it, and unable to find its owner, they prevailed upon their parents to take it home with them.

Back home, they washed and groomed their new pet. The next morning they left it alone in the house with food, water, and their pet cat. Returning later in the day, they discovered that their cat was deceased. Badly deceased in fact. It was also clear that their new pet was probably the culprit.

The following day the parents took the dog to the vet, thinking it wise to have it checked out. The vet informed them that the creature they'd taken in wasn't really a dog at all—it was an African rat. Apparently it had found its way ashore from an oceangoing ship docked along the coast.

A rat is a rat is a rat. It doesn't matter whether it's cleaned and groomed or dirty and scraggly, whether it lives in a sewer or a palace, whether it's cared for or shunned. Wherever it lives, whatever it looks like, however it smells, it will always be a rat.

—Dwight Edwards, *Revolution Within*

POSSIBLE EXIT: *We can dress ourselves up, behave religiously, and do good things, but our nature is still the same—we are still sinners.*

DEPRESSION

❖ The average man of today may have a good deal of fun and pleasure, but in spite of this he is fundamentally depressed.

—Eric Fromm, *The Sane Society*

❖ **POSSIBLE ENTRANCE:** *We suffer so much depression that even parts of the holidays contribute more to the problem than the solution.*

Dr. Cliff Arnall, a British psychologist, has developed a formula to determine the worst day of the year. One factor is the time elapsed since Christmas, when the holiday glow has given way to the reality of credit-card bills. Gloomy winter weather, short days, and the failure to keep New Year's resolutions are also a part of Dr. Arnall's calculations. Last year, January 24 received the dubious distinction of being "the most depressing day of the year."

—Our Daily Bread, 2006

POSSIBLE EXIT: *When you know Christ, you will have "down" days, but you can be on top of them instead of them being on top of you.*

❖ According to the Depression Alliance, "One in five people will be affected by depression at some point in their lives. The World Health Organization estimates that by the year 2020, major depression will be second only to chronic heart disease as an international health burden. Thirty working days are lost due to depression and anxiety for every single day lost to industrial disputes. Not only does depression impact us economically, but it can also lead to some devastating consequences such as suicide. About one in six people who experience severe depression eventually commit suicide, and 70 percent of recorded suicides are by people who have experienced some form of depression. Depression can also strike at any age but is most common between the ages of twenty-five and forty-four years old."

—Preaching to a Shifting Culture, edited by Scott Gibson

❖ Ron Cawthon, a Dallas policeman who was runner-up in Rookie-of-the-Year honors three years ago, battled Trinity [River's] currents, struggling to reach a twenty-three-year-old man who minutes earlier tried to kill himself by jumping two hundred feet from the Jefferson Street Bridge. Later, Cawthon asked the man (no name given) why he jumped. "He woke up this morning," quoted Cawthon as told him by the man himself, "and just felt like he had to do it." Later at Parkland Hospital, the man told officers his wife had left him, he had no money or job and was "tired of living like this."

—Dallas Times Herald, April 15, 1973

Note: This illustration is effective because you can make the observation that there are desperate people like this still today.

DISHONESTY

☺ **POSSIBLE ENTRANCE:** *Dishonesty never pays. Sooner or later, it will catch up to us.*

A lady was speeding and was pulled over by an officer. She didn't have her seat belt fastened, so as soon as she stopped, she quickly slipped it on before the officer got to her window.

After talking to her about speeding, the officer said, "I see you're wearing your seat belt. Do you believe in wearing it at all times?"

"Yes, I do, officer," she replied.

"Well," asked the officer, "do you always do it up with it looped through your steering wheel?

—Source unknown

POSSIBLE EXIT: *Even if our dishonesty doesn't catch up to us here, we will be held accountable for our actions. No one else may know what we've done, but God does, and sin must be punished.*

☺ **POSSIBLE ENTRANCE:** *Dishonesty comes naturally. We practiced it as a child; no one had to teach us.*

There was a knock at the door. When the man answered, he saw a small boy, about five years old. The boy said that something of his had found its way into the man's garage and he needed it back. Upon opening the garage door, the man noticed two things: a baseball and a broken window with a baseball-size hole. He asked the boy, "How do you suppose this ball got in here?"

Taking one look at the ball, one look at the window, the boy said, "Wow! I must have thrown it right through that hole."

—Internet humor

POSSIBLE EXIT: *But wait a minute. Before we laugh at a child's dishonesty, let's look at our own. Have you lied to a police officer about the speed you were driving? Have you lied to a boss about why you were late? Have you omitted any income on your tax return that is impossible to trace?*

☺ One night at dinner, a mother asked her four-year-old son to say grace. Heads bowed and hands folded, everyone waited. After a few moments of silence, the mother look up at him. He glanced at his mother, then over to his father, then back to his mother again. Finally he said, "But if I thank God for the broccoli, won't He know I'm lying?"

—*Our Daily Bread*, 1986

ETERNITY

❖   A master once had a servant he disliked. One day the master said to the servant, "You are the most foolish servant I've ever had. There is nobody more foolish. To prove it, here is a cane. You must carry it with you every day until you find someone more foolish than you to give it to." For years the man carried it. One day the master became ill and was dying. While visiting with him, the master said to the servant, "I wonder where I will spend eternity?" The servant said, "You mean you have lived your whole life here on earth with no thought for eternity?" The master replied, "That's right." So the servant handed the master the cane and said, "Indeed, you are more foolish than I."

—Bob Scrimgeour

❖   High up in the North, in the land called Svithjod, there stands a rock. It is one hundred miles high and one hundred miles wide. Once every thousand years a little bird comes to this rock to sharpen its beak. When the rock has thus been worn away, then a single day of eternity will have gone by.

—Hendrick Willen Van Loon

Note: This illustration would fit heaven or hell in terms of eternity. If using it to speak of heaven the point to be made here is, "Can you imagine what it will be like to be forever with the Lord?"

❖   **POSSIBLE ENTRANCE:** *We tend to look at the future from today forward. But we'd be wise to look at it from the perspective of death backward.*

William Gladstone was considered to be one of Britain's four greatest prime ministers and a committed Christian. A young man once came to him to talk about his future, and he told Gladstone that he was planning to go to Cambridge to get a good education. Dr. Gladstone said, "That is good. A man ought to get a good education. What then?" The man said, "I know after a good education I need practical experience, so I thought I'd go into a law firm in London because that will give me more than I get in a university." Gladstone said, "That's wise. What then?" "I thought what I'd like to do is enter politics. I thought if I got some experience in law I could get a seat in the House of Commons and affect Great Britain." Gladstone said, "That's good. We need men in law who purpose to be there. What then?" The man said, "I thought if I served my party well they'd let me sit where you sit and then I could be Prime Minister." Gladstone said, "Well one man will sit here and if that's what you aspire to, that's good. Then what?" The man said, "I've been keeping a diary and after my career is over

I could write my memoirs and pass to others what I've learned." Gladstone said, "That's good. A man ought to pass on to others what life has taught him. What then?" The man said, "Well, sir, I guess like anybody else, I'll have to die." Gladstone said, "Yes, I don't know about your other plans, but I know about that one. We will all end with a plot of ground. What then?" The man said, "I haven't had a chance to think about that. I haven't had any time to think about religion. I've been so busy thinking about all those other things, I haven't had much time to think about that."

Gladstone said, "Young man, my advice to you is to go home, fall down by the side of your bed and take out your Bible and sit there until you've thought life through to its very end. Only the man or woman who has done that—who can see life from the standpoint of heaven, and time from the standpoint of eternity—can cope with the hard questions of life. Because the basic hard questions of life can only be settled when we see the questions from the light of the long range point of view."

—quoted by Haddon Robinson

POSSIBLE EXIT: *Ask yourself two questions: "Am I certain I'm going to heaven when I die?" When that is settled with a "yes" then ask, "How is that affecting my life today?"*

❖   When English patriot Sir William Russell went to the scaffold in 1683, he took his watch out of his pocket and handed it to the physician who attended him in his death. "Would you kindly take my timepiece?" he asked. "I have no use for it. I am now dealing with eternity."

—Billy Graham, *Unto the Hills*

❖   Why we are here is important. Where we are going is all-important.

—*Our Daily Bread*, 1984

❖   Almost every person with whom I have ever talked in my world travels has believed in life after death.

—Eleanor Roosevelt

❖   After one of the first Russian cosmonauts returned from space, he said, "I didn't see God up there." An American pastor responded in a Sunday sermon by saying, "All he needs to do is to leave the space capsule and take off his space suit. He'll see God!"

—*Our Daily Bread*, 1990

❖ Death is the last chapter in time but the first chapter in eternity.

—*Our Daily Bread*, 2001

❖ **POSSIBLE ENTRANCE:** *We often joke about the hereafter.*

The priest was preparing a man for his long day's journey into night.

Whispering firmly, the priest said, "Denounce the Devil! Let him know how little you think of his evil!"

The dying man said nothing. The priest repeated his order. Still the dying man said nothing.

The priest asked, "Why do you refuse to denounce the Devil and his evil?"

The dying man said, "Until I know where I'm heading, I don't think I ought to aggravate anybody!"

—Source unknown

POSSIBLE EXIT: *We all know the hereafter is not a laughing matter. Where you are going to spend eternity is the most serious issue you will ever address.*

❖ A man decided to make all the necessary arrangements for the day of his funeral. He picked out a burial plot and chose the inscription he wanted carved on his headstone. The minister, who knew the man well, heard that he was busily preparing for the inevitable day. So he went to the man and said, "I understand that you've done everything you can possibly do to provide a resting place for your body. Have you given any thought to a resting place for your soul?"

The man was stunned by the question, for it was true that he hadn't thought about getting ready for the life to come. After listening to the minister explain the gospel, he placed his trust in Christ for salvation and found assurance of eternal life and rest.

—*Our Daily Bread*, 2001

❖ How often on a plane I have heard the hostess ask, "Destination, please?" and always the passengers have an answer. It is the same with eternity.

—Source unknown

❖ I was disturbed when I heard the testimony of a businessman who said he was convinced there was something after death but then admitted that even though he was unable to figure out what it was, he wasn't worried about it. I thought, "Wait a minute. If you haven't resolved the issue of the hereafter, nothing in the here and now actually matters."

—R. Larry Moyer

❖ Jonathan Edwards, the great eighteenth-century Puritan author and preacher, once said, "Some flatter themselves with a secret hope that there is no such thing as another world."

—Mark McCloskey, *Tell It Well*

❖ **POSSIBLE ENTRANCE:** *News magazines consistently remind us of the suddenness of death.*

Time magazine reported on an Aloha Airlines jet that was en route from Hilo to Honolulu when suddenly a gaping hole blew open in the fuselage above the first-class compartment taking a flight attendant with it.

One passenger was quoted as saying, "My life is not in order, and I'm not ready to die."

—Adapted from *Time*, May 9, 1988

POSSIBLE EXIT: *Nothing should keep us from getting ready to die. After all, no one is promised tomorrow.*

Note: Eric Becklin's statement, "My life is not in order, and I'm not ready to die" makes this a powerful illustration. As time progresses, this particular illustration may not be as effective. You can use this line in connection with a recent happening of a similar nature, such as the plane that landed in the Hudson River in January 2009. Explain the happening and then say, "Years ago a man who thought he was going to die was quoted in *Time* magazine, saying . . ." and end with, "I wonder how many of you in this situation would say the same?"

❖ The famous American orator Robert Ingersoll devoted his talents to undermining the Christian faith. It is sad that in his dynamic lectures he so effectively employed sarcasm and humor to twist the truth to gain converts to unbelief. When he died, the brochure for his funeral service carried this statement: "There will be no singing." That certainly was appropriate for one who denied the reality of an afterlife.

—*Our Daily Bread*, 1996

Note: Robert Ingersoll was a noted atheist. Many, though, have never heard this illustration about "there will be no singing." Be on the alert for stories about people, events, etc. different from ones already heard.

EXCUSES

❖ A few boasted of their thefts. P. F., a twenty-eight-year-old Hispanic in Harlem, sounded like a shipping clerk reading off an invoice list as he told *Time* writer B. J. Phillips, "Well, I got a stereo worth four hundred dollars, a dining room set that said six hundred dollars in the window, and some bedroom furniture, but not a whole suite. I got some tennis shoes, and a few things from the jewelry store, but I got there too late for anything really good. I got it all done in half an hour; that's how quick I was working." He paused to add it all up. "I'd put the total somewhere between thirty-two hundred and thirty-five hundred dollars." Any remorse? "I've got three kids and I don't have no job. I had the opportunity to rob and I robbed. I'd do it again. I don't feel bad about it."

—*Time*, July 25, 1977

Note: There are too many figures to use this illustration as is and the costs are outdated. The most effective use of this illustration is to say "A man who stole approximately thirty-five hundred dollars during a blackout in New York City once said, 'I've got three kids . . .'"

❖ **POSSIBLE ENTRANCE:** *We laugh at the excuses others give for their irresponsible behavior.*

Teacher to tardy boy: Why are you so late?
Boy: Well, I always obey the law.
Teacher: Just what do you mean?
Boy: There's a sign in the road that says, "School ahead, go slow."

—Source unknown

POSSIBLE EXIT: *Our excuses may be humorous to us but they are not to God. Sin is very serious. It must be punished.*

☺ An Oklahoma woman was stopped by a highway patrolman for going through a stop sign. "I did go through it," she said, "but I just oozed through."

He looked at her a moment and then said, "Okay, I'll let you go this time, but the next time you see a sign that says ooze, you ooze, but if it says stop, you stop."

—Troy Gordan, *Tulsa World*

☺   A chronic car thief was in court for stealing again. "Why did you take a car this time?" the judge asked.

"Your Honor," he said, "it was parked in front of the cemetery. I thought the owner had died."

—Source unknown

☺   **POSSIBLE ENTRANCE:** *It's part of the human nature that, when we do wrong, we don't accept responsibility. Instead we make excuses.*

Examine the excuses people give for car accidents when they don't want to accept responsibility for them:

- "I told the police that I was not injured, but removing my hat, I found I had a skull fracture."
- "The pedestrian had no idea which direction to go, so I ran over him."
- "The indirect cause of this accident was a little guy in a small car with a big mouth."
- "I was thrown from my car as it left the road. I was later found in a ditch by some stray cows."
- "The telephone pole was approaching fast. I attempted to swerve out of its path when it struck my front end."
- "I was unable to stop in time and my car crashed into the other vehicle. The driver and passenger then left immediately for a vacation with injuries."
- "I collided with a stationary truck coming the other way."
- "A truck backed through my windshield into my wife's face."

—Source unknown

POSSIBLE EXIT: *God cannot excuse sin. He has to punish it.*

Note: An illustration like this is enhanced if instead of reading all eight, you read the four or five best ones.

❖   **POSSIBLE ENTRANCE:** *When it comes to your sin, are you excusing it by attributing it to a person or force outside of yourself?*

When salmon travel hundreds of miles up rivers and streams to spawn where they were hatched, they are acting on pure instinct. They are, in a sense, being driven by uncontrollable force. Man, on the other hand, is different. He cannot use instinct as a valid excuse to account for his actions. He is responsible, and even though he may feel driven, he makes the choices that lead to his downfall.

A young convict who escaped execution through a last-minute decision from a Supreme Court justice looks upon human conduct as of the same order as the salmon. Referring to the murders he committed and to his own fate, he said, "Things just happen." He thinks some kind of force was responsible for his pulling the trigger and killing the two people who happened to be at the scene of the crime at the wrong moment.

—Our Daily Bread, 1984

POSSIBLE EXIT: *God will not accept the excuse, "Things just happen." We must acknowledge, "I have sinned."*

FAME

❖ I think everybody should get rich and famous and do everything they ever dreamed of so they can see that it's not the answer.

—Jim Carrey, comedian

❖ POSSIBLE ENTRANCE: *One of the biggest problems with fame is regardless of how much happiness or security it brings, it doesn't last.*

Tennis champion Hana Mandlikova was once asked how she felt about defeating great players like Martina Navratilova and Chris Evert. She responded, "Any big win means that all the suffering, practicing, and traveling are worth it. I feel like I own the world." When asked how long that feeling lasts, she replied, "About two minutes."

—Our Daily Bread, 1999

POSSIBLE EXIT: *What Christ has for you doesn't last for just two minutes; it lasts forever.*

❖ "I met the big names of baseball," he says, "but I soon discovered that they had troubles like everyone else. I know that my friend, Rocque, was right—that baseball wasn't everything.

"My whole life has taken on a new and higher purpose," he says. "Christ is now first in my life, although I still love baseball and want to do my best. I wish that everyone would experience the thrill, joy, and hope that is mine, something that comes not through seeing your name in the headlines of a newspaper or the temporary fame that baseball can bring, but through a personal meeting with Jesus Christ."

—Felipe Alou, former major league baseball all-star and manager, *Athletes in Action*

❖ Fame is a vapor, popularity is an accident, and money takes wings. The only thing that endures is character.

—O. J. Simpson
in *Sports Illustrated*, 1980

Note: What makes the illustration poignant is that the truth of what O. J. said came back to haunt him.

GREED

❖ A man walked into a convenience store in Kansas and demanded all the money. He wasn't happy with the amount, so he tied up the clerk and worked the counter himself for several hours. He was still industriously working when the police came in and took him away.

—*Fax Daily*, September 25, 1998

❖ **POSSIBLE ENTRANCE:** *Man's basic problem is himself.*

It doesn't matter what you give a man, he will still want more. Instead of being satisfied with what he has, he'll want his neighbor's house, his neighbor's wife, and his neighbor's income. Everything he can get he wants—power and position, wealth and worship.

—R. Larry Moyer

POSSIBLE EXIT: *That's why when God changes us He works from the inside out. He knows our basic problem is bigger than what we do, it's who we are.*

❖ Someone said the difference between Patrick Henry and people today is that Patrick Henry said, "Give me liberty or give me death." People today just say, "Give me! Give me!"

—Joe Falkner, June 1977

❖ A chapter heading in Calvin Miller's book *A Requiem for Love* reads, "A beggar asked a millionaire, 'How many more dollars would it take to make you truly happy?' The millionaire, reaching his gnarled hands into the beggar's cup, replied, 'Only one more!'"

—*Leadership*, Spring 1990

❖ **POSSIBLE ENTRANCE:** *Greed sometimes makes us grab one thing after* *another. Instead of those things giving us freedom, we are trapped by our own greed.*

I was driving to church when I first saw the skunk in the middle of Grand Street, a quiet thoroughfare in my hometown of Lexington, Massachusetts. Skunks are a common sight in the early morning hours, but this one was different. It was violently careening back and forth from one curb to the other, blinded and crazed by what seemed to be a box jammed over its head.

I looked closer. The skunk had apparently raided someone's garbage can during the night, found a cocoa box with a few grains of chocolate in the bottom, and decided to pursue what refreshment remained. But greed had gotten the best of the animal when it stuck its nose far inside, and now the box had become a self-made prison.

—Jones Berkley, *Preaching to Convince*

POSSIBLE EXIT: *Ever feel like that? You reach out for so much, thinking you'll find the thing that satisfies you. Soon you are trapped by your own greed. That trap might be a home you can't afford, a car that is demolished, or an appetite for money that controls you instead of you controlling it.*

☺ A man walked into a bar and saw an old friend dejectedly nursing a drink. "You look terrible," the man said.

"My mother died in March and left me $10,000," the friend replied. "Then in April my father died and left me $20,000."

"Gee, that's tough, losing both parents in two months."

"Then to top it off," the friend said, "my aunt died last month and left me $50,000."

"How sad."

"Tell me about it," the friend continued. "So far this month, nothing."

—Internet humor

GUILT

❖ A pastor told me he counseled twelve to fifteen people within the last two weeks and 90 percent of the problem was unresolved guilt.

—R. Larry Moyer

❖ **POSSIBLE ENTRANCE:** *Our guilt may be for a number of reasons. But it is so real we do all we can to relieve it or escape it.*

The great Indian leader Mahatma Gandhi is an example of a highly successful leader who went through life experiencing an existential debt. When he was a very young teenager, he was married as the result of a prearranged betrothal. He found that he looked forward with great anticipation to the sexual passion the evenings would hold for him and his young bride. At this same time his father was deathly ill, and Mohandas would spend hours by his father's bedside, gently nursing him and providing him with much needed company. On one occasion, after having sat with his father for numerous hours, he was relieved in his vigil by an uncle. Having been relieved of his duties, he was only too anxious to go straight to his marital bed and enjoy the company of his wife. Shortly after having entered his room with his wife, news came that his father had died just moments after he had left. The young Gandhi was gripped by a terrible sense of guilt; he felt that his father had died as a direct result of his lust. This experience created an existential debt in Gandhi's life and had a profound impact on the development of his dark side, thus greatly influencing his style of leadership. His lifelong obsession with nonviolent reform was a subconscious attempt to repay this existential debt.

—Gary McIntosh and Samuel D. Rima Sr., *Overcoming the Dark Side of Leadership*

POSSIBLE EXIT: *God has a better way of dealing with guilt than we have. He wants to remove it now and forever.*

❖ Only God's gift can erase man's guilt.

—*Our Daily Bread*, 1976

❖ **POSSIBLE ENTRANCE:** *Somehow we think our sin will go undetected. But sooner or later, we will pay its consequences.*

Two guys, Jimmy and Johnny, were standing at heaven's gate, waiting to be interviewed by St. Peter.

Jimmy: "How did you get here?"

Johnny: "Hypothermia. You?"

Jimmy: "You won't believe it. I was sure my wife was cheating on me, so I came home early one day hoping to find the guy. I accused my wife of unfaithfulness and searched the whole house without any luck. Then I felt so badly about the whole thing, I had a massive heart attack."

Johnny: "Oh, man, if you had checked the walk-in freezer, we'd both be alive."

—Internet humor

POSSIBLE EXIT: *We laugh, but the consequences of sin are not only fatal, they are eternal.*

Note: When people are laughing they are listening. But we must be careful not to take lightly what God takes seriously. Here, we can admit something is humorous and then immediately address the seriousness of it. In so doing, we have won the ears of the listeners through the Spirit and spoke in a convicting way of their sin.

❖   I spoke with a young couple whose marriage had many times been on the verge of breaking up. Their greatest problem was an inability to live with the past. They couldn't get away from mistakes they had made, sins they had committed, and therefore they lived in guilt day in and day out. Becoming frustrated with the past, they became frustrated with each other.

—R. Larry Moyer

Note: The merit of this experience is to make you think about yours. Counseling matters must be kept confidential. But summarizing the situation and explaining the main problem—"frustrated with the past, they were frustrated with each other"—might be all the illustrative value you need.

❖   A prisoner waiting on death row had a deep sense of guilt. He had killed a man in the presence of the victim's two children during a robbery attempt.

The convict was bothered so much that he refused to allow his lawyer to appeal for a stay of execution. For him, departing this life was an escape from his nagging conscience and the reproach of an angry society. He said, "It's my way out of this living hell."

—*Our Daily Bread*, 1997

❖   In 1971 he killed a man. Even though he was the prime suspect in the murder, no one could prove it, and the case was abandoned. So he got away with it. Or did he?

Nearly three decades later, in failing health and living in a nursing home, he confessed to the crime. A detective who headed the original investigation said, "He was looking over his shoulder for the last twenty-six years, not only for the law, but for his Maker. I think he wants to clear his conscience before he meets his Maker—or try at least."

—*Our Daily Bread*, 1999

❖ The ways we try to deal with guilt are numerous:

1. Rationalization—provide ourselves and others with reasonable explanations for situations that tend to produce guilt or anxiety, damage our self-esteem, or otherwise disturb us.
2. Repression—actively pushing unpleasant or threatening material out of conscious memory.
3. Projection—attributing guilt to others.
4. Compensation—read an extra chapter in the Bible or spend an extra hour in prayer in an endeavor to chalk up points with God.
5. Letting off steam—become angry and take it out on someone or something.

—*His*, October 1969

❖ **POSSIBLE ENTRANCE:** *Let me ask you, where does unresolved guilt takes it greatest toll?*

At the age of fifteen, Robert Garth hit an elderly man on the head to steal money for an athletic uniform. He didn't intend to kill him, but the blow proved to be fatal. The police had no clues. Garth knew that it was very unlikely he would be caught, yet he was miserable. Finally, after fifteen years of mental anguish, he confessed to the police. He was tried, given a relatively light sentence, and sent to prison. There, he trusted Christ as his Savior. Some people said his sentence was too lenient. Robert's reply was this: "I've been incarcerated in a cell for six months. I've been incarcerated in my mind for fifteen years. There is no comparison. The mind was far worse."

—*Our Daily Bread*, 1987

POSSIBLE EXIT: *Try as we might, we can't get the wrongs we do out of our minds. Mental imprisonment can be worse than physical imprisonment.*

❖ Many things can cause guilt. I have met people who live in guilt because they bought a swimming pool that caused their infant's death, a motorcycle that caused their son's accident, or even a boat that resulted in a relative's drowning. Sometimes the guilt drives them to use alcohol or tranquilizers.

—R. Larry Moyer

❖ Guilt is everyone's acquaintance but no one's friend.

—Clyde Annandale, *How to Develop an Evangelistic Sermon*

❖ It is indeed amazing that in as fundamentally irreligious culture as ours, the sense of guilt should be so widespread and deep-rooted as it is.

—Eric Fromm, *The Sane Society*

☺ Police in Los Angeles put a robbery suspect in a lineup. When they asked the suspect to say, "Give me all your money or I'll shoot," the man shouted, "That's not what I said."

—*Fax Daily*, September 25, 1998

❖ **POSSIBLE ENTRANCE:** *We are plagued by the past. We are tormented day and night by people we wish we had never met, thoughts we wish we had never had, words we wish we had never spoken, and things we wish we had never done. We are always trying to escape it.*

One sunny day in September 1972, a stern-faced, plainly dressed man could be seen standing still on a street corner in the busy Chicago loop. As pedestrians hurried by on their way to lunch or business, he would solemnly lift his right arm, and pointing to the person nearest him, intone loudly the single word, "Guilty!"

Then, without any change of expression, he would resume his stiff stance for a few moments before repeating the gesture. Then, again, the inexorable raising of his arm, the pointing, and the solemn pronouncing of the one word, "Guilty!"

The effect on the passing strangers was extraordinary, almost eerie. They would stare at him, hesitate, look away, look at each other, and then at him again, then continue on their ways.

One man, turning to another who was my informant, exclaimed, "But how did he know?"

—Karl Menninger, *Whatever Became of Sin?*

POSSIBLE EXIT: *God has the only answer that works. It's called forgiveness. You can stand before a holy God with a slate that doesn't have a thing on it.*

Note: You don't need to refer to the date of 1972. It's immaterial.

❖ **POSSIBLE ENTRANCE:** *There are many attempted solutions to the problem of guilt. There is only one that removes it.*

Steve Musto counseled prisoners in a prison outside New York City. One corresponded with him. The other day he wrote, "Mr. Musto, I can't put on paper the inner feelings that I now have. My wife had me put in prison, and for the first time in eleven months I wrote her a letter and thanked her." Can you imagine that? But he went on, "I have taken medicine, pills, and shock therapy, and now I realize that I wasn't sick at all. My sins were weighing me down, and I couldn't carry the load by myself. So I took my burdens to the Lord and left them there. I truly believe the Lord spoke through my wife to have me put flat on my back in a prison bunk, so that I would look up. Praise God for His everlasting power."

—This quote was taken from the article "Knowing the Truth" by Lane Adams from the March 1970 issue of *Decision* magazine. ©1970 Billy Graham Evangelistic Association. Used with permission. All rights reserved.

POSSIBLE EXIT: *God is not interested in merely helping you with your guilt. He wants to remove it.*

Note: Be careful to choose from each illustration the substance you need to drive your point home. Here, one may only need to say, "A man who spent time in a prison outside New York City once said, . . ." then use his two sentences beginning with "I have taken" and ending with "by myself."

❖   In the 1950s, psychologists said that guilt was the number one problem in America and would increasingly be so.

Millions of Americans going through inward contortion are proving them right. They are wracked by guilt, and so they try to alleviate the guilt by escape—medicines, liquor, laughter, work franticness, hypocrisy, self-righteousness, and a hundred other things. Guilt wracks America!

—*The Presbyterian Journal*, July 14, 1971

Note: The application here is that psychologists were right. More than fifty years later, guilt is still the thing that wrecks America.

❖   Guilt doesn't help us change our attitudes about ourselves. We are naturally sinful and imperfect and consequently are led to connect wrong thoughts and actions. Then our rebellious actions trigger a fear of punishment, a lowered self-evaluation, or a fear of rejection. In response to this, we either (1) give in and suffer depression and feelings of worthlessness, (2) rebel and fight back by committing even more wrongs, (3) deny we did any wrong and put the blame on someone else, or (4) superficially acknowledge our faults to get rid of the pain, but feel no genuine desire to change.

—Bruce Narramore, *You're Someone Special*

Note: Illustrations make us think not just about illustrations but the content of messages. Bruce Narramore lists four ways we try to resolve guilt. Are there others?

☺ **POSSIBLE ENTRANCE:** *Many times the guilt we feel is only on an emotional level. We don't acknowledge what we've done as being wrong. If given the chance we'd do it again.*

A man with a nagging secret couldn't keep it any longer. In the confessional he admitted that for years he had been stealing building supplies from the lumberyard where he worked.

"What did you take?" his parish priest asked.

"Enough to build my own home and enough for my son's house. And houses for our two daughters. And our cottage at the lake."

"This is very serious," the priest said, "I shall have to think of a far-reaching penance. Have you ever done a retreat?"

"No, Father, I haven't," the man replied. "But if you can get the plans, I can get the lumber."

—Internet humor

POSSIBLE EXIT: *God is interested in more than feelings. He wants us to call the wrongs that we've done wrong, what He calls it—sin.*

☺ **POSSIBLE ENTRANCE:** *Sometimes the attempts we make to deal with our guilt remove the pain; it doesn't remove the problem.*

A man walked into a bar and ordered a drink. He threw it into the bartender's face. The bartender got mad. The man apologized. The bartender forgave him. This happened two more times. Finally the bartender said, "Look, you need help. I'm taking you to a psychiatrist."

They went to a psychiatrist, and he asked the man to lie down on the sofa and offered him a glass of water. After several weeks of help, the man took the water and threw it into the doctor's face. The psychiatrist said, "I thought you said you don't throw water anymore."

The man said, "Oh yes, I still throw water, only I don't feel guilty anymore."

—Haddon Robinson

POSSIBLE EXIT: *You can deal with the pain of guilt by going to church, being good, or doing good works, but Christ wants to deal with the problem. You feel guilty because you are guilty.*

HELL

❖ C. S. Lewis, that great British defender of the faith, wrote, "There is no doctrine which I would more willingly remove from Christianity than this [hell]. I would pay any price to be able to say truthfully, 'All will be saved.'" But Lewis, like us, realized that was neither truthful nor within his power to change.

—K. P. Yohannan, *Revolution in World Missions*

❖ D. L. Moody had shared the claim of Christ with a young man. The man had trouble grasping what Christ had done. At one point he said to D. L. Moody, "If I could see heaven for five minutes I would believe." D. L. Moody's comment was, "If you could see hell for five seconds you would believe."

—Source unknown

❖ **POSSIBLE ENTRANCE:** *If you were to list the most disturbing things about hell, one would stand out above the rest.*

There is a way to stay out of hell, but no way to get out of hell.

—*Our Daily Bread*, 1984

POSSIBLE EXIT: *The number one thing that makes hell what it is—hell—that it's eternal. There is no getting out.*

❖ A chaplain who did not believe in hell was dismissed because,

1. If there is no hell, we don't need you.
2. If there is a hell, we don't want you to deceive us any more.

—Bob Bryant

❖ One day a man in Blackpool, England, thought he detected the smell of burning timber, so he sat down and wrote a postcard about it to the Blackpool fire brigade. "Will you come to my house?" he asked. "I can smell timber burning."

When the firemen received the post card some twenty-four hours later, they thought it was a joke. But as they weren't doing anything anyway, they decided to investigate and see who the practical joker was.

When they arrived you can picture their surprise when they found the house was really on fire! Some timbers under the man's hearth were smoldering so they promptly extinguished them. He was fortunate that the place hadn't burned down, waiting twenty-four hours for the fire department to arrive.

But this is the same attitude that many people take regarding the "everlasting burning." God has given terrific warning but some people don't seem in any hurry to escape.

—C. D. Carter

❖ **POSSIBLE ENTRANCE:** *Do you know who spoke about hell more than any other man in the Bible? It was none other than Jesus.*

When I pastored a country church, a farmer didn't like the sermons I preached on hell. He said, "Preach about the meek and lowly Jesus."

I said, "That's where I got my information about hell."

—Vance Havner

POSSIBLE EXIT: *Why did Jesus speak about hell? Because loving us like He does, He doesn't want us to go there, and came up with a way whereby hell can be avoided.*

❖ The safest road to hell is the gradual one—the gentle slope, soft underfoot, without sudden turnings, without milestones, without sign posts.

—C. S. Lewis, *The Screwtape Letters*

❖ God does not send sinners to hell; they choose to go.

—Milburn Miller

❖ Almost every natural man that hears of hell flatters himself that he shall escape it.

—Jonathan Edwards, "Sinners in the Hands of an Angry God"

❖ Hell is truth seen too late.

—*Pulpit Helps*, January 1997

❖ **POSSIBLE ENTRANCE:** *When we think of hell, our thoughts may be the same as that of a four-time Academy Award winner.*

Four-time Academy Award winner Katharine Hepburn underwent tests at a hospital Thursday and was expected to go home in a few days.

The nature of the ninety-four-year-old actress' illness was not disclosed.

Past health problems include arthritis, pneumonia, and tremors similar to those from Parkinson's disease.

Hepburn was admitted about 6 P.M. Wednesday and was resting comfortably in stable condition Thursday afternoon, Hartford Hospital spokesman James Battaglio said.

"She's up and around and speaking with her physicians," Battaglio said late Thursday afternoon. "Physically she's showing improvement in her overall appearance and her spirit."

Hepburn, who lives in Old Saybrook, is a Hartford native; her father was chief of staff at Hartford Hospital.

In an interview in October 1990, she told the Associated Press, "I'm what is known as gradually disintegrating. I don't fear the next world, or anything. I don't fear hell, and I don't look forward to heaven."

—*Associated Press*, August 2001

POSSIBLE EXIT: *But just because we don't fear something does not change the existence of it.*

HONESTY

☺ **POSSIBLE ENTRANCE:** *Honesty is usually not one of our traits. Even if we are honest in some things, we are not honest in all things, particularly those places where our honesty may hurt us.*

On a job application one question read, "Have you ever been arrested?" The applicant printed the word "No" in the space. The next question was a follow-up to the first. It asked, "Why?" Not realizing he did not have to answer this part, the "honest" and rather naïve applicant wrote, "I guess it's because I never got caught."

—John Maxwell, *Developing the Leader Within You*

POSSIBLE EXIT: *Although he wouldn't have needed to fill out that part and we may call him naïve, we should applaud his honesty. We probably would not have been as honest as he was.*

☺ When a car blew past a stop sign at a busy intersection, my uncle, a Mississippi state trooper, gave chase and pulled the driver over.

"Didn't you see that stop sign back there?" my uncle asked.

"Yeah, I saw it," admitted the driver. "The problem is, I didn't see you."

—Submitted by Michael Hamilton. Reprinted with permission from the September 2006 *Reader's Digest*. Copyright ©2006 by The Reader's Digest Assn., Inc.

☺   Most of my fellow passengers were patient about the flight delay—except one obnoxious couple. The man was practically shouting at the gate agent.

Finally came the announcement: "We are ready to pre-board passengers needing special assistance, passengers with children, and passengers with husbands who act like children."

—Christie Lansang quoted in *Reader's Digest*, January 2006

HOPELESSNESS

❖   When you say a situation or a person is hopeless, you are slamming the door in the face of God.

—Charles L. Allen, *God's Psychiatry*

❖   Tragedy can occur if we assume that a situation is hopeless when it is not. An East Detroit man made such a mistake. Thinking that he had contracted Lyme disease, he assumed that it was contagious and fatal, and that he had passed it along to his wife.

Of course, Lyme disease is neither contagious nor fatal. But because he assumed it was, he shot his wife while she was asleep and then took his own life. According to the *Detroit News*, police said the man left a note saying he felt that this was the only way out of their desperate situation.

—*Our Daily Bread*, 1990

❖   POSSIBLE ENTRANCE: *We often view life as being hopeless. Our thoughts are much like those of Ernest Hemingway.*

Life is a dirty trick, a short journey from nothingness to nothingness. There is no remedy for anything in life. Man's destiny in the universe is like a colony of ants on a burning log.

—Ernest Hemingway

POSSIBLE EXIT: *The Bible never calls life hopeless as long as you understand that hope can be found only one way, through one person—Christ.*

Note: A quote from a literary genius like Ernest Hemingway is timeless.

❖   POSSIBLE ENTRANCE: *Not only do we experience feelings of hopelessness, the older we get, the more those feelings increase.*

Nature has let us down, God seems to have left the receiver off the hook, and time is running out.

—Arthur Koestler, British novelist

POSSIBLE EXIT: *With God, we live in hope, not hopelessness. That hope only increases as we anticipate seeing Christ face to face.*

❖ An article in the *Grand Rapids Press* described a woman who overcame her drinking habit—but only after she admitted she had a problem. She said the "emotional moment" came when she brought herself to say, "I'm Betty, and I'm an alcoholic."

She had been saying that her slurred speech, drowsiness, and other problems were due to the medication she was taking for a chronic ailment. But the family knew the real cause and confronted her. As a result, she finally faced up to her problem. Before that, she was a hopeless case. But when she said, "I'm an alcoholic," there was hope for a cure.

—*Our Daily Bread*, 1994

Note: Anyone who has worked with alcoholics will tell you each must come to the point of admitting, "I'm an alcoholic." Only then can that person be helped. This article in a Grand Rapids, Michigan, newspaper should cause you to think of more current examples you can use.

JUDGMENT DAY

❖ **POSSIBLE ENTRANCE:** *Just the thought of a judgment day makes us uncomfortable. Many of us can identify with one driver's response to an Ohio incident.*

The Ohio highway was unusually crowded. Cars came to a standstill in the night air. Yet the drivers couldn't see what the problem was. As one traveler recalled, "I thought there must have been an accident." He later discovered that a rumor had spread that an image of Christ had been appearing nightly on a nearby soybean tank. Many seemed shaken by what they saw. Others contended that the image was nothing more than a shadow effect created by night lighting and a badly stained, rusty tank surface. The response of one driver was especially noteworthy. When he leaned out of his van window and asked someone what was going on, the bystander looked at him and said, "Jesus is here!" The van driver remarked to a reporter, "For a moment I really freaked out. I was scared. I mean, I wasn't prepared for judgment day."

—*Our Daily Bread*, 1987

POSSIBLE EXIT: *May I ask you . . . suppose Jesus was here—face to face with you. Would you be prepared to see Him?*

❖ The letter began, "Dear taxpayer, in processing your return, we need more information about certain items." If you got a message like that last year, you were one of almost two million Americans chosen for an income tax audit. Such news would hardly be welcomed, even though the Internal Revenue Service says that the vast majority of taxpayers are honest and have nothing to fear. Nevertheless, in the previous year more than two-thirds of those examined by the IRS did owe more taxes. Most people, however, don't really expect to be called in to declare their earnings because only one in every forty-six is checked.

There'll be no random sampling or scientific selection at God's judgment seat! One out of forty-six will be audited—and so will the other forty-five.

—*Our Daily Bread*, 1980

> Note: Have you ever been audited? If you have and can use your experience to help in connection with this illustration, do so. Also, don't forget to use the Internet to update any figures. For instance the ratio in 2002 was 1 in 47 for those with income under $100,000 and 1 in 145 for those over $100,000.

❖ POSSIBLE ENTRANCE: *We try to put off having to experience the consequences of our sin—that day when we will stand before the Lord and answer for all the wrong we have done.*

John had been convicted of highway robbery in Alabama and sentenced to death. The last day of his life had come. The warden awakened him and asked him what he would have for breakfast. "As it is your last day, John, you can have anything you want."

"Thank you, sir. I'd like to have some watermelon."

"But this is December. Watermelons aren't planted yet, much less ripe!"

"That's okay. I can wait."

—Source unknown

POSSIBLE EXIT: *Whether it is today, or ten years from now, there is coming a day when we will be face to face with Him.*

JUSTICE

❖ POSSIBLE ENTRANCE: *Our hearts cry out for justice. This is seen through the parents of a son who died as a result of a mugging in a New York subway.*

Sherwin and Karen Watkins, the Utah tourists whose son died defending them from a gang of muggers in a New York subway, want more than courtroom justice. They want $100 million, too.

The Provo couple has formally notified the New York City Transit Authority of the intent to sue, officials said Wednesday. "He was such a good kid," says Sherwin Watkins, who had taken his family to New York for their annual trip to the U.S. Open Tennis tournament. "He really had his head screwed on straight. He had everything to live for."

—*USA Today*, December 13, 1990

POSSIBLE EXIT: *God's heart is out for justice, too. Sin must be punished, and the punishment of sin is death. Jesus Christ satisfied God's justice by taking our punishment and dying in our place.*

> Note: Always keep the date in mind and current events in mind. Many people would tell you that crime has gone down significantly in New York City but that does not change the relevancy of a family who seeks justice.

❖ **POSSIBLE ENTRANCE:** *Our hearts cry out for justice.*

A few years ago in Scotland, a man murdered a member of his family. But by the time he was brought to trial, the judge decided he'd already punished himself enough, and he let him go. It doesn't take a lot of imagination to guess how the public responded: "What? That's not fair: We want justice! Get that judge out of there, and replace him with a good one who'll uphold the law."

—Bill Hybels and Mark Mittelberg, *Becoming a Contagious Christian*

POSSIBLE EXIT: *God's heart cries out for justice too. A holy God cannot allow sin to go unpunished. He has declared, "The wages of sin is death."*

❖ Have you ever heard anyone say, "I could never live in a country that would build places to punish people—some for the rest of their lives—just because they had done something wrong"? Not very likely! It is obvious that a government is within its bounds when it dispenses justice. "You do the crime, you do the time," is a saying almost everyone agrees with.

—*Our Daily Bread*, 1991

LIFE

❖ In November 1975, the freighter *Edmund Fitzgerald* sank in the cold waters of Lake Superior during a fierce storm. Only a week before the tragedy, chief steward Robert Rafferty had written to his wife, "I may be home by November 8. However, nothing is ever sure." The prophetic irony of his words was noted in a newspaper article listing the twenty-nine crew members who perished in the disaster.

—*Our Daily Bread*, 2005

❖ **POSSIBLE ENTRANCE:** *Have you ever felt on some days that you are the problem and on others days you're the victim?*

Accept that some days you're the pigeon, and some days you're the statue.

—Source unknown

POSSIBLE EXIT: *With Christ you don't have to be the problem or the victim— you can be the victor.*

❖ I don't make plans, because life is short and unpredictable—much like the weather!

—Al Roker

❖ **POSSIBLE ENTRANCE:** *Even at a young age we begin to discover some very powerful feelings about life. A young person put her thoughts into three words.*

Life is stupid.

—Julie quoted by Dawson McAllister in *Please Don't Tell My Parents*

POSSIBLE EXIT: *You know, she's right—life is stupid, until you meet Christ. He is the only One who can make sense out of stupidity.*

❖ The teenager expressed the view of many. Speaking of the wild parties he attended, the sixteen-year-old declared, "Without these parties, my life wouldn't have any purpose."

—*Our Daily Bread*, 1996

☺ From the time an infant first tries to get his toes into his mouth, life is a continual struggle to make both ends meet.

—Internet humor

❖ Do the events of history make any sense? Or is life, as Shakespeare had Macbeth describe it, "A tale told by an idiot, full of sound and fury, signifying nothing"?

—Source unknown

Note: When using illustrations like this, I take the liberty to use the word "fool" instead of "idiot" in an effort to take away the harshness.

LONELINESS

❖ Loneliness is being unaware of the One who is with us everywhere.

—*Our Daily Bread*, 2005

❖ While we were in Illinois for a crusade, a young girl came up and gave me a poem her mother had written titled "Loneliness." I'll never forget the second line. "Is there no one on earth with love I can find?"

—R. Larry Moyer

❖ POSSIBLE ENTRANCE: *Perhaps no one has described loneliness any better than a twenty-nine-year-old single man once did in Topeka, Kansas.*

For myself, I can only describe the world of loneliness as being a gut-level sick feeling in the pit of your stomach. It's so far within yourself you feel you're in a trap and will never be set free.

—*Wichita Eagle and Beacon*, January 14, 1979

POSSIBLE EXIT: *Only one person can set you free. It's the One who said, "If the Son makes you free, you shall be free indeed."*

❖ A school boy in London won first prize for an essay contest. One of the lines from his composition was this: "I believe so many twins are born into the world today because little children are frightened of entering the world alone!" While that young writer's "theological conclusion" is on shaky ground, it does focus on one of man's most nagging problems—loneliness.

—*Our Daily Bread*, 1980

LOST

❖ POSSIBLE ENTRANCE: *If you want to know how God feels about you, just ask yourself the question, "How would I feel if I had a lost child?"*

Six-week-old Crystal Guerrero was kidnapped on December 16, 1993, from a Chicago health clinic. Her parents lived in emotional turmoil for a week, unable to eat or sleep. Then an abandoned baby was found in a church. It was Crystal! She was unharmed and well. Imagine the family's joy, a joy shared by the whole country as the media spread the heartwarming news. The infant was back in her mother's arms just in time for a jubilant Christmas.

—Our Daily Bread, 1995

POSSIBLE EXIT: *God is eager for the day you will come to Him, safe in His arms.*

❖ The newspapers carried the story of a hunter who got lost because he was stubborn. The man had a compass with him but was so confident that he was woodsman enough to find his way without consulting it that he neglected to look at it until it was too dark to see. He had no matches and was forced to bed down in some leaves in the shelter of a rock.

In the morning, he decided again to trust his own gift of being a woodsman. The day wore on, and he made little progress. He decided he had played the fool long enough, so he pulled the compass from his pocket and was soon on the right road home. This man was lost until he admitted that he was lost, and only then was he able to find his way.

If a man will come to the place where he admits to God and himself that he can do nothing for himself, the Lord will immediately reveal to him the way of salvation and will plant new life within, making the man a partaker with the divine nature (2 Peter 1:4).

—Source unknown

Note: I keep emphasizing that illustrations you receive should stir you to think of even better ones from your own experience. This caused me to think of a dear friend who became lost on one of our hunting trips years ago in Colorado. He made it to safety a day later only because he took the first step the night before by saying, "Okay, I'm lost."

❖ One time the pilot of a small plane was flying into Chattanooga and got lost. In a frantic state he got on his radio and asked, "Does anybody hear me? I need help!" Another pilot picked him up and asked, "Where are you?" The man answered, "I don't know. I just flew through some treetops. My propeller hit some trees. My altimeter shows that I am now seven hundred feet above the ground." Air traffic control gave him permission to climb to 4,000 feet, the minimum altitude to fly into

Chattanooga from any direction to clear the mountains that surround the city. When he got to 4,000 feet and got things straightened out, he was then able to fly into Chattanooga. It was discovered he had been a few minutes away from slamming into the side of a mountain several thousand feet high.

—Ted DeMoss and Robert Tamasy, *The Gospel and the Briefcase*

Note: The man knew he was lost but didn't understand fully the consequence of death, which lay ahead of him, had he stayed the course.

LYING

❖ A lie is like a snowball. The longer it is rolled on the ground the larger it becomes.

—attributed to Martin Luther, quoted by Michael G. Moriarty in *The Perfect 10*

☺ "Do you believe in life after death?" asked a boss of his employee.

"Yes, sir," replied the nervous employee.

"Good, because after you left early yesterday to attend your grandmother's funeral, she came in for a visit!"

—Source unknown

☺ "Last week we were studying George Washington, our first president," said the teacher. "Does anyone remember the greatest obstacle that President Washington faced?" A little boy raised his hand. "Yes, ma'am," he replied, "he could not tell a lie."

—King Duncan, *Mule Eggs and Topknots*

❖ Lying makes a problem part of the future; truth makes a problem part of the past.

—Rick Pitino, basketball coach

❖ **POSSIBLE ENTRANCE:** *Our conscience tells us lying is wrong, yet we'd be quick to agree with this Japanese proverb.*

A lie is a useful thing.

—Japanese proverb quoted by Alexander Hill in *Just Business*

POSSIBLE EXIT: *It may be useful, but it still has its consequences. It is a sin that must be punished.*

MAN

❖ **POSSIBLE ENTRANCE:** *Ever notice how prone we are to sin? Our biggest problem is not what we do, it's who we are.*

The difficulty of walking in simple dependence upon the Lord came to mind while I was reading about a mother who went shopping with her two-year-old girl. She said, "We were going down an aisle in the grocery store when all of a sudden my daughter cried, 'Mommy, hurry, hold my hand before I run away.'"

—*Our Daily Bread*, 1974

POSSIBLE EXIT: *Have you been as honest in admitting you run away from God?*

❖ After a horrible crime had been committed against a young girl by six teenage boys, the policeman said this about the youthful criminals: "They are not really evil but are basically good."
The Bible says just the opposite. We are not good but basically evil.

—Source unknown

❖ Man's greatest problem is man himself.

—Billy Graham, Amsterdam Conference, 1983

❖ God without man is still God, but man without God is nothing.

—Source unknown

MATERIALISM

❖ A man one time had a black convertible, which he loved. One day, he loaned it to a friend, and in the matter of a few minutes it was demolished. That which he loved was no more. Our love is to be in Christ, not man or man-made objects. If it is, we will never be disappointed!

—Philip Hook

Note: Put yourself in the person's shoes and assume how he felt—showed it to his friends, took them for rides, polished it frequently, protected it from storms. That way you bring the listener emotionally into the story.

❖ In the summer of 1992, a fire blackened 4,500 acres of forest about thirty-five miles north of Atlantic City. One homeowner saw a fireball with sixty-foot flames come roaring up across the street from his house, before veering away. The Associated Press quoted him as saying, "I've worked twenty-five years for my life here. The thought of having it gone in ten minutes makes you want to stay for the last possible minute."

—*Our Daily Bread*, 2004

☺ These days there are the haves, the have-nots, and the charge its.

—Source unknown

❖ **POSSIBLE ENTRANCE:** *Many times we review our materialistic spirit as a weakness when the Bible would actually call it sin because it is disobedience to a God-given command.*

To lay up treasure on earth is as plainly forbidden by our Master as adultery and murder.

—John Wesley, *The Sermons of John Wesley*

POSSIBLE EXIT: *Why is it sin? First and foremost it focuses our eyes on something that cannot be taken with us. Our greatest need is Someone, not something.*

❖ When an armored truck lost nearly a million dollars, more than half of the money was quickly grabbed by passersby. Apparently they believed the adage, "Finders keepers, losers weepers."

—Adapted from *Time*, April 4, 1988

❖ Mark Petersburg, director of the Christian Embassy in Washington, DC, says, "Hold all you have with a loose grip."

—Bobb Biehl, *The On My Own Handbook*. www.BobbBiehl.com. Used by permission.

Note: This quote is powerful because of its content, not who said it. In using it, it would be sufficient to say, "A person who served as director of the Christian Embassy in Washington once said . . ."

❖ **POSSIBLE ENTRANCE:** *Let me ask you an unusual question. If you wanted to show someone your wealth, what direction would you have them look?*

George W. Truett, a well-known pastor, was invited to dinner at the home of a very wealthy man in Texas. After the meal, the host led him to a place where they could get a good view of the surrounding area.

Pointing to the oil wells punctuating the landscape, he boasted, "Twenty-five years ago I had nothing. Now, as far as you can see, it's all mine." Looking in the opposite direction at his sprawling fields of grain, he said, "That's all mine." Turning east toward huge herds of cattle, he bragged, "They're all mine." Then, pointing to the west and a beautiful forest, he exclaimed, "That, too, is all mine."

He paused, expecting Dr. Truett to compliment him on his great success. Truett, however, placing one hand on the man's shoulder and pointing heavenward with the other, simply said, "How much do you have in that direction?" The man hung his head and confessed, "I never thought of that."

—*Our Daily Bread*, 1992

POSSIBLE EXIT: *Let me ask you, "How much do you have in that direction (pointing upward)? Do you know if you were to die you'd go to heaven?"*

Note: Christians and non-Christians don't know George W. Truett, who died many years ago. Therefore, in using this illustration in most settings it would be better to say, "A man who pastored one of the largest churches in the world at that time was invited to dinner . . ."

❖   If you have something you can't live without, you don't own it, it owns you.

—Albert Schweitzer

❖   There is a line found in the Jewish Talmud that puts it well: "Man is born with his hands clenched; he dies with them wide open. Entering life, he desires to grasp everything; leaving the world, all he possessed has slipped away."

—Charles R. Swindoll, *Living Above the Level of Mediocrity*

❖   It seems that almost all entertainment and even advertisements give just the opposite message. They tell us to enjoy ourselves now, take care of this life, and ignore the next. We've become used to such expressions as "You only live once," or "You only go around once." Richard Pryor, the comedian, said, "Enjoy as much as you can. Even if you live to be ninety that's not as long as you're going to be dead."

—Billy Graham, *Storm Warnings*

❖   "We're enthralled and spellbound by wealth," says sociologist Paul

Schervish, director of Boston College's Center on Wealth and Philanthropy and author of *The Modern Medici*. "We all aspire to be prosperous, to go from rags to riches, to attain the American Dream."

—*USA Today*, August 15, 2006

❖ A magazine article summarized the life of a former NCAA basketball coach and network sports announcer. Throughout his colorful coaching career he had been obsessed with the game and with winning. But years later, stricken with cancer, he came to realize the triviality of the goods and values to which he had been passionately devoted. "You get sick, and you say to yourself, 'Sports means nothing,' and that feels terrible."

Because he had spent little time with his wife and children, he confessed, "I figured I'd have twenty years in the big time, who knows, maybe win three national titles, then pack it in at fifty-three or fifty-four . . . I was going to make it all up to them, all the time I'd been away . . . It sounds so silly now . . . But it went on and on, that insatiable desire to conquer the world."

Have we discovered the triviality of the empty success the world applauds, the futility of being a winner and yet losing the family values and the spiritual values that in the end are all-important? There's still time to redirect our goals. Thanks to our gracious God, right now we can reverse our direction and start living for Christ. That's the life that leaves no regrets.

—*Our Daily Bread*, 2000

❖ Many people today are suffering from what someone has well called "destination sickness," the malady of having everything you've always wanted to have, but not wanting anything you've gotten. You've arrived, but you don't want it when you get there.

—Ray Stedman

❖ **POSSIBLE ENTRANCE:** *Sometimes we are so materialistic, we make "things" goals in lives.*

A car one time had a license plate that said "My Goal."

—Bill Lawrence

POSSIBLE EXIT: *Happiness and eternal life is not experienced when we have found some "thing" but when we find Someone.*

❖ I'm not ready to die because I'd be leaving too much behind.
—Malcolm Forbes, age 70, a week before he died in February 1990

❖ Materialism has nothing to do with the amount; it has everything to do with attitude.
—Howard G. Hendricks

❖ A man once found a dollar bill in the street. Since then he has kept his eyes on the ground, always searching for more. He has accumulated 1,754 pins, 578 buttons, and $2.58, but he has lost the sight of the faces of friends, the loveliness of flowers, the glory of heaven and its blue skies.
—Source unknown

❖ **POSSIBLE ENTRANCE:** *Everything you have can either help you or hurt you. It can help you because you look at it as something to share. It can hurt you because it keeps you from God.*

John Hauberg and his wife live in a stunning home in Seattle. It is built mostly of glass inside and out. Hundreds of glass artifacts decorate the light-flooded rooms, and even the sinks, shelves, and mantelpieces are made of glass. You might think that the Haubergs would be in constant fear that something would break. On the contrary, they invite visitors to roam freely throughout their entire home.

John is also a connoisseur of Native American crafts, but he has donated his entire collection to the Seattle Art Museum. His motive is not to hoard but to share. "I'm not an owner," he says. "I am a caretaker."
—*Our Daily Bread*, 2004

POSSIBLE EXIT: *Look at every thing you have, then ask, "Do I own it or does He?" If you say, "He owns it," it might draw you to God. If you own it, it might draw you away from Him.*

❖ In 1923, a very important meeting was held at the Edgewater Beach Hotel in Chicago. Attending the meeting were nine of the world's most successful financiers: the president of the largest independent steel company, the president of the largest utility company, the president of the largest gas company, the greatest wheat speculator, the president of the New York Stock Exchange, a member of the president's cabinet, the greatest "bear" on Wall Street, head of the world's greatest monopoly, and president of the Bank of International Settlements.

Certainly we must admit that here were gathered a group of the world's most successful men. At least, men who had found the secret of "making money."

Twenty-five years later let's see where these men are: The president of the largest independent steel company, Charles Schwab, died bankrupt and lived on borrowed money for five years before his death. The president of the largest utility company, Samuel Insull, died a fugitive from justice and penniless in a foreign land. The president of the largest gas company, Howard Hopson, went insane. The greatest wheat speculator, Arthur Cutten, died abroad, insolvent. The president of the New York Stock Exchange, Richard Whitney, served time in the Sing Sing Penitentiary. The member of the president's cabinet, Albert Fall, was pardoned from prison so he could die at home. The greatest bear on Wall Street, Jesse Livermore, killed himself. So did the president of the Bank of International Settlements, Leon Fraser.

All of these men learned well the art of making money, but not one of them learned how to live.

—Bobb Biehl, *The On My Own Handbook*. www.BobbBiehl.com. Used by permission.

❖ C. H. Spurgeon said, "I am a foreigner even in England and as such I mean to act. We are simply passing through the world and should bless it in our transit but never yoke ourselves to its affairs." Matthew Henry said, "The world is our passage but not our portion." One thinks of old Bud Robinson, the holiness preacher, who was shown the sights of New York by some of his friends. That night as he prayed he said, "Thank you, Lord, for letting me see New York. And most of all I thank you that I didn't see anything that I wanted!"

—Vance Havner, *Moments of Decision*

❖ Just weeks before he was to collect a $1.5 million inheritance, a forty-three-year-old Australian construction worker died when a wall fell on him. Witnesses said the unfortunate backhoe operator had taken shelter from a strong wind when a brick wall collapsed on him.

—*Our Daily Bread*, 2000

❖ I sit in my house in Buffalo, and sometimes I get so lonely it's unbelievable. Life has been so good to me, I've got a great wife, good kids, money, my own health—and I'm lonely and bored . . . I often wondered why so many rich people commit suicide. Money sure isn't a cure all.

—O. J. Simpson, Hall of Fame football player, *People*, June 1978

Note: Comments like these are invaluable because they come from the side of life where non-Christians live. This quote has become significant because of what happened in his California home years later, including his writing of a suicide note before being taken into custody for the alleged murder of his wife, though he was later acquitted.

☺   I started out with nothing and I've managed to keep all of it.

—Source unknown

❖   The biggest lie on the planet: "When I get what I want I will be happy."— Millington Messenger

—*Pulpit Helps*, October 1998

❖   A man whose every step had been marked by "success," and who had just made $10 million by placing his newly founded company on the New York Stock Exchange, drove his BMW to the top of a mountain and put a bullet in his brain.

—Darius Salter, *American Evangelism*

Note: Here is an example of an illustration that doesn't lose its value. Who or when this happened, doesn't matter because the New York Stock Exchange and BMW keep it relevant.

❖   **POSSIBLE ENTRANCE:** *Sometimes the best thing that could ever happen to us would be to lose everything we have.*

Several years ago, a friend of mine who lived in the Santa Barbara Canyon area of California went through a frightening ordeal. One parched summer, fire swept through the region, devouring thousands of acres of forest and destroying countless homes in the canyon. His home sat at the base of the long canyon. He didn't have much time to prepare his escape, but he had longer than those at the top. He could see the flames and smoke in the distance and knew he had only a short while before his home would become engulfed in fire. He hurriedly made a list of those possessions he most wanted to save. As it turned out, he didn't have time to grab any of them. When the whole ordeal was over, he stood looking at the smoldering heap that was once his home. All that remained was the list he had clutched in his hand. The impact that destructive event had on his family marked each one of them so deeply, they were never the same.

They lost everything, except of course the useless list of items they thought they couldn't do without. The fire, though unbelievably devastating, became a catalyst for changing them into a closer, more grateful family. In short, the change made them different.

—Charles R. Swindoll, *Paul: A Man of Grit and Grace*

POSSIBLE EXIT: *Is everything you have keeping you from taking the long-range view of life? Is it keeping you from seeing your need of Someone, not something?*

❖ I'm telling you that fame and fortune are not what they're cracked up to be.

—Madonna, singer, promoting a new album, *Time*, April 2003

❖ Queen Elizabeth I of England offered her doctor half the British Empire for six months of life when she was dying. Of course, her doctor couldn't give her six seconds.

—D. James Kennedy, *Evangelism Explosion*

Note: This is a great comment. But make sure everyone in your audience catches the point. Add the comment, "She realized as she died that everything she enjoyed could not help her at the moment of death."

❖ **POSSIBLE ENTRANCE:** *Let me ask you a thought-provoking question. How helpful will your possessions be at the moment you die?*

There is a true story that came from the sinking of the *Titanic*. A frightened woman found her place in a lifeboat that was about to be lowered into the raging North Atlantic. She suddenly thought of something she needed, so she asked permission to return to her stateroom before they cast off. She was granted three minutes and then they would have to leave without her.

She ran across the deck, which was already slanted at a dangerous angle. She raced through the gambling room with all the money that had rolled to one side, ankle deep. She came to her stateroom and quickly pushed aside her diamond rings and expensive bracelets and necklaces as she reached to the shelf above her bed and grabbed three small oranges. She quickly found her way back to the lifeboat and got in.

Now that seems incredible because thirty minutes earlier she would not have chosen a crate of oranges over even the smallest diamond. But death had boarded the *Titanic*. One blast of its awful breath had transformed all values.

—Charles R. Swindoll, *Living on the Ragged Edge*

POSSIBLE EXIT: *Having things is nice as long as they are kept in proper perspective. When we die they will be of no help to us. The only thing that matters when the day of death comes is not how much we've had here below but rather if we are properly related to the God above.*

> Note: An illustration like this could be classified under several topics—materialism (as here), death, priorities, etc. Place it in your illustration file under the subtopic you think it should go.

❖ In *The Problem of Pain* C. S. Lewis wrote, "Everyone has noticed how hard it is to turn our thoughts to God when everything is going well. The statement, 'we have all we want,' is a terrible statement if that 'all' does not include God." He goes on to cite St. Augustine, who said, "God wants to give us something, but He cannot. Our hands are full and there is nowhere to put anything."

—Joseph M. Stowell, *The Upside of Down*. Used by permission.

❖ It is stupid to work yourself to death for something that dies when you do.

—Archie Parish

> Note: Change the word "stupid" to "foolish." It communicates the same thing and has a gentler tone, especially for the person guilty of what you're talking about.

❖ **POSSIBLE ENTRANCE:** *A man once observed something we all notice but perhaps haven't thought enough about. Speaking to the issue of materialism he said,*

Of the dozens upon dozens of funerals that I have conducted, I have never conducted one where the casket was occupied by anyone who had anything in his hand.

—Charles R. Swindoll, *Living on the Ragged Edge*

POSSIBLE EXIT: *You leave the world the same way you entered it—nothing in hand.*

❖ Lee Iacocca, not long after leaving the automobile business, said, "Here I am in the twilight years of my life, still wondering what it's all about. I can tell you this: fame and fortune is for the birds."
— Charles R. Swindoll, *Paul: A Man of Grit and Grace*

❖ Everything in life is a rental. Someone else will use your house, car, and office, etc.
— Bill Lawrence

❖ You're in trouble when the things you own begin to own you.
— *Our Daily Bread*, 1996

❖ Mossy Grove, Tennessee—Searchers and dazed survivors went from one shattered home to another Monday, picking through splintered lumber and torn sheet metal for any sign of the missing, after twisters and storms killed at least thirty-six people in five states. More than seventy reported tornadoes cut a path from Louisiana to Pennsylvania over the weekend and into Monday. Seventeen deaths were reported in Tennessee, twelve in Alabama, five in Ohio, and one each in Mississippi and Pennsylvania. More than two hundred people were injured.

"Yesterday, we had a nice brick house and four vehicles. Today, we don't own a toothbrush," said Susan Henry of Mossy Grove, where seven died and at least forty were still unaccounted for.
— *Dallas Morning News*, November 12, 2002

Note: Illustrations like this are always the most effective when they are used at the time they happened and the event is on everyone's mind. However, when the happening is a frequent occurrence like a tornado, they are also effective years later. One can say, "Years ago, a devastating tornado struck Mossy Grove, Tennessee." Then give the facts and the quote.

❖ Henry Kissinger, former U.S. Secretary of State, wrote, "To Americans, tragedy is wanting something very badly and not getting it. But many people have had to learn . . . that perhaps the worst form of tragedy is wanting something badly, getting it, and finding it empty."
— *Our Daily Bread*, 2001

☺ A stockbroker was greatly discouraged because of all he lost as a result

of "Bloody Monday." To comfort himself he decided to go for a ride in his BMW. After driving awhile he had a flat tire. When he opened his car door and stepped out to attend to his flat tire, a car going by ripped off his car door and ripped off his arm. As a policeman came up to him at the scene of the accident he was screaming, "My BMW! My BMW!" The policeman said, "Are you crazy—your arm has been ripped off!" The man looked down to where his arm would have been and said, "My Rolex! My Rolex!"
—Earl Radmacher sermon, "The Practical Value of Prophecy," September 21, 1999

❖ I've never seen a luggage rack on a hearse.
—Source unknown

MONEY
❖ **POSSIBLE ENTRANCE:** *A former pro football defensive tackle, movie star-turned-pastor once testified about what he thought he needed and what he discovered he really needed.*

My life was a wreck after my second divorce. I didn't feel like living, and my life didn't have meaning anymore. I didn't know what I needed. I thought I needed more money. I thought I needed more fame. But what I needed was God.
—Roosevelt ("Rosey") Grier, *The United Methodist Reporter*

POSSIBLE EXIT: *Your need cannot be satisfied by what you need, it can be satisfied only by Who you need.*

☺ One day while Sam Snead, the golf champion, was competing in a Midwest tournament (so the story goes), a fellow stepped up to him in the clubhouse and, hoping to get a little free advice, said, "Mr. Snead, I'd like to ask you a couple of questions about improving my own game." Snead said, "I charge twenty-five dollars a question." The fellow asked, "Well, that's pretty steep, isn't it?" And Snead, said, "Yes, it is. Now, what's your next question?"
—Marion E. Wade and Glenn D. Kittler, *The Lord Is My Counsel*

❖ **POSSIBLE ENTRANCE:** *When we look to money to solve our problems, we discover two things: It is never enough and it doesn't make us happy.*

For Karen Glance, 36, it came down to all those little packets of shampoo. She remembers the morning she opened her bathroom cabinet in St. Paul and counted 150 that had followed her home from hotels in dozens of cities. Says the former apparel executive, "I was a workaholic, a crazy, crazy woman. I was on a plane four times a week. I just wanted to get to the top. All of a sudden, I realized that I was reaching that goal but I wasn't happy. A year would go by and I wouldn't know what had happened."

A few months ago, Glance was shopping in a neighborhood grocery store when she learned that its owner was about to retire. Something fell into place. She looked around the old-fashioned shop, where clerks still climb ladders to retrieve goods from the upper shelves, and she decided on the spot to buy the place. The new proprietor of the Crocus Hill Market may never come anywhere near to matching her old $1,000,000-plus yearly income, but she couldn't care less. Says Glance, "It really comes down to saying, 'Slow down. The value of life might not be in making money.'"

—*Time*, April 8, 1991

POSSIBLE EXIT: *How about you? Have you slowed down enough to realize the value of life is not in money?*

❖ He who has no money is poor, but he who has nothing but money is even poorer!

—*Our Daily Bread*, 1974

❖ Money is undependable. What is there today may not be there tomorrow. Lindsay Crosby, Bing Crosby's youngest son by his first wife, killed himself at age fifty-one. Just prior to his suicide, he discovered that the inheritance he received from his mother, and which he depended on to support his family, had become worthless.

—Adapted from *Parade*, February 25, 1990

☺ I'm a "Take-Charge" Person. Charge It—I'll Take it.

—Bumper Sticker, *Fax Daily*, October 21, 1998

☺ One thing nice about money—the color never clashes with anything you're wearing.

—Russell Pavy, *A Merry Heart*

❖ When I was young, I used to think that money was the most important thing in life; now that I am older, I know it is.

—attributed to Oscar Wilde

122

☺ I've been rich and I've been poor. Rich is better.

—Beatrice Kaufman, American writer and editor

❖ In the pocket of a rich man who had just committed suicide was found $30,000 and a letter, which read in part, "I have discovered during my life that piles of money do not bring happiness. I am taking my life because I can no longer stand the solitude and boredom. When I was an ordinary workman in New York, I was happy. Now that I possess millions I am infinitely sad and prefer death."

—William Hendricksen, *1 Timothy*

❖ **POSSIBLE ENTRANCE:** *Money isn't everything. Here's the proof.*

It can buy you a house, but not a home.
It can buy you a bed, but not sleep.
It can buy you a clock, but not time.
It can buy you a book, but not knowledge.
It can buy you a position, but not respect.
It can buy you medicine, but not health.
It can buy you blood, but not life.
It can buy you a partner, but not a friend.
So you see, money isn't everything.

—Source unknown

POSSIBLE EXIT: *The list of what money cannot buy is far more significant that the list of what it can.*

❖ A businessman was visited by an angel, who promised to grant him one request. The man requested a copy of the stock market page one year in the future. As he was studying the American and New York Stock Exchanges, he boasted of his plans and the riches that would increase as a result of this glance into the future. He then glanced across the page, only to see his own picture in the obituary column. In the light of his certain death, money was no longer important.

—Cross of Life Lutheran Church, "How To Survive Financially," April 29, 2001

❖ As surely as the compass needle follows north, your heart will follow your treasure.

—Randy Alcorn, *The Treasure Principle*

☺ During a sermon our pastor stated that money wasn't important in the afterlife, because in heaven, there is no money. One parishioner whispered to her mother, "Did you hear that, Mom? We're already in heaven."

—Internet humor

❖ The main thing about money [is that] it makes you do things you don't wanna do.

—Lou Mannhiem (Hal Holbrook) in *Wall Street*, the movie

❖ While Americans stamp on their coins, "In God we trust," they often mean, "In THIS god we trust."

—Haddon Robinson, *Making a Difference in Preaching*

ORIGINAL SIN

❖ Just as a climber on a mountaintop can dislodge a pebble that rolls on and accumulates others until it begins to launch an avalanche that will move the whole side of a mountain, so Adam's sin in the garden of Eden dislodged a pebble that has built into an avalanche of sin and death that has swept through our entire race.

—Ray Stedman, sermon on Romans 5:11–21,
"Rejoicing in God," May 1976

❖ **POSSIBLE ENTRANCE:** *Have you ever stopped and asked, "When was the first time you received notice of your death?"*

Your death warrant is, as it were, written into your own birth certificate.

—C. K. Barrett, *The Epistle to the Romans*

POSSIBLE EXIT: *As people who are born sinners, we cannot escape death. Our birth certificate records the date of our birth and reminds us someone will one day record the date of our death.*

❖ **POSSIBLE ENTRANCE:** *All of us know how beautiful babies are. What's depressing is that due to our depravity that beauty is only skin deep.*

The universal tendency to evil has been stated most clearly by a totally secular agency. The clearest statement on original sin that I have ever read comes from the report of the Minnesota Crime Commission.

In studying humanity, the commission came to this frightening and factual conclusion:

"Every baby starts life as a little savage. He is completely selfish and self-centered. He wants what he wants when he wants it—his bottle, his mother's attention, his playmate's toy, his uncle's watch. Deny him these wants, and he seethes with rage and aggressiveness, which would be murderous were he not so helpless. He is dirty. He has no morals, no knowledge, no skill. This means that all children, not just certain children, are born delinquent. If permitted to continue in the self-centered world of his infancy, given free reign in his impulsive actions to satisfy his wants, every child would grow up a criminal, a thief, a killer, a rapist."

—Ray Stedman, sermon on Romans 5:11–21, "Rejoicing in God," May 1976

POSSIBLE EXIT: *We are born inclined to do what is wrong, not what is right.*

PRIDE

❖ **POSSIBLE ENTRANCE:** *Why don't we want to admit to God "I'm a sinner"? There are numerous reasons, but it often comes down to one word—pride. Notice what is at the center of that word—I.*

One wise man said, "Pride is like a beard. It just keeps growing."

—James A. Scudder, *Your Secret to Spiritual Success*

POSSIBLE EXIT: *God is not out to hurt our pride. He is out to destroy it. Because in destroying our pride, He can cause us to see our need and introduce us to Himself.*

❖ Half of the harm that is done in the world is due to people who want to feel important.

—T. S. Eliot

❖ In the summer of 1986, two ships collided in the Black Sea, causing a tragic loss of life. The news of the disaster was further darkened, however, when an investigation revealed the cause of the accident, which hurled hundreds of passengers into the icy waters. The tragedy was not traced to some major problem like a breakdown in radar or thick fog. The blame was attributed to human stubbornness. Each captain was aware of the other ship's presence. Both could have taken evasive action to avert the collision. But according to news reports, neither wanted to give way to the other. It seems that each was too proud to yield and make the first move. By the time they saw the error of their ways, it was too late.

—*Our Daily Bread*, 1988

❖ A factory in North Carolina, which sponsors a radio music show, runs unusual commercials. They plug outstanding employees. Pride raised by hearing their virtues praised to the public has caused the workers to attack their chores with greater vigor, thus increasing production by 125 percent.

—Don MacLean, United Feature Syndicate

☺ Nine-tenths of our suffering is caused by others not thinking so much of us as we think they ought.

—Mary Lyon

☺ **POSSIBLE ENTRANCE:** *At times, we are so impressed with ourselves; all it takes is the right person to put us in our place.*

The following story is told about a United Airlines gate agent in Denver, Colorado, who was confronted with a passenger who probably deserved to fly as cargo.

During the final days at Denver's old Stapleton Airport, a crowded United flight was canceled. A single agent was rebooking a long line of inconvenienced travelers. Suddenly an angry passenger pushed his way to the desk. He slapped his ticket down on the counter and said, "I HAVE to be on this flight and it has to be FIRST CLASS."

The agent replied, "I'm sorry, sir. I'll be happy to try to help you, but I've got to help these folks first, and I'm sure we'll be able to work something out."

The passenger was unimpressed. He asked loudly, so that the passengers behind him could hear, "Do you have any idea who I am?"

Without hesitating, the gate agent smiled and grabbed her public address microphone. "May I have your attention, please?" she began, her voice bellowing throughout the terminal. "We have a passenger here at the gate WHO DOES NOT KNOW WHO HE IS. If anyone can help him find his identity, please come to gate seventeen."

The folks behind him in line began laughing hysterically. Although the flight was canceled and people were late, they were no longer angry at United.

—Mark Rae

POSSIBLE EXIT: *Our pride is not only offensive to others; it's also offensive to God.*

❖   The president of a university once said they had no problems getting funds as long as they promised to name a building after the donor.

—S. Lewis Johnson

☺   **POSSIBLE ENTRANCE:** *Pride can be so much a part of us we don't recognize it for what it is.*

"I have not sinned for some time," said a woman to C. H. Spurgeon.
"You must be very proud of it," he replied.
"Yes, indeed I am," she rejoiced.

—Source unknown

POSSIBLE EXIT: *What about you? Are you proud in areas you don't even recognize?*

❖   **POSSIBLE ENTRANCE:** *Have you ever noticed how pride keeps us looking in the wrong direction?*

C. S. Lewis once said, "A proud man is always looking down on things and people; and, of course, as long as you're looking down, you can't see something that's above you."

—Patrick M. Morley, *The Man in the Mirror*

POSSIBLE EXIT: *Pride keeps us from looking in the most needed direction of all—up.*

❖   **POSSIBLE ENTRANCE:** *I believe some of you would answer the way another woman did when asked why she couldn't trust Christ.*

With a piece of paper in hand, I asked a woman to list the reasons she couldn't trust Christ.
She wrote this:

1. Me
2. Me
3. Me

4. Me
5. Me

—R. Larry Moyer

POSSIBLE EXIT: *Don't let "me" stand in the way of coming to Christ. Remember when He took your place on the cross, "you" were foremost on His mind. He died for YOU.*

❖ Few people need voice lessons to sing their own praise.

—E. C. McKenzie

☺ A local hardware store tries to keep people from becoming prideful. A sign on the door reads, "Shoes required, because you might hurt yourself. Shirts required, because you're not as good-looking as you think."

—Internet humor

❖ Pride is one of the most dangerous and sinister of sins. Writer David Rhodes said, "Pride is a dandelion of the soul. Its roots go deep and if only a little is left, it will sprout again. The danger of pride is that it feeds on goodness."

—James A. Scudder, *Beyond Failure*

❖ Conceit is the only disease known to man that makes everyone sick except the one who has it.

—Source unknown

☺ I had been sports editor of the Port Chester, New York, *Daily Item* only a few weeks when my wife and I went to the movies in downtown Port Chester. The house lights were still on as we walked down the aisle and the thirteen or fourteen people scattered throughout the theater turned toward us and began to applaud. I was stunned. Even though my daily sports column included a photo of me, I had no idea I had become so popular in such a short time.

When the movie was over, one of the patrons came over and vigorously shook my hand. "I'm very flattered that all you people recognize me," I told him. "I'm really amazed and honored."

"I don't know about that," he said, puzzled. "All I know is that a few seconds before you and your wife walked in, they announced that unless there were at least fifteen customers in the theater, they wouldn't show the movie!"

— Submitted by Arn Shein. Reprinted with permission from the
September 1992 *Reader's Digest.* Copyright ©1992 by The Reader's Digest Assn., Inc.

❖   Only sinners can enter heaven!

—Source unknown

☺   We are all proud to some degree. Some are just more humble about it than others.

—Patrick M. Morley, *The Man in the Mirror*

☺   A businessman's success had gone to his head. His constant bragging was beginning to grate on his wife's nerves. After one such session, during which the husband had compared himself favorably with everyone from J. Paul Getty to John D. Rockefeller, he turned to her and asked, "Do you know how many really outstanding business leaders there are in the world today?"

"No," replied the wife quietly, "but I know there is one less than you think."

—Source unknown

Note: In using this illustration, you can change the men's names to more current ones, such as Bill Gates, etc.

☺   Being in show business has its drawbacks . . . The other day I was at one of my favorite eateries and got interrupted mid-bite by someone asking me, "Are you . . . ?"

And I said, "Yes, I'm Dennis Miller. Can we do this later?"

And he said, "Do what later? I wanted to know if you were finished with that ketchup."

—Dennis Miller, *The Rant Zone*

☺   Daughter: "Oh, mother, please tell me if I should accept Bill's proposal?"

Mother: "Why don't you ask your father? He made a much smarter decision about marriage than I did."

—Source unknown

☺ **POSSIBLE ENTRANCE:** *We can become so prideful, we are mindful only of ourselves, not others.*

In his book *Eternity Shut in a Span*, William R. Marshall writes that Goethe and Beethoven were taking an afternoon walk in the Carlsbad Valley, an area in what is now western Czechoslovakia [and now the Czech Republic]. As they strolled along, many saluted them, bowing courteously as they recognized the distinguished pair.

"Isn't it maddening!" exclaimed Goethe. "I simply cannot escape this homage."

"Do not be too much disturbed by it," said Beethoven. "It is just possible that some of it may be meant for me."

—*Our Daily Bread*, 1990

POSSIBLE EXIT: *You may be a gifted person, but there are others who deserve as much or more praise than you.*

❖ God knows best; He hasn't arranged your anatomy so as to make it easy for you to pat yourself on the back.

—George Sweeting, *Who Said That?*

☺ VIP—Pass with Awe!

—Bumper sticker

❖ I always like to hear a man talk about himself, because I never hear anything but good.

—Will Rogers

PROBLEMS

❖ A few months after I made the decision to trust Christ, a kind of mental peace began to develop. Don't misunderstand, I'm not talking about the absence of conflict. What I found in this relationship with Jesus wasn't so much the absence of conflict as it was the ability to cope with it. I wouldn't trade this for anything in the world.

—Used by permission. Josh McDowell, *Skeptics Who Demanded a Verdict*,
p. 92, Tyndale House Publishers, www.josh.org

☺ **POSSIBLE ENTRANCE:** *We often see other people's problems but not our own.*

Said an anxious wife as she watched her husband fishing in a bucket of water in the middle of the living room, "I'd take him to a psychiatrist, but we really need the fish."

—Ken Brousseau Sr.

POSSIBLE EXIT: *God wants you to focus first on your own problem—you are a sinner separated from God.*

❖ Trusting Christ is not the way out of your problems but the way through them.

—R. Larry Moyer

☺ **POSSIBLE ENTRANCE:** *Have you found yourself going to God only when things are going wrong?*

We are often like the boy who was climbing a tree one day, lost his grip, and began to fall. "God save me!" he cried. Part way down, a thick branch caught him by the [pants] and held him fast and he said, "Never mind, God. I'm okay now. I don't need you."

—Marion E. Wade and Glenn D. Kittler, *The Lord Is My Counsel*

POSSIBLE EXIT: *The truth is you need God because even if you never have another problem, you are facing the biggest problem of your life—eternal separation from God.*

☺ No sooner would I open my front door after coming home from work, than my wife would pounce on me with tales of the day's calamities and problems. Finally, one day I sat down with her and said, "Listen, Teddy, before you hit me with the day's disasters—at least let me sit down and eat my dinner."

The very next evening, upon my return from work, my wife greeted me at the door as usual. "Norman, hurry up and eat your dinner," she said. "I have something terrible to tell you."

—Submitted by Norman Wexler. Reprinted with permission from the November 1989 *Reader's Digest*. Copyright ©1989 by The Reader's Digest Assn., Inc.

☺ Occasionally we all feel like the guy in a cartoon who said, "I try to take just one day at a time, but lately several days have attacked me at once."

—John C. Maxwell, *Developing the Leader Within You*

☺ I saw a comic strip of a boy looking out the window as it was raining on the diapers hanging on the line. He was saying, "Is mom ever going to be mad. God is wetting the diapers."

—Source unknown

REBELLION

❖ A man rejects God neither because of intellectual demands nor because of the scarcity of evidence. A man rejects God because of a moral resistance that refuses to admit his need for God.

— Ravi Zacharias, *A Shattered Visage*

❖ A man told of when he was in the service, and one of his jobs was cleaning the restrooms of an enlisted men's club. There were names and writing all over the walls. When a crew had sanded and painted it they put up a sign, "DO NOT MARK ON WALLS." In a few days the walls were covered with writing again. So they sanded it down and painted it again. But they were tired and forgot to put up their sign. This time hardly any names were put on the walls.

—Paul M. Zoschke

❖ Religious history is not a record of man starting with many gods (idolatry) and gradually discovering the one true God. Rather, it is the sad story of man knowing the truth about God and deliberately turning from it.

—Warren Wiersbe, *Be Rich*

❖ Today, people even use Jesus' name to curse by. How strange it would sound if a businessman, when he missed a golf putt, yelled, "Thomas Jefferson!" or a plumber, when he mashed a finger with a pipe wrench, screamed, "Mahatma Gandhi!" We cannot get away from this man Jesus.

—Philip Yancey, *The Jesus I Never Knew*

Note: With an illustration like this you could substitute the famous names with almost any name that your audience could identify with.

❖ Years ago I was camping beside a river. I'd been there only a few minutes when I saw a sign: "No Throwing Rocks into the River." Guess what? Suddenly I was overcome with a tremendous urge to throw at least one rock into the river. It never even occurred to me to throw a rock until I read that sign, but the law of the campsite aroused the rebellion in my flesh.

—Dwight Edwards, *Revolution Within*

REJECTION

❖ Rejection hurts. When presidential candidate Adlai Stevenson conceded the election in 1952, he said he felt like a grown man who had just stubbed his toe. "It hurts too much to laugh, but I'm too old to cry."

—*Our Daily Bread*, 1990

❖ My heart was greatly impressed by something that I heard my mother say. I had been some years seeking Christ, and I couldn't believe that He would save me. She said she had heard many people swear and blaspheme God, but one thing she had never forgotten—she had never heard a man say he had sought Christ, and Christ had rejected him.

—Susannah Spurgeon and Joseph Harrald, *C. H. Spurgeon*

☺ Man overheard talking to a friend: "I'm locked in a major custody battle. My wife doesn't want me, and my mother won't take me back."

—Source unknown

REMEDY

❖ **POSSIBLE ENTRANCE:** *Sometimes the reason we haven't found the solution to our problems is because we haven't identified the problem.*

It isn't that they can't see the solution. It is that they can't see the problem.

—G. K. Chesterton, *The Scandal of Father Brown*

POSSIBLE EXIT: *Our problem is very simple. It is called sin. Because we have sinned we are separated from God.*

☺ **POSSIBLE ENTRANCE:** *Sometimes what keeps us from finding remedies to our problems are our own temptations and sin.*

A couple told me that they were gaining so much weight, they decided to start jogging. But after a few days they gave it up. When I asked why they answered, "We could never make it past the donut shop."

—R. Larry Moyer

POSSIBLE EXIT: *God has the remedies we need. But first we have to face the fact that our own temptations and sin are part of the problem.*

❖ *Consumer Reports* published a booklet with the intriguing title "How to Clean Practically Anything." It offers advice on what solvent to use to remove a wide assortment of stains. Living as I do with drips and drops, that is my kind of book.

Did you know that glycerin will remove stains made by a ball-point pen? Boiling water can remove berry stains. Parents of small children should keep a gallon of vinegar handy to get rid of crayon marks. Bleach works well for mildew. Lemon juice performs minor miracles on rust stains. I haven't tried them all, but I assume that scientists have put these common cleansing agents to the test.

What you will not find in this little book is how to deal with the most serious stain of all—the stain made on your life by sin. Deep, ugly stains made by hostile words and shame-filled actions. Tears won't touch them. Zeal can't erase them. At times we are convinced that we have gotten on with our lives and the sins are gone, but in an unguarded moment we notice the stain seeping through.

The Bible tells us just what we need: "The blood of Jesus Christ His Son cleanses us from all sin" (1 John 1:7). That's the only remedy that works.

—*Our Daily Bread*, 2004

Note: This is another example of an illustration that makes you think. How do people remove stains from their clothes, walls, carpet, etc.? This illustration will allow you to incorporate your testimony about the stains of sin God has removed from your life.

REVENGE
❖ Revenge, need to resist—heal me of this lust of mine of always vindicating myself.

—St. Augustine

❖ **POSSIBLE ENTRANCE:** *You and I are interested in revenge.*

Sarah, the church gossip and self-appointed supervisor of the church's morals, kept sticking her nose into other people's business. Several congregants were unappreciative of her activities but feared her enough to maintain their silence.

She made a mistake, however, when she accused George, a new member, of being an alcoholic after she saw his pickup truck parked one afternoon in front of the town's only bar. She commented to George and others that everyone seeing it there would know that he was an alcoholic. George, a man of few words, stared at her for a moment and just walked away. He said nothing.

Later that evening, George quietly parked his pickup in front of Sarah's house . . . AND he left it there all night.

—Source unknown

POSSIBLE EXIT: *Through the cross, God demonstrated that He is not interested in revenge; He's interested in forgiveness.*

Note: In using this with non-Christians, I'd introduce it with the *Possible Entrance* and then say, "Let me give you an example in the area of gossip, which even Christians can be guilty of."

❖ Minneapolis (Associated Press)—A man who booby-trapped a coffee cup that exploded and burned a fellow worker apparently was angry because coworkers kept dropping things in his coffee, police said. . . .

According to court documents, some employees of the print shop had been regularly dropping bits of paper and other objects into a coworker's coffee cup for several months. The owner of the cup at one point left a note demanding that whoever was tampering with it leave it alone. . . .

—"Coworker linked to booby-trap," *Dallas Morning News*, March 13, 1987

❖ As the mother wept, her husband, Ron, told her his story. As Tyler, their baby, was cooing and playing with his feet in the crib, Ron wrapped the baby's head in plastic wrap. He then sat down for dinner and brushed his teeth before returning to see his son's last breath. He removed the wrap and turned the baby onto his stomach, switched off the light and went to bed. He wanted Amy to be the one to discover the body. "Now we're even," he said.

For what?

Ron said he never forgave Amy for refusing to cut short an ocean cruise with her parents to come home and comfort him when his father died in 1996. So, he said, he decided to marry her, have a child with her, and kill it. He researched SIDS while waiting for her to bond with Tyler. He confessed, he said, because he was haunted by the corpse.

—Story of Ron Shanabarger, who confessed to killing his seven-month-old son, Tyler,
"A Cold Dose of Vengeance," *Time*, July 12, 1999

Note: In this media-driven age, if you find an illustration and are looking for more details, it may be helpful to check the publication's website and do a database search in their archives for the complete article.

❖ One cynic has claimed that there are more lawyers than doctors in the United States, because Americans are much more interested in getting even than they are in getting better.

—Gary Inrig, *Forgiveness*

❖ **POSSIBLE ENTRANCE:** *We are so revengeful. It is amazing the extent to which we carry our ill feelings toward others.*

A mortician at Forest Lawn Cemetery in California told author Gilbert Beers about a man who many years ago spent $200,000 on his own funeral. Estranged from his wife and children, that bitter man squandered all his money on his own burial and left them nothing.

Because the casket and other expenses added up to only $100,000, he ordered that the remaining $100,000 be spent on orchids! Only three people attended that memorial service. What a warped sense of values! What a waste of money!

—*Our Daily Bread*, 1996

POSSIBLE EXIT: *God is not out for revenge. But because He operates so differently than we do, we miss what He wants to do for us. Although we have rejected Him, His response is a contrast to the kind of response we are accustomed to.*

☺ In Battle Creek, Michigan, the defendant before the court was charged with assault. He was being badgered mercilessly by the prosecutor.

"You say you didn't hit the plaintiff, you just shoved him a little?"

"That's right," said the defendant.

"Oh, now, is it?" snarled the prosecutor. "I want you to come down off the witness stand right now and show the jury just how hard you 'shoved' the plaintiff."

The defendant stepped down, doubled the prosecutor over with a hard blow to the stomach, bloodied his nose, and finally knocked him half-conscious to the floor.

Then he turned to the jury and said, "Ladies and gentlemen—about one-tenth that hard."

—Paul Harvey, *Los Angeles Times* Syndicate

☺ In a Dallas newspaper column, a rather well-to-do man was asked, "What are you living for?" His reply was, "To get even."
—Haddon Robinson, *Kindred Spirit*, Winter 1977

☺ **POSSIBLE ENTRANCE:** *We operate out of revenge. Our "watch your back" mentality is seen in many areas of life.*

A patient wasn't taking any chances. Prior to her operation, she taped notes all over her body for the surgeon: "Take your time," "Don't cut yourself," "No need to rush," "Wash your hands," etc.

After surgery, she discovered a new note taped to her, this one from the doctor: "Has anyone seen my watch?"
—Internet humor

POSSIBLE EXIT: *God is not out for revenge. But since sin is offensive to His holiness, it must be punished.*

SELF-EXAMINATION

❖ Kreeft gestured toward the hallway. "On my door there's a cartoon of two turtles. One says, 'Sometimes I'd like to ask why he allows poverty, famine, and injustice when he could do something about it.' The other turtle says, 'I'm afraid God might ask me the same question.'"
—Lee Strobel, *The Case for Faith*

☺ "A lot of people complain about their dumb bosses," says Joey Adams. "What they don't realize is that they'd be out of a job if their dumb bosses were any smarter."
—Internet humor

❖ We are all like the moon; we all have a dark side.
—Attributed to Mark Twain

❖ A man once said, "There never was a crime I couldn't conceive of committing myself."
—Source unknown

❖ **POSSIBLE ENTRANCE:** *Years ago a man had a sobering experience.*

Adolph Eichman, a principal architect of the Holocaust, was normal. In 1961 at Eichman's trial, Yehich Dinur, a survivor from Auschwitz, walked in to testify against Eichman. When he saw him, Dinur began to sob uncontrollably, then fainted onto the floor. Why? Was he overcome by hatred, fear, memories? No! "I was afraid about myself," said Dinur, "I saw that I am capable to do this. I am . . . exactly like he. Eichman is in all of us. Sin is in each of us."

—Charles Colson

POSSIBLE EXIT: *The next time you pick up the paper, recognize that you are capable of any crime someone else has committed. That inclination to steal, kill, destroy is in all of us.*

SELF-RIGHTEOUSNESS

❖ A woman was dying, but she had lived a good and moral life and had never felt she needed a Savior. But when a minister offered to come and talk with her, she allowed him to visit. The pastor explained the way of salvation by grace through faith in Christ. Emphasizing that Jesus died for the sins of everyone in the world, including her, he urged her to trust the Savior.

The woman responded, "Do you mean to tell me that if I'm going to be saved, I have to come to God on exactly the same terms as anyone else— even the most wicked person in the world?" "That's right," the pastor answered, "there's only one way." The woman thought for a moment and then declared, "Well, if that's the case, I want no part of it!"

—*Our Daily Bread*, 2000

❖ **POSSIBLE ENTRANCE:** *We are so self-righteous we see other people making the mistakes, not ourselves.*

As a senior citizen was driving down the freeway, his car phone rang. Answering, he heard his wife's voice urgently warning him, "Herman, I just heard on the news that there's a car going the wrong way on Interstate 280. Please be careful!" "It's not just one car," said Herman. "It's hundreds of them!"

—Internet humor

POSSIBLE EXIT: *Don't look at what the other person is doing, look at yourself. Be willing to say, "I have done wrong. I am a sinner."*

☺ A woman left a service, walked up to a pastor and said, "That was a great message. Everything you said applies to somebody I know."

—Source unknown

☺ During the observance of Animal Week, the fourth graders told about their kindness to pets. Asked what he had done, one little boy said, "I kicked a boy for kicking his dog."

—Source unknown

SELFISHNESS

❖ The man who lives for himself alone will be the sole mourner at his own funeral.

—Billy Sunday

❖ Elisa Morgan, president of MOPS International (Mothers of Pre-Schoolers), shared this insight into a child's view of the world: "Toddler's Creed"

If I want it, it's mine.

If I give it to you and change my mind later, it's mine.

If I can take it away from you, it's mine.

If I had it a little while ago, it's mine.

If it's mine, it will never belong to anyone else, no matter what.

If we are building something together, all the pieces are mine.

If it looks just like mine, it is mine.

—*Our Daily Bread*, 1995

❖ A child when being disciplined said to his father, "I'm not bad. I just want my own way."

—Source unknown

❖ Surveying two hundred middle-class Americans, the eminent UCLA professor discovered that people seek personal advancement from work, personal development from marriage, and personal fulfillment from church. Everything—their perspective on family, church, community, and work—was utilitarian; it was measured by what they could get out of it. Concern for others was secondary.

—Charles Colson, *Why America Doesn't Work*

☺ All the children wanted grapefruit one morning, and there was only one.

"That's all right," Franklin said matter-of-factly. "I'll have it."

—Ruth Bell Graham, *Blessings for a Mother's Day*

❖   Were God to accept the sinner on the grounds of his own righteousness, He would be declaring the death of His own Son unnecessary.

—B. Bayel

SIN

❖   **POSSIBLE ENTRANCE:** *Sometimes we focus so much on the wrongs of others, we fail to see our own sin.*

An employee in the bill-collection department of a large store gave me an insight into human nature. He told me that he repeatedly gets the following response from customers who are delinquent in paying their bills: "I know you must have others who owe a lot more than I do. Get off my back, will you!"

The employee then told me, "They miss the point entirely. Sure, there are a lot of others who owe more. But somehow I have to tell them in a nice way, 'Look, what somebody else owes isn't the issue. Our records say that your account is overdue!'"

The tendency of sinful man has always been to shift attention from himself by pointing the finger at others. Religious people excuse their inconsistencies by referring to the "pagans" around them. And the "pagans" try to sidestep the issue by talking about the hypocrisies of the religious. But God is not fooled by finger-pointers.

When someone else appears to be a greater sinner than we are, it's just an illusion. The sooner we realize that no one owes more to God than we do, the more likely we are to receive His free forgiveness. He extends His pardon only to those who humbly acknowledge that they are hopelessly in debt.

—*Our Daily Bread*, 2004

POSSIBLE EXIT: *When God calls you a sinner, He is not looking at someone else's account. He is looking at yours.*

❖   A little sin will add to your trouble, subtract from your energy, and multiply your difficulty.

—*Our Daily Bread*, 1973

❖   Sidney J. Harris, writer for the North American Syndicate, said, "Once we assuage our conscience by calling something a necessary evil, it begins to look more and more necessary and less and less evil."

—James A. Scudder, *Beyond Failure*

❖ Too many think lightly of sin, and therefore think lightly of the Savior.
—Susannah Spurgeon and Joseph Harrald, *C. H. Spurgeon*

❖ One of the most famous pictures in the world is the *Last Supper* by Leonardo da Vinci. Jesus sits at the table with his twelve apostles. It is said that the artist sought long for a model for the Savior. He wanted a young man of pure, holy look. At length his attention was fixed on a chorister in the cathedral, named Pietro Ban Dinelli. This young man had a very noble face and a devout demeanor. Leonardo used him as a model in painting the face of the Master. Soon after this, Pietro went to Rome to study music. There he fell among evil companions and was led to drink and then into all manner of debasing sins. Year after year the painter went on with his great picture. All the apostles were now painted, save one, Judas the traitor. Da Vinci went from place to place looking for some debased man who would be suitable for a model. He was walking one day on the streets of Milan, watching the faces of the evil men he chanced to meet, when his eye fell on one who seemed to have in his features the character he sought. He was a miserable, unclean beggar, wearing rags, with a villainous look. This man sat as the artist's model for Judas. After the face was painted, Da Vinci learned that the man who had sat for him was his old friend, Pietro Ban Dinelli, the same who had sat a few years before as the model for the Master. Wickedness had debased the beautiful life into hideous deformity.
—J. R. Miller, *Glimpses Through Life's Window*

> Note: It is quite likely this story is a legend. To protect your integrity as a person and communicator, it is important to admit that. At the same time, it can serve as a helpful illustration. Ask your audience, "Can the damaging consequences of sin be seen in your own countenance?"

❖ The Bible will tell you what is wrong before you have done it!
—D. L. Moody quoted in *Our Daily Bread*, 2007

❖ **POSSIBLE ENTRANCE:** *Sin may sound good, taste good, feel good, but its results are deadly.*

A little boy, when his mother was out, got a chair and climbed up to a shelf in the closet to see if there was anything nice. He saw a small white paper parcel. He opened it. It was filled with white powder. The boy tasted it and found it sweet; he took more and then put it up again. His mother came back. The boy soon fell ill and complained to his mother. She asked what he had eaten. He told her he had "tasted some of that sweet sugar in the closet."

"Oh, my boy, it is poison. It will kill you!" she exclaimed. The doctor was sent for and the boy's life was saved. But the boy never forgot that what is sweet may be poison. So with sin.

—*Pentecostal Evangel*

POSSIBLE EXIT: *Don't let Satan deceive you. He is the master of deception. What tastes good now may be fatal later.*

❖   **POSSIBLE ENTRANCE:** *Ultimately, it is not important how others feel about your sin. It is important how God feels about it.*

A man who was convicted of a crime stood in the courtroom with a smile on his face, although all the evidence was against him. One man asked him why he was so happy. "Oh," he said, "it doesn't matter what others think or say. The only thing that concerns me is what the judge says."

—Source unknown

POSSIBLE EXIT: *The important thing is what God, the Almighty Judge, says about our sin.*

❖   A mouse when it is caught in a mousetrap by its tail can continue to eat the cheese. But that won't better its condition any. It certainly won't free him.

Many men know they are guilty and even dread their punishment, but they go on nibbling at their beloved sins.

—C. H. Spurgeon

❖   A physician who directs a venereal disease clinic recently described for me the depressing conditions he witnesses. He said most of his young patients do not come wringing their hands in despair at the awful disease they have contracted; rather, they schedule routine visits to his clinic in order to "cure" what they carry in time for the events of the next weekend.

—James Dobson, *Dare to Discipline*

❖   **POSSIBLE ENTRANCE:** *We often don't see how low sin is taking us until it is too late.*

A company of hunters were eating their lunch up in the Scottish Highlands when one of them spied, on the face of a great precipice opposite, a sheep on a narrow ledge of a rock. He pointed it out to the rest, and one of the guys explained that a sheep had been tempted by the sight of green grass to jump down to some ledge a foot or two from the top of the cliff. Soon, having eaten all the grass there, and unable to get back, there was nothing else for it to do but scramble down to some lower ledge. There in turn it would finish what might be there and have to jump to some ledge yet lower.

"Now it has got to the last," said he looking through the field glass and seeing that below it went the steep cliff without a break for two hundred to three hundred feet.

"What will happen to it now?" asked the others eagerly. "Oh, now it will be lost, and the eagles will see it and swoop down upon it and, maddened with fright and hunger, it will leap over the cliff and be dashed to pieces on the rocks below."

—W. B. Gray

POSSIBLE EXIT: *Sin does the same thing. One step at a time, it takes us lower and lower, farther and farther from God until it takes us to the ultimate death—separation from God forever in what the Bible calls hell.*

❖ You never find in sin that which you enter the sin to find.

—James Borror

❖ On November 9, 1965, the Eastern Seaboard suffered a huge blackout. Coincidently, a similar thing happened in England only on a smaller scale. In America, it was called a "power failure." In England it was called a "power reduction," an obvious understatement. If one did not know the difference one would think a "power reduction" was not as bad as a "power failure," although they meant the same.

We do the same with sin. We call it "human frailties," "weaknesses," "hereditary faults," and "environmental kickbacks." These watered down expressions all mean the same thing—SIN. How much better it is to call SIN by its proper name and acknowledge our need for forgiveness.

—*Our Daily Bread*, 1966

❖ If you have to do wrong to stay on the team, you are on the wrong team.

—Charles R. Swindoll

❖ Years ago when the western United States was being settled, roads were often just wagon tracks. These rough trails posed serious problems for those who journeyed on them. On one of these winding paths was posted a sign that read, "Avoid this rut or you'll be in it for the next twenty-five miles!"

The wise traveler heeded this advice and was spared a lot of trouble. In a similar way, we must steer clear of sinful attitudes and deeds, because once we get into such "ruts," we may be trapped by them for years. Questionable practices that are often repeated invariably lead to unhappy consequences. On the other hand, if we develop godly attributes that are commended by the Scriptures, we will make our way through the wilderness of this world with greater ease and blessing.

—*Our Daily Bread*, 1977

❖ The marvel is, in the biblical view, not that men die for their sins but that we remain alive in spite of them.

—John W. Wenham, *The Goodness of God*

❖ One who has light views of sin will never have great thoughts of God.

—*Our Daily Bread*, 1986

❖ To you, sin may be a small thing; to God it is a great and awful thing. It is the second largest thing in the world; only the love of God is greater.

—Billy Graham, *Angels: God's Secret Agents*

❖ Several years ago in America a bit of deadly botulism poison was found in a particular brand of vichyssoise soup. This is one of the most deadly poisons known to man, and at least one person died and another was paralyzed before the source of the poison was discovered and the contaminated soup destroyed.

Let me ask this question. How much botulism poison was needed to make the soup unsuitable for human consumption? A whole can full? Of course not! Several milligrams? No!

The smallest amount of poison would ruin the can. In the same way, God asks you to take His word that you are a sinner, whether small or great, and to believe that sin has ruined you.

—Source unknown

❖ **POSSIBLE ENTRANCE:** *Have you ever thought how serious your sin might look if you could see it the way others do?*

A drunkard in New Orleans was recently saved in a peculiar manner from continuing his career of dissipation. The young man in question was of a fine family and had splendid gifts but was going down as fast as possible through strong drinking. His friends had pleaded with him, but he had taken their warnings as an insult. One day, one of them, who was a court stenographer, determined to try a new tactic with him. The friend was sitting in a restaurant when the young man in question came in with a companion and took the table next to him, sitting with his back to the friend and not seeing him. He was just intoxicated enough to be talking about his private affairs, and on the impulse of the moment, the stenographer pulled out his notebook and took a full shorthand report of every word he said. The next morning, the stenographer copied the whole thing neatly and sent it to the young man's office. In less than ten minutes the young man came tearing in, his eyes fairly hanging out of the sockets. He couldn't believe he had said those things, but he never drank again.

Most of us would be more willing to stop sinning if we saw ourselves as others see us.

—Source unknown

POSSIBLE EXIT: *Think of the sin you despise in others you know. Do you realize that sometimes they are just as repulsed by your sin?*

❖ Sin is not judged by the way we see it but by the way God sees it.

—*Our Daily Bread*, 1984

❖ Sickness is a terrible thing, more especially when it is accompanied with pain, when the poor body is racked to an extreme so that the spirit fails within us, and we are dried up like a potsherd. But I bear witness that sickness, however agonizing, is nothing like the discovery of the evil of sin.

—Susannah Spurgeon and Joseph Harrald, *C. H. Spurgeon*

❖ Driving along a highway, you are stopped by an accident. A truck driver lies in the wreckage. Half a dozen men from passing cars place themselves shoulder to shoulder and try to lift the bumper. They tug and they pull until you see the veins standing out in their necks, but they cannot free the man. Still they keep straining at the impossible task. Finally, a wrecker drives up and is placed in position to hoist the front of the disabled truck. But the only available spot for the wrecker to attach its hoist is that bumper at which the men are tugging. If the wrecker is to do its work, the men must get out of the way.

If Christ is going to relieve you of the burden of sin in your life, you must get out of the way and let God do it.

—Source unknown

❖ As John Bunyan put it, "One leak will sink a ship; and one sin will destroy a sinner."

Or as Bunyan's contemporary, Jeremy Taylor, said, "No sin is small. No grain of sand is small in the mechanism of a watch."

—Nancy Leigh DeMoss, *Lies Women Believe*

☺ Tom: "That problem you helped me with last night was all wrong, Dad."
Father: "All wrong, was it? Well, I'm sorry."
Tom: "Well, you needn't exactly worry about it, because none of the other daddies got it right, either."

—Source unknown

❖ A woodpecker cut out a nest in the hollow of a telephone pole. No one was aware of it until one day, when everything was perfectly calm, the pole snapped, leaving the residents without service in the wilderness. A boy climbed the twenty-five-foot stub, which was still in the ground, and there discovered what the woodpecker had done. The pole looked fine from the outside but was rotten on the inside.

Many of our lives can look like fine gold on the outside to those whom we confront, but if the inside is not right with God, we will still face tragedy.

—Source unknown

❖ **POSSIBLE ENTRANCE:** *Sin never introduces itself by saying, "Here I am. Come get me."*

Some time ago a scientific magazine wrote about certain alligators that seldom hunt for their victims. Instead they wait for unwary "dolts" to come to them. Being lazy beasts, they just lie near the bank with open mouths, apparently dead. Soon bugs, then flies and other insects light on their moist tongues. Soon bigger game is attracted. A lizard will crawl up to the alligator to feed on bugs. A frog may join the party. Soon a whole menagerie is there, and then there is a sudden earthquake, the giant jaws come together, and the party is over. The subtle attraction of sin is equally fatal.

—*Our Daily Bread*, 1966

POSSIBLE EXIT: *Sin is very subtle. You often don't recognize it because it looks attractive, but it is fatal.*

❖   Whenever a man is ready to uncover his sins, God is ready to cover them.

—*God's Little Devotional Book I*

❖   As Mephistopheles says in *Faust*, "The people do not know the devil is there even when he has them by the throat."

—Haddon Robinson, *Biblical Sermons*

❖   Part of the 1986 Texas sesquicentennial celebrations was a restorative effort on the iron lady statue who caps the dome of the state capital building in Austin.

Once the repair/restoration was completed, an army helicopter was employed to try to lower the heavy statue onto its mount atop the capital dome. For one full day, high winds kept blowing the statue unpredictably so that even the most skilled and persistent helicopter operators could not maneuver the statue into place. The newspaper headline read, "Lady misses the mark."

Likewise, with all of us, no one with even the most persistent effort can maneuver our lives into the place of God's perfection, 100 percent of the time—we miss God's mark.

—Source unknown

❖   **POSSIBLE ENTRANCE**: *You may wonder if you are too big a sinner for God to save. You aren't as long as you can call yourself what He calls you—a sinner—and can call what you have done what He calls it—sin.*

Velma Barfield (the first woman to be executed in the U.S. in twenty-three years) was under the heavy influence of prescription drugs when she poisoned four people. While in prison on death row, she accepted Christ. For the first time in her life, Velma saw herself as a person of worth. Although many factors contributed to her tortured life, she took full responsibility for her actions. In her Bible she wrote, "Sin is being called all kinds of fancy names nowadays, but it's time we come to grips with ourselves and call sin what it really is—SIN."

—Our Daily Bread, 1986

POSSIBLE EXIT: *What are you calling yourself? What are you calling your wrongs? If you can call yourself a sinner and call what you have done wrong a sin, you are not outside the scope of His forgiveness.*

☺ A boy was sent home for stealing pencils off the teacher's desk. The father, who was quite upset, said to him, "Son, why did you steal pencils off the teacher's desk? There was no need for that. I can get plenty of them where I work."

The company had been having trouble with theft.

—Haddon Robinson

☺ Schoolteacher: "This makes five times I have punished you this week. Now, Henry, what have you got to say?"

Henry: "I'm glad it is Friday."

—Source unknown

❖ A man was describing to us how he had been brought up in a godly European home, had come to this country as a young man to seek his fortune, had been converted to Christ, and then had gotten sidetracked. Temptation yielded to another temptation until finally he found himself in what he thought was a hopeless condition. I'll never forget how he described the process.

"It was like being in the ocean when there is a strong undertow," he said. "You don't realize how far you're drifting from shore until all of a sudden you find yourself beyond your depth, trying desperately to swim, but unable to hold your own against the outgoing tide."

—Billy Graham, *How to Be Born Again*

❖ A sin recognized is half-corrected.

—Our Daily Bread, 1983

❖ **POSSIBLE ENTRANCE:** *We make light of sin. We pass it off as easily as a wife did after her fender bender.*

Wife to husband: "I scratched the front fender a little, dear. If you want to look at it, it's in the back seat."

—Source unknown

POSSIBLE EXIT: *We laugh, but let me ask, "When you consider your sin, are you just as light-hearted about it with God?"*

❖ Sin is believing the lie that you are self-created, self-dependent, and self-sustained.

—St. Augustine

❖ The trend away from God may start with incremental steps, but it always grows into open rebellion.

—Ron Blue, *Evangelism and Missions*

❖ One clear, cold March day, I stood at the edge of Niagara Falls. The cataract was garbed in her most glorious winter garments. Some birds were swooping down to snatch a drink from the clear water. My host told me how he had seen birds carried over the brink. They had dipped down for a drink, and ice had formed on their wings. Then they had dipped for another drink and more ice weighed their little bodies. Another dip or two, and they could not rise. Over the falls they went.

Sin is as deceptive as the sparkling water of Niagara's wintry rapids. Dip into it once too often, and we are not able to lay aside every weight and sin that clings so closely.

—Ralph Sockman, *How to Believe*

❖ Many of us trying to get rid of sin are like housewives who destroy the spider's webs without destroying the spiders.

—Sadhu Sundar Singh

❖ Recently a San Diego newspaper contained a story that implied a judge may get impeached for "fixing" his son's parking fines. Why couldn't the judge still sit in judgment over bigger and more serious lawbreakers? (This is what people expect God to do—overlook "parking fine" sinners and only judge the "major leaguers.") The judge cannot do this, for even in the human judiciary system we recognize that if the judge violates the standard of justice he is obligated to uphold, he has no right to judge anyone else by that same standard.

In a similar way, if God were to say to even one "parking fine" sinner, "You are free to go," He would have no basis to send Adolf Hitler or even Satan himself to hell. If even imperfect sinful man recognizes this by impeaching a judge, how much less can a perfectly holy God do what imperfect, sinful man won't even do? Would the Creator have a lower standard of morality than the creature? God cannot grade on a "curve" and still be a perfectly righteous God; the penalty for sin must be paid.

—David Bishop, *Christian Truth and Its Defense for U.S. Marines*, 1997

Note: Allow an illustration like this to cause you to think of a similar event in your experience or reading. Then make the same point David Bishop made.

❖ **POSSIBLE ENTRANCE:** *We try to put our sins behind us. There is only one way to do that.*

You can't put your sins behind you until you face them.

—*Our Daily Bread*, 2001

POSSIBLE EXIT: *And who do you first have to face with those sins? Jesus. Once you deal with your sin before God, He puts your sins behind Him, and you can put them behind you.*

❖ **POSSIBLE ENTRANCE:** *Socrates said what we all know to be true but don't like to admit.*

Men know what is good but do what is bad.

—Socrates

POSSIBLE EXIT: *When you do wrong, it's not because you don't know what is right. You choose to do wrong.*

❖ Paul Harvey told of having a poodle that would beg for candy until one just had to give it a piece. This kept up, and the poodle was quite attracted to the candy and really liked it. Eventually, though, the dog contracted diabetes and had to be taken to the veterinarian every day, seven days a week for several years until finally it died an agonizing death.

—Paul Harvey

☺ **POSSIBLE ENTRANCE:** *We conjecture ways to cover up our sin.*

A little boy told a salesclerk he was shopping for a birthday gift for his mother and asked to see some cookie jars. At a counter displaying a large selection of them, the youngster carefully lifted and replaced each lid. His face fell as he came to the last one. "Aren't there any covers that don't make any noise?" he asked.

—Our Daily Bread, 1980

POSSIBLE EXIT: *God has a far better solution than cover-up. It's called forgiveness.*

❖ That which we call sin in others is an experiment for us.

—Ralph Waldo Emerson

❖ Correctional officials in some states can keep track of nonviolent criminals without having to keep them in prison. They are experimenting with a form of house arrest that uses advanced electronic surveillance devices. One of these systems consists of an electronic transmitter that is worn around the offender's ankle. It triggers an alarm if he violates the rules of his sentence by leaving home early, coming back late, or tampering with the device. Said one offender, "I don't feel like I'm in jail, but I do feel like I'm being watched."

—Our Daily Bread, 1987

Note: What enhances an illustration like this is to use the example of a recent person in the news who has such a transmitter attached to his or her ankle.

❖ The deadliest sins do not leap upon us. They creep up on us!

—Our Daily Bread, 1975

❖ Those of us who lived in Chicago in 1994 remember the hoopla surrounding the execution of John Wayne Gacy, who was convicted of killing thirty-three boys and hiding them in the crawl space under his house. The media wanted to make him out to be some kind of monster who was scarcely a member of the human race. What struck me, however, was how normal he looked. In fact, he looked a lot like someone I know.

Gacy did not have horns. He did not look as if devils were coming out of his body. What got lost in the news stories was that he was an ordinary man with whom all of us, as members of the human family, share a great deal. He was simply a human being who decided to follow perverted sexual desires wherever they might lead.

Gacy is a reminder of some words of wisdom I read somewhere: "Sin always takes you farther than you intended to go, keeps you longer than you intended to stay, and cost you more than you intended to pay."

—Erwin Lutzer, *How You Can Be Sure That You Will Spend Eternity with God*

Note: The truth of this illustration is forever pertinent. It can be effectively used by saying, "As a man reflected on John Wayne Gacy's execution after his conviction for murdering thirty-three people, he observed . . ."

☺ **POSSIBLE ENTRANCE:** *Your sin may be done in secret, but sooner or later it will catch up with you.*

A newspaper reported an unusual incident at a fast-food restaurant. The manager had put the day's cash in a paper bag for deposit that night, but an attendant mistook it for an order and gave it to a couple at the drive-thru window.

A short time later, when the man and woman opened the bag in a nearby park, they were shocked by its contents. They immediately drove back to return it.

The manager had reported a robbery, so police cars and a TV crew were on the scene. How relieved he was to get the money back! He said to the couple, "You should be featured on the evening news for your honesty."

"Oh, please, no publicity!" replied the man nervously. "She's not my wife."

—*Our Daily Bread*, 1996

POSSIBLE EXIT: *No sin goes unnoticed or eventually unpunished. Even if no one here notices, God does.*

☺ Driving along peacefully in her automobile, my neighbor was stopped by a policeman. A cameraman pulled up in another car to snap a picture of the officer giving her a white box.

"Congratulations, madam," the policeman said. "You are the first woman to receive an orchid for Safe Driving Week. We have been following you for some time and want to commend you for observing the laws."

Her picture was in the paper the next day with the caption, "She appeared quite nervous while accepting the orchid." Nervous was hardly the word for it. Her permit had expired, and she was driving without a license.

—The Lutheran Hour Ministries "By the Way"

☺   A San Diego patrolman pulled over a driver and told him that because he was wearing his seat belt, he had just won $5,000 in a safety competition. "What are you going to do with the money?" the officer asked.

"I guess I'll go to driving school and get my license," the man answered.

"Don't listen to him," said the woman in the passenger seat. "He's a smart aleck when he's drunk."

This woke up the guy in the back seat, who saw the cop and said, "I knew we wouldn't get far in a stolen car."

Then there was a knock from the trunk and a voice asked in Spanish, "Are we over the border yet?"

—Internet humor

SINNERS

❖   There are none so good that they can save themselves—none too bad that God cannot save them.

—*Our Daily Bread*, 1983

Note: Communication is saying the same thing in different words. Here is where illustrations help—this is a thought-provoking way of saying no one can save themselves, but God can save anyone.

❖   There was once a man who walked into a drugstore. He was a poor, untidy man, and he said, "If you please, mister, can you give me something for a cold?" The druggist said, "Do you have a prescription?" The man said, "No, but I brought the cold."

When you come to Christ, all He expects you to bring is your sin, not your prescription.

—*The Christian Herald*

Note: This illustration is more effective when you define what you mean by "your prescription"—the number of times you plan to go to church, the life you intend to live, or the commandments you plan to keep.

❖   God knows the path to every heart.

—Source unknown

❖ Unbelievers often comment with various degrees of contempt, "I can't believe God would damn anyone to hell." Those with a biblical view of man, however, exclaim in grateful humility, "I'm surprised God would save any of us!" When we begin to see the human heart as God has been seeing it all along, we are stunned that He would want to redeem the likes of us. We all are truly deserving of nothing but His wrath and judgment.

—Jim Berg, *Changed into His Image*

❖ Jesus came to save the LOST, the LAST, the LEAST!

—*Our Daily Bread*, 1975

☺ There is a tradition to the effect that the comedy writer Noel Coward sent identical notes to twenty of the most prominent men in London, saying, "All is discovered. Escape while you can."

All twenty abruptly left town!

—*Thesaurus of Anecdotes*, edited by Edmund Fuller

☺ **POSSIBLE ENTRANCE:** *We look at others as being sinners, but we don't always admit they learned how to sin by watching us.*

To improve my family's eating habits I stopped buying junk food and replaced it with plain rice cakes. My wife and two children were not enthusiastic about the change. One evening I went to the kitchen after the family was in bed and found my younger child, Ben, smearing frosting on a rice cake. "What are you doing?" I asked, surprised.

"This is how we always eat them," Ben replied. "Mommy showed us."

—Wayne Muhlstein's Web site, http://prosites-waynewatcher
.homestead.com/Support_Did_You_Hear.html

POSSIBLE EXIT: *We might want to ask ourselves, "Have others learned how to do something they shouldn't do by watching us?"*

❖ A Chinese artist was commissioned to portray the parable of the prodigal son. So he chose that part of the story where the wayward boy returns home after having wasted his resources in reckless living. He depicted the father standing by the gate, waiting for his son, who could be seen approaching in the distance.

When the artist showed the painting to a Christian friend, the man exclaimed, "Oh no, you don't have it right at all! The father shouldn't be standing still, he should be eagerly running to meet his son!" "But no Chinese father would ever consider doing that to one who had been so wayward," answered the other in surprise. "Ah," said the Christian, "but this parable depicts the heart of God. He is far more loving than even the best of human parents."

—*Our Daily Bread*, 1989

☺ **POSSIBLE ENTRANCE:** *If many of us were honest, we'd admit we enjoy our sin.*

A little boy was overheard praying: "Lord, if you can't make me a better boy, don't worry about it. I'm having a real good time like I am."

—Source unknown

POSSIBLE EXIT: *But remember that enjoyment is only for a limited time. The kind of joy God provides is forever.*

☺ A little boy was being particularly mischievous in a Sunday school class. After enduring as much as she could bear, the teacher called him to her desk and rebuked him: "Christopher, I'm very much afraid I'll not meet you in heaven!" To which the little rascal replied, "Why, teacher? What have you been doing now?"

—FunnySermons.com

❖ Prostitutes are in no danger of finding their present life so satisfactory that they cannot turn to God: the proud, the avaricious, the self-righteous, are in that danger.

—C. S. Lewis, *The Problem of Pain*

❖ **POSSIBLE ENTRANCE:** *God is not interested in helping you reform your life. He wants to make you into a new person.*

Paul Rader told of an old man who lived in a broken-down shack on a corner lot that was very valuable. He had secured this property before the area was developed, and now it was the section of the city where millionaires built their homes. While dozing off one afternoon on his porch, he was roused by a man who wanted to purchase his land. "What's your price?" he inquired.

"A hundred thousand," came the reply.

"Fine, I'll buy it," said the stranger without hesitation. Before leaving, he handed the owner a check for $10,000 to bind the contract. In the weeks that followed, the old gentleman felt guilty about asking so much for his worthless shack. Thinking he could make it more presentable, he began fixing it up. On the day of the closing, the buyer came to complete the transaction. After the final payment had been made, the old fellow turned to the rich man and said, "Don't you think you've got a nice little place here? See, I've painted it, patched the roof, and put new boards on the floor. You can sure be proud of it." The new owner responded, "I can't use it. It must come down, for I'm going to build a brand-new house!"

—Our Daily Bread, 1975

POSSIBLE EXIT: *God is not saying, "Clean up your act, make yourself presentable, and come to Me." He is saying, "Come to Me, and I'll make you something you have never been—a new person."*

❖ Two flies in a mud puddle can't clean each other.

—Reprinted by permission. No Wonder They Call Him Savior, Max Lucado, 2004,
Thomas Nelson Inc., Nashville, Tennessee. All rights reserved.

❖ All who enter the kingdom of God do so in the same posture, on their knees.

—Alan E. Nelson, Broken in the Right Place

❖ The ultimate proof of the sinner is that he does not know his own sin.

—Martin Luther

❖ A celebrated artist wishing to paint a picture of the prodigal son found a great difficulty in finding a man degraded enough in his appearance to sit as a model. At last he met a man looking terribly wretched and depraved. He told him to come the next day to his studio. The man kept his appointment, but to the artist's great surprise and annoyance he had left off his rags and borrowed better clothes. "Did I not tell you to come just as you were?" asked the artist. "You can go away again. I can't accept you unless you come as you are." Don't try to make an impression when coming to Christ; just give Him an invitation.

—Source unknown

❖ A friend of mine said to a lifeguard in Newport, Rhode Island, "How can you tell when anyone is in need of help when there are thousands of bathers on the beach and in the water, making a perfect hub-bub of noises?" To which he answered, "No matter how great the noise and confusion, there has never been a single time when I couldn't distinguish the cry of distress above them all. I can always tell it."

And that is exactly like God. In the midst of the babble and confusion, He never fails to hear the soul that cries out to Him for help amid the breakers and storms of life.

—"Going Where We've Never Been Before," Columbia Baptist Church, Columbia, KY, March 16, 2003

Note: In using an illustration like this, refer to your experience by a pool or of someone else's experience that is similar to this.

❖ Before you can understand the good news, you first have to hear the bad news.

—John McGahey

❖ It is this passion for autonomy, for independence from God, that prompted C. S. Lewis to write, "Fallen man is not simply an imperfect creature who needs improvement: he is a rebel who must lay down his arms."

—Jim Berg, *Changed into His Image*

❖ The eloquent French evangelist, Paul J. Loizeaux, once exclaimed, "Oh, how hard it is to find sinners! If only I could find one, I have a marvelous message for him."

—*Bibliotheca Sacra*, "Is Faith Enough to Save," January 1942

❖ Preparing to begin a meeting in a large city, famed evangelist Billy Sunday wrote a letter to the mayor in which he asked for the names of individuals he knew who had spiritual problems and needed help and prayer. How surprised the evangelist was when he received from the mayor a city directory.

—Source unknown

Note: Non-Christians do not know who Billy Sunday was. It is also immaterial to the illustration. Just say "An evangelist preparing for a city-wide crusade wrote . . ."

❖   Once when young Henry Moorhouse was walking down the street in Manchester, England, he heard a man calling out from the doorway of a building: "Ladies and gentlemen, come and see the great American pig."

Moorhouse paid the entrance fee and went to look at the remarkable animal. At the command of his master, the animal would pick out letters from the alphabet and spell the words "G-O-O-D-P-I-G." He would also perform other feats—walk on his hind legs and offer to shake his hands with the crowd.

The porker was washed and scrubbed, his hoofs were polished, and he was all dressed up. No one could deny that he was well-trained and well-behaved in every respect. But in spite of his remarkable "culture" and his attractive appearance, the latter proved that he still had the nature of a hog. While out for exercise one day, he slipped from his leash and was soon rolling and grunting contentedly in a large mud puddle.

—Our Daily Bread, 1979

STANDARDS

❖   **POSSIBLE ENTRANCE:** *In order to understand how short we fall of God's standard, we must have an absolute standard to measures ourselves by.*

In his monumental work, *Abraham Lincoln: The War Years,* Carl Sandberg gives an interesting sidelight on that well-known statesman. He says that when Lincoln was traveling from Springfield to Washington for his presidential inauguration, people were impressed by how tall he was. Many men stepped up to the train platform and stood back to back with him to compare their height with his. All but one failed to measure up to the chief executive.

—Our Daily Bread, 1980

POSSIBLE EXIT: *The person whom God puts all of us alongside is Jesus Christ. Alongside of Him we all come up short. We are not perfect—only He is.*

☺   **POSSIBLE ENTRANCE:** *God's standard is not goodness but perfection.*

Roger signed up to play in a kids' baseball league. After his first day of practice, I asked him how he had made out. Grinning from ear to ear, he replied, "The coach says I'm the best of the worst three."

—http://davidsisler.com/07–14–2003.htm

POSSIBLE EXIT: *It doesn't matter how good you have been; as a sinner you are just the best of the worst.*

☺ The kid tried to defend his low marks on his report card. "Father," he said proudly, "I was the highest of all who failed."

—Source unknown

❖ **POSSIBLE ENTRANCE:** *God has a standard. His standard is perfection. But it doesn't matter how good you have been or how religious you are, you can not meet the standard.*

I knew a girl who wanted to be a flight attendant. When she applied for the job they told her she had to be 5'2" tall. When they measured her, she was 5'1" tall. She was one inch too short.

—R. Larry Moyer

POSSIBLE EXIT: *They had a standard. It didn't matter how good or capable she was or how hard she tried; she could not meet their standard. In the same way, you have missed God's standard.*

❖ You can tie a boat to shore using a chain with ten links. But regardless of whether you snip one of the links or all ten links, the boat will drift from shore.

One sin or ten sins can take you away from God. The number isn't important.

—Source unknown

❖ W. A. Criswell, in *The Bible for Today's World*, wrote, "Washington, D.C., is the home of the Bureau of Standards. Every weight and every measure that is used in the United States is a copy of the standard that is kept inviolate by the Bureau in Washington. In that Bureau there is a perfect inch, a perfect foot, a perfect yard, a perfect gallon, a perfect pint, a perfect millimeter, a perfect milligram. Every weight and measure that we have finds its standard in that Bureau in Washington, and all are judged by that standard."
❖ What the Bureau of Standards is to weights and measures, God's Word is to conscience. It shows us His perfect will. So listen to your conscience, but be sure your conscience is being guided by the Bible. Forever settled in heaven, God's Word is our perfect standard!

—Richard W. DeHaan

❖ Basketball goals are often built at different heights. The standard height is ten feet. But many goals are built at eight feet. This gives the shorter guys and the guys who can't jump as well the chance to see what it's like to dunk the ball. Imagine raising the standard height up to twelve feet. Then only the best jumpers could dunk the ball. Imagine raising the hoop up to twenty-five feet. Could anyone dunk it then? No way. Not even the best jumpers or the tallest players.

Trying to dunk the ball on a twenty-five-foot basketball goal is similar to trying to earn your way to heaven. There just is no way that it can be done. To make it, you have to be perfect, and never have sinned. Trusting in Christ is the only way.

—Source unknown

❖   **POSSIBLE ENTRANCE:** *When we compare ourselves with others, we might look pretty good, but compared with God we are filthy.*

Bishop Hugh Gough, frequent speaker at the Keswick conferences, told an interesting story about his dog. He had a Highland terrier that he considered to be "pure white." He took excellent care of the animal, bathing and clipping it often. One morning when he awoke, he looked out the window and discovered that snow had fallen during the night. The ground was covered with a beautiful blanket of white. Just then he saw a dog run across the front yard. It was gray and dirty against the background of the fresh snow. Since his yard was enclosed by a fence, the bishop wondered how a stray dog could have gotten onto the property. To his surprise, his wife told him it was their own white terrier who was running across the yard.

—*Our Daily Bread*, 1981

POSSIBLE EXIT: *We look good only when we look away from Christ. When we look at Christ, we see how sinful we are.*

❖   I live in a house with white siding—at least it looks white most of the year. However, when the snow falls in the winter, all of a sudden my house looks dingy and yellow. What may look "clean" whenever we compare ourselves with other sinners takes on a whole different cast when seen next to the perfect holiness of God.

—Nancy Leigh DeMoss, *Lies Women Believe*

☺   **POSSIBLE ENTRANCE:** *When you consider your sinful condition, let me ask you, "Are you using God's standard or your own?"*

160

A little boy came to his mother, saying, "Mama, I am as tall as Goliath, I am nine feet tall." "What makes you say that?" asked the mother. "Well, I made a little ruler of my own and measured myself with it, and I am just nine feet high," said the boy.

—www.charityadvantage.com

POSSIBLE EXIT: *God's standard is not what you or someone else makes it. It's what God declares it to be—absolute perfection.*

❖   **POSSIBLE ENTRANCE:** *In examining ourselves and our goodness and performance, we often compare ourselves with others. The problem is, regardless of how we compare with others, we still come short of His standard.*

In a certain mountain village about one hundred miles from Paris, a group of American soldiers, consisting of a lieutenant and about forty men, guarded an ammunition dump. The lieutenant received permission to go on leave for two weeks and left the group in the charge of the master sergeant. A few days afterward a motorcycle messenger rode in from General Pershing's headquarters, stating that 2,700 men were to be chosen to march in the peace parades of London, Paris, Brussels, and Rome. But as they read the order they discovered that there were two conditions imposed as standards for selection. The first brought them no difficulty for it stated that every candidate had to have a clean record; no man would be chosen who had been court marshaled. But the second condition gave them pause. The order stated that every man applying had to be at least 1 meter and 86 centimeters tall. No one knew the metric system. Soon a mark of the required height was made on the wall. Now the men no longer could measure themselves by themselves. Several backed up to the mark and were too short. Then someone called for Tall Slim but even he too was short, by no more than one quarter of an inch.

—Donald Grey Barnhouse

POSSIBLE EXIT: *The point is even the tallest of the tallest fell short of the standard. The best of the best of us fall short of God's standard of perfection.*

❖   **POSSIBLE ENTRANCE:** *How do we define morality?*

For many, the standard is "What's moral is what you feel good after. What's immoral is what you feel bad after."

—Ernest Hemingway

POSSIBLE EXIT: *God's standard is not what you feel good or bad about after doing. His standard is based on fact. Whether or not we feel moral or immoral is not the issue. He knows we are immoral. We are sinners.*

❖ In a recent *Nightline* town meeting with gay and lesbian teenagers, Ted Koppel asked, "What do you say when someone says to you, 'The Bible teaches that homosexuality is wrong?'" One teenager answered, "I really don't care. Everything is relative; no one has a right to judge me."

—Robert E. Webber, *Ancient-Future Evangelism*

Note: When Ted Koppel is no longer known, the quote still fits. It expresses what many feel.

TRUTH

❖ Sometimes our greatest problem is not in finding the truth but in facing it.

—*Our Daily Bread*, 1975

☺ A small-town prosecuting attorney called his first witness to the stand during a trial—a grandmotherly, elderly woman. He approached her and asked, "Ms. Jones, do you know me?"

She responded, "Why, yes, I do know you Mr. Williams. I've known you since you were a young boy, and frankly, you've been a big disappointment to me. You lie, you cheat on your wife, and you manipulate people and talk about them behind their backs. You think you're a rising big shot when you haven't the brains to realize you'll never amount to anything more than a two-bit paper pusher. Yes, I know you."

The lawyer was stunned. Not knowing what else to do, he pointed across the room and asked, "Ms. Williams, do you know the defense attorney?"

She again replied, "Why, yes I do. I've known Mr. Bradley since he was a youngster, too. I used to baby-sit him for his parents. And he, too, has been a real disappointment to me. He's lazy, bigoted, and has a drinking problem. The man can't build a normal relationship with anyone, and his law practice is one of the worst in the entire state. Not to mention he cheated on his wife with three different women. Yes, I know him." The defense attorney was also surprised and shocked.

At this point, the judge brought the courtroom to silence and called both counselors to the bench. In a very quiet voice, he said with menace, "If either of you asks her if she knows me, I will throw you in jail and throw away the key!"

—Internet humor

❖ **POSSIBLE ENTRANCE:** *The failure of an eight-year-old boy to tell the truth cost him his life, as reported in the* Chicago Tribune.

Timothy Bates of Brentwood, New Jersey, had eaten tranquilizing pills. The stomachs of the two younger Bates children, who had also eaten the pills, were pumped out. Timothy steadfastly affirmed that he had not eaten any of the pills. He was not treated.

The mother put the three children to bed. The next morning she went to see if they were all right. The two younger children were fine. Timothy was dead.

—Source unknown

POSSIBLE EXIT: *Truth and honesty, as taught in God's Word, are necessities.*

☺ **POSSIBLE ENTRANCE:** *Even when we try to hide the truth, it doesn't change the truth.*

James Fammer tells a story about a woman who acquired wealth and decided to have a book written about her genealogy. The well-known author she engaged for the assignment discovered that one of her grandfathers had been electrocuted in Sing Sing. When he said it would have to be included in the book, she pleaded for a way of saying it that would hide the truth. When the book appeared, it read as follows: "One of her grandfathers occupied the chair of applied electricity in one of America's best known institutions. He was very much attached to his position and literally died in the harness."

—Howard J. Clinebell, *Intimate Marriage*

POSSIBLE EXIT: *We can try to hide the truth that we are sinners, but it doesn't change the truth. We are sinners!*

❖ The best mind-altering drug is the truth.

—Lily Tomlin, actress

☺ **POSSIBLE ENTRANCE:** *We can try to hide the truth, but sooner or later the truth will be revealed.*

A friend of mine had been wanting new kitchen cabinets for a long time, but her husband insisted they were an extravagance. She went to visit her mother for two weeks, and when she returned, she was overjoyed to find that beautiful new cabinets had been installed. A few days later a neighbor came over to visit my friend. After admiring the new cabinets, the neighbor exclaimed, "All of us were so glad that the fire your husband had while you were gone was confined to the kitchen."

—Submitted by Margaret Gunn. Reprinted with permission from the
April 1998 *Reader's Digest*. Copyright ©1998
by The Reader's Digest Assn., Inc.

POSSIBLE EXIT: *In the spiritual realm, the truth cannot be hidden. God already knows everything.*

❖   The truth does not change according to our ability to stomach it.

—Flannery O'Connor, American author

☺   The closest to perfection a person ever comes is when he fills out a job application form.

—Stanley J. Randall

❖   **POSSIBLE ENTRANCE:** *In regard to truth, you may have heard Abraham Lincoln's statement.*

It is possible to fool some of the people all of the time, and all of the people some of the time, but it is impossible to fool all of the people all of the time.

—Abraham Lincoln

POSSIBLE EXIT: *One thing must be added to Lincoln's statement. "It is impossible to fool God at any time."*

WARNING
☺   **POSSIBLE ENTRANCE:** *Some warnings have lightheartedness about them. They are not to be taken seriously.*

My wife and I were vacationing in Alaska. On a tour bus one day, the driver made everyone laugh when he said, "The reason my name is not on the front of the bus is that you have to have made three trips without a collision. I always get to two and can't make the third. Hopefully this time I will."

—R. Larry Moyer

POSSIBLE EXIT: *God's warnings are never like that. There is seriousness about every warning He gives.*

❖ *Life* magazine told about a tragic incident that happened at the small mining town of Saunders in West Virginia. There was one road that leads through the town. At the upper end of the town, slate and coal kept backing up the water for fifteen years, and the people had been warned that if that ever gave way, it could flood and destroy the whole town. The other morning it happened. There was a big sound like a thunderclap, and the water came down wiping out the whole town. At least seventy died. A twenty-nine-year-old mine worker born in that valley pointed to a torn roof and said, "See that, well, the wife and I had the furniture delivered the night before. She went for everything, new carpet, the crushed leather furniture, washer, dryer, bedroom set. I had two cars, too," he said with a shrug. One man said, "I guess we had been warned too many times."

—*Life*, March 10, 1972

❖ On February 20, 1984, a heavily loaded steel truck rumbled across the Lincoln Park Bridge in Youngstown, Ohio. Without warning, the bridge gave way. Two cars and the truck plunged into the gaping hole.

Too late the news leaked out: The bridge had failed to pass inspection in 1983. The city commissioners had ignored the warning—money was too tight to spend on repairing bridges.

—*Take 5 Devotional*, Back to the Bible, January–March 1985

Note: Use this to provoke your thinking. Is there a more recent bridge collapse resulting from an ignored warning?

Chapter 7

Let's Talk About Illustrating Substitution

PAINFUL. SACRIFICIAL. STRIKING. THAT'S how I felt about Christ's death before I had a relationship with Him. He was so abused and yet so loving and forgiving. The words He uttered from the cross stunned me: "Father, forgive them, for they do not know what they do" (Luke 23:34). I could barely fathom His torturous death.

By contrast, the resurrection was comforting, even exciting. He arose. The cross brought me to tears as I thought of His agony. The resurrection made me rejoice.

Then through a combination of things the Lord used, including my own Bible study, I heard two words—"for me." Gradually, I began to understand. He took my place. His death and resurrection became personal. He died *for me* and for all. The cross and resurrection became more than a powerful thought. It was the most important event in history—one that changed my eternal destiny.

Non-Christians need to know that Christ died. But they need to know more than that. They need to know that Christ died *for them*. That's when they begin to understand redemption. If He already paid for my sins, I don't have to pay for them. If something involves a cost and that cost is paid, the one who paid it can offer it as a gift to others.

It makes sense why Christ declared, "It is finished" (John 19:30). God's wrath against my sin is satisfied. Christ made the full payment, not the down payment.

Substitution illustrations are hard to find, but they exist. Watch for them. You might read of a policeman who sacrificed his life by rushing in front of a schoolgirl, pushing her out of the way of a speeding car. Or it may be the story of a fireman who voluntarily entered a building to save an infant he tossed to the firemen below before he became the victim of the flames. Pay particular attention when tragedy strikes. Look for acts of substitution in articles describing an airplane disaster, the destructive path of a tornado, or death caused by inescapable flood waters.

One note. When Christ died on the cross, it was a voluntary death. He chose to die. Some illustrations on substitution are similar. *Most*, however, speak of a person who died for another involuntarily. In other words, in attempting to save another, a person accidentally died. The involuntary part does not have to restrict you from using the illustration. That Christ died voluntarily while others died involuntarily can make the illustration more forceful. Either way, it still remains that one died for another. That is the principle that you are communicating. Keep in mind that few illustrations are perfect. As long as it illustrates the main fact you are communicating it's a usable illustration.

Often the date doesn't matter. It's immaterial to the truth you're illustrating. Years ago, for instance, Dawson Trotman, founder of the Navigators, died as he lifted a drowning girl into a boat then fell beneath the waters of Schroon Lake in New York. She was the second person he had saved that day. The name Dawson Trotman is meaningful to those who know of him or the ministry of the Navigators. It's also interesting to those living in New York who have heard of Word of Life headquartered on Schroon Lake, or may have traveled through the Adirondack Mountains where the lake is located. But being unfamiliar with all those names, ministries, or details doesn't change the truth. The date doesn't enhance the truth of the illustration. One person died for another. That's why when using a substitution illustration you can say, "Years ago, in Dallas, Texas," and need not give the date. Particular details can be helpful. But details such as the date don't always affect the truth behind the illustration.

Christ's substitutionary death can be approached from many directions. You can approach it from the vantage point of a love so great, One died in another's place. Or think of a gift that was purchased through the sacrifice of another. Illustrate that one sinner can't pay for another sinner's sin. Only a perfect person could pay for our sin. Or illustrate whose sins He died for—not one person or a few people but everyone's. Think of the historical significance of such a death—no death ever accomplished more. Think of how sharply His love contrasts to ours. Would we do for another what He did for us? Compare the difference between taking a relatively good person's place or taking the place of a murderer, rapist, or thief. Our love is conditional. His wasn't. The love behind the cross can be illustrated in many ways.

Advance to the resurrection for even more supporting material. Think in terms of quotations, statistics, analogies, as well as stories. The supporting material verifies the truth you're stating and illustrates the miraculous nature of the event.

Again, humorous illustrations are noted with a ☺. Humor in this area is understandably limited. If using humor at all, confine it to such areas as differentiating between His love and ours, or His giving spirit versus our selfish spirit.

Here are helpful illustrations as one proclaims, "Christ died for our sins. Christ arose." (An index of illustration topics can be found at the end of this book.)

Illustrations
About Substitution

BLOOD OF CHRIST

❖ **POSSIBLE ENTRANCE:** *What is the greatest way you can express your love to someone? If you own many homes, you wouldn't say, "I love you, here's my house." Giving up that house is not giving your all—you have other ones. If you're a millionaire, you wouldn't say, "I love you, here's a thousand dollars" because there's more where that came from. What if you say, however, "I love you, and I will give my life in place of yours so you can live." That's something monumental.*

The mortar rounds landed in an orphanage run by a missionary group in the small Vietnamese village. The missionaries and one or two children were killed outright, and several more children were wounded, including one girl about eight years old.

People from the village sent for help to a neighboring town that had radio contact with the American forces. Finally a U.S. doctor and nurse arrived in a jeep with their medical kits. They established that the young girl was the most critically injured. Without quick action, she would die from shock and loss of blood.

A blood transfusion was imperative, so a donor with a matching blood type was required. A quick test showed that neither American had the correct blood type, but several of the uninjured orphans did.

The doctor spoke some Vietnamese pidgin, and the nurse a smattering of high-school French. Using that combination together with much impromptu sign language, they tried to explain to their young, frightened audience that unless they could replace some of the girl's lost blood, she would certainly die. Then they asked if anyone would be willing to give blood to help.

Their request was met with wide-eyed silence. After several long moments, a small hand slowly and waveringly went up, dropped back down, and then went up again.

"Oh, thank you," the nurse said in French. "What is your name?"

"Hung," came the mumbled reply.

Hung was quickly laid on a pallet, his arm swabbed with alcohol, and the needle inserted in his vein. Through this ordeal Hung lay stiff and silent. After a moment, he let out a shuddering sob, quickly covering his face with his free hand.

"Is it hurting, Hung?" the doctor asked.

Hung shook his head, but after a few moments another sob escaped, and once more he tried to cover up his crying. Again the doctor asked him if the needle hurt, and again Hung shook his head.

But now his occasional sobs gave way to a steady, silent crying, his eyes screwed tightly shut, his fist in his mouth to stifle his sobs.

The medical team was concerned because the needle should not have been hurting him. Something was obviously very wrong. At this point, a

Vietnamese nurse arrived. Seeing the little one's distress, she spoke to him, listened to his reply, and answered him in a soothing voice.

After a moment, the boy stopped crying, opened his eyes, and looked questioningly at the Vietnamese nurse. When she nodded, a look of great relief spread over his face. Looking up, the Vietnamese nurse said quietly to the Americans, "He thought he was dying. He misunderstood you. He thought you had asked him to give all his blood so the little girl could live."

"But why would he be willing to do that?" asked the navy nurse.

The Vietnamese nurse repeated the question to the little boy, who answered simply, "She's my friend."

—Col. John Mansur, United States Air Force (retired). Used by permission.

POSSIBLE EXIT: *Jesus Christ was called a friend of sinners. He proved it by dying in our place, giving his life and blood where we should have given ours.*

❖ When evangelist John Wesley (1703–1791) was returning home from a service one night, he was robbed. The thief, however, found his victim to have only a little money and some Christian literature.

As the bandit was leaving, Wesley called out, "Stop! I have something more to give you."

The surprised robber paused.

"My friend," said Wesley, "you may live to regret this sort of life. If you ever do, here's something to remember: 'The blood of Jesus Christ cleanses us from all sin!'"

The thief hurried away, and Wesley prayed that his words might bear fruit.

Years later, Wesley was greeting people after a Sunday service when he was approached by a stranger. What a surprise to learn that this visitor, now a believer in Christ and a successful businessman, was the one who had robbed him years before!

"I owe it all to you," said the transformed man.

"Oh no, my friend," Wesley exclaimed, "not to me, but to the precious blood of Christ that cleanses us from all sin!"

—*Our Daily Bread*, 1994

Note: Illustrations like these are powerful because of the truth and the experience they convey. But when they are this dated, update them by using terminology unbelievers will understand. Do one of two things. Before using the illustration, explain that the blood of Christ has enabled us to be forgiven. Better yet, change Wesley's first comment about the blood of Christ by saying, "He then shared the simple truth that Jesus Christ can forgive any and all sin." Unbelievers are probably not familiar with John Wesley and his impact for the kingdom so simply say "a noted preacher" when you refer to him.

❖ Morality may keep you out of jail, but it takes the blood of Christ to keep you out of hell.

—C. W. Carter, *Syracuse Post-Standard*

❖ **POSSIBLE ENTRANCE:** *Many times we think that the good behavior and proper living that keeps us out of jail will also help us when we stand before God. Not true.*

At the close of a gospel service, an intelligent-looking man came to the minister and said, "I don't see any necessity for the blood of Christ in my salvation. I can be saved without believing in His shed blood."

"Very well," said the minister, "how then do you propose to be saved?"

"By following His example," was the answer. "That is enough for any man."

"I suppose it is," said the minister. "And you propose to do just that in your life?"

"I do, and I'm sure that that is enough."

"Very well. I'm sure that you want to begin right. The Word of God tells us how to do that. I read here concerning Christ, 'Who did no sin, neither was guile found in His mouth.' I suppose that you can say that of yourself too?" [1 Peter 2:22 ASV]

The man became visibly embarrassed. "Well," he said, "I can't say that exactly. I have sometimes sinned."

"In that case you do not need an example but a Savior; and the only way of salvation is by His shed blood."

—Gorden Blount, "The Bread,"
Emmanuel Baptist Church, Pontiac, MI, December 29, 1996

❖ **POSSIBLE EXIT:** *Why won't good behavior help us when we stand before God? Because the smallest sin has to be punished. That punishment is death and eternal separation from God in what the Bible calls hell.*

❖ **POSSIBLE ENTRANCE:** *Something that happened years ago in an African village illustrates what Christ did for us on the cross.*

An African chief ordered a slave to be killed for a very small offense. An Englishman, overhearing the order, offered costly items to spare the poor man's life. The chief answered, "I don't want ivory or gold; I want blood."

The chief ordered one of his men to pull a bowstring and discharge an arrow at the poor slave's heart. The Englishman threw himself in front of the man and received the arrow into his own flesh. He pulled the arrow out and, handing it to the chief, said, "Here is blood; I give my blood for this poor slave, and I claim his life."

The chief turned the slave over to the white man, saying, "Yes, you have bought him with your own blood."

Likewise, we are bought with the blood that Jesus shed on the cross. He paid the penalty that was due us because of our sins. We live because He died.

—L. T. Talbot, *Address on Romans*

POSSIBLE EXIT: *The blood that you should have shed, Jesus shed. You should have died, but He died for you. Jesus was your substitute.*

CALVARY

❖ **POSSIBLE ENTRANCE:** *Some of you may wonder how God can be the God of love in light of all the sufferings you've had to endure. If you want to know if God loves, or whether God loves you, just go back to the cross.*

A man in Dundee, Scotland, who had fallen and broken his back, was confined to his bed for forty years. He never had a day without pain, but God gave him the grace and strength to keep going. His cheery disposition and great love for the Lord inspired all who visited him.

One day a friend asked, "Doesn't the Devil ever tempt you to doubt God?" "Oh yes, he tries—especially when I have to lie here and see my old schoolmates driving by, having a good time with their families. At times it's as if Satan whispers, 'If the Lord is so good, why does He keep you here? Why did He allow you to break your back?'"

When the friend asked how he handled such attacks, the man replied, "I point him to Calvary and to the wounds of my Savior and say, 'Doesn't He love me!' The devil can't answer that, so he flees every time."

—*Our Daily Bread*, 1992

POSSIBLE EXIT: *If you are struggling with the love of God, ask yourself the question, "Would you do for someone what Jesus Christ did for you?" Most of us, if we are honest, would answer, "No."*

❖ Calvary made it possible to escape God's wrath by fleeing to God's love.

—*Our Daily Bread*, 1982

❖ Calvary proves the depth of God's intelligence and love. No one else could have come up with a way whereby God could punish the Son and at the same time pardon the sinner.

—R. Larry Moyer

175

CHRISTIANITY

❖ **POSSIBLE ENTRANCE:** *If most of us were asked, "How do you get to heaven?" we would probably answer in terms of something we have to do. Christianity's answer is in what Someone, namely, Jesus Christ, has already done. One person expressed it this way:*

Every other faith system I studied during my investigation was based on the "do" plan. In other words, it was necessary for people to do something—for example, use a Tibetan prayer wheel, pay alms, go on pilgrimages, undergo reincarnations, work off karma from past misdeeds, reform their character—to try to somehow earn their way back to God. Despite their best efforts, lots of sincere people just wouldn't make it.

Christianity is unique. It's based on the "done" plan—Jesus has done for us on the cross what we cannot do for ourselves: He has paid the death penalty that we deserve for our rebellion and wrongdoing, so we can become reconciled with God.

—Lee Strobel, *The Case for Christ*

POSSIBLE EXIT: *If you want to get to heaven, you cannot trust what you plan to do; you have to trust what He has already done.*

❖ My understanding of Christianity is God in search of lost men, not men in search of a lost God.

—Ronald R. Hatch quoted in *Time, January 15, 1965*

❖ A Hindu man once asked E. Stanley Jones, "What has Christianity to offer that our religion has not?"

He replied, "Jesus Christ."

—Paul Borthwick, *Six Dangerous Questions to Transform Your View of the World*

❖ Christianity is not a negative religion; it is a glorious yes.

—Source unknown

❖ **POSSIBLE ENTRANCE:** *Christianity has no middle ground. It is either the most important truth you will ever hear or it is of no importance at all.*

As C. S. Lewis put it, "Christianity is a statement that, if false, is of no importance, and, if true, is of infinite importance. The one thing it cannot be is moderately important."

—*Our Daily Bread*, 1999

POSSIBLE EXIT: *How do you regard Christianity? Not true and therefore un-important or true and of the greatest possible importance?*

❖   While witnessing for Christ on the streets of a city in California, evangelist H. A. Ironside and his associates were often interrupted by questions from the crowd. It was common, for instance, to have an unbeliever respond to their presentation of the gospel by saying, "There are hundreds of religions in this country, and the followers of each sect think they're right. How can poor, plain people like us find out what really is the truth?" Ironside and his friends would answer something like this: "Did I hear you say there are hundreds of religions? That's strange; I've only heard of two. True, I find many shades of difference in the opinions of those comprising the two great schools. But after all, there are but two. One covers all who expect salvation by doing; the other, all who have been saved by something done."

—*Our Daily Bread*, 1987

❖   A man said to me, "Before I came to Christ, Christianity was a negative religion. Now it is a positive relationship. The reason is rather simple. Before I came to Christ I looked at Christianity through the church. Now I look at Christianity through Christ. The church might fail you. Christ never does."

—R. Larry Moyer

❖   Christianity is above all others the religion of hope. Christ arouses in the most despairing the hope of redemption, promising a new change and better opportunity to the sinner.

—Louis Banks

CHRISTMAS

❖   The most important part of Christmas is the first six letters.

—*Our Daily Bread*, 2005

❖   The famous agnostic lawyer Clarence Darrow once called the celebration of Christmas "a humbug, a public nuisance." He said, "People would be better off if they paid no attention to it."

—Warren Wiersbe, *God Isn't In a Hurry*

❖   **POSSIBLE ENTRANCE:** *Most Americans picture Christ as another Santa Claus.*

Most Americans think of Christ as Santa Claus—He's making a list and checking it twice, going to find out who's naughty and nice. Somehow, though, we think He'll come through with the gifts!

—Haddon Robinson

POSSIBLE EXIT: *Christ will give you the greatest gift you've ever received but not on the basis of whether or not you are naughty or nice.*

❖ Christ was born here below that we might be born from above.

—*Our Daily Bread*, 1988

❖ If you like to ponder past Christmases, go back to the first one.

—Source unknown

❖ **POSSIBLE ENTRANCE:** *Can you imagine celebrating someone's birthday without that special someone being present?*

Two women who were dressed in their finest were having lunch together in a very exclusive restaurant. A friend saw them and came over to their table to greet them. "What's the special occasion?" she asked.

One of the women said, "We're having a birthday party for the baby in our family. He's two years old today."

"But where's the baby?" the friend asked.

The child's mother answered, "Oh, I dropped him off at my mother's house. She's taking care of him until the party's over. It wouldn't have been any fun with him along."

—*Our Daily Bread*, 1990

POSSIBLE EXIT: *Yet that is exactly what we do if we celebrate Christmas without Christ.*

❖ My son, when little, was singing Christmas carols and asked, "Daddy, what does 'ignore' mean?" I said, "It means to not pay attention to someone." He said, "I don't think we should ignore Jesus." I said, "I don't either." He said, "But the song says, 'O come let us ignore Him!'" I said to my wife, "What a message—we sing 'Let us adore Him' and practice 'Let us ignore Him!'"

—R. Larry Moyer

❖ God shook the world with a baby, not a bomb.

—*Christian Clippings*, December 1988

❖ **POSSIBLE ENTRANCE:** *Have you ever considered this? December 25 was just like any other day. Jesus is the one who made it Christmas.*

Two children were busily engaged in trimming a Christmas tree that their father had set up in the living room. As the little boy hung a star on one of the branches, he said to his older sister, "I wish I had been born on Christmas day." "Why?" she asked. "Because Jesus was born on that day." "No, He wasn't," the sister retorted. "When Jesus was born, it was just like any other day. HE made it Christmas!"

—*Our Daily Bread*, 1977

POSSIBLE EXIT: *The sister was right. December 25 was just like any other day. Jesus made it Christmas.*

❖ The best gift in the world was wrapped in a manger.

—*Our Daily Bread*, 1996

CROSS

❖ He died upon a cross of wood and yet created the hill on which it stood.

—Source unknown

❖ It is not barbaric that God laid the penalty for our sins on Himself. It would only be barbaric if He laid the penalty for our sins on somebody else.

—Bishop Michael A. Boughen

❖ In his book *Dare to Believe*, Dan Baumann shares some thoughts that can deepen our gratitude for what the Savior did for us. He wrote, "We have perhaps unwisely and sometimes unconsciously glamorized the cross. Jewelry and steeples alike are often ornamental and attractive but carry nothing of the real story of crucifixion. It was the most painful method of public death in the first century. The victim was placed on a wooden cross. Nails . . . were driven into the hands and feet of the victim, and then the cross was lifted and jarred into the ground, tearing the flesh of the crucified and racking his body with excruciating pain. Historians remind us that even the soldiers could not get used to the horrible sight, and often took strong drink to numb their senses."

—*Our Daily Bread*, 2004

Note: There is no need to quote Don Baumann. Simply use his facts to explain to your audience how gruesome the cross was. It wasn't an attractive piece of jewelry. Illustrations sometimes give you facts you can put into your own words.

❖ On the cross God forsook Christ (Matt. 27:46) so He would not need to abandon you.

—Bill Barnard

Note: An illustration like this is thought-provoking and states truth in a way that is easy to remember. But be careful for a non-Christian audience to explain why Christ said what He did in Matthew 27:46. Emphasize that our sins were placed on Christ, and God cannot look upon sin.

❖ Sixty-one percent of one hundred businessmen said the cross was one of the most significant events in history.

—Billy Graham

❖ If they would have crucified anyone else upon that cross, the earth never would have shook, the temple veil would have never been torn, and man never would have been redeemed!

—R. Larry Moyer

❖ "The cross was not a Favorite Citizen Award handed to Jesus by the Jerusalem Chamber of Commerce."—Rev. George Hill, president of the Church Council in Rochester, NY

—*Look*, "The Battle of the Bible," 1965

❖ **POSSIBLE ENTRANCE:** *What is one of the major ways God wants to use the Bible in your life? The answer is found in the compelling story of how God used a young girl years ago.*

On the stern and rockbound New England coast there lived a little brother and sister who frequently played among the rocks along the shore. One day one of them discovered a natural formation in the rocks above them that resembled a cross. After that, they took great delight in filling the crevices that shaped the cross with dry grass and sticks and setting it on fire to see the beautiful display it made. As the years passed, the girl remained at the old homestead, but the boy went away to seek his fortune. One stormy winter night he returned on a visit to the old home, and he told his sister he had seen signals from a ship in distress out at sea.

Neither of them knew of any way to help the distressed sailors, but then the sister remembered the old cross in the rocks. She gathered a large armful of wood and kindling and hastened to the spot. She filled in the crevices, as in earlier days, and then set the cross on fire.

In a short time, the light of the blaze was shining out through the storm. One of the sailors—who had been cheering his comrades and urging them not to give up—cried out, "The cross! See the light from yonder cross! It will guide us to safety."

They manned the lifeboats and pulled toward the flaming cross. They found the faithful girl, who had remained out in the storm and cold to feed the fire, lying on the shore, frozen to death. She had given her life to direct them to the cross.

—Gospel Herald

POSSIBLE EXIT: *Today, it's the Bible that God wants to use to direct you to the cross where Someone died to save you.*

❖ Christ's birth brought God to man; Christ's death brings man to God.

—Our Daily Bread, 1999

❖ Before electronic bill pay, some of us may have walked into an office to pay a bill—for telephone, electricity, or some other obligation we had incurred. We handed the money to the teller, who counted it, took the bill we owed, and pressed a rubber stamp upon an ink pad, stamped our bill, and handed us a receipt. The company could never collect that specific bill from us again for if they tried to do so, we could produce the receipt, and they would know that the matter has been cleared and that we were free from the obligation forever.

—Source unknown

❖ The Lord Jesus Christ walked up to Calvary, which was God's desk for the payment of the bill of our sins. The account was heavy against us, and the Lord Jesus Christ could settle the account by shedding His blood in dying for us.

—Source unknown

Note: Personalize this. Use an illustration from your experience of paying a bill. Be certain to emphasize that when Jesus paid the debt it was "paid in full."

❖ **POSSIBLE ENTRANCE:** *You struggle with why God allows suffering. So have many others.*

When Corrie and Betsie ten Boom's story and suffering in the German concentration camp of Ravensbruck was vividly brought to life in the book *The Hiding Place*, one scene that always struck me occurs as Betsie leads a Bible class in the midst of the lice-ridden barracks. A woman calls out derisively to the group and mocks their worship of God. She says, "If your God is such a good God, why does He allow this kind of suffering?" She dramatically rips off the bandages from her hand and displays mangled fingers. She says, "I was once the first violinist of the Berlin Orchestra. Did your God will this?"

Everyone is stunned and silent. Then Corrie steps forward and says, "We can't argue that question. All we know is that our God came to this earth, and became one of us, and He suffered with us, and was crucified and died. And that He did it for love."

—Mark R. Littleton, *When God Seems Far Away*

POSSIBLE EXIT: *Christ understands suffering. He suffered for you. One word explains why—love.*

❖ The cross of Christ reveals the love of God at its best and the sin of man at its worst.

—*Our Daily Bread*, 1982

CRUCIFIXION

❖ **POSSIBLE ENTRANCE:** *To completely understand Christ, you must understand His death. Author Philip Yancey wrote a book titled* The Jesus I Never Knew. *Here is how he expressed it.*

Of the biographies I have read, few devote more than ten percent of their pages to the subject's death—including biographies of men like Martin Luther King Jr. and Mahatma Gandhi, who died violent and politically significant deaths. The Gospels, though, devote nearly a third of their length to the climactic last week of Jesus' life. Matthew, Mark, Luke, and John saw death as the central mystery of Jesus.

—Philip Yancey, *The Jesus I Never Knew*

POSSIBLE EXIT: *You will never understand Jesus until you understand the death Christ died. And that death was for you!*

❖ For indeed a death by crucifixion seems to include all that pain that death CAN have of horrible and ghastly—dizziness, cramps, thirst, star-vation, sleeplessness, traumatic fever, tetanus, shame, publicity of shame, long continuance of torment, horror of anticipation, mortification of un-tended wounds—all intensified just up to the point at which they can be endured at all, but all stopping just short of the point that would give to the sufferer the relief of unconsciousness. The unnatural position made every movement painful; the lacerated veins and crushed tendons throbbed with incessant anguish; the wounds, inflamed by exposure, gradually gangrened; the arteries—especially at the head and stomach—became swollen and oppressed with surcharged blood; and while each variety of misery went on, gradually increasing, there was added to them the intolerable pang of a burning and raging thirst; and all these physical complications caused an internal excitement and anxiety, which made the prospect of death itself—of death, the unknown enemy, at whose ap-proach man usually shudders most—bear the aspect of a delicious and exquisite release.

—Used by permission. Josh McDowell, *Evidence That Demands a Verdict*,
p. 205, Campus Crusade for Christ, www.josh.org

Note: Illustrations like this help you explain in your own words the horrible death Christ suffered for our sins.

❖   I cannot personally see anything in the accounts of the crucifixion and burial that is not deeply and profoundly true to expectation. The whole account reads like an actual unvarnished and even naïve transcript from real life.

—Frank Morison, *Who Moved the Stone*

Note: This illustration only becomes meaningful if you point out that Frank Morison was a British trial attorney who said that before he died he would write a book to disprove Christianity. He collected the facts, and much to his surprise became a believer.

❖   What is crucifixion? A medical doctor provides a physical description: The cross is placed on the ground and the exhausted man is quickly thrown backward with his shoulders against the wood. The legionnaire feels for the depression at the front of the wrist. He drives a heavy, square wrought-iron nail through the wrist and deep into the wood. Quickly he moves to the other side and repeats the action, being careful not to pull the arms too tightly, but to allow some flex and movement. The cross is then lifted into place.

The left foot is pressed backward against the right foot, and with both feet extended, toes down, a nail is driven through the arch of each, leaving the knees flexed. The victim is now crucified. As he slowly sags down with more weight on the nails in the wrists, excruciating, fiery pain shoots along the fingers and up the arms to explode in the brain—the nails in the wrists are putting pressure on the median nerves. As he pushes himself upward to avoid stretching torment, he places the full weight on the nail through his feet. Again he feels the searing agony of the nail tearing through the nerves between the bones of the feet.

As the arms fatigue, cramps sweep through the muscles, knotting them in deep, relentless, throbbing pain. With these cramps comes the inability to push himself upward to breathe. Air can be drawn into the lungs but not exhaled. He fights to raise himself in order to get even one small breath. Finally carbon dioxide builds up in the lungs and in the blood stream, and the cramps partially subside. Spasmodically he is able to push himself upward to exhale and bring in life-giving oxygen.

He endures hours of this limitless pain, cycles of twisting, joint-rending cramps, intermittent partial asphyxiation, searing pain as tissue is torn from his lacerated back as he moves up and down against the rough timber. Then another agony begins: a crushing pain deep in the chest as the pericardium slowly fills with serum and begins to compress the heart.

It is now almost over. The loss of tissue fluids has reached a critical level—the compressed heart is struggling to pump heavy, thick, sluggish blood into the tissues—the tortured lungs are making a frantic effort to gasp in small gulps of air. He can feel the chill of death creeping through his tissues. . . . Finally he can allow his body to die.

All this the Bible records with the simple words, "And they crucified him" (Mark 15:24 NASB). What wondrous love is this?

—C. Truman Davis, *Arizona Medicine*, March 1965. Used by permission.

EASTER

❖   At the funeral of a Swiss theologian, his colleagues on the religion faculty served as pall bearers. Each wore a boutonnière; the custom in that community was for each pall bearer to take off his boutonnière and lay it on the ground beside the casket before it was lowered into the grave. The closest friend of the deceased, however, instead took off his boutonnière, crumpled it in his hand, threw it into the grave, and stomped away.

Later, his colleagues asked him the reason for his unorthodox behavior. He explained, "When I realized what death had done to my friend, how death had taken that marvelous mind and caused it to deteriorate, taken that magnificent personality and caused it to shrivel up, I

184

just wanted one defiant act in which I could say, 'Death you are not the final word!'"

That is the message of Easter; death is not the final word. In Christ and His resurrection, life has overcome the power of death.

—*Preaching*, March-April, 1992

❖   At the close of an inspiring Easter morning message, a woman of quiet, steady faith came down the aisle to greet her pastor. Her face carried more than its usual kindly light; in fact, it was radiant as she said, "You have given me new hope today. I have been lame all my life. I shall carry this lameness to the grave, but not beyond that!"

—*Bible Expositor and Illuminator*, September–November, 1973

❖   **POSSIBLE ENTRANCE:** *How do you view Easter? Do you see it as a day you use to attempt to make up and pay for the wrongs you have done? Or do you see it as a day that focuses back on Someone who already paid for your wrongs?*

Hidden deep in Mexico's Sierra Madre Mountains is a tribe of Indians called the Pima. They speak their own language, hunt with machine guns, and live on less than $4 a day. Pima families usually have several children because half of them die before adulthood. Life is hard in their remote part of the world.

Mexicans often make fun of the tribe because of their primitive ways. This makes the Pima angry. Some get drunk, fight, and on occasion, kill. But when their drinking binges are over, the Pimas find themselves flat on their backs, alone—their heads aching and the anger that drove them to drink still there.

Yet as much as the Pima despise their existence, they fear death even more. Why? Because they know they've sinned, and they're not sure if they've been "good enough" to pay for their sins.

To the Pima, Easter is their chance to pay.

—*Breakaway*, April 1996

POSSIBLE EXIT: *Easter does not shout, "You pay for your wrongs!" It exclaims, "Christ has already paid for your wrongs!"*

❖   The return of Easter should be to the Christian life the call of a trumpet. It is the news of a great victory. It is the solution of a great perplexity. It is the assurance of a great triumph.

—Frederick Temple

GIFT

❖ **POSSIBLE ENTRANCE:** *It cost God everything to save you. He had to punish His Son when He should have punished us. But it cost you nothing. It's a gift because He paid the price.*

In the early spring of 1919, a country school near Center, North Dakota, was dismissed early because of a raging blizzard. Hazel Miner, one of the older pupils, started home in a buggy with her two little brothers. In the raging tempest, the buggy turned over and the horse got loose. Hazel wrapped her little brothers in blankets. They got beneath the overturned buggy. As night came on, the blizzard raged. The cold became more intense. The noble girl removed her coat and spread it and herself over the boys. When rescued the next day, the boys were living. The sister had frozen to death.

Now it cost that girl a lot to give her brothers the coat. But all her brothers could do was receive it as a gift.

—Source unknown

POSSIBLE EXIT: *You cannot do anything to get to heaven. The price has already been paid. You must receive eternal life for what it is—a gift from God.*

Note: Illustrations are not divinely inspired and without error. They aren't Scripture. Sometimes you have to change wording. This is as I received it. You could argue the brothers were too cold to know what she was doing and "receive" her gift. So when I use this I explain that to the brothers the coat was a gift, although it cost their sister her life.

❖ I will never forget the first time I saw the Statue of Liberty that adorns the New York harbor. I was awestruck by its appearance and even more by what it represented as it towers 300 feet above the ground Then I was reminded that although the statue was a gift to us, it cost France a lot. Money for the statue was donated by French citizens who wanted to help us celebrate our hundred-year anniversary in 1876.

Although salvation is free to us, it cost God everything. He had to allow His own Son to die in our place, taking the punishment that we deserved.

—R. Larry Moyer

GOSPEL

❖ The gospel is not only the most important message in all of history; it is the only essential message in all of history.

—Jerry Bridges, *The Discipline of Graces*

❖ The gospel is bad news to those who reject it and good news to those who receive it.

—*Our Daily Bread*, 2005

❖ The world has many religions; it has but one gospel.

—George Owen

❖ Tom Landry once said, "The great thing about the gospel is that it is so simple. Anyone can come to the Lord. You don't have to be a Ph.D. to know Jesus Christ."

—Word of Life Annual, 1986

❖ The gospel is amazingly simple and simply amazing.

—Source unknown

❖ Only when I began to realize what my situation was really like did I see the gospel for what it was—extremely good news for people in extremely bad situations.

—Os Guinness, *In Two Minds*

❖ The gospel includes both a welcome and a warning.

—*Our Daily Bread*, 1997

GRACE

❖ Grace is getting what one does not deserve. Once a waiter experienced "grace" after serving a table. The guest's bill came to $10 and he paid his server with a $20 bill. Upon returning with the guest's $10 change, the guest took only $1 for himself and then left a $9 tip. By taking what the waiter "deserved" ($1) and by giving the waiter what he didn't deserve ($9) this generous customer beautifully illustrated "grace."

—Source unknown

Note: When using this illustration, update it with today's standards. For example, use $2 instead of $1.

❖ **POSSIBLE ENTRANCE:** *Most of us remember a spanking. Listen to one man's story that illustrates both the justice and grace of God.*

I vividly remember my last spanking. It was on my thirteenth birthday, as a matter of fact. Having just broken into the sophisticated ranks of the teen world, I thought I was something on a stick. My father wasn't nearly as impressed as I was with my great importance and newfound independence. I was lying on my bed. He was outside the window on a muggy October afternoon in Houston, weeding the garden. He said, "Charles, come out and help me weed the garden." I said something like, "No . . . it's my birthday, remember?" My tone was sassy and my deliberate lack of respect was eloquent. I knew better than to disobey my dad; but, after all, I was the ripe old age of thirteen. He set a new 100-meter record that autumn afternoon. He was in the house and all over me like white on rice, spanking me all the way out to the garden. As I recall, I weeded until the moonlight was shining on the pansies.

That same night he took me out to a surprise dinner. Earlier, he gave me what I deserved. Later he gave me what I did not deserve. The birthday dinner was grace. He condescended in favor upon this rebellious young man. That evening I enjoyed what a proper theologian named Benjamin Warfield called "free sovereign favor to the ill-deserving." I enjoyed grace.

—Charles R. Swindoll, *The Grace Awakening*

POSSIBLE EXIT: *God gives us what we deserve. He sentences us to death and eternal separation from Himself. But then He extends what we do not deserve—forgiveness and eternal life through His Son's death on the cross.*

Note: With an illustration like this you have one of two choices. Either read the story as Dr. Swindoll wrote it or tell it in your own words. Telling it is always better than reading the script, as long as you can do it well.

❖ On the island of Trinidad is famous Pitch Lake—a mineral deposit that is filled with asphalt. Although here and there gas escapes in bubbles from its surface, the substance is hard enough for people to walk on. Workers dig great chunks from the tar-like lake and load train cars full of it to pave the roads of the world.

For more than seventy years, Trinidadians have been taking asphalt out of this crater, yet it never runs empty. It is said that no matter how large a hole is made in this great crater, no cavity will remain after seventy-two hours, for it immediately fills up from below. Workers have drilled as far as 285 feet into the lake and have found that this black, gemlike substance is at least that deep. There seems to be an unlimited supply.

This seemingly endless deposit of pitch can be seen as a picture of God's grace. No matter how great your need, you can't exhaust His love.

—*Our Daily Bread*, 1986

Note: With an illustration such as this, it's important to explain the many good uses tar has and why an unlimited supply is an advantage. Otherwise, the listeners will think about tar as a black, smelly, unattractive mineral instead of the beauty of God's grace.

❖ A church leader died and went directly to the pearly gates. Peter met him and said, "It takes a thousand points to get in. So tell me something about yourself."

"Well," the man said, "until I was twenty-one years old, I never missed Sunday school unless I was sick in bed. I have a string of perfect attendance medals that almost reaches the floor. I was an acolyte, active in the youth group, and I often worked around the church cutting the grass and doing other odd jobs."

"That's extremely good," St. Peter said. "That gives you one point. Tell me something else about yourself."

"Well, I'm seventy years old," he continued. "I attended church regularly, served on the session many times, sang in the choir, and was a speaker on laymen's Sunday one year. I always gave ten percent to the church, and I was a lifelong church member."

"That is truly remarkable," St. Peter replied. "That gives you another point. Tell me something else about yourself."

By this time the man was getting a little desperate, and, if the truth be known, a little irritated. He blurted out to St. Peter, "Look, at this rate the only way I'll ever get into heaven is by the grace of God."

"That's worth a thousand points," answered St. Peter. "And with the two you earned, that makes 1,002. Would you like to come in now?"

—*Focal Point*, Summer 1989

Note: This illustration would be stronger if you deleted the sentence, "And with the two you earned, that makes 1,002." That would enable the listener to know that salvation is *all* by grace, and that human achievement accomplishes *nothing*. Also, the idea of the man talking to St. Peter is heretical, but that is how some non-Christians view what will happen. You could substitute God for St. Peter.

❖ One Saturday morning years ago, I decided to surprise my wife with breakfast in bed. I hurried to a nearby McDonald's and ordered at the drive-thru. When I pulled forward to the pick-up window, I discovered I was about ninety cents short.

Quite embarrassed, I told the lady at the window I had miscalculated and couldn't buy the meal after all. She asked how much I had. When I told her, she smiled and said that would be enough and handed me my order. I told her I'd go home, get the ninety cents, and come right back to pay her, but she told me not to worry about it. I then promised that the next time I came to that McDonald's I would pay the difference. She laughed and told me to just go home, enjoy breakfast, and quit worrying about what I owed. I drove away, grateful for this token of grace.

The next time I drove down that street, looking to grab a fast breakfast, guess where I found myself naturally wanting to go? It was McDonald's—not because I had to or wanted to make up for what I'd done, but simply because I'd received something freely that I in no way deserved, and my heart was unable to remain unaffected by it.

Such is the power of genuine grace in any form.

—Dwight Edwards, *Revolution Within*

Note: Stop and think. Has something similar happened to you that could be used as an illustration of grace?

❖ When God enacts laws, He is on a throne of legislation; when He administers these laws, He is on a throne of government; when He tries His creatures by these laws, He is on a throne of judgment; but when He receives petitions and dispenses favors, He is on a throne of grace.

—C. H. Spurgeon, *Spurgeon's Sermon Notes,*
New Testament

❖ A wealthy English merchant lived on the European continent. He was very eccentric and satisfied with only the best of everything.

So, naturally, he had to drive a Rolls-Royce coupe. It was his pride and joy. But one day, after the car had give years of perfect service, he hit a deep pothole, and the rear axle broke.

This Englishman shipped the car back to the Rolls-Royce plant and was surprised when the car was repaired overnight and returned to him without a bill. Although his warranty had run out, there was no charge. The car was fixed perfectly, all for free.

The owner called the company and inquired about the repair. The reply was, "We have absolutely no record of your Rolls-Royce axle ever breaking. There can be no charge."

The company's commitment to excellence would not permit a flaw to be made known. Therefore, they had repaired the injury immediately and without charge. As if nothing had ever gone wrong.

So it is with God's grace. When we confess our sin, Christ forgives us immediately and without charge. As if nothing had ever gone wrong.

—Steven J. Lawson, *When All Hell Breaks Loose*

❖ **POSSIBLE ENTRANCE:** *You may be asking, "Are my sins too many for God to forgive?" Let me answer that by expressing it the way one man has.*

If man's sin were compared with a thimble, God's grace could be compared with a bottomless ocean.

—Roy B. Zuck

POSSIBLE EXIT: *A thimble gets lost in the ocean. God wants to lose our sins completely.*

❖ **POSSIBLE ENTRANCE:** *We are known for giving favor to those who deserve it—the respectable, law abiding, honest person. God gives His favor to those who not only don't deserve it, but deserve the opposite.*

Let's imagine you have a six-year-old son whom you love dearly. Tragically, one day you discover that your son was horribly murdered. After a lengthy search the investigators of the crime find the killer. You have a choice. If you used every means in your power to kill the murderer for his crime, that would be vengeance. If, however, you're content to sit back and let the legal authorities take over and execute on him what is proper—a fair trial, a plea of guilty, capital punishment—that is justice. But if you should plead for the pardon of the murderer, forgive him completely, invite him into your home, and adopt him as your own son, that is grace.

—Charles R. Swindoll, *The Grace Awakening*

POSSIBLE EXIT: *You will never be able to totally fathom the grace of God. You can only accept it for what it is—favor to those who deserve the opposite.*

❖ What makes Christianity different from all the other religions of the world? Years ago that very question was discussed at a conference. Some of the participants argued that Christianity is unique in teaching that God became man. But someone objected, saying that other religions teach similar doctrines. What about the resurrection? No, it was argued, other faiths believe that the dead rise again. The discussion grew heated.

C. S. Lewis, a strong defender of Christianity, came in late, sat down, and asked, "What's the rumpus about?" When he learned that it was a debate about the uniqueness of Christianity, he immediately commented, "Oh, that's easy. It's grace."

—*Our Daily Bread*, 1997

❖ God's grace is God smiling when there is no reason to smile.

—Charles R. Swindoll

❖ **POSSIBLE ENTRANCE:** *It doesn't matter what sin you have committed or how horrible you feel that sin is, do not look down at yourself for that sin. Instead, I would say what someone else has already said, " . . ."*

There but for the grace of God go I.

—D. L. Moody, *Eternity*

POSSIBLE EXIT: *The same sin you have committed I could just as easily have done.*

❖ World-famous Russian author Aleksandr Solzhenitsyn was sent to a Siberian prison because he criticized Communism. Languishing there under intolerable conditions year after year, he decided to end his life. But suicide, he firmly believed, would be against God's will. He thought it would be better for a guard to shoot him.

So at a public assembly of the prisoners, he sat in a front row, planning to get up and walk toward an exit, compelling a guard to kill him. But to his surprise, another prisoner sat down, blocking his exit. That unknown man leaned over and, to Solzhenitsyn's astonishment, drew a cross on the dirt floor.

The cross! Wondering if that fellow prisoner might be a messenger from God, Solzhenitsyn resolved to endure his imprisonment. There in prison he became a Christian and was eventually set free to bear witness to the world.

Are you in the grip of difficult circumstances? Have you wondered if life is worth living? Focus your heart on the cross—it is the message of God's love, forgiveness, and saving grace for you. Invite the Christ of Calvary with His transforming power into your life. Discover for yourself that the Christ of the cross can change you.

—*Our Daily Bread*, 2005

❖ Behind her were nearly 102 years of life on earth; before her were the endless reaches of eternity. Dena had outlived her peers. I wanted to visit her again, perhaps for the last time. She had been my neighbor when I was a boy. She had known my parents, remembered when I was born, and could tell stories about my family that I was eager to hear. But I was primarily interested in asking Dena one question: "After living more than one hundred years, what is the most important lesson you've learned in life?" So I asked her.

Dena paused, then answered with certainty, "Everything is from the Lord. 'Nothing in my hand I bring, simply to Thy cross I cling.'"

—*Our Daily Bread*, 1993

> Note: Remember, no illustration is perfect. Illustrations must be adapted. This is an effective illustration as you say to people, "If you want to get to heaven, your attitude must be 'Nothing in my hand I bring, simply to the cross I cling.' It's not a matter of what you are offering to Him. It's a matter of what He is freely offering to you."

JESUS CHRIST

❖ Christ is to the godhead what speech is to thought—the expression of it.

—Lewis Sperry Chafer, *Systematic Theology*

❖ **POSSIBLE ENTRANCE:** *Have you ever given serious thought about what it meant for Jesus Christ, who was perfect, to become perfect man so He could die in our place on a cross?*

C. S. Lewis in a radio address brought an interesting interpretation to the meaning of the incarnation: "Lying at your feet is your dog. Imagine, for the moment, that your dog and every dog is in deep distress. Some of us love dogs very much. If it would help all the dogs in the world to become like men, would you be willing to become a dog? Would you put down your human nature, leave your loved ones, your job, hobbies, your art and literature and music, and choose instead of the intimate communion with your beloved, the poor substitute of looking into the beloved's face and wagging your tail, unable to smile or speak? Christ, by becoming man, limited the thing that to him was the most precious thing in the world, his unhampered, unhindered communion with the Father.

—L. D. Weatherhead, *A Plain Man Looks at the Cross*

POSSIBLE EXIT: *If we were honest, we would admit that we would not do for others what Christ did for us. What better way could He have said, "I love you"?*

> Note: This type of illustration becomes more meaningful and interesting if you incorporate a pet dog that you had or have. It's even a place you may be able to incorporate some humor.

❖ If you meet me and forget me you have lost nothing. If you meet Jesus and forget Him you have lost everything.

—Source unknown

❖ If I might comprehend Jesus Christ, I could not believe on Him. He would not be greater than myself. Such is my consciousness of sin and inability that I must have a superhuman Savior.

—Daniel Webster, statesman from New Hampshire

❖ When you know Christ, every day is like living on the edge of a miracle.

—Paraphrased from Gordie Campbell, Elmhurst College

❖ **POSSIBLE ENTRANCE:** *When you know Christ you have all you need. The answer to life is in a Person.*

Art was his life. He had plenty of money and circled the globe to collect the very best. His more than adequate house was filled with Monets, Picassos, and many of the world's finest treasures. But after years of having it all, he found his world shattered when cancer took his wife. To memorialize his love for her, he decided to gather an even better collection in her honor.

The collector's love became focused on his son. They did everything together, and he took pride in all that his son accomplished. It was a sad day when his son went off to fight in the Vietnam war. But not as sad as the day when the news came that his son had been killed in battle. The man was crushed. He lost all interest in collecting. His life was reduced to lonely memories of days gone by with those he loved.

Years later, a knock at his door found him standing face to face with a rather common, slightly tattered person who was holding a picture under his arm. The visitor told the collector that he had been his son's best friend in Vietnam and now made a living as a street painter. He explained that while he was in Vietnam he had painted a picture of his friend and wanted to know if the father might be interested in it. The old man took the picture in his hands and immediately noticed the clear resemblance. The sparkle in his son's eyes brought back a flood of memories. No one would have said that it was great art, but he took the picture tearfully and gratefully. He immediately hung it above the mantel where his favorite picture had hung since before his wife had died.

When the old man passed away, his entire collection went to the most prestigious auction house in London. Needless to say, this created quite a stir among museum curators and wealthy people from around the world. On the day of the auction the room was crowded with the who's who of collecting. The gavel sounded as the hushed crowd that jammed the auction house watched the first picture being unveiled. To everyone's astonishment, it was the picture that the street painter had given to the old collector. The auctioneer waited for a bid. No one moved. He explained that this was a picture of the collector's son who was killed in Vietnam. As the crowd grew restless, the auctioneer explained that the instructions in the will required that this picture be auctioned first.

Finally, to get the bidding started, the auctioneer offered the painting for fifty dollars. Still no one responded—until a voice came from the back of the room from a man who said he was that soldier's friend and, in fact, the painter of the picture. He said he would bid the fifty dollars to get the picture back. The auctioneer called for other bids and, hearing none, gaveled the bids closed as the crowd settled in for the real action.

But to everyone's surprise, the auctioneer gaveled the auction closed. The crowd protested in disbelief. To which the auctioneer replied, "It is the old man's will: 'Whoever takes the son gets it all!'"

We can say the same thing: "Whoever takes the Son gets it all."

—Joseph M. Stowell, *Loving Christ.* Used by permission.

POSSIBLE EXIT: *The answer to life both now and in the hereafter is found in Jesus Christ. When you have Him you have it all!*

❖ It is said that [Hall of Fame baseball player] Ty Cobb was converted late in life and that before he died he said, "I am sorry that I did not receive Christ in the first inning instead of the last."

—Lee Carter Maynard, *Points That Emphasize*

❖ Without Christ we're not ready to die; with Christ we have every reason to live.

—*Our Daily Bread*, 1997

❖ For a long time, I sat in church and never really believed all that I was hearing. Finally, I came to the place where I had to either take Christ completely at His Word or reject Christianity in its entirety. My decision to completely trust Christ, not only for my salvation but with my whole life—friends, studies, dates, money, problems—made a total difference in the type of Christian life that I then began to live. I especially noticed a change in my studies—I had a real purpose in studying and I found that, as I did my part and then just trusted Christ for His peace, I had won the battle. Christ has proven that He is relevant to every area of my life.

—Linda Fulcher, University of Oregon sophomore,
Athletes in Action, Summer 1988

Note: Be careful not to confuse entering the Christian life with living the Christian life. Don't confuse salvation with sanctification. For this reason, when using this illustration in an evangelistic message, I would only use the first two sentences. The remainder talks about her growth as a Christian. Also, who said this is unimportant since no one would know her, and this attitude still is a relevant illustration. It is sufficient to say "An athlete at the University of Oregon once said . . ."

❖   After several years of Communism a man was finally freed: "I had no joy in my freedom. Where could I find peace?"

After learning about Christ at a youth camp he still did not accept Him: "That would mean a rejection of everything I had lived for before."

Then he came under conviction: "For the first time I could see that Christianity involved a Person and not just a philosophy. And I wasn't thinking so much of its power to change the world, but of Christ's power to fill the emptiness in my own life."

He trusted Christ and was called to Christian service as a missionary.

He spent some years in this service: "When I was born again, little did I realize how abundant life in Christ could be."

—*Christian Living*, January 17, 1971

Note: The part of this illustration important in speaking to a lost audience is his conviction: "For the first time I could see that Christianity involved a Person and not just a philosophy."

❖   If you had never known me, you would have missed nothing. If you have never known my Lord, you have missed everything whom to know is life eternal.

—Source unknown

❖   **POSSIBLE ENTRANCE:** *May I ask, "How wealthy are you?" Wealth to God is not a matter of what you have but a matter of Who you know.*

Knowing Christ makes poor men rich. Not knowing Him makes the richest poor.

—*Navigators Book #1* "Life in Christ"

POSSIBLE EXIT: *You don't have anything until you have Christ. Once you have Christ you have everything.*

❖ It would be silly to say that I do not have problems. Everyone does, and I do too, but I have found that if I keep my eyes on Jesus, He gives me the power to walk on top of my problems. He has met my every need. He has never forsaken me. He said, "Lo, I am with you always" [Matt. 28:20], and He has been. He has never disappointed me, and He has given me peace and joy beyond all human understanding.

—Dave Rogan

Note: Who Dave Rogan is, is not important to the illustration. It is effective to say, "One new convert put it this way . . ."

❖ If you have everything but Christ, you have nothing.
If you have nothing but Christ, you have everything.

—Source unknown

The real news came on August 15, 1988, when Jesus Christ made the front cover of *Time* for the sixteenth time. That's got to be a record—especially for an individual who died 1900 years ago!

—Stuart Briscoe, *Mastering Contemporary Preaching*

Note: This illustration produces a powerful idea that the Internet makes it possible to update. As of that date this was the count of how many times Jesus Christ has been on the front page of Time.

❖ Reynolds Price, writing about "Jesus of Nazareth" in *Time* magazine (December 1999), declared that "a serious argument can be made that no one else's life has proved remotely as powerful and enduring as that of Jesus."

—*Our Daily Bread*, 2003

❖ **POSSIBLE ENTRANCE:** *You may not have thought about it, but you live with the reality of Christ every day.*

I read about a man who mentioned something I had not thought enough about. He said that sometimes he encounters people who say they never think about Christ or that Christ has no bearing on their life. He then asks, "When were you born?" When they give the year, he asks, "B.C. or A.D.?"

—R. Larry Moyer

POSSIBLE EXIT: *Since the year of your birth has reference to Christ, you owe it to yourself to find out who this Jesus Christ is.*

❖ His name has not been written into history as much as it has been plowed into history.

—Ralph Waldo Emerson

☺ **POSSIBLE ENTRANCE:** *When you reduce Jesus Christ to a lunatic, be certain you realize what you are saying.*

A man in an insane asylum once said, "I'm Napoleon." Another man said, "Who said?" The man explained, "God did." Another man looked up and said, "I did not."

—Mike Cocoris

POSSIBLE EXIT: *If you reduce Christ to a lunatic, that's the type of man you're saying He was.*

❖ He literally changed the course of human history. Our calendar is divided into B.C., "before Christ," and A.D., from the Latin "Anno Domini," meaning "in the year of our Lord."

—Bill Bright, founder and former president of Campus Crusade for Christ

Note: We currently use what is called a Gregorian calendar, and it is the most widely used in the world. It is a modification of the Julian calendar and eventually came into existence in 1582 after a decree by Pope Gregory XIII.

❖ Kenneth Scott Latourette, former chairman of the Department of Religion at Yale Graduate School, wrote, "That short life of Jesus has been the most influential ever lived. Through Him millions have been transformed and have begun to live the life that He exemplified. Gauged by the consequences that have followed, the birth, life, and death and resurrection of Jesus have been the most important events in the history of man."

—*Our Daily Bread*, 2000

❖ Why is it that you can talk about God and nobody gets upset, but as soon as you mention Jesus, people so often want to stop the conversation?

—Used by permission. Josh McDowell, *More Than a Carpenter*, p. 9, Tyndale House Publishers. www.josh.org

❖ A man by the name of Lamb, considered one of Shakespeare's sharpest interpreters said, "If Shakespeare were to walk into the room, all of us would stand. But if Jesus Christ were to walk into the room, all of us would kneel." Lamb worshipped Christ.

—Haddon Robinson

❖ The simple record of these three short years of active life has done more to regenerate and soften mankind than all the discourses of philosophers and all the exhortation of moralists.

—William Lecky, *historian and skeptic*

❖ Two infidels once sat in a railway car discussing Christ's wonderful life. One of them said, "I think an interesting romance could be written about Him." The other replied, "And you are just the man to write it. Set forth the correct view of His life and character. Tear down the prevailing sentiment as to His drivenness and paint Him as He was—a man among men." The suggestion was acted upon and the romance was written. The man who made the suggestion was Colonel Ingersoll, the author was General Lew Wallace—and the book was *Ben Hur*. In the process of constructing it he found himself facing the unaccountable Man. The more he studied His life and character the more profoundly he was convinced that He was more than a man among men; until at length, like the centurion under the cross, he was constrained to cry, "Verily, this was the Son of God."

—D. J. Burrell

❖ His influence for good has been greater than that of any other person throughout the centuries. The *Encyclopedia Britannica* devotes 20,000 words to Jesus.

—Bill Bright, founder and former president of Campus Crusade for Christ

Note: Remember, illustrations sometimes give you ideas. This should cause a speaker to think, What source do people go to today for information and how many words of that source are devoted to Christ? Here is where the Internet has blessed us. Almost any statistic can be found, making it possible to obtain information about names, people, populations, occupations, and so forth.

❖ A man who was a master climber was asked why he insisted on climbing a large mountain they were looking at. His answer was, "Because it is there." Jesus Christ is there. You must consider Him.

—Haddon Robinson

❖ "A man who can read the New Testament and not see that Christ claims to be more than a man can look all over the sky at high noon on a cloudless day and not see the sun."

—William E. Brederwolf, *The Encyclopedia of Religious Quotations*

❖ Vernon Grounds, former President of Denver Seminary, once said, "If Jesus Christ were insane, would to God all men were insane."

—Haddon Robinson

Note: When I use this quote today, I express the last phrase as "I wish all were insane." That communicates what Vernon Grounds was saying in more relatable language.

❖ Socrates taught for forty years, Plato for fifty, Aristotle for forty, and Jesus for only three. Yet the influence of Christ's three-year ministry infinitely transcends the impact left by the combined 130 years of teaching from these men who were among the greatest philosophers of all antiquity. Jesus painted no pictures; yet some of the finest paintings of Raphael, Michelangelo, and Leonardo da Vinci received their inspiration from Him. Jesus wrote no poetry; but Dante, Milton, and scores of the world's greatest poets were inspired by Him. Jesus composed no music; still Hayden, Handel, Beethoven, Bach, and Mendelssohn reached their highest perfection of melody in the hymns, symphonies, and oratorios they composed in His praise. Every sphere of human greatness has been enriched by this humble carpenter of Nazareth.

—*Our Daily Bread*, 1987

❖ A man who was merely a man and said the sort of things Jesus said wouldn't be a great moral teacher. He'd either be a lunatic—on the level with a man who says he's a poached egg—or else he'd be the Devil of hell.

You must make your choice. Either this man was, and is, the Son of God, or else a madman or something worse.

—C. S. Lewis, *Mere Christianity*

❖ **POSSIBLE ENTRANCE:** *If you consider yourself an atheist, examine this. It takes more faith to believe there is no God than it does to believe in Jesus Christ. A former confessing atheist expressed it this way.*

In light of the convincing facts I had learned during my investigation, in the face of this overwhelming avalanche of evidence in the case for Christ, the great irony was this: it would require much more faith for me to maintain my atheism than to trust in Jesus of Nazareth!

—Lee Strobel, *The Case for Christ*

POSSIBLE EXIT: *Christianity is not based on fiction or feeling; it is based on fact.*

❖ I am a seventeen-year-old student, and I was disappointed by your cover story "Visions of Jesus." It seems that *Newsweek* attempted to find a middle ground in presenting a view of Jesus as a character who could appeal to all people. But that is impossible. Either Jesus was in fact the Son of God, as he claimed, or he was a lunatic. No one who claims to be the Son of God is simply a "good teacher"! Other great religions will never accept Jesus to be who He said He was. If they do, then they are not Jewish, Muslim, or Buddhist. They are Christian.

—Jennifer Rawlings, Gaithersburg, MD, *Time*, April 24, 2000

❖ Jesus was the friend of sinners. He commended a groveling tax collector over a God-fearing Pharisee. The first person to whom he openly revealed himself as Messiah was a Samaritan woman who had a history of five marriages and was currently living with yet another man. With his dying breath he pardoned a thief who would have zero opportunity for spiritual growth.

—Philip Yancey, *The Jesus I Never Knew*

❖ Dr. Erwin W. Lutzer speaks about the uniqueness of Jesus when compared to the leaders of other world religions and political leaders. There is no comparison possible, for Jesus stands alone as God, the Son, who has been raised from the dead and is alive forever more.

Says Lutzer, "During the Russian revolution of nineteen-eighteen, Lenin said that if Communism were implemented there would be bread for every household, yet he never had the nerve to say, 'I am the bread of life. He who comes to Me shall never hunger, and he who believes in Me shall never thirst' (John 6:35).

"Hitler made some astounding claims for the role of Germany on this planet, believing that he was beginning a thousand-year Reich (rule). Despite these outlandish claims he never said, 'He who believes in the Son has eternal life; but he who does not obey the Son shall not see life, but the wrath of God abides on Him' (John 3:36).

"Buddha taught enlightenment; yet he died seeking more light. He never said, 'I am the light of the world; he who follows Me shall not walk in darkness, but shall have the light of life' (John 8:12).

"Mohammed claimed that he and his tribes were descendants from Abraham through Ishmael, another son of Abraham. But he did not say, 'Before Abraham was born, I AM' (John 8:58).

"Freud believed that psychotherapy would heal people's emotional and spiritual pains. But he could not say, 'Peace I leave with you; My peace I give to you; not as the world gives, do I give to you. Let not your heart be troubled, nor let it be fearful' (John 14:27).

"New Age gurus say that all of us will be reincarnated, yet not one of them can say, 'I am the resurrection and the life: he that believeth in Me, though he were dead, yet shall he live. And whosoever liveth and believeth in Me shall never die' (John 11:25)."

—Norman P. Anderson, *So You Want to Go to Heaven?*

Note: Think of your audience. Who are the leaders they would most recognize? Would it be Joseph Smith, founder of Mormonism, instead of Buddha?

❖ "As the centuries pass the evidence is accumulating that, measured by His effect on history, Jesus is the most influential life ever lived on this planet. That influence appears to be mounting."

—Kenneth Scott Latourette

❖ A businessman who scrutinized the Scriptures to verify whether or not Christ claimed to be God said, "For anyone to read the New Testament and not conclude that Jesus claimed to be divine, he would have to be as blind as a man standing outside on a clear day and saying he can't see the sun."

—Used by permission. Josh McDowell, *More Than a Carpenter*, Tyndale House Publishers, p. 14, www.josh.org

❖ Even David Strauss, the bitterest of all opponents of the super-natural elements of the Gospels, whose works did more to destroy faith in Christ than the writings of any other man in modern times—even Strauss, with all his slashing, brilliant, vicious criticisms and his sweeping denials of everything partaking of the miraculous, was forced to confess, toward the end of his life, that in Jesus there is moral perfection. "This Christ . . . is historical, not mythical; is an individual, no mere symbol. . . . He remains the highest model of religion within the reach of our thought; and no perfect piety is possible without His presence in the heart."

—Used by permission. Josh McDowell, *The New Evidence That Demands A Verdict*, p. 321, Thomas Nelson Publishers. www.josh.org

❖ "It is of no use to say that Christ is non-historical." . . . But who among His disciples or among their proselytes was capable of inventing the sayings ascribed to Jesus, or of imaging the life and character revealed in the Gospels?

—Alexander Stewart, *Handbook of Christian Evidences*

❖ Look at Alexander the Great, a truly great military genius; he conquered the world; killed, plundered, conquered. He was so successful that he thought he was a god. In fact, he insisted on his subjects worshiping him. And what happened to him: At the age of thirty-three, he was planning a voyage around Arabia, and he died of a burning fever. Someone once said, "Napoleon bothered God." Maybe Alexander the Great also did when he started to consider himself a god.

How much do we hear about Alexander the Great today? But we do continue to about hear Jesus Christ—every day!

—*Our Daily Bread*, 1993

❖ "You can shut Him up for a fool, you can spit at Him and kill Him as a demon, or you can fall at His feet and call Him Lord and God."

— C. S. Lewis

❖ How petty are the books of the philosophers compared with the Gospels. Can He whose life they tell be more than mere man? If the death of Socrates be that of a sage, the life and death of Jesus are those of a God.

—Jean Jacques Rosseau

❖ **POSSIBLE ENTRANCE:** *Even some of our most well-known leaders of the past were awestruck with Christ and felt that no one compares to Him.*

On the lovely isle of St. Helena the exiled emperor, Napoleon Bonaparte, was once discussing Christ with General Bertrand, a faithful officer who had followed him into banishment and who did not believe in the deity of Jesus. This is what Napoleon said: "Between him and whoever else in the world, there is no possible term of comparison. He is truly a being by Himself. His ideas and sentiments, the truth that He announces, His manner of convincing are not explained either by human organization or by the nature of things. . . . I search in vain in history to find [one] similar to Jesus Christ or anything that can approach the gospel."

—Vernon C. Grounds, *The Reasons for Our Hope*

POSSIBLE EXIT: *If people of that stature were impressed with Him, don't you think you owe it to yourself to find out who Christ is?*

❖ **POSSIBLE ENTRANCE:** *Jesus Christ is called the friend of sinners. People like you and me know they have a friend; He is our friend.*

Many years ago the Prince of Wales visited the capital city of India. A formidable barrier had been set up to keep back the masses of people who wanted to catch a glimpse of royalty. When the prince arrived, he shook hands with some of the political dignitaries who were presented to him. Then, looking over their heads to the crowds beyond he said, "Take down those barriers!" They were quickly removed, and all the people, regardless of social rank, had free access to the heir of the British Empire. Some time later when the prince came to that district again, 10,000 outcasts waited under a banner inscribed with these words: "The Prince of the Outcasts."

—*Our Daily Bread*, 1978

POSSIBLE EXIT: *Think of that. Jesus Christ was a preacher, but He wasn't called the Prince of Preachers. He was called the friend of sinners. He is your friend. Even if you turn you back on Him, He will not turn His back on you.*

❖ When the Prince of Wales visited a city in India many years ago, everyone was occupied with the splendor of his greatness. His name was on every tongue, and he was given great honor. As he was about to return to England, a large crowd including many noblemen came to the railroad station to bid him farewell. From private soldier to mighty merchant, they all fixed their eyes on him as he stood with royal bearing waiting for the approaching train. Suddenly the prince spied a little child on the tracks. Realizing the danger, he instantly rushed forward and picked him up in his arms. When the people saw their royal visitor stoop down to save the youngster, shouts of praise broke forth. He was exalted in their eyes even more than before!

—The Works of Rev. M. L. Fauss

Note: This illustration is similar to the one above yet the circumstances are different. When different messages are given years apart from each other, a different illustration surrounding the same person can be used.

❖ A Chinese scholar who converted to Christ told this parable: "A man fell into a dark, dirty pit, and he tried to climb out but he couldn't. Confucius came along. He saw the man in the pit and said, 'Poor fellow. If he had listened to me, he never would have fallen in,' and he left. Buddha came along and saw the man in the pit and said, 'Poor fellow. If he can climb up here, I'll help him.' And he too left. Then Christ came and said, 'Poor fellow!' And He jumped into the pit and helped him out."

—*Our Daily Bread*, 1999

❖ **POSSIBLE ENTRANCE:** *You may be troubled by the things about God you do not understand. But those things should not depress you, but impress you.*

In a company of literary gentlemen, Daniel Webster was asked if he could comprehend how Jesus Christ could be both God and man. "No, sir," he replied, and added, "I should be ashamed to acknowledge Him as my Savior if I could comprehend Him. If I could comprehend Him, He could be no greater than myself. Such is my sense of sin, and consciousness of my inability to save myself, that I feel I need a superhuman Savior, one so great and glorious that I cannot comprehend Him."

—*Christian Clippings*, August 1989, and Gordon E. Penfold,
Discovering the Lord Leader's Guide

POSSIBLE EXIT: *If Jesus Christ were no bigger than your understanding, He would not be God.*

LOVE
❖ **POSSIBLE ENTRANCE:** *The people we love are often those who measure up to our standards. They look like we think they ought to look, act like we*

think they ought to act, talk like we think they ought to talk. But Jesus Christ was known for such love that in the minds of many, He was always talking to the people He was not supposed to talk to, in the places He was not supposed to be, about the subjects He was not supposed to talk about.

Dr. Clovis Chappel tells the story of a Chicago businessman who many years ago went to Kentucky, met a girl, married her, and brought her back to Chicago. They enjoyed three good years together. Then as a result of stress and depression, she had a mental breakdown and eventually became totally out of touch with reality. Often her screams caused her neighbors to complain. So he moved to the Chicago suburbs to nurse his wife back to health, but she got even worse. Finally, the doctor suggested that he take her back to Kentucky, hoping that something there in that familiar setting would cause her mind to heal. They went there and hand in hand walked through the familiar surroundings, but nothing happened. So they returned to Chicago. When they got close to home, he noticed his wife had fallen asleep, the best sleep she had had in months. When they got home, he gently carried her up the stairs to bed and sat by her during the night. In the morning she awoke, looked around, and saw her husband seated by her side. She looked at him and said, "I seem to have been on a long journey. Tell me, where have *you* been?" He looked at her and gently said, "My sweetheart, I have been right here. Waiting for you all the time."

That's where God is, right here, waiting for you to stop running and come to Him.

—Haddon Robinson

POSSIBLE EXIT: *Jesus Christ was known as a "friend of sinners." You may be running from Him, but He is not running from you.*

❖ Adolf Hitler was obsessed with the eradication of the Jewish race. To be a Jew in Europe in the 1940s was a dangerous condition, because they were hunted relentlessly and sent to concentration camps and gas chambers. Their crime? They were, through no fault of their own, born Jewish. When the Germans took Denmark, Hitler demanded that all the Jewish Danes wear a yellow armband to mark them for the express purpose of deportation to a concentration camp. Legend has it that the king of Denmark, Christian X, was forced to read the decree from the balcony of the Amalienborg Palace. And then, with tears in his eyes, the king proceeded to put a yellow armband on his own arm for all to see. Tradition has it that all the Danish people followed, making it impossible for the German forces to carry out their horrid intentions against the Jews of Denmark.

—Joseph M. Stowell, *Loving Christ.* Used by permission.

❖ Madalyn Murray O'Hair was perhaps the most notorious atheist of the 1900s. Often profane and sarcastic, she was a powerful debater who shouted down her religious opponents.

After O'Hair mysteriously disappeared in 1995, her diaries were auctioned to pay back taxes she owed the federal government. They reveal an unhappy human being who didn't trust even the members of the American Atheists Association. She passed this harsh judgment on herself: "I have failed in marriage, motherhood, and as a politician." Yet she yearned for acceptance and friendship. In her diary she wrote six times, "Somebody, somewhere, love me."

—Our Daily Bread, 2000

LOVE OF GOD

❖ If God had a refrigerator, your picture would be on it.

—Our Daily Bread, 2002

❖ **POSSIBLE ENTRANCE:** *One of the reasons you may be running from God is because you feel He is out to punish you.*

Some time back, newspapers carried the story of a young fellow named William who was a fugitive from the police. The teenager had run away with his girlfriend because the parents had been trying to break them up. What William didn't know was that an ailment he had been seeing the doctor about was diagnosed just after his disappearance. It was cancer.

Here was William, doing his best to elude the police, lest he lose his love, while they were doing their best to find him, lest he lose his life. He thought they were after him to punish him; they were really after him to save him.

—Howard G. Hendricks, Don't Fake It, Say It with Love

POSSIBLE EXIT: *God is not out to punish you. He loves you and wants to pardon you. Don't run from the person who wants to rescue you.*

❖ No individual has any right to come into the world and go out of it without distinct and legitimate reasons for having passed through it.

—George Washington Carver

❖ I was once preaching in St. Louis, and when I got through a man said that he wanted to tell me a story.

There was a boy who was very bad. He had a very bad father, who seemed to take delight in teaching his son everything that was bad. The father died, and the boy went from bad to worse until he was arrested for murder.

When he was on trial, it came out that he had murdered five other people, and from one end of the city to the other a universal cry went up against him. During his trial they had to guard the courthouse, the indignation was so intense. The bereaved mother got just as near her son as she could. As every witness that went into the court spoke against him, it seemed to hurt her more than it hurt her son. And when the jury brought in a verdict of guilty, a great shout went up in the courtroom, but the old mother nearly fainted away. When the judge pronounced the sentence of death they thought she *would* faint away.

When it was over, she threw her arms around her son and kissed him. There in the court they had to tear him from her embrace. She then went the length and breath of the city trying to get permission for his pardon. When he was hanged, she begged the governor to let her have the body of her son that she might bury it.

They say that death has torn down everything in the world, everything but a mother's love. That is stronger than death itself. The governor refused to let her have the body, but she cherished the memory of that boy as long as she lived. A few months later she followed her son in death. When she was dying, she sent word to the governor and begged that her body be laid close to her son's.

That is a mother's love. She wasn't ashamed to have her grave pointed out for all time as the grave of the mother of the most noted criminal the state of Vermont ever had.

—D. L. Moody

Note: The parallel here is "Jesus Christ was not ashamed to associate Himself with you and I as sinners."

❖ The love of God sounds too good to be true, but it is also too great to be missed.

—Max Lucado

❖ He loved us not because we were lovable, but because He is love.

—C. S. Lewis

❖ The love of God is like the Amazon River flowing down to water one daisy.

—F. B. Meyer

❖ It was Abraham Lincoln who said, "God must have loved the common people, since He made so many of them." I would modify that to say, "God must have loved the common people, since He made the way of salvation plain enough to be grasped by all"—yes, even me.

—Our Daily Bread, 1995

❖ Scholar and theologian Dr. Karl Barth had just completed an enviable and extensive trip around the world. He had lectured among the learned, engaged in furious research on several continents, preached in great cathedrals, and witnessed sights that defied description. There had been ample time to walk along the shorelines of several majestic oceans, to meditate in picturesque mountain scenes, to meet with numerous people of bright minds and impressive credentials. It had been the trip of a lifetime, a fitting closure to the man's own achievements and contributions. Upon returning to his homeland, he was asked to state the single most profound thought he had considered during his travels. With a bright smile, the old gentleman responded, "Jesus loves me, this I know; for the Bible tells me so."

—Charles R. Swindoll, *Living on the Ragged Edge*

❖ The true measure of God's love is that He loves us without measure.

—Our Daily Bread, 1975

❖ **POSSIBLE ENTRANCE:** *Years ago a world-renowned person made a very interesting observation.*

The biggest disease this world suffers from is people feeling unloved.

—Princess Diana in *Time*,
September 8, 1997

POSSIBLE EXIT: *If you feel yourself suffering from the absence of love, there is only one remedy. It's not found in a pill or a bottle. It is found in the person of Jesus Christ.*

❖ **POSSIBLE ENTRANCE:** *Most of us would agree with the person who defined love this way.*

Love is not only something you feel. It's something you do.

—David Wilkerson

POSSIBLE EXIT: *God does not say to us, "I feel like I love you." He says, "I know I love you. Here's how I proved it . . ."*

❖ **POSSIBLE ENTRANCE:** *Please understand. God's opinion of you and His love for you is not based on your feeling about Him.*

General Robert E. Lee was asked what he thought of a fellow officer in the Confederate Army who had made some derogatory remarks about him. Lee rated him as being very satisfactory. The person who asked the question seemed perplexed. "General," he said, "I guess you don't know what he's been saying about you."

"I know," answered Lee. "But I was asked my opinion of him, not his opinion of me!"

—Our Daily Bread, 1981

POSSIBLE EXIT: *Why does God love you? Because He loves you. He is not asking you how you feel about Him.*

❖ God's favorite word is—come!

—Robert L. Sterner in Pulpit Helps, August 2000

MERCY

❖ **POSSIBLE ENTRANCE:** *Ask yourself this question: On what basis do I deserve to go to heaven? Unless you understand you don't have any right to go, you don't understand the gospel.*

There is a beautiful story about Thomas Hooker, a respected Puritan preacher and theologian, considered by many in New England to be the father of constitutional liberty. As he lay upon his bed mortally sick in Hartford, Connecticut, the members of his church gathered around his bed and sought to comfort him before he slipped into eternity. "Brother Thomas," they are reported to have said, "yours has been a life of great achievement and piety; now you go to claim your reward." He replied, "I go to claim mercy."

—S. Lewis Johnson Jr.

POSSIBLE EXIT: *Only one thing gets us into heaven—God's mercy.*

☺ **POSSIBLE ENTRANCE:** *If God gave us justice, more of us wouldn't stand a chance. But instead of giving us justice, He extended mercy.*

The story is told of a woman who, after receiving the proofs of her portrait, was angry with the photographer. She stalked back to him and arrived with these angry words: "This picture does not do me justice!" The photographer replied, "Madam, with a face like yours, you don't need justice, you need mercy!"

—R. Larry Moyer

POSSIBLE EXIT: *We can be grateful that God dealt with us in mercy and not justice.*

PROPITIATION

❖ **POSSIBLE ENTRANCE:** *What should the cross and resurrection shout to all of us? It should shout loud and clear, "God is satisfied with His Son's payment for our sins."*

In a certain part of the world when a merchant is selling goods, he does not put a price tag on them. He simply displays his goods on a counter or table. When someone comes along, wishing to buy the item, he begins to lay down money. If the merchant is not satisfied with the price offered, he leaves the money on the table. When enough money is put down to satisfy the merchant, he reaches down and takes it up. When he does, he indicates, "I am satisfied with the payment." When God raised Jesus Christ from the dead, He said to the whole world, "I am satisfied with the payment My Son made for your sins."

—Curtis Hutson, *Salvation Plain and Simple*

POSSIBLE EXIT: *The message behind the cross and resurrection is "You must be satisfied with the thing that satisfied God—His Son's payment for your sins." You must trust Christ and Christ alone to save you.*

❖ The story is told of two boys who were swimming in the lake. One of the boys went out too far, got in trouble, and began to sink. The second boy, seeing his friend in trouble, swam out to save him. He was able to keep the first boy afloat until help arrived, but in the process became exhausted and sank beneath the water. He drowned saving his friend.

Later that day, the parents of the boy who was saved came to the parents of the boy who died saving their son and said, "All we have on us right now is a dollar and eighty-three cents. We know it isn't much, but we hope you'll accept this as our payment to you for the life of our son."

Now if you were the parents who had lost their son, how would you

211

feel? I think you would feel terribly offended and insulted. But this is the way we appear to God when we try to offer Him our acts of human goodness as payment for our own sins. Nothing we can offer God will even begin to make up for what it cost Him to save us. Don't insult God by offering Him your $1.83 when He has given you His precious Son. The cost of our redemption is infinitely high.

—Tony Evans, *Totally Saved*

Note: Remember, illustrations can sometimes serve as a springboard to other ideas. One could take this same point Tony Evans makes and use it in connection with an incident in your community that everyone could relate to.

❖   A man in Henderson, Texas, told of his brother's having polio in 1952. His parents didn't have much money, and it was before the days of medical insurance. After his brother got a brace on his neck, it turned out he also had to have some work done on his teeth. The parents worried about the bill from the orthodontist. It was accumulating all the time. On top of this were all the treatments for polio. The orthodontist found out the parents could not pay his bill because of the treatments for their son's polio. When the parents received the bill they noticed the orthodontist had written "Paid in Full."

—Source unknown

❖   In creation, God shows us His hand; but in redemption, God gives us His heart.

—C. H. Spurgeon, *Spurgeon's Sermon Notes, New Testament*

❖   **POSSIBLE ENTRANCE:** *Why is eternal life a free gift? It is free but not because it did not cost anything. It is free to us because God has already paid the price. It was paid with His Son's blood on the cross. He delivered us, but there was a price for that payment—the death of His own Son.*

When the slave trade was thriving in West Africa, mercenaries would penetrate the interior to capture hundreds of natives. They would then clamp iron collars around their necks to keep them in check until the captives arrived back at the coast for shipment. As they passed through other African villages on their way to the sea, a local chief or king would sometimes recognize a friend or relative. If he were financially able or of a mind to, he could redeem his friend through payment of gold, silver, brass, or money. Out of the practice grew a slang word among the Barnbara tribe of French West Africa that meant "take his head out of the iron collar."

—Source unknown

POSSIBLE EXIT: *We have been redeemed not by silver and gold but by the blood of Christ.*

RESURRECTION

❖ When Nap Clark in Starkville, Mississippi, preached his wife's funeral, they had been married six years. He knew she had cancer when he married her. Following the service, someone said to him, "You must be a great man." He said, "No, I'm not. But I have a great Savior."

—Source unknown

> Note: Don't rely upon non-Christians who are not indwelt by the Spirit to make the proper application. Instead, come out of the illustration saying, "Why could He say that? What did Nap Clark mean by a great Savior? Nap knew he would see her again in the presence of the King. Christ's resurrection guaranteed his wife's resurrection."

❖ Jesus has three basic credentials: (1) the impact of His life, through His miracles and teachings, upon history; (2) fulfilled prophecy in His life; (3) His resurrection. The resurrection of Jesus Christ and Christianity stand or fall together.

—Used by permission. Josh McDowell,
The New Evidence That Demands a Verdict,
Thomas Nelson Publishers, p. 203, www.josh.org

❖ When Christ arose from the dead, He put an exclamation point behind Calvary! If Christ hadn't risen, you are still in your sin.

—R. Larry Moyer

❖ **POSSIBLE ENTRANCE:** *What God did through His Son is illustrated well by something that happened in the California Sierra Mountains years ago.*

Evidence has been found to confirm a survival story that had been doubted for years. In 1957, Lieutenant David Steeves walked out of the California Sierras fifty-four days after his air force trainer jet had disappeared. He related an unbelievable tale of how he had lived in a snowy wilderness after parachuting from his disabled plane. By the time he showed up alive, he had already been declared officially dead by the air force. When further search failed to turn up the wreckage, a hoax was suspected, and Steeves was forced to resign under a cloud of doubt. His original story, however, has now been confirmed. A troop of Boy Scouts found the wreckage of his plane—more than twenty years later.

—*Our Daily Bread*, 1980

POSSIBLE EXIT: *God did not wait twenty-three years. Instead He waited three days. He then took His Son, stood Him before others, and through His Word stands Him before you and says, "Will you believe?"*

❖ **POSSIBLE ENTRANCE:** *Any serious thinker recognizes the fact that in order for Jesus Christ to have supernaturally risen from the grave, He had to be God. Time magazine published an article written by a man named Pinchas Lapide, who, although he does not accept Jesus as the Messiah, thinks it's a possibility that He arose from the grave. Someone responded to his article in a letter to the editor:*

Pinchas Lapide's logic escapes me. He believes it is a possibility that Jesus was resurrected by God. At the same time he does not accept Jesus as the Messiah. But Jesus said that He was the Messiah. Why would God resurrect a liar!

—Eva Zaleckas from Skillman, NJ, *Time*, Letter to the Editor, June 4, 1979

POSSIBLE EXIT: *Stop and think about it. If Jesus Christ was resurrected supernaturally, He must be God.*

Note: You may disagree with this logic and say, "God could resurrect a liar if He wanted to. God can do anything." But don't miss the point that apparently *Time* magazine thought the letter had enough merit to print it.

❖ Konrad Adenauer, former chancellor of West Germany, once told evangelist Billy Graham, "If Jesus Christ is alive, then there is hope for the world. If not, I don't see the slightest glimmer of hope on the horizon." Then he added, "I believe Christ's resurrection to be one of the best-attested facts of history."

—*Our Daily Bread*, 1992

❖ No tabloid will ever print the startling news that the mummified body of Jesus of Nazareth has been discovered in [the Old City of] Jerusalem.

—Peter Marshall

❖ Professor Edwin Selwyn, in his work, *The Approach to Christianity*, said, "The fact that Christ rose from the dead on the third day in full continuity of body and soul, and passed into a mode of new relationships with those who knew Him on earth—that fact seems as secure as historical evidence can make it."

—Bill Bright, *Revolution Now*

❖ Some people on the street were asked by the reporter what epitaph they intended to use on their graves. One lady chose "Here today, here tomorrow," which she says is simple and true.

—Leslie B. Flynn, *What Easter Should Do for You*

❖ A conversation between a Christian missionary and a Muslim illustrates a point. The Muslim wanted to impress the missionary with what he considered to be the superiority of Islam. So he said, "When we go to Mecca, we at least find a coffin, but when you Christians go to Jerusalem, your Mecca, you find nothing but an empty grave." To this the believer replied, "That is just the difference. Mohammed is dead and in his coffin. And all other systems of religion and philosophy are in their coffins. But Christ is risen, and all power in heaven and on earth is given to Him! He is alive forevermore!"

—*Our Daily Bread*, 1985

❖ A world leader once asked Billy Graham, "Do you believe in the resurrection?" He answered, "Yes, and if I didn't I'd have no gospel to preach." The leader answered, "I know of no other hope for mankind."

—Konrad Adenauer, former German Chancellor, to Billy Graham,
taken from "The Peg on Which the Cost of Christianity Hangs" by Ravi Zacharias

❖ **POSSIBLE ENTRANCE:** *Years ago, before there was a cure for diphtheria, it took the lives of many children.*

I read about a family who lost three children to diphtheria in the same week. Only a three-year-old girl escaped the disease. On the following Easter morning, the father, mother, and child attended church. Because the father was the Sunday school superintendent, he led the session when all the classes met together. As he read the Easter message from the Bible, many were weeping, but the father and mother remained calm and serene.

When Sunday school was over a fifteen-year-old boy was walking home with his father. "The superintendent and his wife must really believe the Easter story," said the boy. His father answered, "All Christians do." "Not the way they do!" replied the young man.

—*Our Daily Bread*, 1994

POSSIBLE EXIT: *The resurrection is not just a truth; it is a life-changing truth.*

❖ The resurrection is the Father's "Amen" to the Son's "It is finished."

—*Our Daily Bread*, 1997

❖ POSSIBLE ENTRANCE: *The resurrection is not just an aspect of Christian belief; it is the reason the church of Jesus Christ exists.*

To try to explain [the church] without reference to the resurrection is as hopeless as trying to explain Roman history without reference to Julius Caesar.

—Dr. Daniel Fuller, *Easter Faith and History*

POSSIBLE EXIT: *Without Caesar, there would be no Roman history as we know it. Without the resurrected Christ, there would be no church.*

❖ Some people have not wanted to believe the biblical account of the resurrection, so they offer various theories to explain the empty tomb. One of these is the fraud theory, which claims someone stole the body of Jesus to make it appear that He rose from the dead.

The answer to the fraud theory lies in the fact that Pilate posted Roman guards at the tomb. We read in Matthew 28 that the Jewish leaders bribed these guards to say someone stole the body while they slept. If the guards were asleep, how could they be sure of what happened? An even stronger argument against the fraud theory is the martyrdom suffered by the disciples for their faith in Christ. People do not die for the sake of a fraud.

Another false explanation of the empty tomb is the swoon theory, which claims Jesus never really died. He supposedly lost consciousness on the cross and was put in the tomb. Later He "came to" and escaped.

Answers to the swoon theory are many. The gospel accounts report terrible wounds suffered by Jesus (John 19:30–37). A spear was thrust into his side by a Roman soldier. Also, there is this question: how could a man with nail wounds in his hands and feet and a spear wound in his side move a heavy stone and walk away?

Another false explanation of the empty tomb is the ghost theory, which maintains the disciples imagined they saw Jesus in some kind of vision. This theory holds that the disciples wanted Jesus to be alive so much that they produced a subjective image of Him in their mind's eye.

The disciples, however, were not the "vision-seeing type" and they were certainly not in the "vision-seeing-mood" following the resurrection. They did not expect the resurrection: they scattered in haste and unbelief and hid away in fear of the authorities. Furthermore, when Jesus appeared to the Eleven in the upper room (Luke 24:36–43), He ate with them and invited them to touch Him to find out that He had flesh and bones.

Unbelieving people may argue their pet theories on the resurrection, but the plain statement of facts in the Bible still remains. No one has disproved the biblical account. The only explanation for the empty tomb is the resurrection of the body of the Lord Jesus Christ.

—Fritz Ridenour, *Tell It Like It Is* (Ventura, CA: Regal, 1976). Used by permission.

❖ It may be said that the historical evidence for the resurrection is stronger than for any other miracle anywhere narrated.

—William Lyon Phelps, *Human Nature and the Gospel*

❖ The angel rolled away the stone from Jesus' tomb, not to let the living Lord out, but to let the unconvinced outsiders in.

—Donald Grey Barnhouse

❖ If you think that the resurrection of Christ was a hoax and that someone was just trying to cover up the fact that His body was stolen, do yourself a favor and read *Loving God* by Charles Colson. He explains that twelve of the most powerful men in the United States could not keep the lie together about Watergate for even three weeks. If the resurrection were a lie, no one could have prevented the truth from getting out.

—R. Larry Moyer

❖ Jesus Christ answered His critics at the resurrection. They could no longer say, "If you [are] the Son of God, . . ." (As Satan did in the wilderness and the soldiers did at the cross.) He was who He claimed to be. The resurrection established that as fact!

High atop Mount Coronado overlooking Rio de Janeiro stands a huge statue of Jesus Christ. The stone monument has stood for nearly sixty years, but now it's beginning to crumble. According to *Veja*, a Sao Paulo newsmagazine, "The greatest risk is that a piece of the statue may fall on some tourist. Two million people a year visit Christ the Redeemer."

As Brazilians look for ways to save the statue, perhaps it would be appropriate to point out an important truth about Christ. Even if the statue were to fall, the real Jesus still stands.

—*Our Daily Bread*, 1990

❖ In a joking manner during a discussion on the resurrection of Christ, a Muslim student, studying in Uruguay, said to me, "You poor Christians, you don't know where you're going!" "We go to the tomb of our master and we have his body . . . you go to the tomb of your master and it's . . ."

I noticed his bewilderment and remarked, "Go ahead, say it! It's empty!"

—Used by permission. Josh McDowell, *The Resurrection Factor,*
p. 97, Here's Life Publishers, www.josh.org

❖ **POSSIBLE ENTRANCE:** *The resurrection of Christ is not just good news about Christ; it is great news for all those who know Christ. His victory is also ours.*

British writer Guy King told of standing on a railroad station platform, waiting for a train from London. Another train pulled into the station from the opposite direction, and the members of a soccer team got out. The players were returning from a game in another city. News had not reached home as to the outcome of the game, so those awaiting the team didn't know if they had won or lost. A small boy wiggled his way through the crowd and asked one of the players the score. As soon as he heard it, he ran excitedly up and down the platform shouting, "We won! We won!" That youngster was brimming with joy because he identified himself with the players. In one sense, their victory was his victory.

—*Our Daily Bread*, 1987

POSSIBLE EXIT: *The resurrection of Christ allows everyone who knows Him to be excited.*

❖ Surprisingly, I couldn't refute Christianity because I couldn't explain away one crucial event in history—the resurrection of Jesus Christ.

—Used by permission. Josh McDowell, *The Resurrection Factor*, p. 8,
Here's Life Publishers, www.josh.org

❖ A British agnostic laid out the challenge a few years ago when he said,

"Let's not discuss the other miracles. Let's discuss the resurrection. If the resurrection is true the other miracles are easily explained. If the resurrection is not true, the other miracles do not matter."

—Haddon Robinson

❖ Oxford University was well acquainted with evaluating evidence to determine historical fact. After carefully sifting the historical evidence for the resurrection of Christ, this great scholar said, "I have been used for many years to study the histories of other times, and to examine and weigh the evidence of those who have written about them, and I know of no one fact in the history of mankind which is proven by better and fuller evidence of every sort, to the understanding of a fair inquirer, than the great sign which God has given us that Christ died and rose again from the dead."

John Copley, a professor at Cambridge University, who rose to the highest office in the judgeship in England and was recognized as one of the greatest legal minds in British history, has said, "I know pretty well what evidence is, and I tell you, such evidence as that for the resurrection has never been broken down yet."

Lord Darling, who was another chief justice of England, said, "No intelligent jury in the world could fail to bring a verdict that the resurrection story is true."

I have a friend who graduated first in his university class, a brilliant thinker. Somebody once asked him why he embraced Christianity. My friend replied, "For the simple reason that I cannot refute the resurrection."

I wish everyone would try to refute the resurrection of Christ because that would mean that each would conduct his own investigation. I think of some skeptics in history who started out to disprove the resurrection but when confronted with the evidence came to faith in Christ.

One was Professor Simon Greenleaf. He was professor of law and head of the law department at Harvard University, one of the finest universities in the United States. He had written a book, *The Principles of Legal Evidence*, and three of his students challenged Professor Greenleaf to take his book and apply it to the resurrection of Christ and investigate the reliability of the evidence of Jesus rising from the dead. Professor Greenleaf accepted their challenge. After his study he said, "There's no better documented historical evidence than that for the resurrection of Christ." And he added, "I am convinced that you can convince any jury in England or America that Christ rose from the dead."

I think of two others who were professors at Oxford University. One was Lord Lyttleton and the other was Dr. Gilbert West. They wanted to destroy the "myth" of Christianity. They knew that they must disprove first the resurrection of Christ and, second, the changed lives of the disciples. Dr. West intended to show the fallacy of the resurrection, and Lord Lyttleton was to explain away the radical conversion of Saul of Tarsus, who had tried to destroy first-century Christians. One year later both men had become Christians. In the book that they wrote about their investigation of the evidence for the resurrection, they stated, "Reject not until you have investigated."

—John Maisel, *Is Jesus God?* Used by permission.

❖ The resurrection could not have been maintained in Jerusalem for a single day, for a single hour, if the emptiness of the tomb had not been established as a fact for all concerned.

— Paul Althaus, *Die Wahrheit des kirchlichen Osterglaubens*

❖ Mentioned no less than 108 times, the resurrection of Christ is the crowning miracle of the New Testament.

—Source unknown

❖ Dr. William Ryan Phelps of Yale University has always said, "The test question for the life of Christ is the resurrection."

—John Maisel, *Is Jesus God?* Used by permission.

❖ Historian Philip Schaff, who wrote *The History of the Christian Church*, said, "The definitive test question to Christianity is the resurrection. It is either the greatest miracle or the greatest delusion which history records."

—John Maisel, *Is Jesus God?* Used by permission.

Note: Observe that the above two illustrations come from the same source. Reading is your biggest source of illustrations, and books or articles can render multiple illustrations.

❖ A little boy stood at a show window of a large department store looking at a famous painting of Jesus, which was on display. As the little boy was gazing intently upon the picture, which was familiar to him as he had seen it many times in his Sunday school material, a man came up and stood beside him. That man too began to look at the picture. Noticing him, the little fellow opened up the conversation by saying, "That's Jesus, who came into the world a long time ago to die for us." The man merely said, "Is that so?" That was all that was needed to start the little fellow off on the entire story. He began to tell the familiar story of Jesus' birth. He told about the manger, the shepherds, the wise men, the star, and the angels, then the little fellow told about the trip into Egypt to escape Herod. He omitted none of the details. Then he launched into a description of the ministry of Jesus, which included His parables and miracles. He concluded the narrative by telling of the Lord's arrest, of the unfair trial, and of the crucifixion. The little boy had been well taught in Sunday school and had given accurately all the story up to that point. After describing the death and burial of Jesus he ceased, and both the man and boy stood gazing in silence at the picture. The man turned and walked away thoughtfully. After he had gone a little distance he heard the cry of the little boy behind him. "Hey, mister, wait a minute!" The man stopped as the little fellow came running up breathlessly and exclaimed. "Hey mister! I forgot the most important part about the story of Jesus. He rose from the dead!"

—J. Vernon McGee, *The Empty Tomb, Proof of Life After Death*

❖ Talleyrand, that statesman of France who had been a bishop as a churchman but had denied it all . . . , was a man of intelligence. One day a French philosopher who tried to start a new religion came to him for advice. "My religion is going slow. What am I to do?" Talleyrand replied, "It is a difficult thing to start a new religion. So difficult that I hardly know what to advise. Still, there is one thing that will insure success. Get yourself crucified and rise again on the third day."

—J. Vernon McGee, *The Empty Tomb, Proof of Life After Death*

❖ **POSSIBLE ENTRANCE:** *If there would have been no resurrection, I would not be standing in front of you today. There would be nothing good to tell you. All the news I'd have for you would be of defeat, not victory.*

When I was in my late twenties, I went to Winchester, England, famous for its college and its cathedral. The keeper of the cathedral used to show people around the cathedral. He had been there for many, many years, and he loved to tell the story of how the news of the Battle of Waterloo came to England. There were no telegrams in those days, but everyone knew that Wellington was facing Napoleon in a great battle. A sailing ship sent news to the signalman on top of Winchester Cathedral. He signaled to another man on a hill, and thus news of the battle was relayed by hand semaphore, from station to station to London and all across England. When the ship came in, the signalman on board semaphored the first word—"Wellington." The next word was "defeated," and then the fog came down and the ship could not be seen. "Wellington defeated" went across England, and there was great gloom all over the countryside. After two or three hours the fog lifted and the signal came through "Wellington defeated the enemy." Then all England rejoiced.

There was that day when they put the body of Christ in the tomb. Men might have said, "Everything is ended. All is gone, sin has conquered, man is defeated, wrong has triumphed." But then three days later the fog lifted, Christ rose from the dead, the enemy was defeated.

—Donald Grey Barnhouse

POSSIBLE EXIT: *The news is not "Christ defeated." The news is "Christ defeated the enemy."*

❖   Thomas Arnold, long-time headmaster of Rugby, author of a famous three-volume history of Rome, and appointed to the Chair of Modern History of Oxford, found the evidence highly impressive. "I have been used for many years to study the histories of other times and to examine and weigh the evidence of those who have written about them, and I know of no one fact in the history of mankind which is proved by better and fuller evidence of every sort to the understanding of a fair inquirer than that Christ died and rose again from the dead.

—Haddon Robinson

☺   A minister in Darby, Pennsylvania, tells this one: The four-year-old son of an undertaker was puzzled one Easter morning when he heard about the resurrection. "Do you mean," he asked, "that Jesus really rose up from the dead?" "Oh, yes," the teacher said. The boy shook his head. "I know my daddy didn't take care of him after he died," the boy said. "His never get up again!"

—quoted in *Faith, Hope, and Hilarity: The Child's Eye View of Religion* by Dick Van Dyke

❖   Professor J. N. D. Anderson writes of the testimony of the appearances [of Jesus]: The most drastic way of dismissing the evidence would be to say that these stories were mere fabrications, that they were pure lies. But so far as I know, not a single critic today would take such an attitude. In fact, it would really be an impossible position. Think of the number of witnesses, men and women who gave the world the highest ethical teaching it has ever known, and who even on the testimony of their enemies lived it out in their lives. Think of the physiological absurdity of picturing a little band of defeated cowards cowering in an upper room one day and a few days later transformed into a company that no persecution could silence—and then attempting to attribute this dramatic change to nothing more convincing than a miserable fabrication they were trying to foist upon the world. That simply wouldn't make sense.

—James A. Scudder, *Your Secret to Spiritual Success*

❖ Alger Hiss, a State Department employee, was convicted of Communistic connections on the sole testimony of one, Whitaker Chambers. The defendant was charged with conveying secret documents to a foreign power. If true, this was an act of betrayal of country that was despicable. Therefore, the evidence was considered carefully and seriously. The defense sought to discredit the witness whose testimony was the basis of decision. The court was convinced that the witness was reliable and gave credence to his story when the facts appeared to corroborate his statements.

—J. Vernon McGee, *The Empty Tomb, Proof of Life After Death*

Note: The smoother the transition, the more meaningful it will be. Here, a smooth transition would be, "The witnesses to the resurrection must be deemed reliable when the facts behind the empty tomb corroborate their statements."

❖ The evidence points unmistakably to the fact that on the third day Jesus rose. This was the conclusion to which a former Chief Justice of England, Lord Darling, came. At a private dinner party the talk turned to the truth of Christianity, and particularly to a certain book dealing with the resurrection. Placing his fingertips together, assuming a judicial attitude, and speaking with a quiet emphasis that was extraordinarily impressive, he said, "We, as Christians, are asked to take a very great deal on trust; the teachings, for example, and the miracles of Jesus. If we had to take all on trust, I, for one, should be skeptical. The crux of the problem of whether Jesus was, or was not, what He proclaimed Himself to be, must surely depend upon the truth or otherwise of the resurrection. On that greatest point we are not merely asked to have faith. In its favor as living truth there exists such overwhelming evidence, positive and negative, factual and circumstantial, that no intelligent jury in the world could fail to bring in a verdict that the resurrection story is true."

—Used by permission. Josh McDowell, *The New Evidence That Demands a Verdict*, p. 219, Thomas Nelson Publishers, www.josh.org.

❖ **POSSIBLE ENTRANCE:** *Do you know what makes the resurrection of Christ exciting? For those who know Him, you will carry your infirmities to* *the grave but not beyond it. Joni Eareckson Tada was paralyzed in a diving accident at age seventeen.*

In an article she told about saying to her assistant one day, "File this, Francie, and make copies of this letter, would you? And, oh, yes, would you please pull out the sofa bed one more time?" Her paralysis blocks her body from feeling pain, and the only way she knows something is wrong is when her temperature and blood pressure begin to rise. She intuitively senses something is wrong. Oftentimes it's because she has unknowingly punctured her body or has rubbed against something and suffered a bruise or laceration. Sometimes she has to ask her assistant to undress her and examine her body to see what's wrong.

In the article Joni said she was in the midst of one of these episodes—they happen three or four times a month—and looked up to the ceiling and said aloud, "I want to quit this. Where do I go to resign from this stupid paralysis?"

As Francie was leaving the office that day she ducked out the door, then stuck her head back in and said, "I bet you can't wait for the resurrection."

Joni wrote, "My eyes dampened again, but this time they were tears of relief and hope. I squeezed back my tears and dreamed what I've dreamed of a thousand times—the promise of the resurrection. A flood of other hopeful promises filled my mind. When we see him we shall be like him. . . . The perishable shall put on the imperishable. . . . The corruptible, that which is incorruptible. . . . That which is sown in weakness will be raised in power. . . . He has given us an inheritance that can never perish, spoil, or fade. I opened my eyes and said out loud with a smile, 'Come quickly, Lord Jesus.'"

—David Jeremiah, *The Things That Matter*

POSSIBLE EXIT: *Christ's resurrection guarantees that for those who have trusted Christ, your infirmities are only temporary. One day you will not only be alive; you will be alive and completely healthy.*

☺ A man goes on vacation to the Holy Land with his wife and mother-in-law. Halfway through their trip, the mother-in-law dies. So the man goes to an undertaker, who explains that they can ship the body home, but it'll cost $5,000. Or they can bury her in the Holy Land for $150.

The son-in-law decides to ship her home.

"Are you sure?" asks the undertaker. "That's an awfully big expense. And I can assure you we do a very nice burial here."

The son-in-law explained, "Two thousand years ago they buried a person here, and three days later he rose from the dead. I just can't take that chance."

—Internet humor

❖ What does everyone ask for to confirm anything? One word says it all: evidence. We want fingerprints, blood samples, DNA, eyewitnesses, or anything else that will answer our questions about what happened. The resurrection is not without major evidence. One piece of evidence is a major prophecy of the Old Testament, which aligns perfectly with Christ and rules out any impostors. All one needs is the objectivity and integrity to examine the evidence and let it speak for itself.

—R. Larry Moyer

❖ Philip Schaff, in his *History of the Christian Church*, makes this statement: "The Christian church rests on the resurrection of its founder. Without this fact the church could never have been born, or if born, it would soon have died a natural death. The miracle of the resurrection and the existence of Christianity are so closely connected that they must stand or fall together."

—J. Vernon McGee, *The Empty Tomb,*
Proof of Life After Death

❖ We have an answer from heaven. Along with those visiting Lenin's tomb in the Red Square before those Kremlin walls, I lined up and finally made my way to the tomb. On the right side, on the lower side, and on the left side, you look into the dead and silent face of Nicholi Lenin. He died in 1924 at the age of fifty-four. His death came as a shock to the Communist world. When he died, the Grand Presidium of the Supreme Soviet of Russia gave the announcement to the world, and I quote it verbatim. The Grand Presidium said, "No man has ever wrought as Lenin. He was the greatest teacher of all time. He was the greatest leader among men. He was the author of a new social order. He was the savior of the world." But he is dead! As I walked on this side and that side and the other side, I turned over in my mind that pronouncement of the Supreme Soviet, "He was the greatest teacher, the greatest leader, the author of a new social order. He was the savior of the world." But he is dead. Look at him. He is still and silent in death. Unknown to the Grand Presidium, unknown to the Supreme Soviet that sits in the Kremlin, they spelled their ultimate defeat in the very tense of the word that they used. "He WAS the greatest teacher." But he is dead. "He WAS the greatest leader." Dead. "He WAS the author of a new social order." Dead. "He WAS the savior of the world." He is dead. Look at him.

But with what glory and with what triumph does the Christian stand in this dark world, raise his voice, and lift his face toward heaven and say, "Christ is alive!" He was raised from the dead! There is no tomb before any wall that you can visit and say, "There Christ is buried." Why not? Because He is alive and He reigns in heaven, and someday He shall reign in earth. He is, He is, He is! He IS the greatest teacher of all time. He IS the greatest leader among men. He IS the author of a new social order. He IS the Savior of the world. He IS our coming, reigning King.

—W. A. Criswell

Note: As a historical illustration, this one is powerful. Lenin was the man who turned Russia into a Communist country. Here, all you need to do is use the words the Grand Presidium used in announcing Lenin's death to the world, "He was the . . . , he was the . . . , he was the . . . , he was the . . . ," then use the illustration the same way W. A. Criswell did to say, "But that's the problem, He was the . . . , He was the . . . , He was the . . . , He was the . . . , Christ is the . . . , and He still is today, He is . . . , and He still is today." Review all four with the conclusion, "He still is today."

❖ I agonized and wept with a friend of mine who very suddenly lost his wife. Humanly speaking, her death could have been prevented. Medical personnel never warned her of the side effects of an infection-preventing drug and the need to discontinue taking it if she experienced those side effects. My friends words, however, were, "Jesus was raised. Jesus is alive. And so is my wife."

—R. Larry Moyer

Note: In using a story like this one, you have to read it and not tell it in order to get the full force of Habermas's comments. However, think of non-Christians. Remove any parts of the story that are unnecessary to keep the reading as short as possible. Also remove parts they could not identify with. For example, in this story, the fourth and sixth paragraphs could be removed, and it would make the story stronger.

❖ What can bring a child of the scientific age to accept the historicity of the resurrection? To begin with, he might examine the evidence. Ambrose Flemming, winner of the Faraday Medal and former professor at the University of London, suggested this when he wrote, "Study at your leisure the records in the four gospels of these events and you will see nothing in the certainly ascertained facts or principles of science that forbids belief in this miracle. If that study is pursued with what eminent lawyers have called 'willing mind,' it will engender deep assurance that the Christian church is not founded on fiction . . . but on historical and actual events."

—Haddon Robinson

❖ Dr. Carl F. Henry, one of America's leading contemporary theologians, said of Jesus, "He planted the only durable rumor of hope amid the widespread despair of a hopeless world."

—Source unknown

❖ **POSSIBLE ENTRANCE:** *You might be wondering why the resurrection is so important. Here's the way one person expressed it.*

Theologian Gerald O'Collins put it this way: "In a profound sense, Christianity without the resurrection is not simply Christianity without its final chapter. It is not Christianity at all."

—Lee Strobel, *The Case for Christ*

POSSIBLE EXIT: *If there was no resurrection, I would not be speaking to you today. I'd have nothing to tell you.*

❖ Everyone knows that there are only two inevitabilities in life: death and taxes. The supreme question today, it seems, is not so much what you believe about Easter, but whether or not you have filed your income tax return. At least that is what many think. And so in this week before the IRS filing deadline, it is surely appropriate to consider the more inevitable of those two—not taxes, but death. For resurrection had no meaning if you do not view it against the background of death.

—Ray Stedman, sermon on John 11:25–26, "The Answer to Death"

Note: There is no need to quote Ray Stedman. Use his thought to provide your own thinking particularly when Easter falls just before income tax filing deadline.

❖ John G. Paton, a nineteenth-century missionary to the South Seas, met opposition while leaving his home in Scotland and going to preach to the cannibalistic peoples of the New Hebrides Island. A well-meaning church member moaned to him, "The cannibals, the cannibals! You will be eaten by the cannibals!" Without hesitation, he replied, "I confess to you that if I can live and die serving my Lord Jesus Christ, it makes no difference to me

whether I am eaten by cannibals or by worms; for in that great day of resurrection, my body will rise as fair as yours in the likeness of our risen Redeemer!"
—Michael P. Andrus, First Evangelical Free Church of St. Louis County, Missouri

❖ The resurrection of Jesus Christ is absolutely the best attested fact in ancient history.
—Howard Bushnell in H. A. Ironside's *1 Corinthians*

❖ POSSIBLE ENTRANCE: *What is the best evidence you can have in court? It's an eyewitness. There were many eyewitnesses to the resurrected Christ. Here is one statement.*

If I brought the evidence for the resurrection into court, Jesus Christ would be found guilty of having risen from the dead.
—J. N. D. Anderson

POSSIBLE EXIT: *A person can look at the evidence and say, "I trust Christ." Or "I reject Christ." That person cannot honestly and objectively say, "It never happened."*

❖ It would be terrible to wake up on Sunday morning and not be able to shout, "He is risen," but it would be more terrible to get up and not want to.
—Source unknown

❖ Ten of the followers of Jesus died violent deaths rather than deny what they had witnessed.
—Haddon Robinson

❖ The resurrection of Jesus Christ is a subject of momentous impact. It is either the grandest event since time was or the greatest deception ever foisted on a credulous world. Even Strauss, an opponent of the faith, recognized its significance and spoke of it as a "burning question."
—R. D. Johnston, *Resurrection: Myth or Miracle?*

Note: Illustrations are sometimes more helpful for information's sake or to help state something in different words than they are for illustrative value. This is one example.

❖ It was Dr. Howard Kelly of Johns Hopkins University who said, "What does the resurrection mean to me? A clear hope vested in my risen Savior, which I could not have, had Christ never risen from the dead."
—J. Vernon McGee, *The Empty Tomb, Proof of Life After Death*, Gospel Light, 1968

❖ I readily believe those witnesses who get their throats cut.
—Blaise Pascal quoted by J. Vernon McGee in *The Empty Tomb*

❖ Ten Reasons to Believe Jesus Rose from the Dead

1. A public execution assured His death. As Jesus stood before Pilate, religious leaders accused Him of claiming to be king. The crowd demanded His death. On a hill outside Jerusalem, he was crucified between two criminals (Matt. 27:32–50).
2. A high official secured the gravesite. Because Jesus had predicted He would rise in three days, Pilate ordered the official seal of Rome to be put on the tomb. To enforce the order, Roman soldiers stood guard (Matt. 27:62–66).
3. In spite of the guards, the grave was found empty. On the morning after the Sabbath, the huge stone across the entrance to the tomb had been moved, and Jesus' body was gone (Matt. 28:5–10).
4. Many people claimed to have seen Him alive. The apostle Paul wrote that the resurrected Christ had been seen by Peter, the twelve apostles, more than five hundred people, James, and Paul himself (1 Cor. 15:5–8).
5. His apostles were dramatically changed. When Jesus was arrested, the apostles ran for their lives. But they went through a dramatic change. Within a few weeks, they were standing boldly before the ones who had crucified their leader (Acts 4:1–12).
6. Witnesses were willing to die for their claims. Few would die for what they know to be a lie. Jesus' disciples died for their claims to have seen Him alive and well during the forty days following His resurrection.
7. Jewish believers changed their day of worship. The Sabbath day of rest and worship had been basic to the Jewish way of life. Yet Jewish followers of Christ began worshiping with Gentile believers on the first day of the week, the day He rose from the dead (1 Cor. 16:2).
8. Although Jesus' resurrection was not expected, it had been predicted. The disciples expected Jesus to restore the kingdom to Israel. Their minds were so fixed on the coming of a messianic political

kingdom that they didn't anticipate His establishment of a spiritual kingdom through His death (Isa. 53:10).

9. Christ's resurrection was a fitting climax to a miraculous life. It's appropriate that a life characterized by miracles would conclude with the miracle of resurrection (John 21:25).

10. It fits the experience of those who trust Him. The same Spirit who raised Jesus from the dead also gives new life to us (Rom. 8:11).

—*Campus Journal*, Radio Bible Class, April 1994

❖ Hopelessness means being on the wrong side of Easter.

—Harold E. Kohn, quoted in *Christian Clippings*, February 1988

❖ The blood of Christ is the price of redemption. The resurrection is the proof of it.

—Source unknown

❖ **POSSIBLE ENTRANCE:** *If you were to attempt to destroy Christianity, where would you start? Billy Graham, as one of the most respected preachers in America, said,*

If I were an enemy of Christianity, I'd aim right at the resurrection, because that's the heart of Christianity.

—Billy Graham in *Time*, April 10, 1995

POSSIBLE EXIT: *Do you know what's interesting? No one has ever been able to disprove the resurrection.*

❖ C. S. Lewis [was] a literary genius, a scholar in Medieval and Renaissance literature and a former professor at Cambridge University in England. He had a very strong bias against Christianity and believed Christians to be totally wrong. After evaluating the evidence for Christianity, his knowledge of literary criticism forced him to treat the gospel record as a trustworthy account. He called himself "the most dejected and reluctant convert in all England."

—David Bishop, *Christian Truth and Its Defense for U.S. Marines*, 1997

SUBSTITUTION

❖ While walking in the field one day with my two young sons, a bee from one of my hives made a beeline for the elder boy and stung him just above the eye. He quickly brushed it away and threw himself in the grass, kicking and screaming for help. The bee went straight for the younger son and began buzzing around his head. The next thing I knew he too was lying in the grass, yelling at the top of his lungs. But I picked him up and told him to stop crying. "That bee is harmless," I assured him. "It can't hurt you. It has lost its sting." I took the frightened lad over to his elder brother, showed him the little black stinger in his brow, and said, "The bee can still scare you, but it is powerless to hurt you. Your brother took the sting away by being stung."

—*Our Daily Bread*, 1981

❖ **POSSIBLE ENTRANCE:** *A tragedy that received both national and international attention in 1982 illustrates graphically what it means for a person to lay down his life for another.*

Reader's Digest in its September 1982 issue told about Air Florida Flight 90 that left Washington's National Airport at 3:37 PM on January 13, 1982. It was an icy afternoon as the Boeing 737 cleared for takeoff. Sixteenth in line, the plane began to form ice on its wings. As it took off it cleared two of the bridges across the Potomac and then slammed into the 14th Street bridge. A U.S. Park Police helicopter coming to the rescue saw a balding man with a gray mustache and sideburns. As they extended a lifeline to him, instead of wrapping it around himself, he passed it to a flight attendant. She wrapped it around her arms and was carried to shore. Once again, they returned to the balding man who must have known his time was limited. Once more, instead of wrapping it around himself, he passed it along to another person. Nearly a half hour later, ten minutes after the helicopter's first trip, they returned again to the balding man, but he was gone. When an officer told his wife about it, he said, "He could have gone on the first trip, but he put everyone else ahead of himself. Everyone."

—R. Larry Moyer

POSSIBLE EXIT: *Notice that last word, "everyone." That is literally what Christ did. He died not just for my sins or your sins. He died for the sins of everyone.*

Note: Substitution illustrations all illustrate the same thing—one person dying for another. But they can be approached from different angles depending on the circumstances and quotes within the illustrations.

❖ The Son of God became the Son of Man that He might change the sons of men into sons of God. We are saved by Christ's dying, not by our doing!

—Source unknown

231

❖ **POSSIBLE ENTRANCE:** *Jesus Christ knew we could not save ourselves. Only He could save us. But to do so, He had to die in our place.*

On July 17, 1987, in South Central Texas, during a severe flood, a tidal wave of water overflowed the banks of the Guadalupe River. After a week of sports and fun, three hundred young people, who had been camping along the river, were preparing to go home. A portion of young people were caught by the rising river. The river quickly rose to waist level and knocked them off their feet. Boys carried girls to the trunks of trees and the lower branches of pecan and cypress trees. One boy, hampered by a leg cast, was carried on the back of a friend. Ten young people died. The boy with the leg cast was saved, but the friend who carried him on his back was never seen again. He died in his friend's place.

—R. Larry Moyer

POSSIBLE EXIT: *Had Christ not saved us, we would be facing not just physical death but eternal death in hell. He knew we could not save ourselves. He saved us by dying as our substitute, taking the punishment that we deserve for our sins, and dying in our place.*

❖ The September 1974 issue of *Reader's Digest* told about a bank building on February 1, 1974 in San Pablo, Brazil, that burned all the way to the ground. Six air conditioning units on the twelfth floor had not been wired properly. There were 600 employees in the building at the time, 188 died. One-fourth died when they jumped and fell to their death. One-third died when they went to the top of the building to escape the flames and instead were captured by them. But the reason even more people did not die was because of a twenty-seven-year-old elevator operator who kept going up and down the building, bringing as many as twenty-five to safety every time. She went up to get a fourth load when all of a sudden the power shut off. Hours later, they found her body near the open door of the elevator. She had died in their place.

—R. Larry Moyer

Note: These historical illustrations never lose their value. They are based on verified facts. Illustration like these are particularly pertinent because this type of incident could have occurred today in any major city of the world.

❖ *Reader's Digest* in October of 1979 told about a sailing ship that left a San Diego harbor on July 2, 1978. On that sailing ship was an eighteen-year-old boy and his thirty-eight-year-old uncle. The uncle, who had studied the ways of seamanship, decided to make the 3,000-mile journey and invited his nephew to join him. Ten days later, they found themselves right smack in the middle of Hurricane Fico. During the eye of the storm, they were able to inflate the life raft and floated for four days. Then the raft began losing air. The boy asked, "What can we do?" The uncle responded, "You can't do anything. But I can just get in the water and swim out of sight." He explained to his nephew that with the two remaining water cans at his feet, he could probably last three to four days, and by that time hopefully somebody would find him. What scared the nephew was that he knew his uncle was a man of his word, and he said, "If we have to die, we'll do it together." The uncle insisted, "The only good I can do now in this world is to give you a few more days." The uncle spent the entire morning writing a farewell message on an empty water can. He then handed his wedding ring to his nephew and said, "Will you give this to my son when he's old enough to understand? And try to tell both of my children a little bit about me." With that, he slipped into the water, swam away, and drowned. Two days later, the crew of a tug boat found the nephew and rescued him. His uncle saved him by dying in his place.

—R. Larry Moyer

❖ The January 1976 issue of *Reader's Digest* had an article titled "White Out on Mt. Rainier." It told about a father, his twelve-year-old girl and eleven-year-old boy, who hiked up Mt. Rainier in Washington on Memorial Day weekend in 1968. After starting out on Friday morning, a blizzard struck and the temperature dropped to 22 degrees. The wind was blowing at 60 miles per hour. The three of them tramped around a circle making a depression in the snow, then spread a tarp over the trench. The father helped his son and daughter into their sleeping bags and then placed himself near the opening in case the wind blew the tarp off the trench. On Sunday, at 5:50 AM a search party found the trio; the two children were alive, the father was dead. The girl's reply was, "Dad gave his life for us."

—R. Larry Moyer

Note: I love those illustrations where someone in the story states it for us. The girl's comment, "Dad gave his life for us," provides such a smooth transition into "Christ gave His life for us."

❖ A farmer in North Carolina once drove with two high-mettled horses into town. Stopping in front of one of the stores, he was about to enter when his horses took fright. He sprang in front of them and seized the reins. Maddened by strange noises, the horses dashed down the street, the man still clinging to the bridles. On they rushed, until the horses, wild with frenzy, rose on their haunches, and leaping upon the man all came with a crash to the earth. When people came and rescued the bleeding body of the man and found him in death's last agony, a friend bending tenderly over him asked, "Why did you sacrifice your life for horses and wagon?"

He gasped with his breath, as his spirit departed, "Go and look in the wagon." They turned, and there, asleep on the straw, lay his little boy.

—L. G. Broughton

❖ Arthur "Art" Lee Marple died in an early morning fire because he went through the house helping others get out. After saving his parents, three siblings, and a family friend, it was too late to save himself. He saved others by dying for them.

—Adapted from *Dallas Morning News*, January 22, 2001

❖ Huntsville, Texas—During eleven days, Fred Gomez Carrasco and two cohorts attempted to escape from the state prison. Fifteen were held as hostages. Mrs. Judy Standley and Mrs. Elizabeth Beseda, two of the hostages, each had volunteered to leave with Carrasco if it meant the release of their fellow captives. Rev. Carroll Pickett, their minister, said at their memorial service, "[The two women] loved [the other hostages] so much, they volunteered [to go with Carrasco] if it meant someone could live . . . God, we are thanking You for the lives of two people who loved You, for two people who loved others before they loved themselves . . . [the women gave the other hostages] the greatest love they have ever known."

—*Dallas Times Herald*, August 5, 1974

Note: There may have been more details given here that I failed to copy. One can either research further to obtain more facts or use as much as is told. For example, we don't know how the two died at the hands of the criminals but in many ways it's immaterial to the substitution illustration. However they died, we know they died in the place of others.

❖ Some time ago I was in a pastor's study. He had a narrow piece of wood on his shelf about a foot long. On the wood was a cross. Written below it were the words, "It was for me."

—R. Larry Moyer

❖ **POSSIBLE ENTRANCE:** *Let me ask you something. Suppose you were a pilot of a plane that became disabled. Your course is headed straight toward a residential area as the plane descends. You have a parachute and could jump to safety, but you must do it at an altitude allowing the plane to crash and kill many. Your other option is to fly the plane and guide it toward a vacant area, but there would be no time to jump to safety. You would die, but others would be spared. Which would you do? Let me tell you what one man did.*

Twenty-four-year-old Vinson Kyle Perdue, a United States Air Force pilot, died when his disabled warplane crashed. Instead of parachuting to safety, Perdue apparently stayed with the plane to steer it away from a residential area.

Amy White, who lived near the crash site, was quoted as saying, "I know he went down with that plane so it wouldn't hit anyone's house. It would've hit my house if he didn't maneuver that plane."

—Adapted from *Dallas Times Herald*, August 26, 1981

POSSIBLE EXIT: *Jesus Christ could have parachuted and jumped. In other words, He could have escaped His persecutors and refused to die for us. Instead, He took the punishment for our sins and died so that we could live. He substituted His life in our place.*

❖ When the Communists took over the country of Cambodia, food became very scarce. Many people went hungry and even starved to death. As you might expect, stealing became a real problem. To solve this problem, the Communists began shooting on the spot anyone caught stealing. One day a young boy was caught stealing. Just as a Communist soldier raised his gun to shoot the boy, the boy's mother ran onto the scene. She dashed between her son and the gunman, taking the bullet intended for her son. The soldier was so moved by this demonstration of love that he let the boy go free. Motivated by love, the mother had given her life for her son. In the same way, because God loved us, Christ died in our place, taking the penalty we deserved.

—Source unknown

❖ Skydiver Gareth Griffith, 21, survived a 12,000 foot free fall with a failed parachute when his instructor, jumping with Griffith, used his own body to block Griffith's fall, witness in Orlando said. Michael Castello, 42, died. Griffith was severely wounded.

—*USA Today*, June 25, 1997

❖ During the reign of a certain ruler in the country of Tibet, it was brought to this ruler's attention that an extraordinary amount of stealing was taking place in his country among the people. To stop this trend, the ruler decreed that a severe penalty would be administered to anyone caught stealing. The hand of the thief must be cut off. One of the first persons caught stealing, an old woman, was brought before him. To his alarm, the face of the old woman was that of his mother. For the penalty, now decreed, must be carried out. This ruler ordered that his own hand be cut off instead. The woman, his mother, was set free unharmed. He took the penalty in her place.

—Source unknown

❖ A Dominican DC3 charter plane on a flight to Haiti crashed and caught fire after takeoff. The pilot died, but 27 Canadian passengers, one American, and the other two crew members survived.

Authorities at Las Americas International Airport credited pilot Manuel Lamarche Rey, owner of the twin-engine plane, with saving the lives of the others by skillfully guiding the plane to a flat area to soften the impact of the crash.

Most of the survivors were reported in serious condition at Dario Contreras Hospital and a military hospital at nearby San Isidro Air Force Base. Neither the stewardess, who was Lamarche Rey's wife, Luisa Lourdes, nor co-pilot Jose Peralta, were critically injured, authorities said. The only American passenger also was not seriously hurt.

—*Dallas Morning News*, January 31, 1975

❖ Daniel Bussot-Prieto's parents sailed toward the U.S. from Cuba last week, so the eight-year-old could have a better life growing up in America. But the treacherous Florida Straits intervened with their dreams.

As waves swamped the small motorboat, Daniel's mother lovingly put the family's only life jacket on her son. She knew she, Daniel's father, and the three other adult refugees would face mortal peril on the rough seas. They drowned on August 15. Daniel was saved by the U.S. Coast Guard.

"My parents are in heaven," Daniel said as he left Jackson Memorial Hospital in Miami. He often prays for his parents. But while they were swallowed up by the sea, their dreams live on. Daniel will grow up in freedom with his great-aunt and great-uncle in the Miami suburb of Hialeah.

Daniel suffered second-degree burns over 10 percent of his body from gasoline that spilled on him when the boat overturned. The sea made his wounds more painful. "The gasoline mixed with the salt water," he said from his wheelchair, which he was sharing with several stuffed animals.

Thick socks almost hid the bandages on Daniel's burned feet. He walked tenderly out of the hospital and into a van filled with balloons and gifts marking his release from the hospital. Daniel said his wounds did not hurt.

—Our Daily Bread, 1994

❖ A story is told of an act of heroism that took place when a tornado struck a small town in Texas. The storm struck quickly, and there was little time to seek shelter. One young couple took their baby girl and laid down on their living room floor with their bodies shielding the baby. The storm struck the home and the walls came crashing in. The next day, when rescue parties came to the scene and began to dig away the rubble, they found the bodies of the mother and father—but the little girl was still alive! In a final act of love, they had given their lives so that she might live.

—Source unknown

❖ The following heart-wrenching story was told by Reginald Reimer in a World Relief report.

It was a cold Christmas Eve in Korea. A young mother-to-be, whose husband had been killed in the war, began to feel the pains of labor. She decided it was time to go to the mission clinic a couple of miles away.

As she walked to the clinic, the pains came faster and more intensely than she expected. At a bridge crossing the ravine not far from the clinic, she could go no further. She sought shelter under the bridge and there, without help, gave birth to her firstborn—a son.

The next morning the missionary nurse was on her way to attend Christmas services in the village church. As her jeep crossed the little bridge the engine suddenly died. As the missionary stepped out to take a look, she thought she heard a faint cry from below.

Under the bridge she found the baby, lovingly wrapped in all his mother's clothes. Her lifeless body lay beside him, naked and frozen.

Overcome by what she had found and by the significance of a newborn boy on Christmas morning, the nurse decided she would adopt the little orphan as her own. She named him Kim.

On the Christmas Eve when Kim was turning twelve, his adopted mother decided she would tell him the unusual circumstances of his birth. The next day as they made their way to the village church for the Christmas celebration, Kim asked to stop by the graveyard where his real mother was buried.

The missionary watched as the boy made his way up to the grave. Slowly he began to take off his clothes. First his jacket, then his shirt and trousers—laying them all lovingly and carefully on his mother's grave.

When his adopted mother came up behind him to wrap her own coat around him, she heard him saying, "Mother, you did it for me. You did it for me!"

When we look back at the Christmas story we see an even more profound demonstration of love. We see the Almighty, Sovereign, Glorious, Creator God, stripping Himself of all His visible majesty and power in order to be born into humanity in a dirty animal shelter.

We see Him thirty-three years later, hanging on a rough cross, spilling out His lifeblood, willingly wrapping us in His compassion and forgiveness.

Why? So that you and I may live. His horrible death yields for us abundant and eternal life.

My only response to such amazing love is to take all that I am and have and, like the Korean boy, lay it down and declare, "Lord, You did it for me!"

—David Petrescue in *The Christian and Missionary Alliance*, December 7, 1988

Note: Stories like this are ideally suited for a Christmas Eve service. Be careful to make the gospel clear. Is your message directed to Christians or non-Christians? If it's directed to Christians, the last line of the illustration, "Laying it down and declaring Lord, You did it for me," means living my life for the One who died for me. If your message is directed to non-Christians, "Laying it down and declaring Lord, You did it for me" means trusting Christ alone as the only way to heaven, and that needs to be explained. Don't allow your illustrations to confuse the gospel.

❖ Princeton, British Columbia—A woman who tried to defend her six-year-old son from a cougar mauling was killed when the 59–pound cat attacked her. Cindy Parolin, 36, was killed Monday while horseback riding with three of her children in the wilderness near Princeton, 120 miles east of Vancouver. Six-year-old Steven Parolin was in stable condition with about seventy stitches in his head, relatives said.

—*Dallas Morning News*, August 22, 1996

❖ Once there were two Chinese boys who lived in Hong Kong. They both worked for their father's restaurant. One night while walking home, the younger brother, with a streak of sudden violence, mugged an elderly man and killed him. The older brother, seeing the blood on his brother's clothes, quickly switched shirts. When the police arrived, they arrested the older brother, and he was sentenced to die. The younger brother lived the rest of his life with the thought of his brother dying for his crime.

—Source unknown

❖ Littleton, New Hampshire—Two climbers, frostbitten and starving after wandering aimlessly for three days in the subzero cold of Mount Washington, say, "We were praying that if we were going to die, it would happen soon."

"We couldn't do anything. We were just lying there," Jeffrey Batzer, 20, said from his hospital bed Thursday.

After more than seventy-three hours battling waist-deep snow, winds approaching one hundred miles per hour, and temperatures as low as 28 degrees below zero on the northeast's tallest peak, the two ice climbers were beaten.

"We were trying to die," said Hugh Herr, 17, a high school junior. "We were in such pain . . . The starvation was really bad. At that point, I was ninety percent sure I'd die."

However, at 2 PM Tuesday, a snowshoer found the climbers dazed, frostbitten, and suffering from extreme loss of body heat. Within five hours, they were airlifted by helicopter to Littleton Hospital, where an official called their condition "miraculous."

The two young men say if they don't lose their feet because of the merciless cold, they will join mountain rescue teams in memory of volunteer mountaineer Albert Dow, 27, killed Monday in a freak avalanche while searching for them.

"When I first heard about it, I cried. I just broke down," said Batzer. "For somebody to put his life out on the limb, voluntarily, for us, is something incredible."

At least one hundred people have perished since 1855 on Mount Washington, known for its savage weather. The strongest wind speed on Earth—231 mph—was recorded on the 6,288–foot peak in 1934.

—*Des Moines Register*, January 29, 1982

Note: These two climbers would have been saved even if Albert Dow had not died. But the point of this illustration is, as Batzer stated, "For somebody to put his life out on the line, voluntarily, for us, is something incredible." The point to be made is, "Christ so loved us, He put Himself on a cross instead of nailing us there."

❖ A young man was convicted of murder. He was sentenced to be hanged. For a number of years he had lived in the vilest type of life. Finally, his health was affected and seriously damaged. Sin left its marks and ravages even upon his face. He was prematurely aged. He had always remarkably resembled his father. After sin had aged him, the resemblance was even more striking. In fact, one might say he looked older than his father.

As the date of execution came closer, the father finally secured permission through the governor of the state to spend a few moments alone with his son. They were shut up in that dark prison cell, father and son alone. The father quickly commanded his son, "Take your clothing off as quickly as possible. We're going to change clothing. We resemble each other. I think we can get away with it. I'll put on those stripped prison garments of yours. You put on my street clothes, and when the warden comes you walk out of here as though you were I. Get across the border, get to Canada. Hide yourself, and before the date of the execution, I'll show my identity and then perhaps some day I'll be able to join you." The garments were exchanged, and when the warden came and knocked on the cell, the door opened and the guilty young man walked out to freedom and escaped across the Canadian border. After the son had gone, the father began to think this over. He realized how long the arm of the law may reach. He made a great decision, and his lips were sealed. He never said a word. The appointed execution day came, the black hood adjusted over his face, and the price was paid.

—Source unknown

❖ In a *Time* magazine article (September 16, 1985), Otto Friedrich gave a striking account of the sinking of the *Titanic*, the most luxurious ocean-liner afloat at the time. It weighed 46,328 gross tons and was 3½ city blocks long. For 4,350 dollars, the cost of a trans-Atlantic ticket, travelers could enjoy the ship's elegant furnishings, beautiful draperies, and gorgeous decks.

Those things were not what caught my attention, however. It was instead the accounts of those who died for another as they lowered loved ones into lifeboats as they remained behind. They died in their place. Think of what their loved ones in the lifeboat must have felt and saw as the *Titanic* sank. A substitute had taken their place.

That is what Jesus did for you and for me on the cross. He died in our place. He was our substitute.

—R. Larry Moyer

❖ Then there's eight-year-old Nicholas Berger. His idea of a hero is a little different. Nick's dad, Jim, worked at Aon, a human resources consulting firm on the 101st floor of World Trade Center Tower Two.

At 8:30 AM on Tuesday, September 11, Jim was just a regular guy, in love with his wife, Suzanne, and his three boys—Nicholas, 8, Alex, 6, and Christian, 2. Then a jetliner ripped through the top floors of Tower One. Immediately Jim started ushering his coworkers to the elevators, sending them down to safety. The last anyone saw him, he was headed back for more.

A few minutes later the second plane struck Tower Two. Back home, Suzanne waited beside the phone. "In those initial hours," she said, "as the 'safe' lists were coming out, and his name wasn't on any of them, immediately I started to think, 'Wait a minute, this is Jim Berger. He's saving people.'" Suzanne waited all that day, through the night, and into the next day with no word.

By Wednesday night she was desperate.

"I ran up to the top of the street," she said, "and I just knelt in the middle of the road. And I said 'God, whatever Your will is for me, I have accepted it . . . but I need to know that Jim is home with You.'"

Then Suzanne looked up and saw a brilliant, shining star shoot across the sky. "At that moment I knew he was home. I knew he was in heaven."

In her interview with ABCNews.com Suzanne said she waited until Sunday after church to tell her sons.

"I told them that I believed that their father was in heaven," she said. "And they both just kind of looked up at me, and I expected them to burst into tears."

But Nicholas had something to say. He named the hill they were standing on "Hero Hill." The hill, he said, was "big and strong and has its arms wide open"—just like his father.

Jim Berger is a hero because, given the opportunity to save himself, he chose to save others. What caliber of character does it take to produce that kind of courage?

—*Kindred Spirit*, Spring 2002

Note: Reg Grant, a professor from Dallas Theological Seminary, used this illustration to demonstrate courage and reality. If using it as an illustration of substitution before a non-Christian audience, you'd want to emphasize the theme of love more than courage. Jim's love for his coworkers motivated him to put their safety before his own.

❖ On June 10, 1770, the town of Port-au-Prince, in Haiti, was utterly overthrown by an earthquake. From one of the fallen houses the inmates had fled, except a black woman, the nurse of her master's infant child. She would not desert her charge, though the walls were even then giving way. Rushing to its bedside, she stretched forth her arms to enfold it. The building rocked to its foundation, the roof fell in. Did it crush the hapless pair? The heavy fragments fell indeed upon the woman, but the infant escaped unharmed for its noble proprietress extended her bended form across the body, and at the sacrifice of her own life, preserved her charge from destruction.

—R. Brewin

❖ Karen Zyhowski was taking a wagonload of grass clippings underneath a 2½-foot electric fence when a live wire snapped, coiled around her ankle, and knocked her to the ground. Her seven-year-old daughter, Tara, waved her three-year-old sister to stand back. Then she used one of her rubber thongs to knock the wire off her mother. But her arm touched the wire, knocking her to the ground, and when her head hit the wire she was electrocuted. Tara died in her mother's place.

—Adapted from *Dallas Times Herald*, July 28, 1988

Note: When I use an illustration like this, years after the incident, I often don't refer to the particular issue. I simply say, "*The Dallas Times Herald* once told the story . . ." This kind of incident could have happened today. The date doesn't matter.

❖   Wayne and Red served in the same platoon when the Allied Forces marched across Europe in World War II. Wayne volunteered to be "point man," leading the platoon into enemy territory. Red backed him up.

The two led their men through several battles until they reached the famed "Siegfried Line." They ran across no-man's land and jumped into the enemy trench. When a live grenade exploded in front of them, Wayne, who was in the lead, was wounded by the blast. Seeing his helplessness, Red stepped forward, grabbed Wayne, whirled around, and shielded him from gunfire. A few seconds later Red was hit by an enemy bullet and died instantly. Wayne, who survived, later wrote, "No one has ever valued me more."

—*Our Daily Bread*, 2001

❖   On August 19, 1996, thirty-six-year-old Cindy Parolin and three of her children were riding horses in the Similkameen backcountry, thirty miles northwest of Princeton, British Columbia. Like their mother, six-year-old Steven, eleven-year-old Melissa, and thirteen-year-old David felt a mixture of wonder and excitement as they traveled through the vast wilderness. The four were headed to a cabin to join Parolin's husband and other son for a camping vacation.

As the family rode along, the horses grew increasingly nervous. The cause became starkly clear when a cougar suddenly launched itself from the undergrowth at Steven. The animal missed its mark, landing on the horse just in front of the boy's saddle. The great cat scrambled to hold onto the horse's neck but lost its grip and fell to the ground.

Undaunted, the snarling cougar leaped again and attempted to pull Steven from the saddle. This time it got away with only a sock and shoe, but the contortions of the spooked horse caused the boy to fall to the ground. The cat was on the youngster in an instant, wrapping the struggling child in a clawed death-grip.

Parolin watched the unfolding scene in horror as the cat bared its fangs and then bit into the boy's skull. A knowledgeable outdoorswoman and avid hunter, she knew that her son would be dead in a matter of seconds—his neck broken, skull crushed, or artery lacerated in the lion's terrible jaws. If only she had her rifle . . . But hunting season was weeks away, and Canadian firearms laws made off-season carry all but impossible. She had to act quickly.

Screeching a primal scream, the desperate mother leaped from her mount and rushed to Steven's aid.

With adrenaline-fueled strength, Parolin broke a stout limb from a fallen tree and clubbed the cat away from the child. Now the lion turned its full attention to her, opening a terrible gash in her arm with a swipe of its paw. Spurred by maternal instincts, Parolin fought back. Woman and cougar melded into a blur of flashing claws, teeth, and flailing fists as they wrestled on the ground.

Still thinking of her children, the embattled mother screamed for David and Melissa to grab Steven and run for help. The horses had scattered in the melee, so the older siblings half-carried their bleeding brother more than a mile back down the trail to the family car.

Melissa stayed with Steven in the vehicle while David ran to a nearby campsite for help. He enlisted the aid of Jim Manion who, directed by David, drove to the scene. It had now been more than an hour since his mother had clubbed the cat off his younger brother. On arriving, Manion heard the mother's screams. Moving toward the agonized sounds, he came upon Cindy Parolin, still battling the cougar. She turned to Manion, a look of raging defiance in her eyes.

"Are my children all right?"

"Yes," Manion answered.

On hearing they were okay, she said in a half-whisper, "I am dying now."

Parolin collapsed, but the cat still savaged her body. Although Manion had armed himself with a 12–gauge pump shotgun, he had been afraid to shoot at the cougar for fear of hitting the woman. He fired into the ground nearby, hoping to scare the lion off her limp body. It worked. Now the cougar left the unconscious woman and advanced on Manion.

As the lion slinked toward him, Manion tried to cycle a fresh round into the chamber but his gun jammed. He backed up toward his pickup, desperately working to clear the weapon as the cougar came on.

At the last moment Manion cleared the gun and jacked in a fresh round just as the lion charged. With no time to aim, he leveled the scattergun at the cat and fired from the hip. The charge caught the cougar a bit far back, but it was enough. The lion veered off to the side and disappeared into the dense brush along the road. Later, wildlife officers would find the dead animal lying about 150 feet from the trail.

Manion rushed to Parolin's aid, but she was beyond help, having traded her life for that of her son. Steven survived the near scalping inflicted by the cougar and made a full recovery after receiving seventy stitches in his head. Cindy Parolin was awarded the Star of Courage medal posthumously by the governor general of Canada.

—Don Zaidle, "Killer Cougars," *Outdoor Life*, February 2001. Used by permission.

Note: Know your audience. Illustrations like this one are particularly effective in communities close to wooded areas where mountain lions live. There are so many details given, one gets a good picture of what happened. These details shared effectively enable the audience to see the story. Be careful, however, with being too graphic. The fact that the "lion bit into the boy's skull" might be too much for most audiences.

❖ In Brooklyn some years ago a woman left her baby unattended in the apartment. Fire broke out. Only one fireman would risk his life to save the baby. He got inside the flames but couldn't get out. So he threw the baby out to another fireman, and he himself died in fire as the building crumbled in on him.

Over twenty years later a girl with a young baby was seen kneeling at this man's grave. When asked whose grave it was, the woman said, "This man saved my life."

—Tom Malone, as told by R. G. Lee

❖ One stormy day in August 1908, a switchboard operator in Folson, New Mexico, heard from a subscriber in the uplands that a cloudburst had fallen on Johnson Mesa. Floodwaters were rolling toward Folson. Folson then had a population of about 500 and was situated in a canyon on both sides of the Dry Cinnamon River. Two rivers converged a short distance above the town.

Mrs. Doake, a sixty-eight-year-old hunchback, had time to save herself, but she chose to stand by the switchboard and warn as many as she could. One subscriber, Robert O. Pennenell, carried her message to people who did not have telephones. Scores managed to escape, but the faithful switchboard operator was drowned.

Her skeleton was found several months later and identified by its deformed spine. She was buried in Folson. In 1936, 6,000 telephone employees of the National State Tel-Company paid for the building of a 7,500 pound memorial over her grave.

—Source unknown

Note: This story is effective because it's a historical event. Whenever you can relate it to a recent event people are familiar with, it makes a past experience become more like a current event. What happened then could easily have happened today.

❖ A man lay on the white sand of his private beach, sunning with his wife by his side. He was fifty-five years of age, a successful man, an insurance executive. He was enjoying a vacation. He had recently undergone a complete physical examination and received a clean bill of health. Suddenly, as he rested on the sand, he heard a small voice crying for help. He and his wife saw a little girl on a plastic raft, bobbing up and down on the waves, about 150 feet from shore. The child was being swept into the sea by a high wave.

This man ran into the surf, battled the breakers to swim to the little girl's side. He shoved her back into the raft and began to push it toward shore when he felt a sharp pain. He gave the raft one last hard push, calling to the little girl as she glided away from him: "You've got to help yourself now to get yourself in. I'm dying." She was unharmed—he died. Do you think she could have ever hated him?

—George W. Sinquefield, "The Preciousness of Jesus"

Note: Illustrations like the one above can be used two ways. It can illustrate the brevity of life since the man had just received a clean bill of health. It can also illustrate substitution.

❖ **POSSIBLE ENTRANCE:** *Tornadoes often call for split-second decisions where one lays down his or her life for another.*

On May 23, most of the residents of Saratoga, Texas, were gathered at the community hall for a preschool graduation ceremony. Less than an hour into the program, the father of one of the children glanced out the door. What he saw was death bearing down on his family, and on his town. He yelled that there was a tornado coming. Seconds later at 8:15 PM the tornado struck the town hall. When rescue workers searched through the collapsed structure they found one father huddled over his mother and daughter. He was dead, but two were alive and unharmed.

—*Dallas Times Herald*, May 24, 1987

POSSIBLE EXIT: *Christ's substitutionary death was not a split-second decision. Before we were even born, God devised a plan by which He would redeem the world by letting His perfect Son take our place.*

❖ A seven-year-old girl who pushed her foster brother out of the path of a slow-moving dump truck was run over by the vehicle and crushed to death. Demitra Dorn was hit by the truck about 2:40 PM Thursday as she and the five-year-old boy crossed the street two blocks from their home.

—*Dallas Times Herald*, February 1, 1985

> Note: Demitra died by accident, not intention. She nevertheless died in her foster brother's place. This illustrates substitution. One can strengthen the illustration by saying, "Jesus Christ's substitutionary death was not by accident. He knowingly and purposefully gave His life in our place."

❖ Amos Brown and Debbie West were to have been married today on Brown's eighteenth birthday. But death interrupted.

Six days before he died, Brown and Miss West were walking home when a car stopped nearby. Miss West said they saw a woman leaving the car. A man followed, chasing her.

"I told Amos, 'We need to help that woman, she's in trouble,'" said Miss West.

"At first he said no, but then he gave in and we went across the street to them."

"Amos kept pleading with the man to leave the woman alone, then he jumped on top of the man and pulled him off of her. I helped the woman get up and she kept yelling that she had to get out of here. Then the man started to take off and Amos came up to me.

"He started to hug me, he said 'Debbie . . . Honey.'"

Then he collapsed in his finance's arms. He had been stabbed in the heart. Six days later he died.

—*Kansas City Star*, March 30, 1974

❖ **POSSIBLE ENTRANCE:** *We've all heard of substitutionary death—one person dies for another but no wrong has been committed by the one saved, such as when a person saves another during a violent storm. What makes the death of Christ remarkable is that He is a perfect Person who died for sinners—we who have done wrong and should have taken our own punishment.*

In the 1980s in India, a family had two sons. The older son was very wise and of very good behavior. The younger son was rebellious and continually got into trouble. When he became a teenager he was in a bar one night, and a fight broke out. In a fit of rage, the younger brother broke a bottle in half and with the jagged edge of the broken bottle killed a man in the bar. The crowd became very angry and took off after him in an attempt to beat him to death. The younger brother had no place to hide, so he ran to the home of his older brother. He knocked on the door and said, "Help! The crowd is going to kill me. I have no place to hide." The older brother pulled him inside and then said to him, "Take off your clothes." Immediately, he removed his clothes, and the older brother put them on while the younger brother went to the back of the house. The crowd came and knocked on the door, shouting, "Let us in!" The older brother stood there in his younger brother's clothes, and the crowd did not know it wasn't the same person and immediately beat him, leaving him all but dead. The crowd departed. The younger brother came from the back room, rushed up to the older brother, and said, "What have you done?" He responded, "I am dying in your place."

—Source unknown

POSSIBLE EXIT: *Jesus Christ took the punishment we deserved. He never sinned. He paid the price for our sin by dying as our substitute.*

❖ Ringgold, Georgia—A Catoosa County man is being called a "hero" after giving his own life Saturday afternoon to save his eleven-year-old son.

Randy Lamar Baker, 42, of 97 Lance Road, was killed while he and his son, Chris, were working on a storage building in their front yard, Catoosa County Deputy Coroner Richard Baxter said.

According to Mr. Baxter, the accident happened around 6 PM when the two were jacking up the wood and metal outbuilding to place an axle under it so it could be moved.

Mr. Baxter said that the boy was under the trailer when his father apparently noticed that one of the concrete blocks propping up the building was beginning to crumble, causing the trailer to begin shifting to one side.

Mr. Baker then quickly crawled under the trailer and placed himself between it and his son, allowing the boy to escape with only minor injuries before the weight of the building crushed him, said Mr. Baxter.

"He held the building up until the little boy got out," said Mr. Baxter.

The deputy coroner estimated that the building weighs between 5,000 and 6,000 pounds.

According to Mr. Baxter, Mr. Baker's wife and one of his daughters were on the front porch of their house off Mount Pisgah Road about five miles south of here when they saw the accident happen and called for help.

The father was pronounced dead at the scene. Rescue workers freed his body, and it was taken to Hutcheson Medical Center in Fort Oglethorpe, Mr. Baxter said. The son also was taken to Hutcheson, but was released after being treated for minor cuts and scratches.

The victim, an employee of World Carpet, was the father of two sons and two daughters, Mr. Baxter said.

"The guy is a hero," he added.

—*Chattanooga News-Free Press*, June 15, 1998
Permission to reprint was granted by the Chattanooga Times Free Press.

❖ I met a man in Monmouth, Illinois, who was helping harvest corn years ago. They had the equipment stopped underneath two voltage lines. Suddenly the line touched the equipment. The current started going through the line. A man in his early thirties saw it happening, touched the man's body, and absorbed the force of the current, greater than that used in the electric chair. He absorbed the deadly current in the other worker's place. Doctors said the current went around that other man's heart and the second man took the blow.

—R. Larry Moyer

❖ At a western national recreation area some years ago, a man took his young son fishing but brought only one life vest along. When the boat capsized, he put the vest on his son and pushed him toward shore. "I love you," he said.

—*National Geographic*, August 1991

❖ In early May 1985, Dallas, Texas, was swept with a lot of bad weather. Because the ground was soaked from a great deal of rain that had already fallen, the potential for flash floods was high. More rain fell. Soon the flooding occurred. Houses and cars were being swept away; people were dying. During these floods, the fire chief of a small Dallas suburb, Rowlett, was working to try to save the lives of victims in his community. The man, while attempting to save a woman in the community, was caught by the current, swept downstream, and drowned. He gave his life so others might live.

—Source unknown

❖ Inglewood, California—An apartment manager sacrificed his life by shielding a three-year-old boy from a hail of bullets and died with the child in his arms, police said Monday. Vincent McGowan, 29, was sitting outside the apartment building when a gunman fired four to six rounds from a sidewalk crowded with bystanders Sunday afternoon. McGowan jumped into the line of fire, grabbed little Demone Scott and ran back into the apartment building, police said. "He brought the boy out of the line of fire and died for [him]," said Sgt. Joe Reeves. With the boy clutched in his arms, he ran up one flight of stairs before collapsing from two bullets wounds in the chest.

—*Dallas Morning News*, August 21, 1984

❖ A few years ago, a young man named Mario was walking down the street in Humbolt Park, Chicago. A gang car pulled up along the side of the street, rolled down the window, and aimed a gun at another man walking just ten feet in front of him. Mario saw the gun, but the man it was aimed at didn't. In one swift movement, Mario lunged forward and tackled the man, shielding him with his own body. The gun fired. Mario took the bullets into his own body. He died a few hours later. Mario chose to take that man's place, a man he did not even know.

—Source unknown

❖ A couple of years ago, Joe Delaney was a promising young football star in the NFL. He was home in the off season and passed by a lake. As he did, he noticed three young boys drowning. He jumped in to rescue them. He was able to save one of the boys, but he died in the process.

—Source unknown

Note: Joe Delaney was such an outstanding football player he became the thirty-fourth member of the Kansas City Chiefs Hall of Fame.

❖ In Puntarenas, Costa Rica, a road connects the land with the peninsula. Years ago, a bus carrying fifty students ran off this road when the brakes were broken. The driver could not control the bus, and it fell into the sea. Among the students was a swimming champion. As soon as he could, one by one, he began rescuing from the water each of his fellow students. Ten were saved when he became exhausted. However, he tried to reach another who was nearby, drowning. His last attempt was not successful; he himself drowned. He gave his life saving others.

—Source unknown

❖ James Harrison, a member of the Ouachita Baptist University Choir, was returning home from Europe with his fellow singers. As their plane was landing in Little Rock, Arkansas, it was hit by heavy rains and high winds. The jet skidded off the runway and hit a bank of lights, ripping open the fuselage.

As chaos reigned and flames broke out in the mangled plane, Harrison began to help others. Over and over, he pulled passengers to safety and ran back to the plane for more. On his last trip into the burning wreckage, he was overcome with smoke. He didn't make it out alive.

—Our Daily Bread, 2000

❖ Long Beach, Pacific County—Before they attended his memorial service, the two girls knew Joshua Squibb only as the young man who drowned in the treacherous currents trying to save them.

They knew that he had plunged into the ocean when he heard their screams, that he swam way out to reach them, that he held their heads above water, pushed them toward shore and reassured them with his words: "You can do it. Don't be afraid."

Krystle and her friend Amelia Johnson of Bellevue had spent that sunny Saturday riding horses, shopping, and swimming near Bolstad Beach Approach, the main entrance to Long Beach. They were celebrating the end of seventh grade.

They put on their swimsuits around 3 PM for an afternoon dip. As the shock of the 50-degree surf wore off, they ventured from ankle-deep water to knee-deep. They rode the waves back and forth until they were up to their waists.

"Then a big wave came and picked us up and carried us to where we couldn't touch the bottom," said Krystle.

Squibb had just gotten to the beach with his fiancée, Marcy Sturza, their two-year-old daughter, Bryanna, and his five-year-old son, Lucas.

"We were all splashing and playing, having a good time, and suddenly Josh said, 'Marcy, get the kids out of the water—now!' And he just dove in," Sturza said.

Witnesses said he sped arm over arm to the girls, who by then were barely visible, about a hundred yards from shore. "He told me to float on my back, and he grabbed me and kind of pushed me in," Krystle said. "He kept telling me I was doing really good."

With Krystle floating, more or less calmly on her back, Squibb worked his way to Amelia, who was a little closer to shore.

"He was talking to her and telling her the same things he told me, and then he got swept away. All of a sudden, he was flying past me, and he was gone," Krystle said.

On her back, Krystle drifted out of the current and back toward shore. She touched bottom and staggered out of the water. Amelia, still trapped in the riptide, struggled until Sgt. Mike Cenci, a state wildlife officer, swam out to her and towed her in.

On Tuesday, Squibb's body was found washed ashore on Klipsan Beach, twelve miles north of Long Beach.

—*Seattle Times*, June 26, 2000
Copyright 2000, Seattle Times Company. Used with permission.

❖ Boom! Boom! Thuan cringed as explosions rocked the orphanage. Her parents had been killed years ago, and now the war had found her again. Suddenly, several foreign soldiers rushed into the building. One of them picked up Thuan to carry her to a waiting helicopter. As he ran, a hand grenade landed near them. The soldier pushed Thuan away and threw himself on the grenade, absorbing its blast. After that, things were a blur of soldiers running, a bumpy helicopter ride, a crowded city, and then the relative quiet of a new orphanage.

Many months later, Thuan was adopted by a family in a country far away. Though she was a stranger in a strange land, the Jeffersons, whom she now knew as "Mom and Dad," treated her with a gentle kindness that overcame her fears. They took her to church and Sunday school and taught her about Jesus.

"Mom," she said one day, "my Sunday school teacher says that when a sinner asks Jesus to forgive him, God adopts him into His family. Why would God want to do that?"

Mother looked at Thuan thoughtfully. "Let me tell you a story, honey," she said at last. "Many years ago, God gave us a son whom we named Michael, and we loved him very much. Mike grew into a fine young man, and when our country called upon him to serve, he went into the army without complaint. He was sent to a country far away, and there he was killed saving the life of a little girl." Mother paused as she went over to a desk and took out a picture. "This is Mike," she said, showing it to Thuan.

Thuan studied the picture. The young man looked vaguely familiar. Suddenly, she understood. "I was the little girl he saved, wasn't I?" she gasped.

Mother nodded and hugged her close. "A Red Cross worker told us your name, and we had you traced. Since our son died to save your life, we considered you the most important person in the world, and we wanted you to be part of our family," she said. "Now we love you with all our hearts. It's the same way with God. His only Son died to save you from your sins, and now God wants to make you part of His family."

—http://forums.christiansunite.com

❖ **POSSIBLE ENTRANCE:** *Mark Twain's book* Tom Sawyer *is a classic. A scene from that story helps us understand what Christ did for us.*

In Mark Twain' book *Tom Sawyer*, we read how Tom's girlfriend Becky had ripped a page in the teacher's anatomy book. When the teacher discovered the ripped page, he began to go around the room asking each student if they were guilty. Tom knew that Becky would give herself away. So just as the teacher was getting to Becky, he stood up and said, "I did it!" The teacher gave him a lashing. He took Becky's punishment

—From *Tom Sawyer* by Mark Twain

POSSIBLE EXIT: *The punishment for our sin is far greater than a lashing. It is physical death. Jesus Christ in essence said, "Crucify Me when you should crucify them."*

❖ A girl in Gary, Indiana, had been terribly burned in a flash fire. She lingered between life and death, and any hope of being restored to a place of usefulness depended upon a delicate and extensive skin graft. When a call was issued for a volunteer to give skin, a young boy responded. The operation took place in a day when our more advanced techniques were unknown, and during the surgery complications set in and the boy died. But through the gift of himself he made it possible for that young lady to be completely restored. What a debt of gratitude must have filled her heart!

—*Our Daily Bread*, 1982

❖ Thirty-six-year-old Jerry Dean Burdette drowned after saving an eleven-year-old boy and two other people who were trying to rescue him.

Burdette helped the would-be rescuers and then went back for the boy, who was about 100 yards offshore. After getting the boy to safety, Burdette was pulled underwater by the strong current.

—Adapted from *Post Tribune*, September 11, 1978

❖ As the hard-working manager of a McDonald's restaurant, DeWayne Bible always cared about his workers and looked after their welfare.

On Sunday he gave up his life for them, shot to death after he persuaded gunmen who held up the restaurant to take him hostage instead of a young woman employee, police said.

His mother, Pearle M. Bible, said her son often called the store when he was off duty to make sure everyone was all right.

"He would check on them all of the time," Mrs. Bible said. "He was always considerate. He's that kind of person."

Sgt. Fred L. Jackson, a spokesman for the Marion County Sheriff's

Department, said Bible, 24, was shot to death Sunday morning when the bandits raided his restaurant and demanded a hostage as they made their getaway.

—*Herald Democrat*, Sherman, Texas, November 1985

❖ A man and his fiancée were approached by two men with guns and ordered into their apartment building. The man told his fiancée to run. She did, and was able to escape. But the gunmen shot the man in the back and killed him. He gave his life for his fiancée.

—Adapted from *Dallas Times Herald*, June 19, 1983

❖ Twenty-seven young people died when the bus they were riding in collided with a truck going the wrong way. One boy survived because his brother shoved him through a window just before the bus erupted in flames. Joshua was near the door when he saw his brother, Aaron, on the floor and ran back to help him. Aaron survived; Joshua did not. He died in place of his brother.

—Adapted from *USA Today*, May 19, 1988

Note: Incidents like these have timeless value in illustrating the substitutionary death of Christ. They show the importance of being a reader and keeping a file. When time permits, examine archives to get more details.

❖ An incident that took place several years ago in California illumi-nates what Jesus did on the cross in order to solve the problem God had in dealing with the sin of humanity. A young woman was picked up for speeding. She was ticketed and taken before the judge. The judge read off the citation and said, "Guilty or not guilty?" The woman replied, "Guilty." The judge brought down the gavel and fined her $100 or 10 days. Then an amazing thing took place. The judge stood up, took off his robe, walked down around in front, took out his billfold, and paid the fine. What's the explanation of this? The judge was her father. He loved his daughter, yet he was a just judge. His daughter had broken the law, and he couldn't simply say to her, "Because I love you so much, I forgive you. You may leave." If he had done that, he wouldn't have been a righteous judge. He wouldn't have upheld the law. He loved his daughter so much that he was willing to take off his judicial robe and come down in front and represent her as her father and pay the fine.

—Used by permission. Josh McDowell, *More Than a Carpenter*, pp. 114-115,
Tyndale House Publishers, www.josh.org

❖ Washington—Rows of loafers, wingtips, and pumps—38,000 pairs of shoes—ringed the Capitol reflecting pool Tuesday, bearing silent witness to the number of people killed each year by guns. The relatives and friends who placed them there called for stricter gun laws.

"We know we don't have to live this way. We have the spirit to change," said Richard Haymaker, an organizer of the event, called "Silent March."

Haymaker was host to Yoshihiro Hattori, 16, a Japanese exchange student killed October 17, 1992, in Baton Rouge, Louisiana. Hattori went to the wrong house looking for a party.

A homeowner was acquitted in the death but was ordered to pay Hattori's parents $653,000.

Many of the shoes were placed in the display by those paying tribute to loved ones.

"There's a lot of memories in those shoes," Judy Becker-Darling said tearfully as she fingered the size-13 Docksiders her husband Frank once wore.

He was killed January 25, 1993, by a gunman outside CIA headquarters in McLean, Virginia.

Becker-Darling says her husband saved her life. He told her to get under the dashboard when gunfire broke out. Then bullets shattered the back window of their Volkswagen Golf.

"I'm here because of him."

The shoes will be laid on the Capitol lawn today. Later, they will be donated to homeless shelters and other charities. The destination for some is war-torn Sarajevo, Bosnia-Herzegovina.

—*USA Today*, September 21, 1994

Note: In using an illustration like the above, do not bring up the purpose of the shoes around the Capital reflecting pool. Stricter gun laws are a controversial issue. Instead, go directly to the January 25, 1993, substitution illustration and cite it as one that appeared in USA Today.

❖ In the spring of 1985, a series of violent storms roared across the United States. A postal worker who saw a tornado bearing down on a baseball field where a Little League game was in progress grabbed his niece and another child from the stands, forced them into a ditch, and threw himself on top of them. When the tornado touched down, the man was swept away to his death, but the children survived. He saved them by dying for them.

—Adapted from *Time*, June 10, 1985

Note: An illustration like this stresses the importance of watching the news. This is especially true after disasters, when stories of heroic acts in which one person risks his or her life for another are more common.

❖   A young couple tried to hide behind a file cabinet when a gunman broke into an office building. The gunman found them, however, and twenty-eight year old John Scully died from gunshot wounds when he covered his wife with his body to protect her. She sustained non-life-threatening injuries.

—Adapted from *Dallas Morning News*, July 5, 1993

❖   Challis, Idaho—Donald Johnson, one of four Canadians aboard a light plane that crashed in Idaho's rugged wilderness country May 5, gave his fifteen-year-old daughter his heavy coat, saving her life but forfeiting his own.

Johnson, of Estevan, Saskatchewan, froze to death that night.

"All four passengers survived the initial crash," Mrs. Johnson said. "As it grew bitterly cold, her father gave his heavy coat to her," said Custer County Sheriff Sid Teuscher, who brought the survivors down from the mine about 45 miles southwest of here. "When they woke up the next morning, he was frozen."

The group was on a flight from Livingston, Montana, to Boise, Idaho, when the pilot apparently became lost in the high mountain range.

—*The Detroit News*, May 27, 1979

❖   In Brookhaven, Mississippi, county sheriff James Posey, 37, exchanged himself for a woman and three children being held hostage. Posey was later shot to death by the hostage-taker. The woman and children were unharmed.

—*Herald Palladium*, September 30, 1982

❖   Robert Head, an elementary school crossing guard in Brownwood, Texas, was helping children across the street. As one five-year-old girl stepped into the crosswalk, Mr. Head saw a car speeding into the intersection. He knew that the little girl would certainly be killed. He ran into the street and pushed her out of the way. Mr. Head saved her life, but he himself was struck and killed.

—Source unknown

❖   In Hillsdale, Michigan, eleven-year-old Brenda Hallbrook was found crying. Her brother James, age two, was found sitting in a puddle of water. Brenda said her parents, Ballard and Carolyn, heard the storms and lay on top of their children in a hallway. Ballard and Carolyn Hallbrook died. (Result of a series of tornadoes that struck eleven southern and midwestern

255

states and Colorado, worst in forty-nine years and left at least 310 persons dead.)

—*Kansas City Star*, April 5, 1974

Note: This substitution illustration does not have the same amount of detail as the others. I would use it when time constraints make it necessary.

❖ In the winter of 1975, the *Chicago Sun-Times* pictured a couple at a table kissing. The caption read, "Roderick A. Hinson gets a snack and a smack from Jacqueline Y. Nash in East Cleveland, Ohio, after he served her three-day jail sentence for possession of an unregistered gun. Hinson, 26, said it was his fault that she had the gun and, 'A jail is not a good place for a lady.' The judge said the substitution was unusual, but legal."

—*JET*, a Johnson Publication, January 23, 1975

❖ From *Leadership* magazine comes the story of an old Japanese farmer who had just harvested a rice crop that would make him rich. His farm was on a high plain overlooking the village at the ocean's edge. A mild earthquake had shaken the ground, but the villagers were used to that, so they took little notice.

The farmer, looking out to sea, saw that the water on the horizon appeared dark and foreboding. He knew at once what it meant—a tidal wave. "Bring me a torch, quick," he shouted to his grandson. Then he raced to his stacks of rice and set them ablaze.

When the bell in the temple below rang the alarm, the people scrambled up the steep slopes to help save their neighbor's crop. But the farmer met them at the edge of the plain, shouting, "Look! Look!" They saw a great swell of water racing toward them. As it crashed ashore, the tiny village below was torn to pieces. But because that farmer willingly sacrificed his harvest, more than four hundred people were spared.

God the Father also gave up something He held dear—His only Son. As a result, millions have experienced salvation through faith in Him. How thankful we should be for Jesus Christ—God's sacrifice!

—*Our Daily Bread*, 1990

❖ Evangelist Billy Sunday used to tell the story of a great plague that swept Paris and killed thousands of people. It baffled the skill of the doctors of that day. After a consultation, several doctors agreed that the only way to diagnose and eventually end the plague was for one of them to examine thoroughly the body of one who had died. This, however, would mean certain death for the examining physician. A famous French surgeon arose and said, "Gentlemen, I will make the examination." He wrote out his will, stepped into the room of a patient who had just died from the plague, and made the diagnosis. He recorded the results on a piece of paper, which he placed in a jar of vinegar for all to read. Within six hours, the doctor himself was dead, but the lives of thousands were spared through his sacrifice.

—*The Best of Billy Sunday*

Note: Who told this true story is unimportant. What matters are the historical facts. So one can begin by explaining, "Years ago a great plague swept Paris killing thousands of people . . ."

❖ On March 5, 1994, Deputy Sheriff Lloyd Prescott was teaching a class for police officers in the Salt Lake City Library. As he stepped into the hallway he noticed a gunman herding eighteen hostages into the next room. With a flash of insight, Prescott (dressed in street clothes) joined the group as the nineteenth hostage, followed them into the room, and shut the door. But when the gunman announced the order in which hostages would be executed, Prescott identified himself as a cop. In the scuffle that followed, Prescott, in self-defense, fatally shot the armed man. The hostages were released unharmed.

God dressed himself in street clothes and entered our world, joining us who are held hostage to sin. On the cross Jesus defeated Satan and set us free from the power of sin.

—Greg Asimakoupoulos, Concord, CA, in *Leadership*, Summer 1994

❖ **POSSIBLE ENTRANCE:** *Most of us can identify with the love a mother feels for her child. We have witnessed it and been the recipients of it. That love is there before the child was ever born.*

Melbourne, Australia—A nurse from Bristol, England, who refused radiation treatment for liver cancer to protect her unborn child died with her husband at her beside and their two-week-old son getting stronger, hospital officials said today.

The Royal Women's Hospital said Sheryl Skirton, 35, died Wednesday night, ending a drama that climaxed when Mrs. Skirton gave birth to the boy aboard a British Airways 747 minutes after it landed in Melbourne from Bristol.

—*Dallas Times Herald*, August 25, 1983

POSSIBLE EXIT: *She gave her life to protect her unborn child. What makes the love of God profound is that He died for rebellious sinners.*

❖ During a robbery and kidnapping attempt, Gus Polidor, a former major league baseball player, was killed while trying to save his one-year-old-son. At age 33, he saved his son by dying for him.

—Adapted from *USA Today*, May 1, 1995

❖ In the spring of 1998, in Jonesboro, Arkansas, two boys, ages eleven and thirteen, set off their school fire alarm and then opened fire on their classmates as they evacuated the building, killing four girls and a teacher. Shannon Wright, a 32-year-old English teacher, stepped in front of one of her sixth-grade students to shield her from the bullets. The girl survived, but Wright died. The teacher gave her life for the student.

—Adapted from *Time*, April 6, 1998

❖ The week, February 3, was once selected as clergy week. That date marks the anniversary of the sinking of the troop ship *USS Dorchester*. In World War II four chaplains on that ship made the ultimate sacrifice when they gave their life jackets to soldiers who had none. When the ship sank they drowned while the four soldiers lived.

—Source unknown

❖ The "miracle girl" of Flight 255 has been identified.

A Philadelphia grandfather recognized the lone survivor of the Northwest Airlines crash as his little four-year-old, brown-eyed granddaughter.

Anthony Cichan arrived at C. S. Mott Children's Hospital in Ann Arbor on Monday, finally able to feel some joy after learning that his son, daughter-in-law, and grandson died in the crash of Northwest Flight 255.

In a deeply emotional moment, Cichan positively identified the little survivor who lay wrapped in gauze bandages as Cecilia Cichan of Tempe, Arizona. He had felt sure even before arriving that the girl was his granddaughter because of two distinct characteristics—her purple nail polish and a chipped front tooth.

Rescue workers pulled the child, wearing a summer dress, from the burning wreckage Sunday after hearing her cries. She was found prone, clutched in the arms of a woman believed to be her mother.

"There were three or four plane seats around her and one body cradling her," said Dr. John Gary Giradot, 26, an intern at Dearborn's Oakwood Hospital, who helped firemen and ambulance workers rescue the child.

"We cut off the seat buckle. I could see she had good color and she was breathing well. She was in shock. We were in and had her out of the wreckage in fifteen minutes."

None of the airliner's other 151 passengers survived.

—*Detroit News*, August 18, 1987

Note: It is difficult to prove this woman died in her child's place voluntarily. But that is true for numerous substitution illustrations. When necessary, one can safely say, "We do not know if that was a purposeful substitution. But we do know Christ's death was purposeful. He chose to die for us."

❖ Think once again about the passengers on United Airlines Flight 93 whose plane crashed into that Pennsylvania field on September 11, 2001. Unlike the passengers on the planes that flew into the World Trade Center, those on Flight 93 knew they were going to die. Facing certain death, they gave profound and heroic meaning to their lives by diverting the hijackers' plan and thus saving an untold number of people on the ground.

—Ronald Heifetz and Martin Linsky, *Leadership on the Line*

Chapter 8

Let's Talk About Illustrating Saving Faith

I COULDN'T GET IT out of my mind. The billboard displayed a cross with Jesus nailed upon it. That, though, wasn't what captivated me. It was the three words alongside the cross—"It's your move."

God has done His part. On the cross, Jesus Christ, the perfect Son of God, took our place. He was our substitute. The third day Christ arose, proving He had conquered both sin and the grave. The payment for our sin was completely and forever made.

That payment must be accepted. It's our move. The gift of eternal life provided through Christ's death and resurrection is free, but it must be received.

How does one receive that gift? The Gospel of John answers that question. John explains his purpose for writing the book in John 20:31: "But these are written that you may believe that Jesus is the Christ, the Son of God, and that believing you may have life in His name." The word John used ninety-eight times to communicate what one must do to receive eternal life is the word "believe."

Believe means to trust, depend, rely on. As we depend on doctors to cure us or depend on chairs to hold us, we must come to God as sinners, understand His Son died for us and arose, and trust in Christ alone to save us. I so trust Christ to save me that my attitude is, "If He cannot save me, I am going to hell. Nothing else can get me to heaven." He alone is my salvation. I acknowledge the truth of Acts 4:12, "Nor is there salvation in any other, for there is no other name under heaven among men by which we must be saved." The word in our English language that communicates what the Bible means by believe is the word "trust." We need to invite the lost to trust in Christ alone to save them.

In one-on-one evangelism, as well as speaking publicly to lost people, don't use misleading phrases such as "invite Jesus into your heart," "give your life to God," or "pray to receive Christ." They are not used in any evangelistic context in the Bible. Scripture exhorts the lost to believe—to trust in Christ alone to save. When speaking, consistently use the terminology "trust in Christ."

Illustrations here help communicate what the Bible means by believe. Unfortunately, we have mangled the biblical use of the word "believe." Statements are made such as, "I believe it's going to rain," "I believe I'll probably be able to visit you tomorrow," "I believe we have decided to go to the movie." All these communicate hope or speculation, not assurance or guarantee. Eternal life is a guaranteed offer to those who believe. Jesus said, "He who believes in Me has everlasting life" (John 6:47).

Lost people must understand they are trusting a *Person* to save them—not their good works, their church attendance, or a system of taking the sacraments. They must trust a person—Christ—as their only way to heaven. The One who died for them and satisfied the wrath of a holy God against their sin is the only one who can save them. Salvation is trusting Christ to get us to heaven. Illustrations help convey this.

In my one-on-one presentations of the gospel people have said, "I believe all that." I've agreed, "I think you do. You believe there was a historical Christ. You believe He died on a cross and that He rose again. But my fear is that you're trusting your own good life to save you." Some have responded, "Sure." I then say, "But that's the point. Believe means you must trust Christ to save you—the One who died for you."

But we must trust Christ *alone*. I am not trusting Christ plus any amount of good living, but trusting Christ alone to save me.

Many do not understand the free nature of the gift of eternal life. Eternal life is a gift to be received, not a goal to be achieved. Unless I'm willing to receive the gift, I cannot receive eternal life. Illustrations can convey the freeness of eternal life and the fact that saving faith is as simple as receiving a gift.

Good illustrations can communicate that eternal life is a gift. They should point to trust in a Person, and to the inability of good works to save us. They communicate to the lost, "It's your move," and "Here's what it means to 'believe on the Lord Jesus Christ, and you will be saved'" (Acts 16:31).

Here are helpful illustrations for saving faith. (An index of illustration topics can be found at the end of this book.) Once more, humorous illustrations are noted with a ☺.

Illustrations About
Saving Faith

ASSURANCE OF SALVATION

❖ In his book *Dare to Believe*, Dan Baumann illustrates this unique experience of knowing that something is ours, yet longing to enjoy it more fully. He explained at Christmastime he would always do a lot of snooping, trying to find the gift-wrapped presents and figure out what was in them. One year he discovered a package with his name on it that was easy to identify. There was no way to disguise the golf clubs inside. Baumann then made this observation: "When Mom wasn't around, I would go and feel the package, shake it, and pretend that I was on the golf course. The point is, I was already enjoying the pleasures of a future event; namely, the unveiling. It had my name on it. I knew what it was. But only Christmas would reveal it in its fullness."

—*Our Daily Bread*, 1988

❖ **POSSIBLE ENTRANCE:** *Let me ask you a question that all of us ought to ponder: "If you were to die today, would your relatives know where to find you?"*

John B. McFerrin, a noted preacher in the South, was dying. He was ready to die, and he was eagerly looking forward to being with the One he had loved and served so faithfully. His son, also in the ministry, spent as much time as possible at his father's bedside. But one Saturday he found it necessary to leave him because he had to fill a preaching assignment in another city. Well aware of his father's grave condition, he was hesitant about going. Sensing his son's reluctance, McFerrin encouraged him to be on his way. "Son, you'd better get started," he said. "Don't worry about me. I'm feeling some better today. But if I should slip away while you're gone, you'll know where to find me!"

—*Our Daily Bread*, 1987

POSSIBLE EXIT: *Why could he say that? Was it because he had been a preacher? No, because that will not get you to heaven. Was it because he had lived a good life? No, because that will not get you to heaven. It was because he had trusted Christ.*

❖ The French emperor Napoleon was one day reviewing his troops when his horse bolted out of control. He was in danger of being hurled to the ground, so a young private leaped from the ranks and quickly calmed the animal. "Thank you, Captain," said Napoleon—thus bestowing upon the private an instant promotion. Smiling proudly, the soldier inquired, "Of what regiment, sir?" "Of my guards," replied Napoleon as he dashed down the lines. Immediately assuming his new rank, the private-turned-captain walked over to join a group of staff officers. "What is this insolent fellow doing here?" remarked one of them. "I am a captain of the guards," the young man replied. "You rascal, you're just a private. What makes you think you're a captain?" At that the young man pointed to the emperor and confidently responded, "He said it!" "I beg your pardon, Captain," the officer answered politely, "I was not aware of your promotion." That young soldier did not feel like a captain, nor did he wear the insignia of a captain. All he had was the word of Napoleon. But that was enough.

—*Our Daily Bread*, 1984

❖ **POSSIBLE ENTRANCE:** *When you trust Christ, you are just as certain of heaven as the people who are already there.*

I am now enabled to rely upon His precious promises and to feel that I am as safe, though not as holy, as the greatest saint in heaven.

—Susannah Spurgeon and Joseph Harrald, *C. H. Spurgeon*

POSSIBLE EXIT: *When you trust Christ, knowing you are going to heaven is not a guess; it's a guarantee. You are as certain of heaven as though you're already there. His word says so!*

CHURCH
❖ People in Amsterdam were asked the question, "What are the first words that come to your mind when you think of church?" Two different people answered, "Empty and frightening."

—R. Larry Moyer

> Note: An illustration like this helps you identify with people's understanding of church. It also allows you to address the frustration that "church is frightening, and yet how do I get to heaven if I don't attend?"

☺ As a dental hygienist, I always encourage patients to floss. During one cleaning, the dentist I work with asked my patient if he was "flossing religiously." "Well," the man hedged, "I floss more often than I go to the synagogue."

—Source unknown

☺ **POSSIBLE ENTRANCE:** *We are of the opinion that you need to attend church to get to heaven. That's both frustrating and confusing.*

A little boy spied a large bronze plaque in the foyer of his church and asked the pastor what it was for. The pastor replied, "It has on it the names of all the members of this church who have died in service." The little boy asked, "Which one, the eleven o'clock or the seven o'clock?"

—Source unknown

POSSIBLE EXIT: *I have news for you. It doesn't matter which service of the church you attend or how many services you attend, your church attendance will not get you to heaven.*

COMING OF CHRIST

❖ Upcoming event: The second coming of Christ! Be prepared!

—*Pulpit Helps*, February 2003

❖ POSSIBLE ENTRANCE: *Our minds sometime go to the Lord's coming, and when it does, the question "When is He coming?" pops into our minds. Instead ask the question, "Where am I going?" Here's how one person put it.*

It's not when the Lord is coming but where you're going when He comes that concerns me.

—Milburn Miller

POSSIBLE EXIT: *Suppose Christ had come yesterday. Where would you be today?*

☺ POSSIBLE ENTRANCE: *Trust Christ. This way if Jesus returns today, you won't have to wish you had been prepared.*

During the Easter service of 1949 a woman and her son sat in a motion picture theater in Tacoma, Washington, watching the Cecil B. de Mille film, *The King of Kings*. The scene was the crucifixion of Christ, and the film showed the sky darkening, the earth shaking, and rocks falling. She whispered to her boy, "That is the way it will be when Jesus comes back." At that moment a quake jolted the whole Puget Sound area; the walls of the theater began to sway and the seats trembled.

"Oh no!" cried the mother. "Not yet!"

—This quote was taken from the article "Future Shock" from the June 1973 issue of *Decision* magazine. ©1973 Billy Graham Evangelistic Association. Used with permission. All rights reserved.

POSSIBLE EXIT: *If Christ returned today, would you be forced to exclaim, "Oh no, not yet!"*

❖ I'm not looking for something to happen; I'm looking for Someone to come.

—Vance Havner

❖ **POSSIBLE ENTRANCE:** *God is very serious about His Son's return.*

Over one-fourth of the Bible talks about the return of Christ to the earth.

—Pastor Jim Rose

POSSIBLE EXIT: *Could it be that you've missed one of the most important messages of the Bible—Jesus is coming.*

❖ The next best words to "In My Father's house are many mansions" (John 14:2) are the words "I will come again, and receive you unto Myself" (John 14:3).

—Source unknown

CONVERSION

❖ To paraphrase Martin Luther King Jr., I may not yet be the man I should be or the man, with Christ's help, I someday will be—but thank God I'm not the man I used to be!

—Lee Strobel, *The Case for Christ*

❖ The *Akagi* pitched and rolled in the rough seas as the white surf whipped across the flight deck in the predawn blackness. The crews were hard pressed to keep their planes from sliding into the sea. The time was 5:30 AM. The day was the 7th of December. The year was 1941.

I stood in the commander-in-chief's quarters. "I am ready for the mission," I said.

Vice Admiral Nagumo stood to his feet and grasped my hand hard in his. "Fuchida," he said, "I have confidence in you."

After a final briefing with the men, I climbed to the command post above the flight deck. My plane was in position, its red and yellow striped tail marking it as the commander's plane.

Just before I climbed into the plane, the officer in charge of the maintenance gang presented me with a white cloth headband. "This," he said, "is from the maintenance crew. Take it to Pearl Harbor."

Fifteen minutes later 185 fighter bombers and torpedo planes were in the air, the 6 aircraft carriers now tiny streaks on the surface of the water beneath us. We were the first wave of the 359 planes that I led toward Pearl Harbor 275 miles to the south.

By 7:30 AM we were over the northern tip of the island. There was still no sign that anyone knew we were in the air. If we had the advantage of surprise, the torpedo planes would strike first. Then the level bombers would attack. In the event of resistance the dive bombers were to attack first to confuse and attract enemy fire.

At 7:49 I gave the signal for a surprise attack, but the signal was misinterpreted. At 7:55 the dive bombers tore in on Hickam Field, Ford Island, and Wheeler Field. Two minutes later the torpedo planes zeroed in on battleships in the harbor. At about 8:00 fighter planes [fired their machine guns at close range on] the air base, and then the level bombers began to drop their cargoes of death on the battleships.

Suddenly it was a though a giant hand had smashed at my plane. A gaping hole appeared on the port side. The steering mechanism was damaged but, before returning to the carrier, I managed to drop two bombs on the USS *Maryland*.

During the war, I faced death three times. Once when I was flying on reconnoiter between Formosa (now called Taiwan) and China, I was informed that we were lost and that we had only ten minutes of fuel left. We were flying above water and, when our fuel was gone, we hit the water near a Chinese junk. On another occasion I crash-landed in a jungle. A third brush with death came during the Battle of Midway. Following surgery, I was confined to a hammock on the *Akagi* when it was attacked by American planes. The side of the ship where I was lying was blown out by a bomb. I was thrown into the ocean and picked up by one of the destroyers.

When the war ended, I was bitter and disillusioned. I had spent twenty-five years in the Japanese navy, and adjustment to civilian life did not come easily. I took up farming near Osaka, Japan.

I had had very little place in my life for religion. But now, living in close relation to the earth, I began to think in terms of a Creator-God. I had never been an atheist, but I had grown to manhood without any formal religion. In the Japanese navy the former "War Catechism" was the sum total of my ideology.

I began to think too that there must be a reason why I was still alive. Of the 70 officers who took off from the *Akagi* that December 7 morning, I was the only one to survive the war.

Then one day I saw in a list of Japanese war prisoners returning from the United States the name of a lieutenant whom I had known very well. I went to Uraga Harbor to meet him and to ask him about the treatment of prisoners of war in American camps.

My friend told me a story about a young American woman who had visited that particular camp regularly and had done what she could to make life more bearable for the prisoners. When one of the prisoners asked why she was so kind to them, she said, "Because my parents were killed by Japanese soldiers."

This did not make sense to the prisoners. The young woman, who was no more than twenty years old, explained, "My parents were Christian missionaries in the Philippines when the war broke out. They were captured and ordered shot as spies. They spent their last thirty minutes of life praying for their captors. At first I was bitter when I heard what had happened, but my hatred has been washed away by Spirit-directed love for all men, even my enemies."

It was a beautiful story, but I could not understand it.

Not long afterward, while leaving a railroad station in Tokyo, I was handed a tract by an American. It told the story of Jacob DeShazer, a member of the Doolittle squadron that bombed Tokyo on April 18, 1942. In the tract DeShazer told how, while a prisoner of the Japanese for forty months, he had received a Bible. He began reading it and surrendered himself to Jesus Christ.

Soon after receiving that tract, I read an editorial in a Tokyo newspaper about the Bible being the world's best seller. Impelled to buy a copy of the Bible, I began to read the New Testament. In the gospel of Luke, I came across the words, "Father, forgive them; for they know not what they do." These were the words of Jesus on the cross as He prayed for the people who were putting Him to death!

It was then that I understood the source of the American woman's concern. That very day I decided to become a follower of Jesus.

I struggled for some time with the problem of making known my conversion to Christianity. Then one day I saw an automobile belonging to an evangelistic group parked at the curb of one of Osaka's busiest streets. The automobile was equipped with a loudspeaker. I asked permission to speak, and as a crowd collected, my voice boomed out, "I am Mitsuo Fuchida who led the air raid on Pearl Harbor. I have now surrendered my life to Jesus Christ."

The next day newspapers carried headlines: "From 'War Catechism' to the Bible." What I'd said had a mixed reception. Some people denounced me as an opportunist. Some said that I was betraying my ancestors. Some encouraged me. A Communist coal miner wrote me a polite letter, urging me to have nothing to do with Christianity. He concluded his letter by saying, "Peace is only attained through Lenin."

It was not Lenin but Christ who changed my life and gave me "peace that passes understanding." I, who had been steeped in militarism, found the true peace. No other could fill that God-shaped blank in my life.

(December 7 marks the anniversary of the Japanese attack on the U.S. Naval Base at Pearl Harbor on Oahu Island, Hawaii, that brought the United States into the Second World War. Captain Mitsuo Fuchida was general commander of the air squadron that performed the raid. In 1952 Fuchida told John A. Barbour the story of that attack and of how, after the war, he found peace through knowing Jesus Christ. Fuchida became a Presbyterian lay minister. Before his death in 1969, he traveled thousands of miles, preaching the message of peace through Jesus Christ.)

—Mitsuo Fuchida (as told to John A. Barbour), "I Led the Attack on Pearl Harbor," *Decision*, December 1991. Used by permission of the John A. Barbour family.

❖   The advertising slogan for the Louisiana tourist industry is, "Come as you are. Leave different!"

—*Preaching*, July–August 1998

❖   **POSSIBLE ENTRANCE:** *You may have a lot of questions on your mind that are keeping you from coming to Christ. Why not come to Christ? You'll be surprised how many of those questions will disappear.*

In his delightful little book *Inward Ho!* Christopher Morley writes, "I had a million questions to ask God. But when I met Him, they all fled my mind; and it doesn't seem to matter."

—Warren Wiersbe, *Why Us?*

POSSIBLE EXIT: *Your questions are important. But come to Christ and you'll find your questions are resolved.*

❖   The Devil can make a good man; but only God can make a Christian.

—Source unknown

❖   **POSSIBLE ENTRANCE:** *You may feel like you're too big of a sinner for God to save and even question whether you can get your life turned around. Let me encourage you with what God did in the life of one man who was on death row.*

In his book *The Case for Faith*, Lee Strobel tells the story of William Neal Moore, a confessed murderer. He killed a seventy-seven-year-old man during a robbery attempt. Shortly after being imprisoned, two people told him about the love of Christ. He received God's free gift of forgiveness and eternal life.

—R. Larry Moyer

POSSIBLE EXIT: *God shows no partiality. What God did in Billy Moore's life He can do in yours.*

Note: Be sure to make the gospel clear. Always make sure you clearly state the issue for the sinner: "You must come to Christ, recognize that Christ died for you and rose from the dead, and trust Christ alone to save you."

DECISION

❖ Evangelist D. L. Moody told a story about a minister who was preparing a sermon on the urgency of receiving Christ without delay. After studying for some time, the preacher fell asleep in his chair and had a strange dream in which he overheard a conversation among several demons. They were huddled together, trying to devise a scheme for leading people of earth into hell.

One of the evil spirits said, "Let's tell people that the Bible is not the Word of God and that it can't be trusted." The others responded, "That isn't enough." Another spoke up, "Let's tell them that God doesn't exist, that Jesus was only a good man, and that there really is no heaven or hell." Again the others responded negatively. Finally, a third demon said, "Let's tell people there is a God, a Savior, and a heaven, and a hell. But let's assure them that they've got all the time in the world to be saved, and encourage them to put off the decision." "That's it!" the others shouted gleefully.

—*Our Daily Bread,* 1999

❖ You can't give Christ a definite maybe; it has to be a definite yes or a definite no.

—Billy Graham

❖ E. Stanley Jones states it graphically, "If you don't make up your mind, then your unmade mind will unmake you."

—J. Allan Peterson, *The Myth of the Cross*

❖ **POSSIBLE ENTRANCE:** *When you stand before God, what He was decided about you will be dependent on what you have decided about Him.*

The agreement you want with God *then* has to be made *now*.
—Douglas M. McCorkle, former president of Philadelphia Biblical University

POSSIBLE EXIT: *What you want God to do with you after death is determined by what you have done with Him before death.*

DISBELIEF

❖ At the University of Chicago Divinity School each year they have what is called "Baptist Day." It is a day when all the Baptists in the area are invited to the school because they want the Baptist dollars to keep coming in. On this day each one is to bring a lunch to be eaten outdoors in a grassy picnic area. Every "Baptist Day" the school would invite one of the greatest minds to lecture in the theological education center. One year they invited Dr. Paul Tillich.

Dr. Tillich spoke for two and a half hours, proving that the resurrection of Jesus was false. He quoted scholar after scholar and book after book. He concluded that since there was no such thing as the historical resurrection, the religious tradition of the church was groundless, emotional mumbo-jumbo, because it was based on a relationship with a risen Jesus, who, in fact, never rose from the dead in any literal sense. He then asked if there were any questions.

After about thirty seconds, an old, dark-skinned preacher with a head of short-cropped, woolly white hair stood up in the back of the auditorium. "Docta Tillich, I got one question," he said as all eyes turned toward him. He reached into his sack lunch and pulled out an apple and began eating it. "Docta Tillich" . . . crunch, munch . . . "My question is a simple question," . . . crunch, munch . . . "Now I ain't never read them books you read" . . . crunch, munch . . . "and I can't recite the Scriptures in the original Greek" . . . crunch, munch . . . He finished the apple. "All I wanna know is the apple I just ate—was it bitter or sweet?"

Dr. Tillich paused for a moment and answered in exemplary scholarly fashion: "I cannot possibly answer that question, for I haven't tasted your apple."

The white-haired preacher dropped the core of his apple into his crumpled paper bag, looked up at Dr. Tillich, and said calmly, "Neither have you tasted my Jesus."

The 1,000 plus in attendance could not contain themselves. The auditorium erupted with applause and cheers. Dr. Tillich thanked his audience and promptly left the platform.

—Source unknown

☺ As some people were walking through a cemetery, they noticed a tombstone that said, "I told you I was sick."

—Source unknown

❖ The rejection of Christ is often not so much of the "mind," but of the "will"; not so much "I can't," but "I won't."

—Used by permission. Josh McDowell,
The New Evidence That Demands a Verdict,
p. xi, Thomas Nelson Publishers, www.josh.org

DISTRACTION

❖ William H. Hinson tells us why animal trainers carry a stool when they go into a cage of lions. They have their whips, of course, and their pistols are at their sides. But invariably they also carry a stool. Hinson says it is the most important tool of the trainer. He holds the stool by the back and thrusts the legs toward the face of the wild animal. [They] maintain that the animal tries to focus on all four legs at once. In the attempt to focus on all four, a kind of paralysis overwhelms the animal, and it becomes tame, weak, and disabled because its attention is fragmented.

—John C. Maxwell, *Developing the Leader Within You*

☺ While Milgrom waited at the airport to board his plane, he noticed a computer scale that would give your weight and a fortune. He dropped a quarter in the slot, and the computer screen displayed, "You weigh 195 pounds, you are married, and you are on your way to San Diego." Milgrom stood there dumbfounded.

Another man put in a quarter and the computer read, "You weigh 184 pounds, you are divorced, and you are on your way to Chicago."

Milgrom said to the man, "Are you divorced and on your way to Chicago?"

"Yes," came the reply.

Milgrom was amazed. Then he rushed to the men's room, changed his clothes and put on dark glasses. He went to the machine again. The computer read, "You still weigh 195 pounds, you are still married, and you just missed your plane to San Diego!"

—Source unknown

☺ **POSSIBLE ENTRANCE:** *Distractions can be costly.*

Joe Arsenis robbed a store in Nashville, Tennessee, then fled on foot. When he heard someone chasing him, he turned around as he was running to see who it was. He ran smack into a concrete pole and knocked himself out. He was sentenced to five years.

—*Tidbits*, October 13, 1995

273

POSSIBLE EXIT: *That's humorous, but when distractions keep us from thinking about the most important issue of life, they are not humorous at all.*

☺ **POSSIBLE ENTRANCE:** *Distractions are often humorous. You may be able to identify with this:*

Recently, I was diagnosed with A.A.A.D.D. (Age-Activated Attention Deficit Disorder). This is how it manifests itself.

I decide to wash my car. As I start toward the garage, I notice that there is mail on the hall table. I decide to go through the mail before I wash the car. I lay my car keys down on the table, put the junk mail in the trash can under the table, and notice that the trash can is full. So I decide to put the bills back on the table and take out the trash first but then I think, since I'm going to be near the mailbox when I take out the trash anyway, I may as well pay the bills first. I take my checkbook off the table, and see that there is only one check left. My extra checks are in my desk in the study, so I go to my desk where I find the can of Coke that I had been drinking. I'm going to look for my checks, but first I need to push the Coke aside so that I don't accidentally knock it over. I see that the Coke is getting warm, and I decide I should put it in the refrigerator to keep it cold. As I head toward the kitchen with the Coke, a vase of flowers on the counter catches my eye—they need to be watered. I set the Coke down on the counter, and I discover my reading glasses that I've been searching for all morning. I decide I better put them back on my desk, but first I'm going to water the flowers. I set the glasses back down on the counter, fill a container with water, and suddenly I spot the TV remote. Someone left it on the kitchen table. I realize that tonight, when we go to watch TV, we will be looking for the remote, but nobody will remember that it's on the kitchen table. So I decide to put it back in the den where it belongs, but first I'll water the flowers. I splash some water on the flowers, but most of it spills on the floor. So I set the remote back down on the table, get some towels, and wipe up the spill. Then I head down the hall trying to remember what I was planning to do.

At the end of the day, the car isn't washed, the bills aren't paid, there is a warm can of Coke sitting on the counter, the flowers aren't watered, there is still only one check in my checkbook, I can't find the remote, I can't find my glasses, and I don't remember what I did with the car keys. Then when I try to figure out why nothing got done today, I'm really baffled because I know I was busy all day long, and I'm really tired. I realize this is a serious problem, and I'll try to get some help for it, but first I'll check my e-mail.

—Internet humor, author unknown

POSSIBLE EXIT: *When it comes to considering your need of Christ, distractions can be fatal.*

ETERNAL LIFE

❖ In 1981, Ida's Pastry Shoppe in Jenison, Michigan, advertised this special offer: "Buy one of our coffee mugs for $4.79 and fill up your cup for a dime each time you visit."

But the owners never expected that twenty-five years later, four long-time customers would still be getting their cup of java every day—for 10 cents.

You won't find many deals like that anymore. But Jesus offered something far greater to the woman at the well (John 4:10). He said, "Whoever drinks of this water will thirst again, but . . . the water that I shall give him will become in him a fountain of water springing up into everlasting life" (vv. 12–14).

—*Our Daily Bread*, 2006

❖ POSSIBLE ENTRANCE: *A man eulogized in* Newsweek *expressed what we all feel.*

You may have never heard the name of Sir Isaiah Berlin. When he died in 1997, Arthur Schlesinger eulogized him in *Newsweek* as "very likely the most sparkling man of the twentieth century." Born in Latvia, Berlin eventually became an Oxford professor and was noted for his extraordinary academic achievements. He was admired by people from every level of society.

Ironically, in that same issue of *Newsweek*, Sir Isaiah was quoted as saying, "I'm afraid of dying, for it could be painful. But I find death a nuisance. I object to it . . . I'm terribly curious. I'd like to live forever."

—*Our Daily Bread*, 1998

POSSIBLE EXIT: *How many of us would admit we'd like to live forever—especially in the presence of God?*

❖ The truest end of life is to know that life never ends.

—William Penn, founder of Pennsylvania

☺ POSSIBLE ENTRANCE: *We want to live forever, especially if it is in a place where all of our problems are over. Sometimes we just aren't sure we're going to make it.*

I plan to live forever—so far so good!

—Bumper sticker

POSSIBLE EXIT: *The Bible doesn't say you can hope you are going to live forever. It says you can know you're going to.*

❖ **POSSIBLE ENTRANCE:** *Most people are convinced you have to work you way to heaven.*

On a flight from Dallas to New York in preparation to attend Amsterdam '86, I had a chance to speak to a man about Christ. After I explained the gospel to him he said, "I've had many people tell me you have to work or earn your way to heaven. You are the first one who told me that it is a gift."

—R. Larry Moyer

POSSIBLE EXIT: *May I say loudly and clearly what the Bible says. Eternal life is a gift. It is free.*

ETERNAL SECURITY

❖ A woman who accepted Christ's gift of salvation said, "What a wonderful feeling it is not to wonder anymore."

—R. Larry Moyer

❖ **POSSIBLE ENTRANCE:** *It doesn't matter how many good things happen in life. Life at its best is temporal. The most important thing is to know you are going to be with Christ forever.*

Recently, the Carolina Hurricanes, formerly known as the Hartford Whalers, won their first Stanley Cup in franchise history by beating the Edmonton Oilers. While the fans in Raleigh, North Carolina, were as excited as ever, Glen Wesley was also exuberant, but he has his priorities in order.

Wesley, a veteran defenseman for the Carolina Hurricanes, had played in over 155 postseason games yet without a championship. Among all of the active players in the NHL, Wesley had gone the longest without winning the Stanley Cup.

Prior to the final game, Wesley was asked about his lack of a title. "I always say 'God knows,'" Wesley said. "I trust that, and I know that if it's His will, then great—but if not, I've had a great ride. I don't hold that as a priority.

"My eternal salvation is far more important to me—it's more important to have that eternal security and one day be at the feet of the Lord—than to be at the foot of the Cup," he said. "Life here on earth is temporary, and heaven is eternal."

—www.carolinahurricanes.com

POSSIBLE EXIT: *What good is winning the Stanley Cup without Christ? Wesley has it right. "Life here on earth is temporary, and heaven is eternal."*

Note: Make sure your audience knows that this is a hockey team and the Stanley Cup is the championship trophy.

❖ A small boy was walking with his father by a river, watching some workers who were knocking out the temporary props from under a bridge. "Look, Dad!" he said. "Why are they doing that? Won't the bridge fall down?" "No," replied his father, "it will just settle down on those big stone pillars. They will give it the permanent support it needs."

—*Our Daily Bread*, 1987

Note: The application here is "Our salvation has permanent support."

❖ You may tremble on the Rock, but the Rock will never tremble under you.

—Pastor Guy Parrish, Church Central Muskogee, Muskogee, OK

Note: This illustration is effective. But you must first introduce the fact that Jesus Christ is often referred to as the Rock of our salvation. That's because He is the one we must trust in as our only way to heaven. Then give the illustration. Always remember you are talking to non-Christians who probably don't know some of these terms.

☺ When Dan Reeves, star halfback for the Dallas Cowboys and later coach for the Atlanta Falcons, went to the hospital to see his wife and new-born son for the first time, he was thrown for a big loss. Rushing into the hospital room, he asked to hold his son, Michael. "Not on your life," his wife said emphatically.

Reeves looked as if a blitzing linebacker had just nailed him in the backfield. "Why not?" he asked.

"You fumble too much," his wife replied.

—Dallas Cowboys newsletter

Note: The point to be made is that God never fumbles. We can trust Him. You can trust Him to get you to heaven. Once you are His, He will not drop you.

☺ **POSSIBLE ENTRANCE:** *When you trust Christ, how do you know you will be in His presence forever? The answer is, "He said so." If He said it, that's all the proof you need.*

God says to me in John 6:37, "Him that cometh to me I will in no way cast out." I have read that in the Greek. A Greek professor, preaching in an old country church, said, "That verse says, 'Him that cometh to me I will in no wise cast out.' But in the Greek it means, 'Him that cometh to me I will never, no never, no never, no never, no never cast out.'"

An elderly lady came to him after the service and said, "Well, He may have to say it five times for your professors, but one time is enough for me."

—Curtis Hutson, *Salvation Plain and Simple*

POSSIBLE EXIT: *Christ tells us many times in the Bible that when we trust Him, we are eternally secure. But even if He had said it only once, that would have been enough.*

Note: I always update illustrations like these and use modern English.

❖ You do not come to Christ to make a promise; you come to depend on His promise. It is the faithfulness of God and not your own that gives the gift of grace.

—Erwin Lutzer, *How You Can Be Sure That You Will Spend Eternity with God*

❖ **POSSIBLE ENTRANCE:** *Why are you forever secure the moment you trust Christ? It's not because you are holding Him but because He is holding you.*

A mountain climber in the Alps had come to a treacherous place in his ascent. The only way to advance was to place his foot in the outstretched hands of the guide who had anchored himself a little way ahead of him. The man hesitated a moment as he looked below to where he would certainly fall to his death if anything went wrong. Noticing his hesitation, the guide said, "Have no fear, sir. In all my years of service my hands have never yet lost a man!"

—*Our Daily Bread,* 1990

POSSIBLE EXIT: *If your salvation was dependent on you holding God, you could lose eternal life because you might lose your grip. Remember it is God holding you. He's never dropped anyone and never will.*

❖ I asked a woman I had just led to Christ, "Where would you go if you were to die right now?" She answered, "Heaven." I then said, "Where would you go if you died ten years from now?" She answered, "If I'm safe now, I'll be safe then."
—R. Larry Moyer

❖ Recently I heard of a gospel worker who walked up to two men and handed them a tract. One of the men smiled and asked, "Life insurance?" The Christian worker replied, "Yes, for time and eternity."
—Erling C. Olsen, *Meditation in the Book of Psalms*

❖ In a sermon, Juan Carlos Ortiz spoke of a conversation with a circus trapeze artist. The performer admitted the net underneath was there to keep them from breaking their necks, but added, "The net also keeps us from falling. Imagine there is no net. We would be so nervous that we would be more likely to miss and fall. If there wasn't a net, we would not dare to do some of the things we do. But because there's a net, we dare to make two turns, and once I made three turns—thanks to the net!"

Ortiz makes this observation: "We have security in God. When we are sure in His arms, we dare to attempt big things for God. We dare to be holy. We dare to be obedient. We dare, because we know the eternal arms of God will hold us if we fall."
—*Leadership,* Fall 1990

❖ If you think you can earn your salvation, you think too highly of sheep. If you think you can lose your salvation, you think too lowly of the Shepherd.
—Source unknown

Note: Be sure the audience understands that the Bible calls us sheep and calls Christ the shepherd.

❖ **POSSIBLE ENTRANCE:** *Sometimes we struggle with being forever secure in Christ because we forget one thing: just as we would not abandon our children, God does not abandon His.*

Tim Allen Duncan beat to death a fourteen-year-old girl on September 25, 1994.

Mr. Duncan's mother, Vicky Mann, said her son, who had admitted using drugs before the murder, also was a victim.

"I think it is tragic that the two youngest people who were at an all-night drug party for adults are the ones whose lives were ruined," she said. "They say he has no remorse, but he has told me, 'I would die if it would bring that little girl back to life.'"

Ms. Mann said she plans to continue to visit her son regularly. "I'm his mom," she said. "I will not abandon him."

—Dallas Morning News, January 30, 1998

POSSIBLE EXIT: *When God's children do wrong, He loves us even more than we love our own children. Just as we do not abandon them, God does not abandon us.*

❖ Martin Luther was once asked if he felt saved. He replied, "No, I don't feel saved, but my confidence in Christ's promise is greater than my doubts!"

—Erwin Lutzer,
How You Can Be Sure You Will Spend Eternity with God

❖ When I was a college sophomore on a summer missions trip in Europe, our ship docked for a short time in Cobh, Ireland. Among the people who came aboard to sell their wares was a quaint little Irish lady with some handmade lace. Talking with a distinguished-looking customer, she shared the reality of her salvation through Jesus Christ and her eagerness for heaven. The man chided her a bit about her assurance of heaven. He said it was presumptuous and perhaps even egotistical to think that she was good enough to be sure of heaven. I'll never forget her radiant response: "Oh, sir, you mistake me. You see, it is not my reputation that is at stake. It is Jesus Christ who made the promise." The man did not have a clue about the gift of eternal life through Christ. But the Irish lady correctly understood that God, on whom she had focused her faith, would keep her secure in Christ.

Earl D. Radmacher, *Salvation*

❖ Dr. Henson used to say, "The Lord takes you and puts you into the Father's hand, and then He covers you with His other hand. How are you going to get out?"

—John G. Mitchell, *An Everlasting Love*

Note: Who Dr. Henson was is immaterial to this illustration. Just say, "A person one time made this thought-provoking statement, . . ."

❖ Because my daughter is a flight attendant, I am blessed with a parent's pass for my personal use. For a small service charge, I may fly wherever the airline flies. There's one drawback, however. I must be on "standby." That means I'm allowed on board only if there's space available. Until then, my luggage is set aside and labeled "Status Pending." While the paying passengers board, I must wait, wondering if my name will be called. I can never be certain of a seat because available space isn't guaranteed.

—*Our Daily Bread*, 2001

Note: Instead of using this illustration as it is, use the idea but draw one from your own flying experiences or the experience of someone you know.

❖ Someone asked the great financier J. P. Morgan, "What is the best collateral a person can give for a loan?" Morgan replied, "Character." God's character is the best collateral we can have that our eternal salvation is secure in Christ.

—Warren Wiersbe, *The Intercessory Prayer of Jesus*

❖ A number of years ago, Jim Kaat, a star pitcher for the Minnesota Twins baseball team, was asked by a sportswriter what it meant to be a Christian and a professional athlete. Kaat answered by relating an experience that had taken place on the pitcher's mound a couple of weeks earlier. It was at the end of a crucial game—a game the Twins needed to win if they were to have a chance at the league championship. Kaat needed to get only one more batter out and the Twins would win the game. He said that as he prepared to throw the ball the thought went through is mind, "I'm sure glad my destiny isn't riding on this next pitch!"

—*Our Daily Bread*, 2001

❖ If "save forever" doesn't mean forever, then we don't have a gospel that is truly "good news" to a lost world.

—Tony Evans, *Totally Saved*

FORGIVENESS
❖ In Miami, Florida, a woman who offered a man $1,000 to kill her husband was arrested, pleaded guilty to a charge of attempted murder, but walked out of the criminal court a free woman. The reason for her release: the husband she sought to destroy had bailed her out of jail and then

pleaded with the court not to punish her, insisting that she "just got mixed up."

The judge, in telling the woman that she would not be sentenced, said, "I don't know anybody in the world who would take a woman back after she paid someone to kill him." Turning to the husband the judge said, "You're not uneasy sleeping out there in the same house with her?"

"Not a bit," the husband replied.

Sinners paid Judas to betray Christ and nailed Him to a cross, and yet He said, "Father, forgive them they know not what they do" (Luke 23:24 ESV).

—Robert L. Summer

Note: The application here would be, "Here was a man who forgave the person who tried to kill him. You and I nailed Christ to a cross. It was for our sins He died. Yet He is willing to take us back and give us a complete forgiveness and even let us into the same 'house.'"

❖ **POSSIBLE ENTRANCE:** *Human nature is such that we often have the power to pardon, but not the desire.*

One of the captive followers of the Duke of Monmouth was brought before James the Second. "You know it is in my power," said the king, "to pardon you." "Yes," said the man, who well knew his cruel character, "but it is not in your nature."

—C. H. Spurgeon

POSSIBLE EXIT: *With God, it is not only within His power to forgive, it's also within His nature.*

☺ **POSSIBLE ENTRANCE:** *By our nature, when others do wrong to us our first thought is revenge.*

A six-year-old comes crying to his mother because his little sister pulled his hair.

"Don't be angry," the mother says, "your little sister doesn't realize that pulling hair hurts."

A short while later, there's more crying, and the mother goes to investigate.

This time the sister is bawling and her brother says, "She knows now."

—Todd Cartmell, *Keep the Siblings,*
Lose the Rivalry

POSSIBLE EXIT: *When we wrong God, His first thought is forgiveness, not revenge.*

❖ **POSSIBLE ENTRANCE:** *You may wonder, "How much can God forgive?" To answer that question you need to ask this question, "How much does God love?"*

We pardon in the degree that we love.

—*Leadership*, Fall 1980

POSSIBLE EXIT: *Since God's love has no limits, neither does His pardon.*

❖ When one goes up north in the winter, one might look at a junkyard and see item after item of nothing but worthless trash. And yet overnight, because of a snowfall, the appearance of that junkyard can so change that nothing is seen except a soft blanket of white snow. This is how it is when the Lord covers our transgressions and makes us whiter than snow.

—Kirk Mueller

> Note: Two things would help this illustration come alive for a non-Christian audience. First tie it to a specific snowstorm you or they have experienced. Next mention items of "junk" the snow covers such as an abandoned car, broken table, old bicycle. The snow covers it all. Parallel that to specific sins that God's forgiveness covers, with the emphasis "His forgiveness covers it all."

❖ I love the way a person expressed it when he said, "God dropped my sins into the depth of a sea and then He put up a 'No Fishing' sign." No one can bring them to the surface.

—R. Larry Moyer

❖ Perhaps you have seen an electronic computer used to calculate mathematical problems. What happens if you get your information confused or make an error? You can press the cancel button! Automatically, all of the information is eliminated from the apparatus. You can begin your calculation again without trying to sort out previous mistakes! In fact, there is no record of the previous information; it is lost forever!

That is what happens to our sins when God forgives us! The consequences often remain, but the guilt (the legal condemnation for the offense) is gone.

—Erwin W. Lutzer, *Failure: The Back Door to Success*

❖ **POSSIBLE ENTRANCE:** *When God writes forgiveness over our debt of sin, He writes it with a pen, not a pencil. It can't be erased.*

There lived for many years in a Scottish village a doctor noted for his skill and piety. After his death there was found written across many of his accounts: "Forgiven—too poor to pay." In selling the estate, his wife said, "These accounts must be paid," and sued for the money. The judge asked, "Is this your husband's handwriting in red?" She replied, "Yes." "Then," said the judge, "there is not a tribunal in the land that can obtain the money where he has written 'Forgiven.'"

—Source unknown

POSSIBLE EXIT: *No one can alter God's forgiveness. When He declares "forgiveness" it cannot be reversed.*

❖ A person asked the pastor, "What does forgiveness mean?" He answered, "It means all your files have been deleted."

—Billy Graham

❖ **POSSIBLE ENTRANCE:** *Once you trust Christ, you can never be punished for your sins. You cannot take the punishment when the punishment has already been taken.*

Many years ago, a father and his daughter were walking through the grass on the Canadian prairie. In the distance, they saw a prairie fire. They realized it would engulf them. The father knew there was only one way of escape: they would quickly build a fire right where they were and burn a large patch of grass. When the huge fire drew near, they then would stand on the section that had already burned. When the flames did approach them, the girl was terrified, but her father assured her, "The flames can't get to us. We are standing where the fire has already been."

—Erwin W. Lutzer, *Failure: The Back Door to Success*

POSSIBLE EXIT: *Judgment cannot fall where judgment has already been. The punishment for sin has already been taken. Since God punished Christ for your sin, God can now forgive you.*

❖ A young convert from Madagascar had become a zealous worker for Christ. Whenever he spoke the name of Jesus, his bright eyes filled with tears. A missionary who heard about him wanted to know if this was really true. So he put the young man to the test and saw the startling effect. Deeply moved, he asked him, "How can this be?" "How can it not be?" replied the young man. "He has died for me, and my every sin is forgiven!"

—*Our Daily Bread*, 1987

❖ Søren Kierkegaard appeared to grasp what the forgiveness of sins means to a Christian. When the thought of God does not remind him of his sin, but that it is forgiven, and the past is no longer the memory of how much he did wrong, but of how much he was forgiven—then that man rests in the forgiveness of sins.

—Haddon Robinson, in *Focal Point* newsletter

❖ After the death of Abraham Lincoln, Mrs. Lincoln sorrowfully asked John F. Parker, the president's bodyguard, "Why were you not at the door to keep the assassin out?"

Parker lowered his head and said, "I have bitterly repented of it. I did not believe anyone would try to kill so good a man. The belief made me careless. I became so interested in the play, I failed to see the assassin enter the presidential box."

"You could have seen him. You had no right to be careless." Having said this, Mrs. Lincoln covered her face with her hands and wept uncontrollably.

Recovering her composure, she said to Parker, "Go now. It's not you I can't forgive. It's the assassin."

Tad Lincoln, who heard his mother, said, "If Pa had lived, he would have forgiven the man who shot him. Pa forgave everybody."

—Adapted from Elizabeth Keckley, *Behind the Scenes, or, Thirty Years a Slave and Four Years in the White House*, 1868

Note: The application here would be, "What Tad really meant was, 'Pa forgave anyone.' So, too, Christ forgives anyone, anywhere, of anything."

❖ "I sentence you to life without parole in the state penitentiary," the judge said.

A wave of nausea came over me as I thought of spending the rest of my life in prison, of being isolated from everyone and everything that was important to me. I thought that my life was over.

As a child, I had dreams about my future—dreams of being a professional football player, of raising a family, of having my own business.

But my dreams were obscured by a home life of violence, alcoholism, and sexual abuse.

My parents drank heavily and argued frequently. Often their arguing led to physical abuse. I vividly remember one incident when I was thirteen. My parents were into a heated argument. Their bedroom door was shut, but I heard every word. Next came the familiar sound of dad hitting mom, followed by a thud as mom crashed to the floor. That night she had to be rushed to the hospital. When I saw her the next morning, she had white tape plastered across her broken nose and battered cheeks. Her face was swollen, and she looked at me sadly through blackened eyes.

From a very young age until far into my teens, I was bruised by sexual abuse from other family members. I often felt guilty and responsible for what was happening to me. After the acts were carried out, I was threatened not to tell anyone. I remember being left alone and crying.

As the abuse continued, I began to feel more like an object than a person. Eventually I was able to escape the pain in my own life because I started seeing the world as full of objects using other objects.

My hopes and dreams were further diluted through involvement with drugs and alcohol. I began drinking and doing drugs at age fourteen. I remember my first encounter with marijuana. While riding in a car with several friends, I was asked if I'd ever smoked marijuana.

"Sure," I lied, not wanting to be the oddball in the crowd.

"Here, roll some up," they said. After smoking the joints, I felt the drug settling into my system. The more I smoked, the less I cared. The less I cared, the better life seemed.

But I soon learned that drug addiction was not cheap. It wasn't long before I couldn't support my growing drug habit by lying to my parents about why I needed money, so I turned to crime. I started by stealing petty stuff.

As my drug habits worsened, so did my crimes. But my crimes ended abruptly late one hot July night in 1977. All was quiet outside the home I was burglarizing. Inside was a different scene. While rummaging through a closet for valuables to steal, I was confronted by the owner. A struggle ensued, and I stabbed the woman, killing her.

I was arrested and charged with capital murder. Conviction of the charge carried a maximum penalty of death, with "life without parole" as the only alternative.

At my trial the jury foreman read the verdict: "We find the defendant, Ted A. McGinnis, guilty, and fix his punishment at death by electrocution." When mitigating circumstances were considered, the judge reduced my sentence to life without parole. Next to death, prison was the only place for me.

In prison my discouragement gave way to depression, and I was transferred to the system's psychiatric unit. One day, while wandering around the drab, cramped hospital ward, I was approached by a fellow inmate who invited me to go chapel the next Sunday.

"Why not?" I replied. Actually, I thought that some women might be at the service. As I entered the chapel that Sunday, I saw that my thoughts were correct—several young women were present. A couple of young men were busy setting up sound equipment for the service. Everyone was smiling and greeting one another.

Soon the room was filled with singing. As I looked around, I saw convicted criminals—the undesirables of society—taking an active part in the service. I began to feel a strange and uncomfortable sensation deep inside me. I wanted to run, but the prison rule was that whoever attended had to stay until the service was over.

The preacher was in his mid-twenties. His fiery red hair seemed to light up the room as he preached. I don't remember his name, but I'll remember his message forever. He spoke of the Savior who wanted to forgive my sins, of God who could heal all my broken dreams and put my life together again. I forgot all about the women. All I could think of was Jesus, the Savior whom the preacher was talking about. As the sensation inside me grew, I became more uncomfortable.

The preacher asked if anyone wanted to receive forgiveness for his sins. No one moved, but I felt a raging inside me. Could God really forgive me and heal me? What would people think of me if I responded? I'd heard how some convicts viewed others who'd gotten "jailhouse religion."

"Last call," the preacher said.

Without giving myself time for another thought, I rose from my seat and dashed to the front. With tears streaming down my cheeks, I gave my life to Jesus Christ. The strange, uneasy sensation I'd felt was replaced by a peace I'd never experienced before. The person whom society had condemned, God restored. The tool Satan had used to harm and destroy lives could now be used by God to minister to others.

After my conversion I learned that knowing and serving Christ brings blessings. I feel that I've been blessed beyond anything imaginable.

God saw my loneliness in prison and brought Marilou Coley into my life. We met in 1985 through a mutual friend. Soon we realized that we loved each other and requested permission to marry. We were denied permission because the rules didn't permit inmates sentenced to "life without" to marry. But we knew that God had put us together and that he'd work it out for us. We prayed and left it in his hands. Before long the rules were changed, and we were married in April, 1986. After almost five years of marriage we feel more blessed than when we met.

God has also made it possible for me to know the joy of being a father. My son, Wayne, from a relationship before I became a Christian, and Marilou's daughter, Amber, have been a great blessing to me. Because of my family, there are no more lonely days for me. Even when we are apart, my thoughts are with them.

One of the greatest blessings I've had is being used by God to lead others to the glorious liberty found in Christ Jesus. When one young man first became my cell mate, he was into drugs, and gambling heavily. I began to tell him about Jesus Christ, and it wasn't long before he felt convicted by the Holy Spirit. He even asked me to stop praying for him and to stop telling him about the Lord because he almost always lost all his goods when he played cards, and he was having trouble sleeping.

Finally he told me that he was going to go to chapel with me. I was surprised when he stood up during the service and told how God was dealing with his heart. He said he was tired of fighting God's call to him; that night he gave his life to Jesus.

As I've been privileged to present the gospel to lost and lonely men, I've learned that the love of God reaches not only to the uttermost, but even to those who are considered the "guttermost."

I'm still in prison doing "life without." But, thank God, I've been set free from the sin that ripped apart my life for many years. God gave me a pardon that no one can take away.

Though I look out my cell window and see fences of razor wire, I can look inside myself and see freedom from my sinful and pain-filled past.

> — This quote was taken from the article "I'm in Prison for Life, but I'm Free,"
> ©1990 Ted A. McGinnis in the January 1991 *Decision* magazine, pp. 4-5.
> Used by permission.

Note: Remember, make the gospel clear. The story reads, "That night he gave his life to Jesus." Instead, clearly present the gospel by saying, "That night he trusted Christ." Also, this is a long story. But sometimes it is best to file the whole story, and then when you use it, choose the parts you want. Having more facts than you need is easier than not having enough facts to understand the story. You can always delete from what you know but you can't add to what you don't know.

❖   It should be easy for me to forget what God chooses not to remember.

—R. Larry Moyer

Note: Many people experience God's forgiveness but can't forgive themselves. This a helpful way to explain the beauty of God's forgiveness: if what we have done is no longer on His mind, it doesn't have to be on ours either.

❖   A theology professor was watching five boys playing in his yard when he noticed one of them with a BB gun, taking aim in the direction of his window! The next thing he heard was the shattering of glass; then he saw the boys running off in all directions. The teacher had the window replaced immediately. He found out that a lad by the name of Dave White had pulled the trigger, so he waited for an opportunity to meet him. But though the other boys drifted back to play in the yard again, Dave stayed away. Then one day the man saw him in a store. Greeting him in a friendly manner, he found him to be rebellious, tense, and scared. He said to him kindly, "Dave, I paid for the window, and as far as I'm concerned everything is all right. Come back and play." But the young fellow still didn't return. Finally, however, he timidly rejoined his playmates. And when he saw the professor smile at him warmly, he relaxed. At last he realized that he had been forgiven and was fully accepted by the one he had wronged.

—*Our Daily Bread*, 1979

Note: There is no need to mention he was a theology professor. "Professor" is what non-Christians will identify with.

❖   The two Greek philosophers Plato and Socrates were discussing God's attitude toward sinful man. Socrates said to Plato, "I expect a holy God can forgive sin, but I can't conceive how."

—Lance B. Latham, *The Two Gospels*

☺   A man was telling a companion about an argument he'd had with his wife. "Oh, how I hate it," he said. "Every time we fight she gets historical." "You mean hysterical," replied the friend. "No, I mean historical," he insisted. "She drags up everything from the past and holds it against me!"

—*Our Daily Bread*, 1980

Note: The application here is, "God never brings up the past. He does not become historical."

❖   A man who was serving a lifetime sentence in the Oklahoma State Penitentiary escaped. The warden, Jerome J. Waters, offered the fugitive $1,500 if he would surrender himself at the gates of the prison.

There was a catch, however, to the offer. The reward was to be earned and saved by the escapee by doing work in the prison. "If he comes we will see that he does not get out again. Justice will prevail," said the warden.

How different is the offer God makes to all the fugitives from divine justice. There is no catch to His offer.

—Source unknown

❖   When Methodist minister William Sangster was addressing Christmas cards, a friend noticed one name and remarked, "Don't you remember how he slighted you?" Sangster responded, "Oh yes, I remember, but I have remembered to forget."

—Haddon Robinson

> Note: The application here is that God, knowing all, knows all we've ever done. But the beauty of forgiveness is, "He remembers to forget."

☺   I was explaining to a new convert that not only his sins in the past but also those in the future are forgiven on the basis of the cross. He said, "I bet you that's why they call Him Almighty, isn't it?"

—R. Larry Moyer

❖   Written by a widow on her adulterous husband's gravestone in an Atlanta, Georgia, cemetery: "Gone, but not forgiven."

—*San Antonio Express News*, December 28, 1975

> Note: The application here is, "We keep records. God doesn't."

❖   They say that the first time Sawat went to the top floor of the hotel, he was shocked. He had never dreamed it would be like this. Every room had a window facing into the hallway and in every room sat a girl. Some looked older and they were smiling and laughing, but many of them were just twelve or thirteen years old—some even younger. They looked nervous, even frightened.

It was Sawat's first venture into Bangkok's world of prostitution. It all began innocently enough, but soon he was caught up like a small piece of wood in a raging river. It was too powerful for him, too swift, and the current too strong.

Soon he was selling opium to customers and propositioning tourists in the hotels. He even went so low as to actually help buy and sell young girls, some of them only nine and ten years old. It was a nasty business, and he was one of the most important of the young "businessmen."

Sawat became a central figure in one of the world's largest and most loathsome trades: Thailand's sex industry. It is estimated that over 10 percent of all girls in Thailand end up in prostitution. The top floors of most hotels are used by them, as are the back rooms of many bars. Though the practice is discouraged by the royal family, many poorer rural families sell their young daughters to pay off family debts. Who knows what happens to many of these frightened ten-year-olds when they have outlived their usefulness?

Sawat disgraced his family and dishonored his father's name. He had come to Bangkok to escape the dullness of village life. He found excitement, and while he prospered in this sordid life, he was popular. But then the bottom dropped out of his world. He hit a string of bad luck: he was robbed, and while trying to climb back to the top, he was arrested. Everything went wrong. The word spread in the underworld that he was a police spy. He finally ended up living in a shanty by the city rubbish dump.

Sitting in his little shack, he thought about his family, especially his father. He remembered the parting words of his father, a simple Christian man from a small village in the south, near the Malaysian border: "I am waiting for you." Would his father *still* be waiting for him after all he had done to dishonor the family name? Would he receive him home after disregarding all he had been taught about God's love? Word had long ago filtered back to his village about his life of crime and sin.

Finally, he devised a plan.

"Dear Father," he wrote, "I want to come home, but I don't know if you will receive me after all that I have done. I have sinned greatly, Father. Please forgive me. On Saturday night I will be on the train that goes through our village. If you are still waiting for me will you tie a piece of white cloth on the po tree in front of our house?"

During the train ride he thought over his life of evil. He knew his father had every right to refuse to see him. As the train finally neared the village he was filled with anxiety. What would he do if there was no white piece of cloth on the po tree?

Sitting opposite Sawat was a kind stranger, who noticed how nervous his fellow passenger had become. Finally, Sawat could stand the pressure no longer. The story burst out in a torrent of words. He told the man everything. As they entered the village, Sawat said, "Oh, sir, I cannot bear to look. Can you watch for me? What if my father will not receive me back home?"

Sawat buried his face between his knees. "Do you see it sir? It's the only house with a po tree."

"Young man, your father did not hang *one* piece of cloth . . . look! He has covered the whole tree with pieces of white cloth!" He could hardly believe his eyes. There was the tree, covered, and in the front yard his old father was dancing up and down, joyously waving a piece of white cloth! His father ran beside the train, and when it stopped at the little station he threw his arms around his son, embracing him with tears of joy. "I've been waiting for you!" he exclaimed.

—Taken from *The Father Heart of God.* Copyright © 1985 by Floyd McClung, Jr. Published by Harvest House Publishers, Eugene, Oregon 97402. Used by permission.

Note: Build this up as much as possible to illustrate God's forgiveness. You might say, "God would have so many white scarves hanging on His tree of forgiveness, it would be difficult to see the tree. All you'd see would be the white scarves. He's saying to you, 'Please, please come home.'"

❖ **POSSIBLE ENTRANCE:** *One of the reasons we struggle with forgiveness is that we forget that God's love is such a contrast to ours—thankfully.*

By contrast, we are often half-hearted in our acceptance of people by either directly or indirectly reminding them of their past. This makes them feel that they don't quite belong. For example, a minister was visiting a rich man who had adopted a twelve-year-old boy he had taken in from the streets. While the two men were talking, the boy, now fifteen, came into the room. After a casual greeting, the father went to the closet, pulled out a pair of tattered old shoes, and said, "Fred was wearing these when I found him." The minister saw that the teenager was embarrassed and deeply hurt. But the father went on, "I think it's good for him to be reminded every once in a while of his condition when I took him in." Silently the pastor prayed, "Thank You, Lord, for accepting me fully. Thank You for not dragging out my old shoes!"

—Our Daily Bread, 1981

POSSIBLE EXIT: *God doesn't remind you of your sins. When He forgives, that's it, it's a done deal. This is what helps us to forgive ourselves. If our sins are not on His mind, they don't have to be on ours.*

❖ God's and man's forgiveness of Jake Bird, convicted of the ax and knife murder of a mother and daughter on October 30, 1947, of Tacoma, Washington, bears dramatic witness to the saving grace of God.

God put it into the heart of the son-in-law of the murdered woman to visit Mr. Bird in his prison cell. The grieving man told the prisoner that God would forgive his sin and save his soul upon the condition that he trust Jesus Christ as his Savior. After some three hours of listening to God's precious plan of salvation, the prisoner gave the rest of his life to Christ.

Two years later Jake Bird was hanged for his crime. The guard who stayed with him his last eight hours of life reported Jake's testimony as follows:

"You know, a lot of fellows would be awful nervous if they were me, knowing what they were going to do in a few hours. But I'm not. You see, I'm going home to be with my Lord, so I'm not scared."

"After a while," the guard related, "he said he felt like singing, so he got up and walked back and forth in the cell singing some old gospel songs."
—Booklet on the topic of grace by Willard M. Aldrich

Note: Be certain to make the gospel clear. This author uses the terms "gave his life to Christ." We should always say "trusted Christ." Salvation is not our giving our lives to Christ. It is Him, giving His life to us.

❖ It's a good thing our local library gives a grace period before it starts charging for overdue books. My family checks out books by the dozen, and sometimes we forget to get them back on time.

Recently one of my daughters passed the grace period—by more than three weeks. When I went to pay the fine, I asked if we could get credit for the grace period and pay just for the days after that. I was told, however, that once the grace period ends, the full penalty is due.
—*Our Daily Bread*, 1994

Note: Some think they have gone too far for God to save them. The use of this illustration is that God's grace never ends unless we end first (die). Until then, His grace is available.

❖ **POSSIBLE ENTRANCE:** *Many people are afraid of God. They see Him as their enemy, not as their friend.*

C. H. Spurgeon illustrated this tendency in his book *All of Grace*. He told of a minister who went to the home of a poor woman to give her some money that she desperately needed. When he knocked at her door, she did not answer. He felt sure she was home, so he knocked again. Still no response. After more knocking, he left. On Sunday, he saw her in church and said, "I called at your home last Friday. I suppose you were not at home, for I knocked several times, and you did not answer. I had some money for you." "What time were you there?" she asked. "About noon," the minister replied. "Oh dear," said the woman, "I heard you. But I did not answer. I thought it was my landlord calling for the rent."
—*Our Daily Bread*, 1987

POSSIBLE EXIT: *God is not out to collect on something we owe. The debt has been paid. He is out to pardon. The question is will you let Him?*

❖ British Bible teacher and lecturer David Pawson says, "I have talked to the most devout Muslims who pray five times a day, have journeyed to Mecca, have fasted during Ramadan, and are more devout than many Christians. But when I ask, 'Do you know if your sins are forgiven?' they've said, 'We don't. We just have to hope for the best.'"

—*Our Daily Bread*, 1996

GOD

❖ The small house was simple but adequate. It consisted of one large room on a dusty street. Its red tiled roof was one of many in this poor neighborhood on the outskirts of the Brazilian village. It was a comfortable home. Maria and her daughter, Christina, had done what they could to add color to the gray walls and warmth to the hard dirt floor: an old calendar, a faded photograph of a relative, a wooden crucifix. The furnishings were modest: a pallet on either side of the room, a washbasin, and wood-burning stove.

Maria's husband had died when Christina was an infant. The young mother, stubbornly refusing opportunities to remarry, got a job and set out to raise her young daughter. And now, fifteen years later, the worst years were over. Though Maria's salary as a maid afforded few luxuries, it was reliable, and it did provide food and clothes. And now Christina was old enough to get a job to help out.

Some said Christina got her independence from her mother. She recoiled at the traditional idea of marrying young and raising a family. Not that she couldn't have had her pick of husbands. Her olive skin and brown eyes kept a steady stream of prospects at her door. She had an infectious way of throwing her head back and filling the room with laughter. She also had that rare magic some women have that makes every man feel like a king just by being near them. But it was her spirited curiosity that made her keep all the men at arm's length.

She spoke often of going to the city. She dreamed of trading her dusty neighborhood for exciting avenues and city life. Just the thought of this horrified her mother. Maria was always quick to remind Christina of the harshness of the streets. "People don't know you there. Jobs are scarce and the life is cruel. And besides, if you went there, what would you do for a living?"

Maria knew exactly what Christina would do, or would have to do for a living. That's why her heart broke when she awoke one morning to find her daughter had gone. She also knew immediately what she must do to find her. She quickly threw some clothes in a bag, gathered up all her money, and ran out of the house.

On her way to the bus stop she entered a drugstore to get one last thing. Pictures. She sat in the photograph booth, closed the curtain, and spent all she could on pictures of herself. With her purse full of small black and white photos, she boarded the next bus to Rio de Janeiro.

Maria knew Christina had no way of earning money. She also knew that her daughter was too stubborn to give up. When pride meets hunger, a human will do things that were before unthinkable. Knowing this, Maria began her search. Bars, hotels, nightclubs, any place with the reputation for street walkers or prostitutes. She went to them all. And at each place she left her picture—taped on a bathroom mirror, tacked to a hotel bulletin board, fastened to a corner phone booth. And on the back of each photo she wrote a note.

It wasn't too long before both the money and the pictures ran out, and Maria had to go home. The weary mother wept as the bus began its long journey back to her small village.

It was a few weeks later that a young Christina descended the hotel stairs. Her young face was tired. Her brown eyes no longer danced with youth but spoke of pain and fear. Her laughter was broken. Her dream had become a nightmare. A thousand times over she had longed to trade these countless beds for her secure pallet. Yet the little village was, in too many ways, too far away.

As she reached the bottom of the stairs, her eyes noticed a familiar face. She looked again, and there on the lobby mirror was a small picture of her mother. Christina's eyes burned and her throat tightened as she walked across the room and removed the small photo. Written on the back was this compelling invitation. "Whatever you have done, whatever you have become, it doesn't matter. Please come home."

She did.

—Reprinted by permission, *No Wonder They Call Him Savior,* Max Lucado, 2004, Thomas Nelson, Inc., Nashville, Tennessee. All rights reserved.

❖ Long before we ever think of Him, He thinks of us.

—John Phillips

Note: An illustration like this becomes helpful whenever you change the tense— "Long before we ever thought of Him, He thought of us. He wanted to save us from our sin."

❖ **POSSIBLE ENTRANCE:** *God is so impossible to find that many of us would echo the sentiment of this teenager.*

Where is God? I'm sick of hanging on to nothing.

—Dawson McAllister, *Please Don't Tell My Parents*

POSSIBLE EXIT: *Could it be, though, that in attempting to find God, we've not looked in the right place? We put our focus on what we want Him to do for us instead of what He has done for us.*

☺ Two shipwrecked sailors were adrift on a raft for days. In desperation, one knelt down and began to pray. "Oh, Lord, I haven't lived a good life. I've drunk too much. I've lied. I've cheated. I've gambled. I've caroused with women. I've done many bad things, but Lord, if you'll save me, I promise . . ."

"Don't say another word!" shouted his shipmate. "I think I just spotted land."

—Source unknown

❖ As to some things we may be in doubt: as to His Being there can be no uncertainty.

—Lewis Ransom Fiske, *Man-Building: A Treatise on Human Life and Its Forces*

❖ **POSSIBLE ENTRANCE:** *Because of the negative feelings we may have about God or religion, we are running from the Person who is here to help us.*

Several years ago an Eastern paper reported this story:

One evening a woman was driving home when she noticed a huge truck behind her that was driving uncomfortably close. She stepped on the gas to gain some distance from the truck, but when she sped up, the truck did too. The faster she drove, the faster the truck did.

Now scared, she exited the freeway. But the truck stayed with her. The woman then turned up a main street, hoping to lose her pursuer in traffic. But the truck ran a red light and continued the chase.

Reaching the point of panic, the woman whipped her car into a service station and bolted out of her auto screaming for help. The truck driver sprang from his truck and ran toward her car. Yanking the back door open, the driver pulled out a man hidden in the back seat.

The woman was running from the wrong person. From his high vantage point, the truck driver had spotted a would-be rapist in the woman's car. The chase was not his effort to harm her but to save her even at the cost of his own safety.

Likewise, many people run from God, fearing what He might do to them. But His plans are for good not evil—to rescue us from the hidden sins that endanger our lives.

—*Leadership*, Summer 1986

POSSIBLE EXIT: *You may feel religion has done you a lot of harm. But God is not out to harm. He is out to help.*

❖ **POSSIBLE ENTRANCE:** *It is the Bible that needs to dictate your view of who God is, not the daily newspaper.*

A twenty-year-old woman had been murdered by her husband in her mother's kitchen. The man then shot his eighteen-month-old son (who survived) and finally killed himself. In the hours that I sat with the grieving mother at the funeral home she repeated over and over, "God wanted my daughter murdered."
—David Scholer pamphlet "Why Does God Allow Evil and Suffering?"

POSSIBLE EXIT: *If you want to know whether God wants people to live or die and how He feels about anyone, anywhere including you, go back to the cross.*

❖ **POSSIBLE ENTRANCE:** *Sometimes people are not as convinced there is no God as they say they are.*

I was flying from Dallas to St. Louis. The plane lost air cabin pressure and all the oxygen masks came down. A woman seated in front of me remarked, "If you were an atheist, something like this would sure make you think."
—R. Larry Moyer

POSSIBLE EXIT: *Don't wait for a near-death experience to make you question whether or not there is a God. Resolve that issue today by going back to two pivotal events in history—the cross and the resurrection.*

❖ If there is no God, why is there so much good? If there is a God, why is there so much evil?
—Augustine quoted by Lee Strobel in *The Case for Faith*

❖ **POSSIBLE ENTRANCE:** *Perhaps you have difficulty with the amount of bloodshed spoken of in the Bible. You may feel like this person did when he said,*

The Bible tells us to be like God, and then on page after page it describes God as a mass murderer.
—Robert A. Wilson, *Right Where You Are Sitting Now*

POSSIBLE EXIT: *Before you call God a mass murderer, examine what God allowed His Son to do because of your sin. Then ask, "Does this person strike you as a mass murderer?"*

☺ A college student was in a philosophy class, which had a discussion about God's existence. The professor presented the following logic:
"Has anyone in this class heard God?" Nobody spoke.
"Has anyone in this class touched God?" Again, nobody spoke.
"Has anyone in this class seen God?" When nobody spoke for the third time, he stated, "Then there is no God."
One student thought for a second and then asked for permission to reply. Curious to hear this bold student's response, the professor granted it, and the student stood up and asked the following questions of his classmates:
"Has anyone in this class heard our professor's brain?" Silence.
"Has anyone in this class touched our professor's brain?" Absolute silence.
"Has anyone in this class seen our professor's brain?"
When nobody in the class dared to speak, the student concluded, "Then, according to our professor's logic, it must be true that our professor has no brain."
The student received an "A" in the class.

—Internet humor

❖ **POSSIBLE ENTRANCE:** *We wrestle with the question, "How can a loving God allow someone to go to hell?" One person put it this way:*

If there is a God who allows people to go to hell, I would never want to spend eternity with him. I choose hell.

—Paul Borthwick, *Six Dangerous Questions to Transform Your View of the World*

POSSIBLE EXIT: *But please don't overlook one truth. When someone goes to hell, that person chose to go. God does not turn His back on us. We turn our backs on Christ.*

❖ **POSSIBLE ENTRANCE:** *God wants us to come to Christ. But we have to decide to come. The danger we face is that instead of giving in to the pleadings of the Holy Spirit, we refuse Christ, and God has to give us up to our own unbelief. Here is how a noted Christian author and professor named C. S. Lewis expressed it:*

C. S. Lewis said, "There are two kinds of people: those who say to God 'Thy will be done' and those to whom God says, 'All right then, have it your way.'"
—Rick Warren, *The Purpose Driven Life*

POSSIBLE EXIT: *Which kind of person are you? One who has said to God, "Thy will be done. I'm coming to Christ." Or are you one to whom God might one day say, "Thy will be done."*

☺ One day, a six-year-old girl was sitting in a classroom. The teacher was explaining evolution to the children. The teacher questioned a little boy:

Teacher: Tommy do you see the tree outside?
Tommy: Yes.
Teacher: Tommy, do you see the grass outside?
Tommy: Yes.
Teacher: Go outside and look up and see if you can see the sky.
Tommy: Okay. (He returned a few minutes later.) Yes, I saw the sky.
Teacher: Did you see God?
Tommy: No.
Teacher: That's my point. We can't see God because He isn't there. He just doesn't exist.

A little girl spoke up wanting to ask the boy some questions. The teacher agreed.

Little Girl: Tommy, do you see the tree outside?
Tommy: Yes.
Little Girl: Tommy do you see the grass outside?
Tommy: Yehhhs!
Little Girl: Did you see the sky?
Tommy: Yehhhs!
Little Girl: Tommy, do you see the teacher?
Tommy: Yes
Little Girl: Do you see her brain?
Tommy: No
Little Girl: Then according to what we were taught today, she doesn't have one.
—Source unknown

❖ One married woman was typical. "My mom died of cancer when I was young, and at the time I thought I was being punished by God," she told a counselor. "Tonight I realized that God loves me—it is something

I've known but couldn't really grasp. Tonight a peacefulness came into my heart."

—Lee Strobel, *The Case for Faith*

❖ Pastor William E. Sangster told of an experience in his youth when he went on a vacation with some friends. Within a short time he had spent all the funds given him for the trip, so he wrote home for more. His father, thinking he should teach his son the value of money, did not respond to the requests. Sangster's companions wondered why he had been turned down and suggested several reasons. Young William said to them, "I'll wait till I get home, and he'll tell me himself."

—*Our Daily Bread*, 1984

Note: The application here is "Once we trust Christ, one day we will be home. All of our questions will be answered."

❖ A magazine from the Long City Mission carried the story of George Woodall, a missionary to the inner city. One day he led a young woman to trust the Lord Jesus as her Savior. A little later she came to him and said, "I keep getting worried. I wonder, has God really forgiven my past?" Mr. Woodall replied, "If this is troubling you, I think I know what He'd say to you. He'd tell you to mind your own business." "What do you mean?" she inquired with a puzzled look. He told her of a little book he had read in which the author said that Jesus had made our sins His business. When He took them away, He put them behind His back, dropped them into the depths of the sea, and posted a notice that read, "No fishing!" Although that author had taken some liberties in stating the truth in everyday language, the woman got the point and was greatly helped. She understood that when our sins are covered by the atoning blood of Christ, they are blotted out completely and forever.

—*Our Daily Bread*, 1980

Note: For a non-Christian audience, I would not stress the missionary occupation of this man. I would say, "A man who was a student of the Bible once led a young woman to Christ." Then tell the story.

GOOD WORKS

❖ **POSSIBLE ENTRANCE:** *We are convinced that to get to heaven we have to be good. That raises the question, "How good is good enough?"*

Bishop Taylor Smith once sat in a barber's shop and told the barber that faith in Christ alone could save him. The barber did not agree, and after being further questioned, the barber said that he was doing the best that he could and that was good enough. When the barber was done, the bishop got up and another man took his place. The bishop asked the barber, "May I shave this man?" The barber said, "No, you aren't a barber." "But," Smith replied, "I'll do the best I can." The barber replied, "But your best is not good enough."

—Bishop Taylor Smith

POSSIBLE EXIT: *You have to be more than good. You have to be perfect. The best person has failed. That's why God cannot accept you based on what you've done for Him. He can only accept you based on what He did for you on a cross.*

☺ **POSSIBLE ENTRANCE:** *We are so convinced we get to heaven through our good works, we start imagining what we will present to God when we see Him face to face.*

St. Peter greets a man at the pearly gates. "What have you done to deserve entry into heaven?" he asks.

"Well, on my trip to the Black Hills, I came upon a gang of tough bikers threatening a young woman," says the man. "So I went up to the biggest, meanest biker and punched him in the nose. Then I kicked over his bike, yanked his ponytail, and ripped out his nose ring. When I finished with him, I turned to the rest of the gang and said, 'Leave this woman alone or you'll have to answer to me!'"

St. Peter was impressed. "When did this happen?"

"Just a couple of minutes ago."

Source unknown

POSSIBLE EXIT: *You can do the most heroic thing imaginable, but that will not get you into heaven. If you do not accept eternal life as a gift, God will not give it to you.*

❖ Grace doesn't get rid of works, it produces them; it doesn't make them unnecessary, it makes them possible.

—*Our Daily Bread*, 1974

❖ I always felt the harder you worked the higher you went.

—A new convert in Clearwater, Kansas

❖ Senator Phil Gramm of Texas said in 1990, "Balancing the budget is like going to heaven. Everybody wants to do it. but nobody wants to make the trip."

—from a television interview

Note: If people know Phil Gramm, use his name. If they don't, and as years pass they won't, all that is needed here is to say, "A former United States senator said, . . ."

☺ Many years ago, Dr. Walter L. Wilson was in Grand Rapids, Michigan, for a Bible conference. As was his custom, he visited Radio Bible Class and was invited to give a brief message to the staff. He told of an unusual conversation he had with a man who took exception to his presentation of the gospel. "You make no provision for human effort," the unbeliever complained. "Personally, I believe I am saved by good works!" "Shake hands, brother!" answered Wilson. "So do I!" The faultfinder expressed great surprise. "You mean you actually believe you are saved by good works?" "Yes, indeed!" replied Wilson with a victorious smile. "Jesus' good works—not mine."

—*Our Daily Bread*, 1983

❖ When an especially good person dies, an older friend of mine from the mountains of North Carolina often comments, "If she ain't going to heaven, there's no use the rest of us even trying."

—Source unknown

❖ We are saved by God's work, not by good works.

—*Our Daily Bread*, 1983

❖ Human goodness may be likened to a canoe. A canoe is a lively little boat for its purpose—to be used on rivers and lakes in calm waters. It is admirably suited for young people or a beautiful day or evening in June. But the canoe is not suitable at a seaport or to cross the ocean. It is a totally unfit boat for such a purpose. The trip from New York to France cannot be made by a canoe, even in the month of June when the ocean is generally calm.

So the human character is admirably suited to take an individual around the daily course of life in the midst of a sinful world, but it is a totally depraved thing for the passage from earth to heaven. If a canoe be judged by all canoeists to be the best canoe that was ever made, it is still insufficient for the ocean passage. If a human character be judged by all men to be the best human character that ever developed, it is still insufficient for the passage from death to life, from earth to heaven.

—Source unknown

HAPPINESS

❖ Millionaires seldom smile.

—Andrew Carnegie quoted by Robert J. Morgan in
Nelson's Complete Book of Stories, Illustrations & Quotes

❖ Princess Diana, beautiful, famous, and wealthy, won the admiration of millions but found simple happiness elusive.

—*Dallas Morning News*, August 31, 1997
(written after her death in a car accident August 30, 1997)

❖ Not long ago, I was riding double on a motorcycle with a friend of mine in Newport Beach, California. We were talking, laughing, and having a good time.

As we were riding along, two women pulled alongside us in a new Lincoln Continental. For two blocks, at twenty miles an hour, they just stared at us. Finally the lady on the passenger side rolled down her window. "What right do you have to be so happy?" she yelled out. Before we could reply she rolled up her window and they sped away.

—Used by permission. Josh McDowell, *The Resurrection Factor*, p. 2,
Here's Life Publishers, www.josh.org

☺ A wife once told me that her husband jumps out of bed each morning, happy as ever. When she one time asked him, "How can you be so happy this early in the morning," he replied, "Because so far, so good.

—R. Larry Moyer

❖ I have made many millions, but they have brought me no happiness.

—John D. Rockefeller

HEAVEN

❖ The man who expects to go to heaven should take the trouble to learn what route will get him there.

—*Pulpit and Bible Study Helps*, April 1991

❖ CEO's Toughest Question—*60 Minutes* reporter Dan Rather interviewed Jack Welch, the outspoken former CEO of General Electric and author of a new book called *Winning*. At the end of the interview, Rather asked Welch, "What's the toughest question you have ever been asked?" Welch thought for a moment, then he responded, "Do you think you'll go to heaven?" "How did you answer the question?" Rather asked.

"It's a long answer," the CEO replied, "But I said that if caring about people, if giving it your all, if being a great friend counts—despite the fact that I've been divorced a couple of times, and no one's proud of that. I haven't done everything right all the time. I think I got a shot. I'm in no hurry to get there and to find out any time soon."

—*Leadership*, Fall 2005

❖ Your final exit will be your greatest entrance.

—*Pulpit Helps*, October 2003

❖ **POSSIBLE ENTRANCE:** *Some people don't view heaven as a very exciting place.*

George Bernard Shaw once explained, "Heaven as conventionally conceived, is a place so inane, so dull, so useless, and so miserable that nobody has ever ventured to describe a whole day in heaven, though plenty of people have described a day at the seashore."

—Harlan D. Betz, *Setting the Stage for Eternity*

POSSIBLE EXIT: *Don't go by your perception of heaven. Go by the explanation the Bible gives.*

☺ A good doctor can help you so you won't die. A bad doctor sends you to heaven.

—Raymond L., age 10

Note: This could be used to make the point "Although humorous, the child was wrong. Only Christ can take you to heaven."

☺ There are a lot of questions the Bible doesn't answer about the hereafter. But I think one reason is illustrated by the story of a boy sitting down to a bowl of spinach when there's a chocolate cake at the end of the table. He's going to have a rough time eating the spinach when his eyes are on the cake. And if the Lord had explained everything to us, what's ours to come, I think we'd have a rough time with our spinach down here.

—Vance Havner, *Moody Monthly*, June 1974

❖ A Christian dentist once took his dog along to his office one Saturday morning. He had trained the dog to stay in the waiting room and not come into the surgical area. The dentist was witnessing to a man who was a patient. The patient said, "Sometimes I wish you could show me what heaven is going to be like." The dentist said, "Oh, I can now." So he called his dog (Duke) into the room and the dog sat at his feet, placed his head in the dentist's hands and just looked up at his lord and master.

That's what it will be like in heaven—looking at our Lord and Master.

—Ed Davis, pastor

☺ POSSIBLE ENTRANCE: *We only think we know how fantastic heaven is going to be. When you get there it will be so overwhelming you will wish you had arrived sooner.*

A woman died and went to heaven—which was more beautiful than she'd ever imagined. She couldn't wait to show it to her husband (when he eventually arrived) because he was an eternal pessimist.

A year later her husband joined her and she took him on a tour.

"The sky, the flowers, the music, the people—heaven is truly heaven, isn't it?" she exclaimed.

He surveyed Paradise briefly, then said, "Sure. And if it weren't for you and your doggoned oat bran, we'd have been here five years sooner."

—John Wood

POSSIBLE EXIT: *But a bigger issue than when will you arrive is, "Will you arrive?" If you were to die today, do you know for sure you'd go to heaven?*

❖ Joy is the serious business of heaven.

—C. S. Lewis

❖ POSSIBLE ENTRANCE: *Numerous discussions center around what heaven is going to be like. We miss the whole point.*

The emphasis of the Bible is not when we're going but Who we're going to be with.

—Jim Rose, pastor

POSSIBLE EXIT: *The thing that makes it heaven is being in the presence of Christ Himself.*

❖ When Pepper Martin was the hero of the World Series for the St. Louis Cardinals, he was asked what was his greatest ambition in life, and he replied, "To go to heaven."

—Billy Graham, *Is There Life After Death?*

❖ A prepared place for prepared people!

—Source unknown

☺ **POSSIBLE ENTRANCE:** *We go through an experience every week that I can use to explain the question we have about heaven.*

A small daughter was shopping with her mother. She was impressed with the automatic doors. As they approached a store, she asked her mother, "Will it open for me?"

—*Pulpit Helps*, June 1998

POSSIBLE EXIT: *When you think of heaven's door, you're probably asking, "Will it open for me?" There is only one way you can be certain it will—trust Christ.*

❖ **POSSIBLE ENTRANCE:** *When you know Christ, it gives you a whole new perspective on death. It is something you can look forward to with excitement.*

A nine-year-old girl who had leukemia was given six months to live. When the doctor broke the news to her parents outside her hospital room, the youngster overheard his words. But not until later did it become obvious to everyone that she knew about her condition. To everyone's surprise, her faith in Christ gave her an attitude of victory. She talked freely about her death with anticipation in her voice. As she grew weaker, it seemed that her joy became more radiant. One day before she sank into a final coma, she said to her family, "I'm going to be the first to see Jesus! What would you like me to tell Him for you?"

—*Our Daily Bread*, 1978

POSSIBLE EXIT: *If today you were given six months to live, could you look forward to death with excitement?*

❖ He who wants all heaven in his head is going to get his head split.
—Sir Wilfred Frenfell

Note: If there is a question whether someone will understand an illustration like this, share it with a friend or two prior to speaking. I have done that numerous times and found it helpful. When one friend heard the above illustration, he thought he understood it but wasn't sure. So when I use it, I precede it with the words, "There is no way our minds can totally comprehend heaven. A person once said . . ."

❖ A man who was dying said to his friends in his last moments, "It's the most beautiful thing I've ever seen."
—Jimmy Leonard Sr.

❖ Heaven's delights far outweigh earth's difficulties.
—*Our Daily Bread*, 1982

❖ **POSSIBLE ENTRANCE:** *Jackie Gleason, the highest-paid clown in American history, expressed what many of us feel. He said " . . ."*

A national magazine carried the autobiographical story of Jackie Gleason, the highest-paid clown in history. It told of his rise from poverty to plenty. In the midst of the article was a startling comment. Jackie Gleason said, "There is one thing of which I am desperately afraid. That is, that I may never make heaven."
—Haddon Robinson

POSSIBLE EXIT: *If you understand the greatest message of the Bible, you need not fear you won't make heaven. You can be 100 percent certain you will be there.*

❖ God's children never say goodbye for the last time.
—*Our Daily Bread*, 2004

❖ In April 2004 I was flying to Manila, Philippines, to train pastors in evangelism and public speaking. The journey was long (seventeen hours of flying time alone), besides a three-hour layover in Japan. It was a tiring journey and had an element of danger in it, as all traveling does.

The woman who sat alongside me the whole way from Detroit was from Manila and was visiting her family. She was going in the summer so she could spend time with her niece and nephew who were out of school. As I engaged in conversation with her, I found her open to the gospel and had the privilege of leading her to Christ. When we landed in Manila, the pilot of the plane said, "We have now arrived in Manila. Welcome home." She looked at me and said, "I've been waiting to hear those words, 'welcome home.'" I thought, *Isn't it going to be exciting when we see the Savior face to face and we hear Him say that to us, "Welcome home"?* That comment she made brought back to me in a fresh way what an exciting day that's going to be.

—R. Larry Moyer

❖ A refugee from Hitler says that so many tales were told about America that his whole family felt they knew the country well. So settled was their knowledge and love of the land he had not yet seen that as he departed for America his mother said to him, "You are going home, and I am staying in a foreign land."

The Christian who realizes the tyranny of life in this world is glad to escape to the land that is fairer than day. When our loved ones go before us, we are forced to say, with tears for ourselves, "You are going Home and I am staying in a foreign land."

—Donald Grey Barnhouse

❖ Mrs. Thomas A. Edison said that, when her famous husband was dying, he whispered to his physician, "It is very beautiful over there."

—John Myers, *Voices from the Edge of Eternity*

❖ Before I had gone to Dallas Seminary, I had never even been to Texas, let alone the city of Dallas. I did not know what it was like at all. But I had connections with the place through mail, and I had a room in the dorm reserved for me. Although I had never been there before and had never seen it, I came and found a room prepared for me. I had a reservation. In the same way, Jesus has gone away to prepare a place for us in the Father's house. There is a place for me! It's reserved, waiting for my arrival.

—D. Jonathan Graham

Note: Illustrations provoke ideas. Instead of using Dallas Seminary, think of a similar illustration from your experience.

☺ Dear Pastor, I would like to go to heaven someday because I know my brother won't be there.

> —Stephen, age 8, Chicago, quoted by Sumner Wemp, August 1998

Note: This can be used in an effective way to say, "Humorous. But it raises a serious question. Who is going to get to heaven and why?"

☺ **POSSIBLE ENTRANCE:** *Ask the average person, "What do you have to do to get to heaven?" Some of the answers may be surprising, particularly if you ask a child.*

My assistant's child was in the office one day. To get to know him a bit, I thought I would use the occasion to question him about his salvation even though my assistant had assured me he had trusted Christ. So I asked him, "Do you know beyond a doubt that you are going to heaven?" He answered, "Yes." Then I asked, "Well, what do you have to do to go to heaven?" He quickly answered, "Well, you have to believe that Jesus died for you." Then he stopped abruptly and said, "Well, first you have to die!"

> —R. Larry Moyer

POSSIBLE EXIT: *Yes, you do have to be dead. But upon death, what determines whether or not a person goes to heaven? What do you have to do to get to heaven?*

❖ A girl was cast on a bed of suffering and was about to die. She spoke in anticipation about seeing the Lord. Someone said, "What will be the first thing you'll say when you see Him?" She replied, "I'm going to look at Him and say, 'I know You!'"

> —S. Lewis Johnson

❖ More than thirty-five years ago, my family moved into a new house—a place we called home until recently when my mother sold it.

Pleasant memories of the home where we grew up made it hard to part with. But one thing mother told me makes it easier. She said that when the family first moved into the brick house Dad was so fond of, he told her, "This is my last move. My next move is up."

> —*Our Daily Bread*, 1996

❖ Which is the longest day? That depends on the part of the world in which you live. In New York, the longest day is fifteen hours. In London, it is sixteen hours, in Stockholm, Sweden, it is eighteen hours. In Farse, Finland, it is twenty-two hours. In Woodbury, Norway, the longest day lasts for two months. In Spitzbergen for thirty-two months, but in the New Jerusalem, it lasts forever, for "there shall be no night there."

—Source unknown

❖ Earth is the land of the dying; heaven is the land of the living.

—*Our Daily Bread*, 1983

❖ **POSSIBLE ENTRANCE:** *When we have trusted Christ, regardless of how death comes, only what is good awaits us. While on earth He's been with us; at death we have the certainty we'll be with Him.*

In April 2001, missionaries Jim and Roni Bowers and their children, Corey and Charity, were shot out of the sky by a Peruvian jet that mistook them for drug traffickers. Of all the bullets that were fired that day, a single bullet pierced the fuselage of the missionary airplane, hit Roni in the back and entered the head of seven-month-old Charity, killing them both instantly. Speaking of that terrible moment, Jim Bowers said, "Nothing bad happened to them. They got to heaven quicker than we did."

—Ray Pritchard, *He's God and We're Not*

POSSIBLE EXIT: *Losing his wife and child were hard. But Jim knew with certainty two things. First, they were in heaven. As he said, "They got to heaven quicker than we did." And second, he knew that one day he would join them.*

> Note: In speaking to a non-Christian audience, I would not make an issue of the fact that these people were missionaries. Help your audience identify with the fact that they were just people like us. I would say, "In April 2001, a couple by the name of Jim and Roni Bowers and their children, all of whom had trusted Christ, were shot out of the sky . . ." The other advantage of this is it discourages the audience from thinking that because these people were missionaries, they got to heaven.

HOPE

❖ **POSSIBLE ENTRANCE:** *We have tried everything, and we are disappointed, angry, without any certainties about the future. All of us need hope.*

Years ago a S-4 submarine was rammed by a ship off the coast of

Massachusetts and sank immediately. The entire crew was trapped in a prison house of death. Every effort was made to rescue them but all failed. Near the end of the ordeal, a diver placed his helmeted ear to the side of the vessel and heard a tapping from inside. He recognized it as Morse code. It was a question, forming slowly: "Is . . . there . . . any . . . hope?"

—Charles R. Swindoll, *Simple Faith*

POSSIBLE EXIT: *When you come to Christ, you have hope and not disappointment. Someone has said, "Life without Him is a hopeless end. Life with Him is an endless hope."*

❖   During the American Civil War, a soldier boy lay wounded on a hard-fought field. The roar of the battle had died away, and he rested in the deathly stillness of its aftermath. Off over the field flickered the lanterns of the survivors searching for wounded ones who might be carried away and saved. This poor soldier watched, unable to turn or to speak, as the lanterns drew near. Then a light flashed in his face and the surgeon bent over him, shook his head, and was gone. By and by, the party came back and again the kindly surgeon bent over him. "I believe if this poor fellow lives till the next sundown, he will get well." In a moment the surgeon was gone, but he had put a great hope in the soldier's heart. All night the words kept repeating themselves. "If I live till sundown, I shall get well." He turned his head to the east to watch for the dawn. At last the stars went out, the east quivered with radiance, and the sun arose. Intently his eye followed the ark of the day. He was getting weaker—could he live till sundown? He thought of his home . . . "If I live till sundown I shall see it again. I will walk down the shady lane. I will drink again at the old mossy spring." He thought of his wife, mother, and other loved ones. That hope kept him alive.

—J. R. Miller, *Glimpse Through Life's Window*

❖   Robert, 47, and his wife, Paula, 51, were found shot to death in their suburban home in Philadelphia. They were socially prominent and lived in affluence. Paula had phoned a state trooper and said, "My husband begged me to kill him. I did it. I shot him, and now I am going to kill myself!" The trooper tried to keep her talking while he radioed a patrol car to go to the scene of the tragedy. Seeing his purpose, she said, "You're not going to keep me on the phone until someone interferes. We made this agreement, and I'm going to keep it."

Ten minutes later the officers entered the home where murder and

311

suicide had just occurred. They found a note that contained these forlorn words: "We have no hope for the future."

—Told by speaker Hyman Appelman

Note: This is an example of a dated illustration that is not limited by time. It could easily have happened today. Begin the illustration by saying, "An incident years ago reminds us of how people today still feel. In fact had I not told you, you would have thought I read this in yesterday's newspaper."

❖ The young parents, she is 23 and he is 25, said that their sweet smiling daughter developed pneumonia nearly two years ago. When they took her to the local hospital, a routine blood count revealed she had leukemia. Her doctors advised immediate transfer to Roswell Park.

After two weeks of intensive therapy in the hospital, Jody was well enough to go home. Now she returns once a month for additional tests and treatment. Between the once-a-month visits to the hospital, she sees her local doctor in Endicott.

Mr. and Mrs. Hillis are over the shock of Jody's having leukemia. "We live from day to day," confesses Mrs. Hillis, "but we are hopeful."

Their home is in Endicott, New York. They had brought the child to Roswell Park Memorial Institute. "We have a chance to beat leukemia now."

—*Look*, May 5, 1970

Note: The application here is "All of us need hope." But when the Bible speaks of hope—it has the idea of certainty. When we place our trust in Christ, we have the certainty we are going to be with Him forever.

❖ The best is yet to be.

—John Wesley quoted by Randy Alcorn in *Heaven*

❖ Whatever our vision, most of us expect heaven to be a better place. Evangelist Billy Graham has said he can't wait to get there. "I look forward to the reunion with friends and loved ones, who have gone on before. I look forward to heaven's freedom from sorrow and pain."

—Billy Graham, *Just as I Am*

❖ The natural flights of the human mind are not from pleasure to pleasure but from hope to hope.

—Samuel Johnson

❖ **POSSIBLE ENTRANCE:** *Some people aren't excited about heaven because they have a distorted perspective of what it will be like.*

Science fiction writer Isaac Asimov writes, "I don't believe in an afterlife, so I don't have to spend my whole life fearing hell, or fearing heaven even more. For whatever the tortures of hell, I think the boredom of heaven would be even worse."

—Randy Alcorn, *Heaven*

POSSIBLE EXIT: *Heaven will be anything but boring. In fact, no mind can completely comprehend the grandeur of it. That is probably one of the reasons the Bible doesn't tell us more about what heaven will be like. God knows that our finite minds wouldn't understand.*

❖ **POSSIBLE ENTRANCE:** *The way to heaven is so simple and free, we find it hard to believe. We wonder, as with most offers, if there isn't some fine print we've overlooked.*

Recently I received a magazine sweepstakes letter that addressed me by name and repeatedly mentioned a $500,000 prize. It spoke of instant wealth and a lifetime of leisure. Finally, at the bottom of page 2, in very small print, I found the part I was looking for. As required by law, the letter told me that the approximate numerical odds of my winning the prize were 1 in 80 million. Now that's remote!

—*Our Daily Bread*, 1999

POSSIBLE EXIT: *With Christ there is no fine print. The way to heaven is simple and free.*

JUSTIFICATION

❖ Suppose that a man rented a field from another and promised to pay a hundred dollars for the rental. The agreement is signed, the day of payment comes. If the harvest has been poor because of drought, pest, unseasonable storms, or poor fertilizers, the man who rented the field may wish that he had not signed the agreement. He may wish that the owner would take half of the harvest instead of demanding cash. But the agreement has been signed; there is nothing to do but abide by it. If, however, the owner should say that he would accept fifty bushels of corn instead of money, there is an end to the agreement. If the owner should say that he would accept twenty bushels of grain instead of the money, there is an end to the matter. If the owner should say that he would free the man from his debt provided that the debtor sign for him, then that would be the end of the matter. It is the owner who must be satisfied.

God must be satisfied in the matter of our sin. Justification is expression of the fact that God declares Himself fully satisfied by virtue of what the Lord Jesus Christ has done for us.

—David J. Riggs, http://mywebpages.comcast.net/davidriggs01/briefvs.htm

> Note: This illustration should encourage you to think of examples you can use from your community. Your listeners may not identify with the rental of a field, but what analogies would work?

❖ An old man owned land with a cabin on it. A millionaire came and offered him a tremendous figure and gave him $1,000 down payment.

The old man fixed it up, but the millionaire was not impressed. "I bought it for what I'm going to make it, not what is already there."

—H. A. Ironside

> Note: Use this illustration to think of your own. Mention a place you enjoy going and imagine you have a cabin in need of much repair. Then using someone your audience will know, insert that name as the millionaire who buys it. Continue the illustration. Drive home the point that justification means God does not want to repair us. He wants to make us a new person—one who stands 100 percent righteous in His sight. That's the meaning of justification.

❖ **POSSIBLE ENTRANCE:** *When you come to Christ, you come as a sinner. After you come to Christ, you're still a sinner. But you are a sinner who is completely accepted by God.*

The children of God are not perfect, but they are perfectly His children.

—D. L. Moody, *Decision*, February 1987

POSSIBLE EXIT: *Why are you perfectly His children? Because God places His Son's righteousness upon you in such a way that when God looks upon you He no longer sees your sin. All He sees is the righteousness of His Son.*

❖ Recently my son and I were driving in a thunderstorm when our car was struck by lightning. Immediately the car's horn blared uncontrollably, the lights on the dashboard blinked crazily, the car no longer accelerated, and we smelled smoke from all the wires that had just been fried. And yet, although we saw the flash and heard the rifling crack of thunder, we never felt a thing. Inside that car, we were safe.

The wrath of God is far more real and powerful and destructive than that lightning. But on the cross, Jesus took in His own body the full fury of the bolt of that wrath, wrath that we had earned. We who are "in Christ" are utterly safe from any possibility of God's wrath striking us. In Christ we'll never feel a trace of the agony He had to bear to perfectly preserve us from the fiery assault of God's wrath. "Jesus paid it all, all to Him I owe."

—Dwight Edwards, *Revolution Within*

> Note: If there has been a recent thunderstorm, refer your audience to it and then add, "A man once told of an experience he had during that kind of a storm that illustrates how we can find safety from God's wrath in Christ." Then tell the story. The recent storm will give more meaning to the storm experience of Dwight Edwards.

☺ **POSSIBLE ENTRANCE:** *When we hear the word "justification," we have no idea what it means. You will be able to identify with something that happened years ago.*

A humorous incident related by John H. Gerstner in his book *A Primer in Justification* clarifies the issue. He wrote, "To illustrate how far our twentieth century is from what the sixteenth century considered the heart of the gospel, let me relate a true, though almost unbelievable, incident. I was once speaking to a group of business people on justification, and there was a journalist in attendance representing a local newspaper. I preached justification emphatically, clearly, earnestly, and I hoped, persuasively. It was, therefore, rather discouraging to learn from the newspaper account that I had spoken the night before on the theme of 'Just a vacation by faith!'"

—*Our Daily Bread*, 1985

POSSIBLE EXIT: *In some ways that is what justification is—a vacation by faith. Because you can relax, enjoy life and eternity because you stand before God as perfect as His own Son. This is what justification really is.*

❖   In many cases, God's true acceptance of us in Christ and the inheritance we have in Him simply isn't taught. However, ignorance of the Word of God is not the only reason for this condition. Many people who know the Bible intimately experience the same thing. I was speaking to the student body of a seminary one time. In the course of discussing the Christian's identity in

Christ, I asked a series of questions. "How many of you are as righteous and acceptable in the sight of God as I am?" Every hand in the auditorium was raised. "How many of you," I asked again, "are as righteous and acceptable in the sight of God as Billy Graham?" This time about half of the audience raised their hands. "How many of you are as acceptable and righteous in the sight of God as the apostle Paul?" There were around ten percent of the hands raised. "Now here's the really tough one," I said. "How many of you in the sight of God are as righteous and acceptable as Jesus Christ?" Only three hands were raised out of an entire auditorium of seminary students.

Mind you, this was not a case of ignorance. These men were attending a fine seminary. Every person in that audience could have defended aggressively the doctrine of justification by faith. They had the truth in their heads, all right. But did they have the truth in their hearts? It is a perfect illustration of the principle that a person can know what the Bible says but not necessarily know what it means. I wonder: Would you have raised your hand?

I finally told that group of students the same incredible truth that I am laying before you. "I'm going to say this to you straightforward, so there's no chance you'll miss it," I began. "If you are a true Christian, then you are as righteous and acceptable in the sight of God as Jesus Christ!" You should have seen some of their faces! I think some of them feared that lightning would strike me on the spot!

—Bob George, *Classic Christianity*

Note: This kind of illustration lets you use names of people your audience can identify with and would be appropriate to compare their righteousness against.

❖ Some years ago a poor, elderly woman was approached by a skeptic. The man said sarcastically, "Well, Betty, you claim you're one of the saints. Tell me what you mean by that. Are you trying to say you're well versed in religion?" "No, sir, I'm not a scholar nor a theologian," replied the Christian, "but I'm positive about one thing—I'm saved by grace. That's enough to make me happy in this life and bring me safely to heaven." "Is that all you know about it? Can't you at least explain a little more what being saved by grace means?" the man insisted. Betty thought for a few moments and then answered, "Why, it means that because the Lord stood in my shoes at Calvary, I'm now standing in His!"

—*Our Daily Bread*, 1979

Note: Some illustrations like this one are helpful in their entirety, or for just one thought-provoking line. Here one could say, "A person one time explained justification by saying, 'Since He stood in my shoes at Calvary, I'm now standing in His.'"

MISUNDERSTANDING

❖ Murphy's Law: Once you've explained something so clearly nobody can misunderstand, somebody will.

—Wilbur Rutledge

☺ POSSIBLE ENTRANCE: *Misunderstanding can be costly.*

Needing to shed a few pounds, my husband and I went on a diet that had specific recipes for each meal of the day. I followed the instructions closely, dividing the finished recipe in half for our individual plates. We felt terrific and thought the diet was wonderful—we never felt hungry! But when we realized we were gaining weight, not losing it, I checked the recipes again. There, in fine print, was, "Serves 6."

—Submitted by Barbara Currie. Reprinted with permission from the July 2005 *Reader's Digest*. Copyright ©2005 by The Reader's Digest Assn., Inc.

POSSIBLE EXIT: *Misunderstandings can be costly. But the most costly misunderstanding of all is when one misunderstands what you have to do to get to heaven. Although the Bible explains it clearly, sometimes we either haven't heard it clearly or read it carefully.*

☺ POSSIBLE ENTRANCE: *Sometimes when we lay out requirements for entering something or doing something, they are as clear as they could be and may still lead to misunderstanding.*

I have to admit that when restaurants started using the sign, "No shoes, no shirt, no service," for a moment I was confused and misunderstood. Being a rather simple-minded person, my initial thought was that they were saying, "We have no shoes, no shirt, no service." The shoes and shirt part didn't bother me. I already had those. But I wouldn't understand why they wouldn't give any service, when that is what I came there for. I quickly learned that the sign meant, "If you have no shoes, no shirt, you will receive no service."

—R. Larry Moyer

POSSIBLE EXIT: *But when it comes to how to enter that place God calls heaven—His house—the instructions are clear and leave no room for misunderstanding.*

REGENERATION

❖ POSSIBLE ENTRANCE: *God's not interested in making you into a changed person, but a new one. He's not interested in what you can do with your life, but what He can do with it.*

London businessman Lindsay Clegg told the story of a warehouse property he was selling. The building had been empty for months and needed repairs. Vandals had damaged the doors, smashed the windows, and strewn trash around the interior. As he showed a prospective buyer the property, Clegg took pains to say that he would replace the broken windows, bring in a crew to correct any structural damage, and clean out the garbage. "Forget about the repairs," the buyer said. "When I buy this place, I'm going to build something completely different. I don't want the building. I want the site." Compared with the renovation God has in mind, our efforts to improve our own lives are as trivial as sweeping a warehouse slated for the wrecking ball. When we become God's, the old life is over (2 Cor. 5:17). He makes all things new. All He wants is the site and permission to build.

—*Leadership*, Summer 1983

POSSIBLE EXIT: *God is not interested in the building you can build on your site, but the building He can build on it.*

❖ Reformation is turning over a new leaf. Regeneration is receiving a new life.

—*Our Daily Bread*, 1986

❖ POSSIBLE ENTRANCE: *If we try to reform ourselves we only make our condition worse, not better.*

In Owen Sound, Canada, a police constable received a call from a lady who complained, "I have a skunk in my basement." He replied, "The thing to do is to very carefully place a trail of bread crumbs leading from the basement to your yard outside." She agreed to this plan and hung up.

That afternoon, the same constable received another call from the same woman. "I did what you told me," she reported. "Now I have two skunks in my basement."

—Neil Ashcraft

POSSIBLE EXIT: *God is not interested in reformation. He is interested in regeneration. He doesn't want to make you into a better person. He wants to make you into a new person.*

❖ A little boy asked, "Why is it that when I open a marigold it dies, but if God does it, it's so beautiful?"

Before the question could be answered the boy said, "I know! It's because God always works from the inside."

—www.baptistbanner.net

❖ Regeneration is not a change of the old nature, but an introduction of a new nature.

—C. H. Spurgeon

❖ The following story was told by William E. Biederwolf, former president of Winona Lake Bible Conference. A young sculptor worked painstakingly on the statue of an angel. When the great Michelangelo came to view it, the artist hid nearby and waited to hear the master's comment. Michelangelo looked intently at the sculpture with breathless suspense. At last he said, "It lacks only one thing." Hearing this, the young artist was heartbroken. For days he could neither eat nor sleep. A friend became so concerned for him that he went to Michelangelo to ask what the statue lacked. The master replied, "It lacks only life; with life it would be perfect."

Some people are like that statue. Outwardly, they have an admirable appearance. They are good by the standards of the world. They live moral, exemplary lives. They are respected citizens who are active in charitable functions. They are faithful members in their churches. But never having been born again, they lack one thing—spiritual life. The Bible tells us that "God has given us eternal life, and this life is in His Son. He who has the Son has life; he who does not have the Son of God does not have life" (1 John 5:11–12 NIV).

—Our Daily Bread

RELIGION

❖ POSSIBLE ENTRANCE: *Some of us have no time for religion. We'd agree with well-known personality, Ted Turner.*

"I was saved seven or eight times, but when I lost my faith I felt better about it," Ted Turner said when speaking to a group of humanists. He was raised, he said, in an extremely religious environment, including six years in a Christian prep school with Bible training and daily chapel services and regular meetings with evangelists.

—Erwin W. Lutzer, *How You Can Be Sure You Will Spend Eternity with God*

POSSIBLE EXIT: *If Ted Turner feels he was saved seven or eight times, it causes us to wonder if he knows what the Bible means by saved. Here's why; let me explain what being saved means.*

❖ **POSSIBLE ENTRANCE:** *Religion tends to confuse us. We can identify with the boy who was asked about his church preference.*

The country boy went to a big city college and had a little trouble filling out all the forms. When he called home to tell his mother, she said, "Well, son, just what did you put down?" He said, "I did pretty good, except for the part where they asked me my church preference. I put down 'red brick' because I wasn't sure what they wanted."

—*Fax Daily*, January 26, 1999

POSSIBLE EXIT: *What would you say if I told you God's first and foremost concern is not your church preference? Don't ask, "Do you belong to a church?" The better question to ask is "Do you belong to Christ?"*

❖ **POSSIBLE ENTRANCE:** *Some feel we'd be better off if there was no religion. They might agree perhaps with what Karl Marx once said:*

The first requisite to the people's happiness is the abolition of religion.

—Karl Marx

POSSIBLE EXIT: *God is not interested in talking to you about religion. He is interested in talking with you about salvation. Please don't confuse the two.*

☺ **POSSIBLE ENTRANCE:** *Sometimes what keeps us from Christ is our fear that if we come to Christ and then start coming to church to learn more about Him, we might become a religious fanatic. We'd like to avoid that if at all possible.*

The minister captured the undivided attention of the congregation when he related the following incident: "I stopped in a coffee shop the other day and sat at the counter next to a man reading the newspaper. He glanced at my apparel and then wanted to know where my church was. When I pointed in the direction of the Episcopal church on the corner, he said, 'Why, that's the church I go to myself.'"

"Isn't that strange?" I replied. "I've been preaching there for five years and I don't believe I've ever seen you."

"Come on now, preacher," he shot back. "I didn't say I was a fanatic."
—http://jmm.aaa.net.au/articles/8465.htm

POSSIBLE EXIT: *At this point God is not asking you, "How many times will you come to church?" He is asking you, "Will you come to Christ?" Please don't confuse coming to church with coming to Christ.*

❖ When questioned why he proselytized in the arena of politics but not religion, [Gandhi] responded, "In the realm of the political and social and economic, we can be sufficiently certain to convert; but in the realm of religion there is not sufficient certainty to convert anybody, and, therefore, there can be no conversions in religions." Now that's helpful, isn't it? Even Gandhi didn't find certainty in religion.
—Andy Stanley, *Since Nobody's Perfect . . . How Good Is Good Enough?*

❖ Some people endure religion. Others enjoy salvation.
—Source unknown

❖ Religion, while putting its adherents on the road to destruction, offers them a first class ride all the way there. C. S. Lewis observed, "Indeed the safest road to hell is the gradual one—the gentle slope, the soft underfoot, without sudden turnings, without milestones, without signposts."
—Mark McCloskey, *Tell It Often, Tell It Well*

Note: Keep in mind you are speaking to non-Christians. Since they would not know who C. S. Lewis is, it would be helpful to say, "C. S. Lewis, one of the greatest thinkers of his day and author of *The Chronicles of Narnia.*"

☺ **POSSIBLE ENTRANCE:** *Pride often keeps us from Christ. Sometimes it is the pride of admitting we have been a member of a church for a long time but have never understood the gospel.*

Two churches were trying to merge. The problem was these were from two different denominations. Finally one man said, "Well, my mother and father were Baptists, my grandparents were members of the church, as were my great-grandparents, and nobody is going to make a Christian out of me now!"
—Source unknown

POSSIBLE EXIT: *We laugh, but sometimes this is our attitude.*

❖ There are only two kinds of religion in the world—the kind that you carry and the kind that carries you.

—Haddon Robinson

❖ It is natural to be religious. It is supernatural to be Christian.

—W. M. Craig

❖ I was speaking once to a Jewish man on a plane. While talking about religion he said, "It just seems to me that a lot of people have hurt their fellow man in the name of religion."

—R. Larry Moyer

Note: This is helpful in identifying with people's negative attitudes about religion. In using this illustration in personal evangelism as well as evangelistic speaking, my response is, "That's why it's important not to confuse religion with Jesus Christ. Religion has done a lot of people a lot of harm, but Jesus Christ is out to help you, not hurt you."

❖ A Chinese Christian leader, C. K. Lee, spoke to an American audience and afterward invited questions. He gave a memorable answer to a student who asked, "Why should we send Christianity to China when it has Confucianism?"

Mr. Lee said, "There are three reasons. First of all, Confucius was a teacher and Christ is a Savior. China needs a Savior more than she needs a teacher. In the second place, Confucius is dead and Christ is alive. China needs a living Savior. In the third place, Confucius is one day going to stand before Christ and be judged by Him. China needs to know Christ as Savior before she meets Him as judge."

—Norm Lewis, *Priority One*

❖ **POSSIBLE ENTRANCE:** *For some of us religion means absolutely nothing. We may look at it as an opportunity to take out of the offering plate more than we put in. After author Josh McDowell came to Christ, he shared,*

About the only thing I got out of my religious experience was seventy-five cents a week: I would put a quarter into the offering plate and take a dollar out so I could buy a milkshake!

—Used by permission. Josh McDowell, *The New Evidence That Demands a Verdict*, p. xxiii, Thomas Nelson Publishers, www.josh.org

POSSIBLE EXIT: *Because of these feelings, we miss two things. When God wants us to come to Christ, He is talking about a relationship, not religion. Second, at this point God's concern is not what you have to give Him. It is what He has to give you—free.*

Note: In using this illustration, update the present cost of a milkshake.

SALVATION

❖ Once you put salvation on the basis of works, you can never be sure you have a relationship.

—Haddon Robinson

❖ You may have had a bad start in life, but you need not have a bad ending.

—*Our Daily Bread*, 1982

❖ I pray for you to remember that the genuine faith that saves the soul has for its main element, trust—absolute rest of the whole soul—on the Lord Jesus Christ to save me, whether he died in particular or in special to save me or not, and relying, as I am, wholly and alone on him, I am saved.

—C. H. Spurgeon, *The Forgotten Spurgeon*

❖ **POSSIBLE ENTRANCE:** *We are accustomed to working for or earning everything we have, so many people's thinking is skewed into believing that you can work your way to heaven by noble efforts and good works.*

One night I watched a news interview of a wealthy person who had made a large gift to a foundation. I agonized when the donor indicated that he thought his act of goodness would merit him something in terms of going to heaven.

—R. Larry Moyer

POSSIBLE EXIT: *No amount of money will get you to heaven. Nothing you do or offer to God will get you to heaven.*

❖ When the jailer said, "What must I do to be saved?" Paul didn't say, "Do, Try, Work, Go, Heed, Serve."

—Ben Bailey

Note: Remember that communication is saying the same thing in different words. Let this illustration cause you to think about other ways to say the same thing. For example, I have said, "When Paul answered the jailer's question, "What must I do to be saved?" He used six words. But those six words were not, "Begin going to church every Sunday" or "Live an honest and good life" or even "Obey the Ten Commandments each day." They were, "Believe on the Lord Jesus Christ."

❖ King Christian of Denmark, then eighty-five years of age but still agile, stood at the corner of the street waiting for an electric car to go by. Suddenly two little girls, one four years of age and the other five, started to run across the track. A car was bearing down on them, but they knew it not. Onlookers screamed with terror, so certain did it seem that the little ones were to be crushed underneath the wheels. Just at that moment the old man leaped forward and grasped them by the arms and drew them to a place of safety. A few minutes and the little girls were telling everyone that they had been saved from death by the king.

—W. B. Riley

Note: This is not a substitution. But the powerful thought behind the illustration is that we too have been saved from death by the King! You can then explain how Jesus did it—by substituting His life in our place.

❖ A man in Australia had reached the very last of his resources without finding a speck of gold. There was nothing to do but to turn back, while a mouthful of food was left, and retrace his steps as best to the nearest point. The last day's fruitless work left him too weak and exhausted to carry his heavy load back to camp. So he just flung them down and staggered over the two or three miles of desert, guided by the smoke of the campfire. Next morning early, he braced himself up to go back and fetch his tools. The way seemed twice as long as usual, for his heart was too heavy to carry. Then he caught his toe against a stone deeply embedded in the sand and fell down disgusted and exhausted. Then he noticed that the stone he tripped on had a certain brilliance about it. He went and got his pick and dug up the stone, which brought him $8,000.

Many of us would get further in life if we would stop trying to paddle our own way, and fall down at the feet of the Master.

—Louis Banks

❖ I deserve to be damned; I deserve to be in hell; but God interfered.
—John Allen of the Salvation Army as quoted in *Wycliffe Commentary*

❖ If we could gain our own salvation, Christ would not have died to provide it.

—*Our Daily Bread*, 1974

❖ Oh, the many times that I have wished the preacher would tell me something to DO that I might be saved! Gladly would I have done it, if it had been possible. If he had said, "Take off your shoes and stockings, and run to John O'Groat's," I would not even have gone home first, but would have started off that very night, that I might win salvation. How often have I thought that, if he had said, "Bare your back to the scourge, and take fifty lashes"; I would have said, "Here I am! Come along with your whip, and beat as hard as you please so long as I can obtain peace and rest, and get rid of my sin." Yet that simplest of all matters—believing in Christ crucified, accepting His finished salvation, being nothing, and letting Him be everything, doing nothing but trusting to what He has done—I could not get a hold of it.

—Susannah Spurgeon and Joseph Harrald, *C. H. Spurgeon*

> Note: The language in this illustration makes it too old to use. But the idea behind it ought to arouse your thinking. You can use Spurgeon's thought to generate an illustration that says, "If God said to us, 'To get to heaven you have to go to church,' we would go to church every Sunday. If God said, 'To get to heaven you have to live a good life,' we'd attempt to lead the best life possible [continue with other examples pertinent to the way people in your church are thinking]. But when God says, 'My Son died for you. He's already paid for your sins. I can give you eternal life free,' that is so simple we can't get it."

❖ Congressman Bill Archer, former head of the House Ways and Means Committee, displayed a plaque in his Capitol Hill office. It read, "God so loved mankind that he didn't send a committee."

—Jack Egan in *U.S. News & World Report*

❖ In a recent issue of *Living Today*, the official publication of the Presbyterian Church of Australia, the question was posed, "What is the basis for your hope of heaven?" The following were the most popular responses:

I have always lived a good life.
I have been a good family person.
I'm not as bad as the person down the street.
I have always tried to be kind to everyone.

An analysis of the answers showed the prevailing opinion to be, "Good people go to heaven."

—J. Oswald Sanders, *Heaven Better By Far*

Note: If you are about to preach an evangelistic message, a month ahead, conduct your own questionnaire with people in your community. This will add more weight to your illustration because it will demonstrate how the people around your listeners have answered.

❖ **POSSIBLE ENTRANCE:** *If a child wants to ask you this question that he asked his mother, how would you answer?*

A husband came home from work and found his wife in tears. The father asked, "What's wrong." His wife replied, "Jeffrey," who is their ten-year-old, "asked me a question I couldn't answer. He asked me if I knew God." The husband said, "Why didn't you tell him you're a member of our church." She answered, "Because he didn't ask me that. He asked me if I knew God." The husband said, "Why didn't you tell him you've been baptized." She said, "He didn't ask me that. He asked me if I knew God."

—Source unknown

POSSIBLE EXIT: *That is my question to you—not "Have you gone to church or been baptized?" but "Do you know God?" Notice I didn't say, "Do you know about God? But do you know God?"*

❖ **POSSIBLE ENTRANCE:** *Salvation costs a lot. But the good news of the gospel is that someone else has paid the price.*

The thrilling story of the rescue of Morris Baetzold from a rocky cave in Hanckler, Ohio, was told in newspapers throughout the nation. The boy's seemingly hopeless entrapment brought to Hanckler members of the National Capital Cave Rescue team, members of the National Speleological Society, and an expert rescue team from the U.S. Bureau of Mines in Cane City, Kentucky, near Mammoth Cave. Cave experts were flown in from Washington and a lot of rescue equipment was brought.

In commenting on the great expenditure of time and money to rescue the boy, Fire Chief Paul Chodera said, "Our services and the voluntary services of the rescue squads were free. After all, what is a life actually worth? I estimate the total cost of the rescue of the boy was around two-hundred-and-fifty-thousand dollars. After twenty-five and a half hours, Morris was brought up from what would have been his tomb."

—Source unknown

POSSIBLE EXIT: *It cost $250,000 to save the boy. But it costs the boy nothing. Someone else paid the price. It cost God everything to save you. He had to crucify His Son when He should have crucified you. But it cost you nothing. Eternal life is free because Christ has already paid the price.*

❖   A man in a car stopped to ask a pedestrian the way to a certain street. When the man told him the way, the driver asked doubtfully, "Is that the best way?" The man replied, "That is the only way."

—Billy Graham, *Unto the Hills*

❖   We err greatly if we require others to "get good" before we help them "get God."

—Charles Stanley

❖   All America waited anxiously. Many of us prayed. Captain Scott O'Grady's F-16 had been shot down as he was flying over Serbia. Had he been killed or captured? Was he seriously injured? The hours ticked by. Five days passed. On the sixth day another pilot picked up a faint message from O'Grady's radio. He was alive, managing somehow to hide from hostile soldiers.

Immediately all the resources needed for a daring rescue operation were set in motion. O'Grady was snatched up to safety by a helicopter—and the U.S. rejoiced. *Newsweek* magazine reported that the weapons and machinery used for the rescue of that one pilot were valued at $6 billion.

—*Our Daily Bread*, 1996

Note: The way you come out of this illustration is to explain that, although it cost America $6 billion, it cost O'Grady nothing.

☺ **POSSIBLE ENTRANCE:** *Ask the average person, "What do you have to do to get to heaven?" Many would not know what to say. One reason is they don't know whose word to take for it.*

An evangelist was holding revival services in one of our western cities. He wanted to mail a letter, so he left his motel room in search of the post office. On the corner was a newsboy, and he stopped to ask him how to find it. He got a prompt, clear answer. "Thank you," said the preacher, "you're a bright youngster. Do you know who I am?" The boy looked at him for a moment and replied, "I'm sorry I don't, sir." The minister then explained that he was an evangelist preaching that week in a nearby church. He invited him to attend, saying, "If you come tonight, I'll show you the way to heaven." "No thank you, sir," said the newsboy politely. "I'm afraid I couldn't take your word for it—you don't even know the way to the post office."

—*Our Daily Bread*, 1979

POSSIBLE EXIT: *If you want to know how to get to heaven, you have to know whose word to take for it. You have to know who to believe. The best person to ask is the one who lives there. So if you want to know how to get to heaven, ask Christ because He lives there. Here is what He tells us in the Bible . . .*

❖ Good works cannot add to the gift of salvation. Suppose your best friend were to surprise you with a beautiful gift, and let's suppose your response would be that of immediately digging into your purse or wallet for a couple of bills to help pay the expense. What an insult it would be! Suppose the gift was an expensive coat, and you offered back five dollars. This would result in wounding the giver. Say you offered a quarter, or a nickel, or even a penny! No, the smaller the gift, the greater the insult. You must accept gifts freely. If you pay even a penny, it is not a gift. It is that way with salvation. Even a small attempt to pay for our salvation forfeits our receiving it. We will never be able to say one day in heaven, "Look what Christ and I did!" It will be all Him—none of me. As God says in His word, "For by grace are ye saved through faith, and that not of yourself; it is the gift of God, not of works, lest anyone should boast."

—D. James Kennedy, *Evangelism Explosion*

Note: An illustration like this is powerful because of the thought "even a penny spent would prevent it from being a gift." Eternal life is completely free.

❖ In the life of Teddy Roosevelt, when some of his men were wounded and dying, he needed medical help. He went to the Red Cross and said, "I need to buy some medical supplies." She said, "Sorry, you can't." He said, "Look, money is no issue. Name the price. I'll pay it."

She said, "You can't. But I can give them to you." He took the medical supplies that saved many of his men.

—Ralph Marks, Hollywood, Florida

Note: It's helpful to point out that Teddy Roosevelt was a lieutenant colonel of the Rough Rider Regiment during the Spanish-American War.

❖ One day I was passing a little house at the intersection of a highway, in which a flagman for the railroad was sitting. I looked through the window and saw him reading what we would commonly call a family Bible. And though it said on the door "No Admittance," I boldly went through the door.

I said to the flagman, "When I looked through the window and saw you reading that Book, I just had to come in and pass a word of greeting to you."

"Oh," he said, "I read that Book a great deal."

"But," I replied, "are you saved?"

"No, I'm not."

"Well, why aren't you saved?"

"I never could be good enough to be saved."

"Friend," I said, "if God would make an exception in your case, and give you salvation outright as a gift, would you receive it?"

"I don't know what brand of fool you think I am, that I wouldn't take a gift like that."

So I said to him, "Pick up that Book and turn to John 10:28."

It took him a good while to find it, and he read, "I give unto them eternal life and they shall never perish . . ."

"Now, take Romans 6:23."

And he found that and read, "The wages of sin is death; but the gift of God is eternal life through Jesus Christ our Lord." He laid the Book down and said to me, "Stranger, I don't know who you are, but you've done more for me today than any other man."

"What have I done for you? I've got you in a trap. You told me that if it was a gift, you'd accept it. Now," I said, "what are you going to do about that?"

"Well," he replied, "I will accept it right now."

And he did. We had a word of prayer, and I went on my way.

That's the simplicity of it, dear friend. The gift of God is eternal life through Jesus Christ. Now, what are you going to do about that?

—Lewis Sperry Chafer, founder of Dallas Theological Seminary

Note: Illustrations stir ideas. Lewis Sperry Chafer's line here is priceless— "Friend," I said, "if God would make an exception in your case, and give you salvation outright as a gift, would you receive it?" You can use this illustration as it is, or use the idea to build an illustration around something expensive people purchase such as a house, car, etc. Then ask, "If someone made an exception in your case and wanted to give you that outright as a gift, would you receive it?"

The point you would eventually make is if you wouldn't turn down something else when it's free, why turn down eternal life when it's free?

❖ Ted Turner, successful broadcasting entrepreneur, asked a provocative question of his good friend Vartan Gregorian, president of the Carnegie Corporation: "You're a big fund-raiser. What's the largest gift ever?" Gregorian told him that it was the $500 million donation Walter Annenberg had made to education. Turner replied, "How about a billion? I'm going to give a billion tonight." And he did, promising $100 million annually to fund United Nations programs for the next ten years.

Turner's impressive philanthropy received worldwide attention and applause. After all, it was the largest gift on record globally. Or was it? What about the Bible's record of God's gift to the world of His "only begotten son"? (John 3:16).

—*Our Daily Bread*, 2002

❖ Anyone, even a half-breed with five husbands or a thief dying on a cross, was welcome to join His kingdom. The person was more important than any category or label.

—Philip Yancey, *The Jesus I Never Knew*

❖ **POSSIBLE ENTRANCE:** *People say, "It sounds too good to be true" and therefore conclude it probably is not true. They are not always right.*

A recent promotion by H&R Block offered walk-in customers a chance to win a drawing for $1 million. Glen and Gloria Sims of Sewell, New Jersey, won the drawing, but they refused to believe it when a Block representative phoned them with the good news.

After several additional contacts by both mail and phone, the Simses still thought it was all just a scam, and usually hung up the phone or trashed the special notices.

Some weeks later, H&R Block called one more time to let the Simses know the deadline for accepting their million-dollar prize was nearing and that the story of their refusal to accept the prize would appear soon on NBC's *Today* show.

At that point, Glen Sims decided to investigate. A few days later he appeared on *Today* to tell America that he and his wife had finally claimed their million dollars.

Sims said, "From the time this has been going on, H&R Block explained to us they really wanted a happy ending to all this, and they were ecstatic that we finally accepted the prize."

God wants a similar ending as He offers salvation to every unbeliever.

—*Leadership*, Summer 2002

POSSIBLE EXIT: *It may sound too good to be true that eternal life is free. But it is. The reason it is free is because Christ paid the price.*

❖ The truth of the matter is that salvation is not a "give" proposition at all; it is a "take" proposition. We don't give our hearts, lives, wills, or anything else to God in order to get Him to save us. This would be a form of bribery, a way of meriting or deserving to be saved. But God says salvation is *"not of ourselves"*—and especially, it is not offering anything to God.

—Ray Stanford, *Handbook of Personal Evangelism*

❖ One of the latest forms of a safe has a device on which is a number of letters. To open the safe it is necessary to point to a number of letters on the indicator. And usually a word is used, and only that word will open the safe. So a sinner will point in vain for salvation to words such as "works" or "church" or "religion," etc. Only one word will open the way, and that word is "Jesus." Neither is their salvation in any other . . . I am the way . . .

—Source unknown

❖ Back in 1822, Caesar Malan was visiting at the home of a friend in Brighton, England. One evening he said to the daughter of his host, "I wish you were a Christian, Charlotte." The young woman resented his speaking to her on the subject, so he felt it best to drop the matter for the moment. What he had said disturbed her; however, the next day she told him she would like to be converted but did not know how. He explained the way of salvation but noticed that she was determined to "clean up her life and do what she could to first establish her own righteousness." She wouldn't receive the freely offered "righteousness of God" (Romans 10:3). Finally, he said, "Charlotte, Charlotte, you must give yourself to the Savior just as you are!" "What? You certainly don't mean that God will accept me without any works of my own, do you?" "I mean just that," was the reply. Nothing more was said then but shortly afterward Charlotte called upon the name of the Lord as her Savior. To describe how it all happened she wrote her famous hymn, "Just as I am, without one plea, but that thy blood was shed for me, and that thou bid'st me come to thee, Oh Lamb of God, I come! I come!"

—Kenneth W. Osbeck, *101 Hymn Stories*, Kregel Publications

❖ An old man testified that it took him forty years to learn three simple things: that he couldn't do anything to save himself, that God didn't expect him to, and that Christ had done it all.

—King's Business

❖ A few years ago I visited Casa Loma, "Toronto's Fairy Castle." Never before had I seen such a fabulous building designed for a residence. Its dining room can seat 100 guests. Its kitchen is spacious enough to feed a regiment. The library, eighty feet long, was built to hold 100,000 books.

I was informed that it cost Sir Henry Pellatt in excess of $1 million to build this marvelous dwelling, in which he hoped to entertain royalty. Before completing it, however, he encountered financial troubles and sold his castle home to the city of Toronto.

While gazing at Casa Loma, I envision it being sold at auction. A small lad steps up to the auctioneer and cries, "Stop the sale; I want to buy it outright." "But son," explains the auctioneer, "you don't have enough money to buy Casa Loma." "Oh, yes, I do!" protests the child as he draws from his pocket a shiny new Canadian penny and offers it to the auctioneer.

Such a child, thought I, would be not more foolish than those who hope to acquire salvation from God through their meager good deeds. They are blind—both to the value of salvation and to their own spiritual bankruptcy.

Salvation is a gift of God through faith in His Son, Jesus Christ. God is too rich to sell salvation; but if He did, we would be too poor to buy it.

—L. D. Kennedy

Note: Use the principle behind the illustration instead of the actual facts of the illustration.

❖ **POSSIBLE ENTRANCE:** *God's standard is not goodness; it is perfection. It doesn't matter how good you have been. Consider your own life and how you have lived. You cannot be as perfect as God demands.*

A man had serious trouble with his eyes, and his family physician advised him to see a noted specialist. The physician told him, "You'll need a lot of money. The fee will be very large." Deciding to use all his life's savings if need be, he made the appointment. After examining his eyes, the specialist told him that a delicate operation was absolutely necessary. Then he remarked, "I doubt that you can afford my fee, and I never accept less than my stated charge." The man replied, "Then I'm afraid I'll have to go blind. I can't even borrow enough to pay you."

The doctor continued, "You can't come up to my terms and I can't come down to yours. But there is another course open to us. I can perform the operation *gratis*. And that is what I am willing to do."

—Our Daily Bread, 1978

POSSIBLE EXIT: *You cannot come up to God's standards. He cannot come down to yours. But He can provide salvation free of charge, and that He is willing to do.*

❖ If we were to walk into a souvenir shop and I said to you, "I've bought you a souvenir. It's already paid for. You just go pick it up," that would be like what Christ did. He bore the wrath, pain, punishment your sin deserved. Everything is paid for. But—you have to pick it up!

—R. Larry Moyer

❖ Christ didn't lose His life; He gave it!

—Source unknown

❖ If God had given me nothing beyond salvation, He would still have given me all that mattered.

—Source unknown

Note: It doesn't matter who said this, whether an athlete, TV personality, homeless person or the local librarian. It is truth at it's best.

❖ When an engineer designs a suspension bridge, he has to keep in mind three important factors. First, he must figure on the dead load, which is the weight of the structure itself. Second, he must take into account the live load, or the amount of tonnage that the bridge will bear. And third, he must allow for the wind load. This is the stress that the superstructure can take from high wind velocities.

God's marvelous salvation provides for three similar needs in our lives. The "dead load" corresponds to the burden of sin. Many a person has crumbled under the weight of his own guilt-laden soul. But God assures us that by faith in Christ we stand secure in His perfect righteousness (see Romans 4:22–25). The "live load" suggests our need for daily cleansing, and for the grace to keep us useful and strong in our service for the Lord. That too was anticipated by the Father when He sent His Son to die on the cross. The Bible tells us that the blood of Jesus keeps on cleansing us from all sin (see 1 John 1:7). The "wind load" reminds us of those periods of crisis when we are subjected to the great stress of adversity and trial. But because of our position in Christ, secured for us by His death and resurrection, we know that nothing shall be able to separate us from the love of God (see Romans 8:39).

—Our Daily Bread, 1979

❖ Never turn down anything that's free.
—Bobb Biehl, *The On My Own Handbook*. www.BobbBiehl.com. Used by permission.

❖ If our greatest need had been information,
God would have sent us an educator.
If our greatest need had been technology,
God would have sent us a scientist.
If our greatest need had been money,
God would have sent us an economist.
If our greatest need had been pleasure,
God would have sent us an entertainer.
But our greatest need was forgiveness,
So God sent us a Savior.

—Anonymous quoted by Charles R. Swindoll in *The Grace Awakening*

❖ An elderly man who had never gone to school decided he wanted to learn how to read. His greatest desire was to read the Bible so that God could speak to him through His Word. But learning to read wasn't easy. Just becoming familiar with the alphabet was hard work. For several years this dedicated Christian kept at it. Finally he was able to read—a little at first and eventually the entire New Testament. A few days after he had finished the last book of the Bible, he stopped by to talk with a friend. With tears in his eyes, he said, "It was worth all that effort just to be able to read John 3:16."

—Our Daily Bread, 1988

❖ God's acceptance of me is not based on the depth of my sincerity but on the death of His Son.

—Source unknown

❖ Snake expert and zoo director Gerald de Bary was called an expert in handling snakes. One of the jobs he seemed to especially enjoy at Salt Lake City's Hogle Zoo was cleaning the snake cages.

During his chores one night he came to the cage of a South African puff adder. As he opened the deadly snake's cage he suddenly felt dizzy. The reptile struck as he fell, clamping its fangs into his arm.

He called the night watchman for help, instructing the man to find some snakebite serum. In the frantic attempt to find an antidote, the watchman and others forgot that serum and a syringe were in a refrigerator barely an arms length from where the stricken zoo keeper lay. He died thirty-two hours later.

—*Life*, February 7, 1964

Note: The application here would be, "There is no reason to die and be forever separated from God. Your way of eternal salvation is within reach—all you have to do is trust Christ."

❖ **POSSIBLE ENTRANCE:** *The greatest thing about trusting Christ is that regardless of how the story of your life began, you know how it is going to end.*

I was in the Phoenix airport making an airline connection as I traveled back from a speaking engagement. As I was waiting to board my plane, I struck up a conversation with "Jerry." Jerry was a small man, probably in his early sixties, and had experienced a lot of life. I came to find out that he had grown up in Ohio (my neck of the woods), and had worked as a common laborer in many different jobs. He had been a butcher, worked in construction, driven a truck, and worked on a farm, along with a few other odd jobs along the way. His hands and face showed the wear of a tough life. He was somewhat opinionated on just about every topic, and a little rough around the edges. Yet he seemed to be a "good ole boy" with a sensitive side, and you could tell that down deep he really wanted to do the right thing.

I was able to turn the conversation around to spiritual things and came to believe that Jerry had indeed trusted Christ as a young man while he served in the Navy. But the thing that I will never forget about Jerry was his answer to my question, "What caused you to trust Christ?" Jerry's answer was, "I like the way the story ends."

—Doug Cecil, *DTS Connection*, Spring 2005

POSSIBLE EXIT: *How is your story going to end? The time to decide is not later. It is now!*

❖ Augustine recognized that Paul's words touched everything. There was nothing he had which he had not received. If this was so, then all was of grace. His description of the Christian as "a hallelujah from head to foot" is a thumb nail sketch of the joy and gratitude of a redeemed memory. "Let me not tire of thanking you," he wrote, "for your mercy in rescuing me from all my wicked ways."

—Os Guinness, *In Two Minds*

❖ If God keeps inviting you to a life of grace, mercy, love, etc. and you keep saying, "Excuse me," one day He will have to look at you and say, "Excuse me, I never knew you."

—Source unknown

❖ On September 8, 1974, daredevil Evel Kneivel attempted to jump the Snake River Canyon in Idaho using a specially designed vehicle that resembled a motorcycle, ran on steam, and was equipped with a parachute. The government refused to let him perform the stunt on public property, so he bought land and "jumped" from his own private property over a spot in the canyon 500 feet deep and a quarter mile wide. Despite all the expensive preparations, Kneivel fell (literally) short of his goal. The parachute deployed early, and the "motorcycle" and its rider landed in the canyon. Surprisingly, Kneivel suffered only a broken nose.

—Adapted from "Evel Kneivel Jump Site—Twin Falls, Idaho," Idaho Tourism, http://www.idahobeautiful.com/south-central/evel-knievel-jump-site-twin-falls-idaho.html

Note: The application here is, "Although we give it our hardest try we are afraid we might come short of what it takes to get to heaven."

❖ One man told me he had been advised to join a certain church to be saved. He was told by someone else that he had to be baptized in a particular church. Still others spoke vaguely about trying to obey the Sermon on the Mount. And one of his friends said he needed to go through a period of intense sorrow for sin before he could expect God to save him.

Frankly, I don't blame that confused man for saying to me, "I don't want to read any pamphlets or tracts. Show me right from the Bible how I can be saved." So we started reading passages in Romans and discussing them. By the time we reached the fifth chapter, he said, "It's clear to me now. All I need to do is place my trust in Jesus Christ." He did, and he found peace.

—*Our Daily Bread*, 2004

Note: Again I emphasize that illustrations from others make you think of your own. Think of people you have spoken to and who have been confused. Then end with, "The Bible tells us one way to be saved and repeats it many times—believe the Lord Jesus Christ. We must trust in Christ alone to save us."

❖ **POSSIBLE ENTRANCE:** *Any offer, any gift can be rejected or returned. But the most foolish mistake anyone could make is to reject the gift of eternal life.*

During the World War II blitz in London, a woman stood by an open window in the top story of a blazing building. An escape ladder was quickly run up. A brave fireman made his way to the top. He leaned with outstretched arms to take the woman to safety, but she retreated in terror. The flames enveloped her, and the noble fireman returned without her. Weeping, he said, "I tried to save her, but she wouldn't let me."

—Hyman J. Appelman

POSSIBLE EXIT: *The problem was not that he could not receive her. That's what the outstretched arms were all about—his way of saying come to me. The problem is she would not receive him. Christ will receive anyone. That's what His outstretched arms on the cross were all about. It was His way of saying, "Come to Me." But there are those who will not receive Him.*

❖ A mother, knowing that her sick child needed some fresh fruit, went to a wealthy prince who lived nearby. In his royal vineyards were some of the choicest grapes to be found anywhere. She scraped together what little money she could and made her way to the estate. Finding the caretaker, she offered to buy a cluster of the luscious grapes but was turned away with a curt, "They are not to be sold! Do you think the prince grows these to be peddled by a huckster?" Not easily discouraged, however, she returned several times, only to have her offer rejected again and again. When the plight of this humble peasant came to the attention of the princess, she asked to see her. Reaching for a basket, she filled it with some of the finest fruit of the vineyard and placed it in the hands of the anxious mother. "My husband does not sell his grapes," she said, "but he is always ready to give them away to the poor and needy."

—*Our Daily Bread*, 1974

Note: An illustration like this is helpful to bring out the fact that God will not "sell" us eternal life if we have are good, go to church, are baptized, etc. It has to be received as a gift, completely free.

❖ Martin Luther said that the most damnable and pernicious heresy that has ever plagued the mind of man was the idea that somehow he could make himself good enough to live with an all-holy God.

—Darius Salter, *American Evangelism*

❖ Look for yourself, and you will find in the long run only hatred, loneliness, despair, rage, ruin, and decay. But look for Christ and you will find Him, and with Him everything else thrown in.

—C. S. Lewis, *Mere Christianity*

❖ As Luther pointed out, it is natural to assume that God will not give us something as wonderful as the redeeming presence of Christ unless we do Him a favor first.

—Alister McGrath,
Evangelicalism and the Future of Christianity

❖ My lowest days as a Christian (and there were low ones—seven months' worth of them in prison, to be exact) have been more fulfilling and rewarding than all the days of glory in the White House.

—Charles Colson, *Loving God*

Note: Whenever you are not certain of the facts behind a person you are quoting, be certain to do your research. A few words about a person (for example, that Charles Colson was indicted in the Watergate scandal) can lend tremendous credibility to the quote.

❖ That reminds me of what theologian John Gerstner once said. "Christ has done everything necessary for [the sinner's] salvation. Nothing now stands between the sinner and God but . . ."

But what? What is this roadblock that stands between so many people and their salvation by the gracious, forgiving God?

That roadblock, he continued, is "the sinner's 'good works!'"

—D. James Kennedy, "How to Know for Sure You're Going to Heaven" tract

❖ I read a beautiful story of a little fellow who was born blind. His name was Charlie. He was about eight or nine years of age when a famous specialist looked at his eyes and said, "I see no reason why little Charlie should not be able to see." He performed the operation, took his delicate instruments and clipped away that old filmy stuff that prevented his sight, and placed thirty-two bandages around his eyes and head and said to his mother, "Take off one bandage each day. Don't take off more than one at a time, because if you do, the light will be so strong it will blind him again. "

The mother followed instructions until at last there was one bandage left. She went to the phone, called the doctor and said, "I want you to come out and see the results of the operation." The doctor hurried out, and when he looked at little Charlie, he said, "Let the first thing he sees be something beautiful; he will never forget it. It will make a lasting impression upon him."

They took him to a flower garden. Little Charlie stood facing a bush of roses as the last bandage was removed. He said, "Mother, why didn't you tell me it was half so beautiful."

She said, "I tried to, Charlie, but you were blind and couldn't see."

—Monroe Parker

❖ What a night for the Minnesota Twins baseball team in 1987! They had just defeated the Detroit Tigers and won the American League pennant for the first time in twenty-two years. More than 50,000 people, young and old, crowded into the Metrodome to welcome their victors home from Detroit. Banners were waving, horns were blaring, the crowd was cheering. There were even tears of joy.

The players were surrounded by members of the news media. One reporter in the crowd called out to Greg Gagne, the Twins' star shortstop, and commented, "This has got to be the greatest moment of your life." Quietly Gagne replied, "Actually, no. That was the moment I asked Jesus Christ into my life."

—*Our Daily Bread*, 2001

Note: It's important to keep the gospel clear. The Scriptures do not use the terminology "Ask Jesus Christ into your life." In terms of salvation, we are exhorted to "believe"—trust in Christ alone. So it would be best to use poetic license and say, "That was the moment I trusted Jesus Christ as Savior."

❖ A group of tourists were visiting an old historic church in Philadelphia. The man who was the keeper of the premises gave them a key to the front door so that they might walk in and examine its interior. When they put the key in the lock, they twisted and they turned yet nothing happened. After a few minutes of trying, the keeper appeared and said, "Oh, I forgot to tell you it isn't locked. Just lift the latch and walk in!"

That is all that's necessary for salvation. No human efforts will get you to heaven. All you need do is lift the latch by trusting Christ to save you, and walk in.

—R. Larry Moyer

❖ There is a saying that goes, "The only way up is down." That's also true when it comes to salvation. To go up to heaven, you must go down to the feet of Christ. That is, you must trust in Christ's love to save you.

—Source unknown

> Note: Don't assume a non-Christian knows what you mean by "Go down to the feet of Christ." Use the phrase but then put it in words that a non-Christian will understand.

❖ I did not understand all about the plan of salvation. I do not understand all about electricity either, but I don't intend to sit in the dark until I do.

—Vance Havner

❖ Living without God means dying without hope!

—Source unknown

❖ A couple of years ago I knew about Jesus, but now I really know Jesus Himself.

—Johnny Cash, *Campus Life*, March 1973

❖ **POSSIBLE ENTRANCE:** *It is not what you have done that will get you to heaven. It's Who you know.*

While conducting an eight-day Bible conference in a southern city, I was informed by my hotel that due to a demand for space I could use their accommodation for only three days of my stay, and that other hotels in the community were equally crowded. A Christian businessman hearing of our problem shared instructions that after my three days in the hotel, I should go to another hotel where space would be available for me. Arriving at the registration desk I found a dozen others ahead of me. As each made his request for a room, he was informed they had no space available. Nobody in the line received a room, even though some of them had confirmed reservations. When the desk clerk took my name, he fumbled through some papers and replied. "Yes, we have a room for you."

340

The businessman who had secured the room for me was in a position to do favors for the hotel, and they could not afford to turn away a request from one of his friends. I had secured a room on another man's name and favor.

—John Walvoord

POSSIBLE EXIT: *He got the room because he knew the right person. In order to get to heaven, you have to know the right Person. You have to be personally related to God through trusting Jesus Christ as your Savior.*

❖ John Wesley, that uncrowned king of eighteenth-century England, strove for years to make himself acceptable to God by his own effort and religious duties. His words when he received the Savior have become historic. "I felt my heart strangely worried. I felt that I trusted Christ and Christ alone for salvation. And an assurance was given me that He had taken away all my sins."

—Edwin Adams, "Religion but Not Right with God" tract

❖ Heaven goes by favor. If it went by merit, you would stay out, and your dog would go in.

—Mark Twain

❖ As the gospel was being presented to a woman, she explained she had tried her best to please God. Then she added, "But I'm afraid God will never accept me."

The Christian talking with her said, "I agree with you. He never will."

A look of astonishment came over the woman's face, for she had not expected such a response.

The believer then explained, "No, He never will, but God has accepted His Son, and if you join yourself to Him through faith, you will find God's favor!"

—*Our Daily Bread*, 1997

❖ Anyone can devise a system whereby good people can go to heaven; only God can devise a plan whereby bad men who are His enemies can enter heaven.

—Lewis Sperry Chafer, founder of Dallas Theological Seminary

❖ The missionary had been a good friend to the Indian pearl diver.

He had spent many hours together sharing salvation with the diver. The Indian could not understand anything so precious being free. In making preparation for the life to come, the diver was going to walk to Delhi (900 miles) on his knees. He thought this would buy heaven for him. The missionary said "You can't buy it when Jesus has died to buy it for you." The diver couldn't understand or accept the free salvation. Before he left, he gave the missionary the largest, most perfect pearl he had ever seen. The missionary wanted to buy it. The diver, upset, said that the pearl was beyond price, his only son had lost his life to get it, and its worth was in the life blood of his son. Suddenly the diver understood. God was offering him salvation as a free gift. It is so precious, no man could buy it. It had cost God the life blood of His Son. The veil lifted—he understood at last.

—Source unknown

❖ Salvation is not try, but trust; not do, but done!

—*Our Daily Bread*, 1981

❖ A boy always used to brag about his brother, how good he was, how athletic he was, etc. One day at school a friend said to him, "You're always bragging about your brother. What is it you enjoy most about your relationship with him?" The boy's response was, "Oh, just to know him."

—Source unknown

❖ Salvation is a gift to be received, not a goal to be achieved.

—Source unknown

❖ Thou has made us for Thyself, O God, and our hearts are restless until they find rest in Thee.

—St. Augustine

❖ God is like a righteous judge who condemns murderers to death in the electric chair. But He is also a loving God, who then steps from behind the judicial bench, takes off His judicial robes, and goes to the electric chair for us (through Christ, His Son). But the warden asks me, "Do you accept this death in your place?" If I don't, I still have to die for my sin. But if I do accept it, then I'm free forever.

—Source unknown

❖ Six-year-old Anthony Bernardino of El Monte, California, was flying a kite when he suddenly stepped into a two-foot wide construction hole, plunging twenty-eight feet and touching off a seven-hour rescue drama. He was unable to save himself and was in need of a higher power, which came when workers bored a parallel shunt and carefully dug under the boy and then brought him to the surface.

—*Life*, March 17, 1972

Note: Here again is a story so relatable that when it happened is immaterial. It's a situation that could occur today. It is sufficient to say, "Years ago a six-year-old boy in California . . ."

❖ Let us suppose that a plane comes down in the waters south of New Zealand. [These waters sometimes average 68 degrees Fahrenheit.] The pilots know there is no other plane, no ship, and no land within a thousand miles. Three men are cast into the water: One is able to swim only a few hundred feet; the second can manage to stay afloat an hour or two; the third is the world champion long-distance swimmer. Is it sensible for the champion to show the first man his best swimming stroke? What if the champion said, "Take me as an example"? These men do not need an example, they need a savior. One will drown in two minutes, a second will drown in two hours, and a third will drown in fifteen hours.

So it is with men. They do not need an example; they need a Savior. A convict is like the man who can swim only a few strokes; the average man is like the man who can swim for a while; the very, very good man is like the man who can swim for fifteen hours. But all three are doomed to die.

—Donald Grey Barnhouse

Note: This illustration can be particularly helpful if you are speaking in a setting that is located near a large body of water.

❖ **POSSIBLE ENTRANCE:** *The things we go to for help often don't help us. They only plunge us deeper into sin.*

A young woman addicted to heroin wrote this note, which was found by the police in a phone booth. "I am twenty years of age and for the past two years I have been wandering through the nightmare of a junkie. I want to quit but I can't. Jail didn't cure me. Nor did hospitalization help me for long. The doctor told my family it would have been better and indeed kinder if the person who first got me hooked on drugs had taken a gun and blown my brains out. And I wish to God she had. My God, how I wish it. Someone—please help me."

—*Bible Expositor and Illuminator*, Winter 1972

POSSIBLE EXIT: *It doesn't matter who you are or what you've done; God is waiting for you to say, "Please help me."*

❖ **POSSIBLE ENTRANCE:** *When we think of what happens in our own families, we begin to understand how simple it is to come to Christ.*

It is amazing what God uses to show us that only He can save. A mother once said that as she struggled to understand the simplicity of salvation, she was reminded of an incident in the life of her son. When finished playing in the dirt, he communicated with simple words and desperate looks that he could not clean himself. The Lord used that to show her that we came to Christ, dirt and all. He forgive us and cleanses. We cannot cleanse ourselves.

R. Larry Moyer

POSSIBLE EXIT: *God is not saying, "Clean yourself up and then come to me." You will never be clean enough for God to accept you. All you can do is come to Christ with all your dirt and your sins, and let Him cleanse you.*

SATISFACTION
❖ Some time ago, Pastor R. I. Williams phoned in his sermon topic to the *Norfolk Ledger-Dispatch*. When asked what it was, he said, "The Lord Is My Shepherd." "Is that all?" inquired the man at the other end of the line. The minister replied, "That's enough!" Apparently his meaning was misunderstood, for the following words appeared on their church page of the paper: "Rev. R. I. Williams' subject at the morning service will be: 'The Lord is My Shepherd—That's Enough!'" The pastor smiled when he read this, but he liked the idea so much that he used the expanded version as his sermon title that Sunday.

—*Our Daily Bread*, 1976

❖ Don't waste any sympathy on me. I am the happiest person living.

—Fanny Crosby, a blind hymn writer

❖ Carl Sagan (scientist/author) commenting on the new optimism on life elsewhere in the universe: "It's nice to think that there is someone out there that can help us."

—PBS documentary
"Chariots of the Gods? Unsolved Mysteries of the Past," Spring 1978

Note: A helpful way to use this illustration would be to say, "There is Someone out there who can help you. He can get you through this life on earth. He can get you to heaven."

❖ I've never seen a person turn away from Jesus and be happy. I've never seen a person turn to Jesus and regret it.

—Billy Graham, *Pulpit Helps*, January 1999

❖ Christ can take the place of anything, but nothing can take the place of Christ.

—*Our Daily Bread*

SUCCESS

❖ There is no future more disastrous then the success that leaves God out.

—*Christian Clippings*, November 1987

❖ **POSSIBLE ENTRANCE:** *It doesn't matter how much success you've enjoyed. It will mean nothing when death comes to you.*

Dennis Barnhart was president for an aggressive, rapidly growing company, Eagle Computer, Inc. His life is a study in tragedy. From a small beginning, the firm grew incredibly fast. He decided they should go public. The forty-five-year-old man, as a result of this first public stock offering, became a multimillionaire virtually overnight. Then for some strange reason, while in his red Ferrari only blocks from the company headquarters, he drove his car through seventy feet of guard rail into a ravine and died.

A *Los Angeles Times* account read, "Until the accident at 4:30 Wednesday afternoon it had been the best days for Barnhart and the thriving young company, which makes small business and personal computers. Eagle netted $37 million from the initial offering of 275 million shares. The stock, which entered the market at $13 a share, quickly rose as high as $27 before closing at a price of $15.50."

—Charles R. Swindoll, *Living on the Ragged Edge*

POSSIBLE EXIT: *When death strikes, how will the newest gadget, the value of your stocks, or the amount of your success benefit you? In no way!*

❖ **POSSIBLE ENTRANCE:** *The question is not whether you are climbing the ladder of success, the question is whether your ladder is against the wrong wall.*

A man climbed the ladder of success only to find out he had his ladder against the wrong wall.

—Dr. Howard Hendricks

POSSIBLE EXIT: *If success leaves God out, it could be more appropriately called failure.*

TRANSFORMATION

❖ A friend once showed an artist a costly handkerchief on which a blot of ink had been made. "Nothing can be done with it now; it is absolutely worthless." The artist made no reply but carried it away with him. After a time he sent it back, to the great surprise of his friend, who could scarcely recognize it. In a most skillful and artistic way he had made a fine design in India ink, using the blot as a basis, making the handkerchief more valuable than ever. A blotted life is not necessarily a useless life. Jesus can make a life beautiful though it has been marred by sin.

—*Christian Clippings*, January 1990

❖ Many years ago the head of a rescue mission in London accepted the challenge to debate a well-known skeptic, but with this condition: he would bring with him 100 people who would tell how believing in Jesus had changed their lives. He invited his opponent to counter with witnesses to the benefits of unbelief. On the appointed day the believer came with his 100, but the skeptic never showed up.

—*Our Daily Bread*, 1999

❖ The beat-up old car sits on the used-car lot, rusty and forsaken. Years of abuse and hard driving have taken their toll on the formerly shiny automobile.

A man walks onto the lot and is attracted to this rust bucket. He plunks down cash, and the salesperson hands over the keys while saying, "I'm selling you this car 'as is.'" The new owner just smiles; he knows his cars, and he's about to restore this castoff to its former beauty.

Across town, a troubled woman sits in forlorn sadness, contemplating where she went wrong. Years of abuse and hard living have taken their toll on what was once a vibrant young girl. She's been mistreated by others so many times that she feels she has little value anymore. And after making her own mistakes and living with her own bad choices, she's sure she will be left on life's junk heap forever.

But then someone tells her about Jesus. Someone mentions that Jesus specializes in castoffs, that He is waiting to transform anyone who trusts Him—even her. Someone tells her that Jesus will take her "as is." She believes. She trusts. And Jesus begins to restore another lost person to the abundant life He has promised.

—Our Daily Bread, 2004

TRUST

❖ **POSSIBLE ENTRANCE:** *There are times we must place our trust in something outside of ourselves to get us to a particular destination.*

The man who'd led the first successful trans-Atlantic balloon flight, Maxie Anderson, lifted off from San Francisco with his son Kris aboard a 75-foot-tall, helium-filled balloon known as the Kitty Hawk. Four days and 3,100 miles later, they set down at Matane, Quebec, in the first nonstop balloon crossing of North America and the longest balloon voyage over land in history.

—The Norm Hitzges' Historical Sports Almanac, May 12, 1980

POSSIBLE EXIT: *What were they doing? They trusted the balloon to get them across North American and the Atlantic. God is asking you to trust in Christ alone to get you to heaven.*

❖ You can walk on the third, fourth, or fifth floor of a building. You didn't see the floor when it was being built, you don't even understand what all it is made of, yet you accept it for what it is, reckon it to be true, and step out on it.

In coming to Christ you might not understand why He would save you or all the details surrounding His substitutionary death and resurrection. But you must accept Him for who He is and trust the One who died for you to save you.

—R. Larry Moyer

Note: This illustration can be adapted into any location in which you are speaking. The key is to make the audience relate to this simple illustration of trust.

❖ Jesus said, "Come and see," not "See and [then] come."

—Source unknown

❖ The pith, the essence of faith, lies in this—a casting of oneself on the promise.

—C. H. Spurgeon, *Spurgeon at His Best*

❖ **POSSIBLE ENTRANCE:** *Christ loves you, and the cross proves it. God is now asking you to trust Christ, the One who died for you and arose and opened up your only way to heaven. Other people can't save you, but He can and will.*

A group of botanists went on an expedition into a hard-to-reach location in the Alps, searching for new varieties of flowers. One day as a scientist looked through his binoculars, he saw a beautiful, rare species growing at the bottom of a deep ravine. To reach it, someone would have to be lowered into that gorge. Noticing a local youngster standing nearby, the man asked him if he would help them get the flower. The boy was told that a rope would be tied around his waist and the men would then lower him to the floor of the canyon. Excited yet apprehensive about the adventure, the youngster peered thoughtfully into the chasm. "Wait," he said, "I'll be back," and off he dashed. When he returned, he was accompanied by an older man. Approaching the head botanist, the boy said, "I'll go over the cliff now and get the flower for you, but this man must hold on to the rope. He's my dad!"

—*Our Daily Bread*, 1983

POSSIBLE EXIT: *He knew he could trust his dad because he knew his dad loved him. You can trust Christ to get you to heaven. He loves you—His death on the cross proves it.*

❖ A man fell over a cliff and caught himself on a branch. He looked up and saw an angel. The angel said, "Do you believe I can save you?" The man said, "Yes, I believe you can save me." The angel said, "Do you believe I will save you?" The man said, "Yes, I believe you will save me." So the angel said, "Okay, let go." You may believe He can save you. You can believe He will save you. That doesn't mean you've trusted Him to do it.

—Haddon Robinson

348

Note: As I heard Haddon Robinson give this illustration, there would have been no question in the listener's mind that by "He," Dr. Robinson meant Jesus Christ, not the angel. When speaking to non-Christians you want to be equally clear as to who you are referring to with your pronouns.

❖ **POSSIBLE ENTRANCE:** *God is asking you to trust in Christ alone as your only way to heaven.*

The Bluewater Bridge is the east-west link between the U.S. and Canada. It connects Port Huron, Michigan, and Sarnia, Ontario. The bridge was completed in October 1938 at a cost of $3.25 million. It is nearly 1¼ miles in length and 38 feet wide. It has a vertical clearance of 152 feet to allow huge ocean vessels to pass underneath. In 1982 the bridge carried 2,831,514 vehicles across.

—Bluewater Bridge publicity brochure

POSSIBLE EXIT: *Yet, whether it be a tiny Volkswagen or a big Mack truck, each one must trust the bridge to get it to the other side. Whether you are a criminal or a good moral person, you must trust Christ as your only way to heaven.*

Note: Find out about a bridge that your audience would be familiar with and come up with your own illustration.

❖ **POSSIBLE ENTRANCE:** *It is not enough to understand that Christ can save you. You have to trust Him to do that.*

In 1893, engineer George Ferris built a machine that bears his name—the Ferris wheel. When it was finished, he invited a newspaper reporter to accompany him and his wife for the inaugural ride. It was a windy July day, so a stiff breeze struck the wheel with great force as it slowly began its rotation. Despite the wind, the wheel turned flawlessly. After one revolution, Ferris called for the machine to be stopped so that he, his wife, and the reporter could step out. In braving that one revolution on the windblown Ferris wheel, each occupant demonstrated genuine faith. Mr. Ferris began with the scientific knowledge that the machine would work and that it would be safe. Mrs. Ferris and the reporter believed the machine would work on the basis of what the inventor had said. But only after the ride could it be said of all three that they had personal experiential faith.

—*Our Daily Bread*, 1984

POSSIBLE EXIT: *When they looked at the Ferris wheel, they understood it could hold them. When they sat down on it, they trusted it to do it.*

❖   At one point on the Iowa-Illinois border, there is a bridge known as the MacArthur Bridge. Built just after World War II, the bridge serves the purpose of crossing a wide section of the Mississippi River. Due to its age and structure, a reasonable weight limit is placed upon vehicles crossing the river. Now every driver of a large truck who approaches that bridge must make a decision—to trust the bridge or not. It isn't enough to know the bridge is there, or even agree that it can hold the truck safely. They must drive out onto the bridge. They demonstrate biblical faith when they depend upon the bridge to hold them up. In the same way, you must depend upon Christ alone for salvation.

—Source unknown

❖   Two men were flying over the jungle when their plane began to crash. Both men had parachutes attached to their backs. One man was confident that the parachute would land him to safety once he jumped, but the other man did not trust that the parachute could save him. The next day a search party found the two men. One was alive and well because he had trusted the parachute when he jumped. The other man was found dead inside the wrecked plane with his hand on the pull cord of the unopened parachute. He never allowed it the chance to do what it was made to do.

—Source unknown

❖   A man in Enid, Oklahoma, was in a boat when it capsized. As soon as the boat capsized, a buddy of his emptied a gas tank and threw him the empty tank. The man rested his body on the tank and trusted it to save him, and it did.

—*The Tulsa Tribune,* June 12, 1976

Note: As with other illustrations, this could occur today as easily as it did in 1976. Therefore, the date does not matter. One can tell the story without any reference to when it occurred.

❖   Some years ago, a man in Texas received word that he had inherited a large fortune from a relative in England. This Texan, a recluse living in poverty, had never heard of the English relative. Even though he was on the verge of starvation, he wouldn't believe the news. His refusal to believe didn't change that fact that he was heir to a million dollars; instead, disbelief deprived him of enjoying the money. He died starving and poverty stricken. The objective truth remained, but he missed out on its benefits because he failed to claim them in faith.

—Paul Little, *How to Give Away Your Faith*

❖ **POSSIBLE ENTRANCE:** *An advertisement of an item many of us use frequently, especially in the summer months or on picnics, Igloo ice chests, illustrates what the Bible means by believe.*

The Broadback River in Northern Quebec—Sixty miles from civilization, Brian Chutka, Bill Moore, and Ned Pitta were on the trail of the world's record brook trout. For two idyllic days they fished their way down river. Then it happened! A violent storm erupted. Gale-force winds and three-foot waves flipped their canoe like a pancake. They clung to the boat in the 50-degree water, but as it began to go under . . . up popped their Igloo ice chest. Bill struck out for shore, nearly drowning before Brian reached him with the buoyant Igloo ice chest. Ned clung to a small corner of the submerged canoe. They floated helplessly for three hours before reaching shore. After six days in the wilderness, the men were finally spotted by rescue planes. Brian Chutka and Bill Moore are still after that big brookie, and when they catch it, they'll bring it home in an Igloo ice chest . . . the one that saved their lives.

—Igloo ice chest advertisement

POSSIBLE EXIT: *They knew they couldn't save themselves. They had to trust the ice chest to save them. Spiritually we have to admit we cannot save ourselves and trust in Christ alone to save us.*

❖ I am writing this deep in a Swiss valley. A cable car swings on a thin wire overhead. It carries thirty-two people and is moving over an awful abyss at a height of 5,000 feet. I doubt if one person in that car knows how it works—how thirty-two people can be conveyed in a box of metal and glass over a great ravine on one steel wire. Does the wire move, or only the car? But how can the car go steeply upward with no rack and pinion principle involved at all? They do not know. They do not care. Soon they will land on the mountain peak and enjoy the most heavenly views. It will avail them, though none of them understands. Yes, but somebody understands. The genius who conceived it—he understood. The artificer who made it— he understood. The engineers who maintain it—they understand. Heaven help those poor souls in the car if somebody does not understand! So it is with the cross. It can avail for those who do not understand it so long as they trust themselves to it.

—W. E. Sangster

❖ In a burning building in Harlem, New York, a small girl perched on the fourth-floor window sill. The firemen could not get the ladder truck between the buildings, and they could not persuade her to jump into a net she could not see. Her father arrived and shouted through the bull horn that there was a net and that she should jump. Jump she did, and she was so completely relaxed that she did not break a bone in a four-story fall. She trusted her life completely to her father. She knew his voice, and she knew what he said was best.

—*Focal Point*, Summer, 1989

❖ Bernie May of Wycliffe Bible Translators wrote, "As an airplane pilot, from the first time I sat in the beginner's seat beside my instructor I was taught to 'trust' my instruments. 'Your instincts will fool you,' my instructor rightly told me. 'You must learn that even though you may feel you are flying south, if your compass says you are flying east, you'd better believe it.' Later, as I took my instrument training, I was taught the danger of trusting my feelings. Often when a plane is surrounded by swirling mist and being buffeted by strong winds, you may feel you are in a dive and be tempted to pull back on the controls. But if your instruments say you are flying level— or even climbing—you'd better believe them. To pull back on the controls might put you into a steep climb, which would cause the plane to stall, drop off in a spin, and leave you out of control."

—*Our Daily Bread*, 1986

❖ One woman on crutches struggled to escape her office on the sixty-fourth floor of the World Trade Center's Tower Two. A group of her fellow employees tried to carry her but made slow progress.

"They had me over their shoulder for five or ten flights and just couldn't do it," she recalled.

Finally a coworker she knew only as Louis hoisted the woman on his shoulder and carried her down the stifling stairway. When they reached the fifteenth or twentieth floor, a security guard told them they were out of danger and urged Louis to leave the woman and make his way down to the street. Louis refused.

"He carried me down all fifty-four flights and then out of the building," the woman said, ". . . And he stuck with me until . . . I could go in an ambulance."

That woman had no choice but to lean on someone she barely knew to help her down the stairs. Her rescuer proved worthy of her trust.

—James A. Scudder, *Your Secret to Spiritual Success*

❖ **POSSIBLE ENTRANCE:** *For years the Houston Astrodome was one of the most popular sports arenas in Texas. Games would be filmed from a gondola suspended above the playing field.*

When a news reporter would crawl onto the 27,000-pound gondola suspended more than 300 feet above the playing field in the Houston Astrodome, he did more than believe that the five-inch thick cable will hold him. He literally entrusted his life to those cables. There is genuine faith.

—Gary Hauck, Houston, Texas

POSSIBLE EXIT: *The reporters knew if the cables did not hold them they were doomed. We have to so trust in Christ to get us to heaven that we realize if He can't get us to heaven, we are doomed.*

❖ I once illustrated the act of faith by the experience of a friend who was in an upper room of a hotel at night when the building took fire. He seized the escape rope that was in his room, swung out of the window and lowered himself in safety to the sidewalk. He had a good opinion of that rope during the day when he saw it coiled up by his bedside, but it was only an opinion. When he believed on the rope and trusted himself to the rope, it saved his life.

—T. L. Cuyler

❖ A circus man in Buffalo, New York, who was a tightrope walker, was visited one afternoon by a family he knew well. He was off duty, so he asked the girl, about ten years old, if she believed he could carry her across the tightrope and back again.

"Yes, I believe you can."

"Will you trust me to do it?" asked the circus man.

"No, I'm afraid not."

He turned to the brother, about fourteen years of age. "Do you believe I can carry you across the tightrope and back again?"

"Yes, I believe you can," responded the boy. "Will you trust me?" asked the circus man. "Yes, right now," and the circus man picked up the boy and carried him across the rope and back again.

What was the difference? The girl accepted it as true, the man could do it, but she did not trust him to do it. The boy trusted the circus man to carry him.

—Source unknown

❖ This piece was heard on National Public Radio's "Morning Edition" on November 2, 1988: "In 1958, America's first commercial jet air service began with the flight of the Boeing 707. A month after that first flight, a traveler on a piston-engine, propeller-driven DC-6 airliner struck up a conversation with a fellow passenger. The passenger happened to be a Boeing engineer. The traveler asked the engineer about the new jet aircraft, whereupon the engineer began speaking at length about the extensive testing Boeing had done on the jet engine before bringing it into commercial service. He recounted Boeing's experience with engines, from the B-17 to the B-52. When his traveling companion asked him if he himself had yet flown on the new 707 jet airliner, the engineer replied, 'I think I'll wait until it's been in service awhile.'"

—*Leadership*, Fall 1989

> Note: The point to be made here is, although he was an engineer for Boeing and knew the plane could do it, he did not trust the airliner to get him where he wanted to go.

❖ Suppose we were to go to the Grand Canyon and I were a tightrope walker. I could stretch a rope from one edge of the canyon to the other. And I could look at you and say, "Do you think I can walk across that rope?" You say, "No!" I do it, then I say, "Do you think I could take a wheelbarrow across?" You say, "No." I do it, then I say, "Do you think I can take a wheelbarrow with two hundred pounds of weight in it across?" You say, "No." I do it. Then I say, "You're less than two hundred pounds. You think I can carry you across?" You say, "Well, if you could carry two hundred pounds across, you certainly can carry me across." Then I look at you and say, "Okay, get in."

When you're willing to get in, that's faith—trusting me to do it. Saving faith is trusting Christ with your eternal destiny.

—Cliff Bassett, Elysburg, Pennsylvania

❖ Two teenagers were in a boat on Long Island Sound when suddenly a storm came up. As the waves grew larger, the craft was tossed about and the boys could no longer control it. Finally it capsized, and they were thrown into the water. One of them could swim very well, but the other could not. When the good swimmer came to the surface, he immediately looked for his buddy. Seeing him floundering nearby, he rushed to his aid. But before reaching out to rescue him, he shouted, "I can't help you until you stop kicking and thrashing around. Just trust me, and let me save you! Otherwise you'll drown!" The sinking boy understood. Ceasing all efforts of his own, he allowed his companion to bring him safely to shore.

—*Our Daily Bread*, 1975

❖ A little girl had asked her father what *faith* meant, and he had told her to wait for his answer. One day he was doing something in a cellar, the entrance to which was a trap door in a passage. The child called out to him, "May I come down to you, Father?" "Yes," he said.

The little girl was going to descend when she found that the ladder had been taken away. "I can't get down," she cried out. "There is no ladder." "Jump down," her father answered, "and I will catch you." The child hesitated. She could not see her father and below her everything seemed dark. "But I can't see you, Father. I can't see anything," she said.

"I can see you," was the reply. "Jump and I shall be sure to catch you. My arms are wide open, dear." She took him on faith and jumped.

—J. R. Gregory

☺ "As I understand it, doctor, if I believe I'm well, I'll be well. Is that the idea?"

"It is."

"Then, if you believe you are paid, I suppose you will be paid."

"Not necessarily."

"But why shouldn't faith work as well in one case as in the other?"

"Why," he said, "there is considerable difference between having faith in providence and having faith in you."

—Horace Zimmerman

Note: Non-Christians may not know what you mean by providence. This would be a helpful illustration if you changed it to say, "There is a considerable difference between having faith in God and having faith in you."

❖ I have accepted Christ's sin payment for my sin problem!

—Source unknown

Note: Many "trust" illustrations have their limitations. The part you want to consistently drive home is that you must trust in Christ alone as your only way to heaven.

Chapter 9
Your Illustration Check List

WITH YOUR MESSAGE COMPLETED and illustrations chosen, use the check list on the following page to ask yourself questions about the support material you are going to use.

1. Is the support material sufficient? (Your tendency is to have too little, not too much.)
   ☐ Yes   ☐ No

2. Are the illustrations relevant to a lost audience?
   ☐ Yes   ☐ No

3. Are the illustrations easy to explain and easily understood?
   ☐ Yes   ☐ No

4. Does each illustration address a particular point you wish to communicate?
   ☐ Yes   ☐ No

5. Do the illustrations have the proper amount of detail? (Not too little, but not too much.)
   ☐ Yes   ☐ No

6. Are names and dates used only when necessary?
   ☐ Yes   ☐ No

7. Is there a mix of serious and humorous illustrations?
   ☐ Yes   ☐ No

8. Could the humor be offensive to anyone in attendance?
   ☐ Yes   ☐ No

9. Are the illustrations well balanced and varied?
   ☐ Yes   ☐ No

10. Is the humor properly placed throughout the message?
    ☐ Yes   ☐ No

11. Are the illustrations believable?
    ☐ Yes   ☐ No

12. Do the illustrations grab attention, make my listeners sit up and listen?
    ☐ Yes   ☐ No

13. Have I walked into and out of each illustration effectively?
    ☐ Yes   ☐ No

Index of Illustration Topics

A

Acceptance/Rejection 40
Achievements 40
Assurance of Salvation 264
Atheists 42

B

Blame 43
Blood of Christ 172

C

Calvary 175
Christianity 176
Christmas 177
Church 265
Coming of Christ 266
Confusion 44
Conscience 44
Consequences of Sin 46
Conversion 267
Cross 179
Crucifixion 182

D

Death 48
Decision 271
Denial 79
Depravity 80
Depression 82
Disbelief 272

Dishonesty 84
Distraction 273

E
Easter 184
Eternal Life 275
Eternal Security 276
Eternity 85
Excuses 89

F
Fame 91
Forgiveness 281

G
Gift 186
God 294
Good Works 300
Gospel 186
Grace 187
Greed 92
Guilt 93

H
Happiness 303
Heaven 303
Hell 100
Honesty 102
Hope 310
Hopelessness 103

J
Jesus Christ 193
Judgment Day 104
Justice 105
Justification 313

L
Life 106
Loneliness 108

Lost 108
Love 205
Love of God 207
Lying 110

M
Man 111
Materialism 111
Mercy 210
Misunderstanding 317
Money 121

O
Original Sin 124

P
Pride 125
Problems 130
Propitiation 211

R
Rebellion 132
Regeneration 317
Rejection 133
Religion 319
Remedy 133
Resurrection 213
Revenge 134

S
Salvation 323
Satisfaction 344
Self-examination 137
Self-righteousness 138
Selfishness 139
Sin 140
Sinners 153
Standards 158
Substitution 230
Success 345

T
Transformation 346

Trust 347
Truth 162

W

Warning 164

Notes

Chapter 1: Why Illustrate?
1. Dwight Pentecost, *The Parables of Jesus* (Grand Rapids: Kregel, 1998), 12.
2. Haddon Robinson and Torrey Robinson, *It's All in How You Tell It* (Grand Rapids: Baker, 2003).
3. Ralph Waldo Emerson cited in Michael J. Hostetler, *Illustrating the Sermon* (Grand Rapids: Zondervan, 1989).
4. C. H. Spurgeon, *Lectures to My Students*, vol. 3 (Grand Rapids: Zondervan, 1954).
5. Ibid.
6. Mark Wiskup, *Presentation S.O.S.: From Perspiration to Persuasion in 9 Easy Steps* (New York: Business Plus, 2005).

Chapter 2: Why Humor?
1. Charles R. Swindoll, *Living on the Ragged Edge* (Nashville: Thomas Nelson, 2005).
2. Norm Miller and Helen Koolman Hosler, *Beyond the Norm* (Nashville: Thomas Nelson, 2005).

Chapter 3: How Do Illustrations Help Communicate?
1. Warren Wiersbe and David Wiersbe, *The Elements of Preaching* (Wheaton, IL: Tyndale House, 1986).
2. C. S. Lewis, *God in the Dock: Essays on Theology and Ethics* (Grand Rapids: Eerdmans, 1994).
3. Michael Hostetler, *Illustrating the Sermon* (Grand Rapids: Zondervan, 1989).

Chapter 4: Where Do You Find Illustrations
1. Jay Adams, *Pulpit Speech* (Grand Rapids: Baker, 1971).